This volume is sponsored by
the Center for Chinese Studies
University of California, Berkeley

THE MAGISTRATE'S TAEL

Tien-shih-chai hua-pao, case 1, vol. 3, p. 26, detail

The Magistrate's Tael

Rationalizing Fiscal Reform in Eighteenth-Century Ch'ing China

Madeleine Zelin

UNIVERSITY OF CALIFORNIA PRESS   BERKELEY · LOS ANGELES · LONDON

University of California Press
Berkeley and Los Angeles, California

University of California Press, Ltd.
London, England

© 1984 by
The Regents of the University of California
Printed in the United States of America

1   2   3   4   5   6   7   8   9

Library of Congress Cataloging in Publication Data

Zelin, Madeleine.
  The magistrate's tael.

  Bibliography: p.
  Includes index.
    1. Finance, Public—China—History.   2. Fiscal
policy—China—History.   3. China—History—Ch'ing
dynasty, 1644–1912.   I. Title.
HJ1402.Z44   1984   336.51   83-13515
ISBN 0-520-04930-6

To my parents,
Murray and Rita Zelin

CONTENTS

TABLES

PREFACE

Not long ago, all courses in modern Chinese history in the United States began with the firing of the first cannon of the Opium War. Even for Chinese scholars, the year 1840 has become the dividing line between ancient and modern in the evaluation of their country's past. The indigenous evolution of the Chinese polity has been obscured by a single-minded focus on its failure to respond to the challenge of Western imperialism. Recent work on population growth, commercialization, and the development of handicraft industries and agricultural specialization has shattered an image of a static late-imperial economy. But in the political realm, the spectre of the decaying Ch'ing empire, so deeply imprinted on the minds of nineteenth-century chroniclers, still survives. Although we no longer speak of "unchanging China," the paradigm for understanding China's early-modern experience remains a weak, corrupt imperial state, barred from innovation by an archaic philosophical heritage. As a result, we often overlook the complexity of that experience and deny ourselves the opportunity to explore the real roots of China's nineteenth- and twentieth-century decline.

This book is about China before the "coming of the West." It is also about corruption, but more important, it is about change. The first century of Manchu rule in China was more than just a page in the history of barbarian adaptation of Chinese political forms. It was a period of vigorous reform that had important implications for the potential development of a strong, modern Chinese state.

The main arena of reform in the early Ch'ing was fiscal policy. Building on China's preexisting tradition of bureaucratic rule, the new Manchu dynasty endeavored to use fiscal reform to enhance the power of the monarchy and strengthen the institutions of centralized government. They drew a clear distinction between the inner and the outer court that was reflected in the separation of the imperial purse and the state treasury. Efforts to forge a direct relationship between subject and ruler were accompanied by policies designed to diminish the power of the gentry and local strongmen whose mediating role under former dynasties had weakened the authority of the state. In order to improve tax collection, tax assessment was simplified and the land and head taxes were merged. At the same time, the Ch'ing clearly delineated which revenues were to be the province of local and of central administration, and they established a system of annual accounting to monitor revenue collection and utilization and ensure central-government supervision of all state income.

Taken together, these measures constituted a major step forward in the evolution of China's administrative apparatus. However, they could not contend with the underlying weakness of late-imperial finance. Corruption and tax evasion were a continuous threat to the fiscal stability of the early Ch'ing state. Chinese rulers in the seventeenth and eighteenth centuries faced many of the same problems as their contemporary counterparts in Europe: a weak agricultural fiscal base, poorly articulated distinctions between public and private revenues, and intense competition, both within and without the bureaucracy, for the limited surplus product of the realm. The existence in China of a mature bureaucratic system of rule, as well as the innovations introduced by the Manchu dynastic founders, exacerbated these problems by demanding morality in fiscal administration without providing sufficient funding at the local level to accomplish this goal. The great achievement of China's early-eighteenth-century reformers was the creation of a fiscal system which not only answered the needs of traditional political economy, but had the potential to develop into a system of government finance suited to the requirements of a strong centralized state.

The culmination of early Ch'ing fiscal reform was the "return of the meltage fee to the public coffers" (*huo-hao kuei-kung*), implemented during the reign of the third Ch'ing emperor, Yung-cheng. Officials in each province were authorized to collect a fixed percentage surcharge (*huo-hao*) on all regular land and head taxes remitted to the central government. This *huo-hao* was then retained in the province of origin to provide officials with substantially increased salaries (*yang-lien*) as well as "public-expense funds" (*kung-fei*) with which to carry out certain administrative responsibilities and projects of benefit to the local area.

Although the concept of *huo-hao kuei-kung* was simple, its rationalizing impact on the structure of Chinese fiscal administration was enormous. At the level of intrabureaucratic relations, the provision of adequate funds for local officials eliminated the need for institutionalized government corruption. The existence of a reliable source of funds for public expenses made it possible for officials to undertake the budgeting of local expenditure and engage in the long-range planning of local construction projects. Moreover, with income guaranteed, local governments were able to take on as their own responsibility many of the services and public works either neglected or relegated to the private sector during the last decades of imperial rule.

Many of the problems addressed by this new fiscal system were the legacy of the preceding dynasty. The Ming had seen several efforts at cleaning up corruption, but, except in the case of the "Single Whip" reforms, no attempt was made to restructure the fiscal apparatus of the state. The monetization of taxation, which was a major goal of the Single Whip reforms, became an important factor in the crisis that made reform necessary in the early Ch'ing. However, differences in the operation of government during the two dynasties largely account for the latter's ability to introduce such dramatic changes in fiscal institutions.

Although the bureaucratic structures of the two regimes were similar, ideological appeals seem to have played a far greater role as the basis for decision making as well as in the assessment of official behavior during the Ming. Even more important was the role of the emperor in the two regimes. The Ming dynasty is famous for its elimination of the post of prime minister, an act that is generally seen as vital to the rise of autocracy in the late imperial period. Nevertheless, most late Ming rulers were little more than puppets of those members of the literati who manned the upper echelon of the central bureaucracy.[1] On the other hand, the early Ch'ing rulers, as aliens, were far less fettered by traditional modes of interaction between emperor and court. Moreover, the Manchus brought to China new notions of imperial authority which in practice placed the emperor in a much more central position than he was accorded by traditional Confucian notions emphasizing the ritual centrality of the monarch. The direct role played by the early Ch'ing emperors in the formation of policy often contributed to the introduction of new ideas and new techniques in government. By the early eighteenth century, that role was reinforced by new institutions such as the secret-palace-memorial system, which both improved the emperor's access to information and his control over administrative affairs. Finally, the Ch'ing bureaucratic apparatus itself was far more centralized than that of the Ming, a fact that facilitated empire-wide reform and imperial direction of its implementation.

These conditions made possible the rational approach to solving China's fiscal crisis that was adopted during the 1720s and 1730s, but they did not guarantee that such bold measures would be undertaken. Each of the emperors during the so-called High Ch'ing was an able and dedicated ruler. However, differences in their personalities and in the political climate during their reigns had a profound effect upon the way in which they dealt with the problems of fiscal administration. The Ch'ien-lung emperor, last of the High Ch'ing triumvirate, deliberately sought a balance between the overly lenient policies of his grandfather, the K'ang-hsi emperor, and the excessive harshness that marked the reign of his father, the Yung-cheng emperor.[2] It was not merely style that distinguished these two great rulers. K'ang-hsi reigned in an environment in which Manchu legitimacy was not yet established. His notorious refusal to attack corruption may have grown out of the necessity to placate a predominantly Chinese bureaucracy not yet reconciled to Manchu rule.[3] His son no longer had to fear recriminations from officialdom or the literati. By the time the Yung-cheng emperor took the throne, China was united and at peace, and almost eighty years of Manchu rule had left no other realistic focus of loyalty for an elite whose status depended as much on imperially conferred ranks and degrees as on local wealth and influence. The Yung-cheng emperor was a tough and pragmatic man, but it is unlikely that he could have taken the steps that he did to rationalize administration and combat corruption and gentry privilege had he ruled at an earlier time.

In part, the peace and prosperity of the High Ch'ing must be attributed to the *huo-hao kuei-kung* reforms. Unfortunately, despite its contribution to China's early modern development, *huo-hao kuei-kung* ultimately failed. By the nineteenth century, China was indeed a country ravaged by corruption and torn by centrifugal forces which the government was increasingly powerless to resist. Nevertheless, the nature of our inquiry into modern Chinese history is changed dramatically when we realize that the "traditional" Chinese monarchy, which appears so resistant to change in the century of Western ascendency, was not always so. We must learn to look at China in the late-imperial period as a dynamic state, struggling to devise its own formula for rational and efficient bureaucratic rule. If the *huo-hao kuei-kung* reforms were a failure, then we must ask why.

Nineteenth-century Chinese intellectuals sought the roots of bureaucratic corruption in the declining moral qualities of China's official class, and modern critics have tended to follow suit. Faced with the evidence in government statutes of strong sanctions against officials found guilty of fiscal malfeasance, scholars have postulated that the government was too weak or too lazy to enforce its own regulations, or that the force of custom was too great for any agent of the throne to overcome. In the end we are left with the unsatisfying notion that China was corrupt because China was corrupt. Such an explanation, or lack thereof, provides us with no basis upon which to judge the actual capacities of the late imperial state. Even more important, it allows us neither the data nor the analytical framework within which to compare the problems faced by Chinese dynasties with those of other premodern societies, or with those of Chinese governments in the twentieth century.

Personalities did, of course, play a role in the demise of *huo-hao kuei-kung*, as they did in its implementation. The Ch'ien-lung emperor, more than any of his predecessors, was a product of a Confucian education and a prisoner of Confucian myths of kingship.[4] His desire to be judged a benevolent ruler led him to approach Yung-cheng's reforms with hesitation. On the one hand, he feared that support of *huo-hao kuei-kung* might be seen as contrary to the way of the ancient sages. On the other hand, he dared not reverse the policy so painstakingly implemented by his own father. In the end, Ch'ien-lung's efforts to satisfy both imperatives were indeed damaging to *huo-hao kuei-kung*, but they were not solely responsible for the reemergence of institutionalized corruption in the late Ch'ing. More important were the constraints imposed on rational fiscal administration by the structure of the late-imperial socioeconomic system. If we are to understand properly the decay of the Chinese empire, then we must examine the impact of that system on the breakdown of imperial control of corruption. The gradual demise of *huo-hao kuei-kung* provides an excellent example of the limits of reform in the late-imperial period. Its analysis will alert us to the ways in which the government evaluated the task of maintaining adequate levels of revenues and the techniques that it used to do so. If the government did try to eliminate corruption and failed, then a study of the reform process should enable us to comprehend more fully the tensions within the late-imperial polity that led to China's nineteenth- and twentieth-century decline.

ACKNOWLEDGMENTS

Many people have given generously of their time and energy to help with this study. I am most indebted to Professor Frederic Wakeman for his constant encouragement, criticism, and insights during the writing of this work and throughout my career. Beatrice Bartlett, Philip Kuhn, Alan Ware, Jonathan Spence, David Keightley, James Polachek, and Wolfram Eberhard have read all or part of the manuscript and I hope the version before them now succeeds in reflecting their suggestions for its improvement.

Funding for this project was provided by the Fulbright Foundation, the Social Science Research Council, the National Endowment for the Humanities, and the Columbia University Council for Research in the Humanities. Most of the materials used were situated in Chinese archives. I wish to express my special gratitude to Dr. Chiang Fu-tsung, Mr. Peter Chang, Mr. Chuang Chi-fa, Mr. Li T'ien-ming, and Ms. Wang Ching-hung of the National Palace Museum in Taiwan and to Mr. Huang Hsiao-ts'eng, Mr. Chu Te-yuan, and Mr. Liu Kuei-lin of the Number One Historical Archives in Peking for their patience and assistance. I also wish to thank Professors Wei Ch'ing-yuan, Chiang Kuei-ke, and Ch'en Chieh-hsien for their advice and aid with textual problems.

Finally, I would like to thank my family for their unceasing support of and interest in my work. My parents have never failed in their faith in me, even when I abandoned biochemistry to study something so exotic as Chinese. My husband, Alan Ware, has shared all my burdens with me, and has been my most perceptive and friendliest critic. And my son, Iain, whose birth coincided with the completion of this book, has taught me how precious one's working time can be.

I

THE ROOTS OF
FISCAL INSTABILITY

IN THE ANNALS OF LATE-IMPERIAL CHINESE HIS-
tory, few emperors have achieved the fame of the second Ch'ing
ruler, K'ang-hsi (1661–1722). His legendary humanity and benevolence as a ruler were given ample expression during a reign that
lasted sixty years. Although the final decades of K'ang-hsi's rule
were tainted by one of the most celebrated succession crises in
China's long imperial past, he is best remembered as the emperor
who brought peace to the land and restored conditions in which
good government and the pursuit of learning could flourish. Little
known or discussed is the negative legacy that K'ang-hsi bestowed
on the empire. Yet the way in which this legacy was handled was to
have a tremendous impact on the future of the Ch'ing dynasty and
the development of the Chinese state.

When the K'ang-hsi emperor died in 1722 he left a state treasury
containing only 8 million taels of silver.[1] This sum, equal to about
27 percent of the central government's total annual tax revenues,[2]
could in no way be compared with the empty treasuries and royal
indebtedness of K'ang-hsi's eighteenth-century European counterparts. Nevertheless, within the context of late-imperial Chinese
economic thought such a figure was to be deplored. This was a political system that worshipped the balance of expenditure against

income and considered central-government reserves essential lest man be unprepared for the ravages that nature could bring.

Depleted treasuries were certainly not new to China. In fact, their existence was so common that they played a central role in the traditional "dynastic cycle" explanation of the collapse of imperial regimes. When the talents and virtue of the imperial line were declining, when officialdom was becoming corrupt, and when the pressure of population growth was beginning to strain the resources of both the land and the state, it was expected that the imperial coffers would shrink. The previous Ming dynasty had presented a classic case of fiscal strain, resulting in increased surtaxes, popular resistance, growing military expenditure, and finally, inability to cope with foreign invasion. However, in 1722 the Ch'ing dynasty was not dying. On the contrary, there had been no major internal disorder since the defeat of the Three Feudatories and the pacification of Taiwan in the 1680s. Under the devoted sponsorship of the late emperor, scholarship and the arts were once again approaching the high standards of previous dynasties. For the most part, almost eighty years of Manchu rule had won for the alien conquerors the confidence and loyalty of China's native population, especially the important scholar-gentry elite. To stimulate the economy and rehabilitate the areas devastated by nearly a century of rebellion and warfare, both the dynasty itself and private entrepreneurs were engaged in large-scale land reclamation and resettlement. Reforms were also being undertaken in administration and fiscal policy. The vigor of the dynasty was demonstrated even in the succession crisis, for the empire survived unscathed and even strengthened. The factionalism that surrounded the various princely contenders remained limited to small coteries of supporters and did not spread to engulf the entire bureaucracy. The emperor who emerged from the contest, Yung-cheng, was an independent, energetic, and able ruler whose achievements as monarch far outweighed the questionable means he may have used to accede to the throne. Clearly, this was not an era of imperial degeneration and declining official morale.

The strains on imperial finances had, in fact, been reduced since the early years of Ch'ing rule. At that time, even in areas firmly under imperial control, popular sentiment against the newly imposed barbarian authority continued to be reflected in tax resistance and arrears.[3] Forty years passed before the whole of China was pacified and could be relied on for regular tax payments to the imperial treasury. In the areas most affected by warfare and rebellion, notably Szechuan, it was not until the mid-eighteenth century that productivity, and consequently tax remittances, reached the levels realized during the Ming dynasty.[4] However, none of these problems are comparable with the burdens imposed on early Ch'ing finances by the initial commitments of their conquest. Military expenditures used up most of the state's revenues during the early decades of Manchu rule. According to one estimate, of the 15.7 million taels spent during the first year of the Shun-chih reign (1644–61), over 13 million taels went toward military supplies and soldiers' pay. Furthermore, total expenditures exceeded the annual income of the court by almost a million taels.[5] Under these conditions, little was spent by government on public works or the general welfare.

State revenues did increase by the end of the Shun-chih period, to almost 30 million taels by Shun-chih 17 (1660),[6] though part of this new income had to provide for the increased expense of governing an expanded territory. One important element in these expenses was the payments made by the state to support the Three Feudatories which grew out of Manchu efforts to subdue parts of the empire's southern provinces. The Chinese generals sent to accomplish this task established instead quasi-independent satrapies which nevertheless continued to require provisioning and revenue support from the central government. During the Shun-chih reign that grant grew to 5 or 6 million taels per year. By the time of K'ang-hsi this sum had doubled and came to encompass about one-third of the annual income of the Ch'ing state.[7] Thus, although the dynasty recognized the need to counteract official corruption and tax evasion, the main obstacle to fiscal stability during the years of Manchu dynastic consolidation was excessive expenditure, especially military expenditure. Once peace was restored in the realm, the expectation was that fiscal balance would be restored and that the size of the state's coffers would match the glory of the regime in other spheres.

When the Yung-cheng emperor came to the throne in 1723, that dream of a vigorous and prosperous empire seemed on the verge of realization. More than a generation had passed since a major military expedition had added its burden to the state treasury[8] and the Manchu court itself was notoriously frugal, being loath to make the same mistakes as its profligate predecessor.[9] When the new emperor looked at his father's treasury he did not revel in the accumulation of 8 million taels, but was concerned about revenues several times that amount that should have been there but were not. Their absence was not the result of a dynasty spending beyond its means, but of a fiscal administration in which taxes that ought to have been sent to the central government were being dissipated elsewhere. Moreover, the Board of Revenue treasury was not the only one exhibiting shortages. The fiscal independence of the other government ministries in Peking, an inheritance from the Ming, had also left its mark. Even a cursory examination brought to light deficits in the stores of almost every treasury in the capital, in addition to serious discrepancies in central-government accounts.[10]

In some respects the problem of central-government finances was no more than a reflection of the developing crisis in provincial and local fiscal administration. If the central government was not receiving a large portion of its annual tax quota, it was because these lower agencies of the Ch'ing bureaucracy were not sending it on. Investigations into the state of provincial finances disclosed widespread arrears, some dating back a decade or more. Deficits in provincial and local treasuries were enormous. In Shantung the chou and hsien showed shortages exceeding 600,000 taels.[11] Shansi equaled that sum merely by taking account of those deficits so old that those responsible were no longer living or so surrounded by corruption that the guilty parties could not be determined.[12] In Kiangsi, the debts of individual officials ranged from ten thousand taels to as much as forty thousand taels each, and the unassigned deficit raised that province's liabilities by an additional one hundred twenty thousand taels. In Chekiang, the financial commissioner's treasury alone showed a shortage of three hundred thousand taels.[13] Grain reserves also reflected the disorder in local finances. Granaries which according to the records were stocked to overflowing to guard against famine and to stabilize rice prices were found to be half empty. Some granaries did not exist at all except in the accounts of those officials charged with their maintenance.[14]

Behind the façade of Ch'ing power and prosperity was a fiscal system whose foundations were extremely fragile. Within a structure that was one of the most rational of its time, a fiscal tug-of-war was being waged between the central government and local governments, and between both and the representatives of the various interests among the local population on whom they depended. That the system had survived at all was a function of the adaptability of those who participated in it. How much longer Chinese finances could have persisted in this way we shall never know. For in 1723 one of the first acts of the new emperor was to declare total war on deficits and those who caused them. How Chinese finances reached such a state we can begin to discern by looking back at the development of fiscal administration in the late Ming and early Ch'ing.

The Legacy of Late-Ming Fiscal Reform

Like most preindustrial societies, China relied on levies on the produce of the land for the major portion of its tax revenues. Therefore, it is not surprising to discover that China faced many of the same problems encountered by other states attempting to assess and collect a reliable income from a tax base composed largely of small agricultural units. Where China differed from both its Asian and its European counterparts was in the degree of bureaucratization of the tax system.

In England, China's chief nemesis in the nineteenth century, the crown had, by the eighteenth century, come to rely primarily on indirect duties on the commercial sector of the economy. More comparable to China are France and Japan. In Japan, direct taxes on the land continued to be the main source of *daimyo* income, but collection was based largely on community self-assessment of tax quotas set in the *han* capitals. In France, not only the land tax, but commercial taxes as well, were collected primarily by tax farmers, who had a legitimate role within the French fiscal system. In both instances, the state's main interest was receipt of its quota. In the case of Japan, the solidarity of the village unit and the fact that the rural elite had been largely removed to castle towns seem to have prevented gross inequalities in assessment. These factors, as well as the already high rate of Japanese land taxes and the comparatively small size of Japanese administrative units, can probably account for the low level of corruption evident in the tax system. On the other hand, in France the chronic royal shortage of funds due to the twin demons, waste and warfare, made the French government willing to mortgage its taxes to tax farmers who would advance funds to the court on the strength of future receipts. In none of these countries was a large bureaucracy employed to determine the productivity of the land and who owned it, and to collect from each individual taxpayer the government's share. Likewise, in each of these three states those who governed below the level of the central government did so largely with their own resources and formed a power base separate from the throne.

In China, the state was also concerned with collecting its quotas, but here the early growth of the bureaucratic state, the demise of a feudal-style aristocracy, and the relative weakness of rural communal institutions were combined with increasing rationalization of the tax-collection process, culminating in the highly centralized fiscal structure of the early Ch'ing. Tensions certainly existed between local, provincial, and metropolitan interests, but at least in theory China's vast territory was administered by a unified civil service, funded by taxes collected by and for the government itself. To a large extent it was the very sophistication of the Chinese bureaucratic and fiscal system that was its downfall.

By the eighteenth century, the main source of funds supporting the Chinese bureaucracy came from the land and head tax (*ti-ting ch'ien-liang*). For the most part, this and other direct taxes were collected by county-level magistrates with the aid of clerks and yamen runners who, with the exception of a small number of the latter, were unsalaried, though regular members of the subbureaucracy. Technically, all such revenues were the property of the central government. However, as we shall see, a portion of these taxes was left in the provinces to pay official salaries as well as certain local- and provincial-government expenses. Hence, on paper at least, China had one of the most rational and centralized fiscal administrations in the world.

This had not always been the case. During the Sung dynasty (960–1278) provincial-government expenses were derived largely from the income of official estates granted to the incumbent for the duration of his term in office. By the Ming dynasty this system had been eliminated, but the distinction between public and private in fiscal matters was still unclear. Only slightly less ambiguous was the distinction between central- and local-government revenues. Although taxes were classified as either *ch'i-yün* (those to be sent to the central government) or *ts'un-liu* (those to be retained by the locale), these terms were often applied arbitrarily and items covered by each varied.[15] Even retained income could be earmarked for the purchase of local products for shipment to the capital,[16] and inasmuch as all deposits in granaries and treasuries were considered ultimately to be the property of the emperor, no funds could be disbursed without an imperial decree.[17] At the same time, within the central bureaucracy each ministry received its own income directly from a multiplicity of tax-distribution points throughout the provinces. What seems to have saved this system from collapse was the predominance of taxation in kind and the existence of corvée obligations among the local populace, which provided local government with ample material and manpower resources.

Despite the government's claims to centralized control of tax utilization, the Ming fiscal system as a whole was very decentralized. This contradiction can be chiefly attributed to the founder of the dynasty, who saw the Chinese economy as eternally undifferentiated and nonexpanding. This vision, combined with his distrust of bureaucrats, found its expression in the main vehicles for Ming tax collection and assessment, the *li-chia* and *liang-chang*.[18] Both of these innovations were designed to protect the rural population from illegal claims on their resources and guarantee the delivery of taxes to the central government. This was to be achieved by reducing the influence of local government in the tax-collection process and by increasing local self-regulation. In the end they did neither, but though they gradually disappeared as formal taxation devices, many of the problems in Ch'ing tax collection evolved from them.

Under the *liang-chang* system, collection of the grain tax and its transportation were completely removed from the magistrate's control and relegated to local magnates whose personal wealth was sufficient to ensure that taxes would be remitted in full. However, largely as a result of its independence from the local administration, this system provided rich opportunities for the development of tax farming. The establishment of a separate tax-collection structure with its own staff could have provided the foundation for a specialized tax administration. However, the fact that the post of *liang-chang* was considered a kind of corvée, and was never integrated into the regular administrative hierarchy, deprived it of its rationalizing potential.[19] By 1421, with the increasing monetization of the economy and the transfer of the capital away from China's rice-producing heartland to Peking, the *liang-chang* system began to decline in importance. Its tax-collection functions were gradually taken over by the *li-chia*, and the ultimate receipt and transportation of the taxes to the capital once again became the duty of the magistrates.[20]

Though the *li-chia* originally played an important part in the allocation of corvée, by the late Ming it was primarily a system of rotating responsibility designed to prompt tax payments (*ts'ui-k'o*). Responsibility for the tax quota of an entire artificial "neighborhood" fell to the incumbent holding the rotating post of *li-chia* headman. Few commoners wanted this job, because failure of one's "neighbors" to pay their taxes in full often resulted in bankruptcy for the headman's household. However, by interposing an informal tax-collection structure between the individual and the state, the *li-chia* made possible the arrogation of this tax-prompting power by unscrupulous gentry and commoners who saw in it a chance for profit. This was usually accomplished with the tacit consent of the magistrate, whose sole concern was to see that the tax quota was remitted in full. The result was frequent falsification of the receipts given to taxpayers and the collection of illegal surcharges on a large scale.[21]

During the last few decades of the sixteenth century a series of measures were undertaken independently by a number of officials throughout China, aimed at alleviating some of the weakness of the Ming system of tax collection. Known collectively as the Single-Whip reforms, these measures were designed to simplify and consolidate the diverse taxes levied on the people and to convert payments in kind and in labor service to payments in silver. Unfortunately, a lack of centrally directed coordination of the reforms meant that commutations were often confused and arbitrary and rates varied from place to place. Although tax payments were commuted to silver, the myriad categories into which they had been divided when paid in kind remained. As the censor, Liu Yin-tung, pointed out in the first year of the new Ch'ing dynasty, "There are hsien with a regular quota of around three thousand taels, but it is divided into over forty designations. One item may require payment of only 1.6 or 1.7 taels, but surcharges of twenty or thirty taels are added on."[22] Nor was any effort made to consolidate the large number of agencies to which the taxes from a particular place were due.[23] Moreover, the failure to deal with inequalities inherent in the head tax led to a series of localized efforts at equal corvée which extended from the sixteenth century well into the period of Ch'ing rule.[24]

What the Single-Whip reforms did accomplish by converting taxes to cash payments, was to subject local finances to a degree of scrutiny that was inconceivable when taxes consisted largely of goods and services. If Ch'ing peacetime deficits were more shocking or attracted more attention than those in the past, it was in part because they were more visible. Still worse was what this visibility meant for the operation and financing of local government. Prior to the Single-Whip reforms, the staffing of local yamen and the provision of stationery, firewood, and so on was carried out through corvée labor and levies in kind. So long as these goods and services were provided in kind, there was considerable flexibility in local fiscal management and it was very difficult for agencies outside the locale to ascertain the extent of such resources or try to take a share. Once they were commuted to silver, the logistical obstacles to commandeering local revenues were overcome. As a result, the central government, the army, and even members of the imperial household began to appropriate the resources once used to operate local administrative units.[25] The effect was to leave local government with a bare minimum of legal sources of funds at its disposal. Expected now to hire yamen staff and purchase yamen supplies, local and provincial officials gradually worked out a new system of funding, one that was responsible for much of the shortages and corruption that plagued the bureaucracy in 1723.

Bureaucratic Solutions to Structural Problems

Until the eighteenth century, few men in a position to influence imperial policy recognized or were willing to acknowledge that it was genuine need among local- and provincial-level officials that prompted irregularities in the Chinese fiscal system. For many years, temporary but far more immediate causes of shortages, such as war and rebellion, tended to mask the defects in the system itself. Moreover, the success of the local bureaucracy in compensating for its difficulties, at least for the time being, made the paucity of funding available for local use seem less acute than it was. However, most important was the political economy of traditional China. Formulated at a time when taxes were paid in kind, when officials still came from a privileged class with independent means, when informal or customary claims on the labor and productivity of the masses were generally recognized, and when little was expected of government, it now perpetuated myths that no longer accorded with Chinese realities.

Kuo-chi min-sheng were the watchwords of Chinese political economy in imperial times. Translated in modern terminology as fiscal administration and people's livelihood, they are better understood as a dual exhortation to provide enough taxes for the government to function without depriving the people of the means of subsistence. Because government was seen as existing to transform not the physical landscape but rather the moral landscape of the kingdom, it was not unreasonable that low taxation would be seen as a basic principle of good government.[26] Rule by moral example was an inexpensive form of government. If the ruler, and by extension his representatives in the field, were virtuous, the populace would follow suit. Small outlays would be necessary for waterworks and for armies directed at external enemies, but large internal peacekeeping forces would normally be unnecessary, the people would be hardworking and content in their occupations, and harmony would reign over the land.

Of course, such ideal conditions rarely existed, but they did produce a formula for evaluating fiscal matters that was accepted by most officials in late-imperial times. Given the low level of taxation in China, it was expected that the people would pay their taxes in full. If they did so, officials need only manage the proceeds frugally for both the state and the people to prosper. If, instead of prosperity, the government was faced by mounting deficits, it could be due only to two factors: either taxes were not being received from the people or they were being received and subsequently dissipated through mismanagement or official peculation.

Beliefs such as these were not conducive to a fundamental restructuring of the imperial system of taxation and finance. Rather, reformers tended to attack each symptom individually in a manner that kept the basic framework of government finance intact. This is not to belittle the importance of such changes, as we shall see in the case of the reforms undertaken in the early Ch'ing.

Officials could and often did use the pretext of taxpayer default to cover a myriad of their own fiscal misadventures. In late-imperial China, however, claims that taxes had never reached the magistrate's yamen were to be taken seriously. In an economy chiefly composed of small landholders, where even the very wealthy generally owned no more than a few hundred acres, taxpayers were particularly vulnerable to the vagaries of nature. Flood or drought could easily deprive whole counties of the ability to pay their full quota. Most dynasties dealt with temporary disabilities of this kind by granting tax remissions and by allowing the less fortunate to spread their liability out over a number of years. This sort of taxation on the installment plan became extremely widespread during the Ch'ing for dealing with arrears of all kinds.[27] The frequency of natural disaster and the remissions and relief that they necessitated constituted one of the reasons that Chinese governments would prefer to keep a net surplus and not simply a balance of expenditure and income in their treasuries.

Less easily controlled were instances of deliberate nonpayment. Grouped under the category of tax resistance (*k'ang-liang*) in the tax codes, these could range from refusal to pay taxes as an open political protest to secretly bribing yamen personnel to lower obligations or expunge arrears from the yamen records. Once these moves were discovered, however, punishment coupled with retrieval of the arreared sum was the usual prescription. Real inability to pay could be wrongly assigned to this category and dealt with in the same way, especially when an area failed in its petition for disaster-zone status, when tax records were tampered with so that an inordinately large portion of the quota was levied on a locale's weaker inhabitants, or when surtaxes and illegal levies made it impossible for the peasantry to pay its regular tax obligations.

Both of the above instances concern the failure to pay taxes. Far more insidious were cases where the taxpayers had fulfilled their obligations to the state, but the state received little or none of the funds collected. Such cases usually involved embezzlement by intermediaries and were grouped under the heading of *pao-lan* or tax farming. Tax farmers were local yamen functionaries, members of the local elite, or simply local gangsters who contracted with the peasants to collect and pay their taxes for them. In its purest form this meant that, in return for a small fee, the peasant was saved the time and expense of carrying his taxes to the county seat. However, peasants often were coerced into entrusting their taxes to tax farmers or were prevented from turning in their own taxes by strongmen who, in cooperation with local yamen functionaries, controlled the county's tax-collection centers.[28] In either case, the tax farmer could keep all or a portion of the taxes collected, depriving the government of its quota and making the taxpayer appear to be in arrears.

Even when the government did receive the people's taxes, this did not guarantee that the full amount would be applied to the functions of government for which they were intended. Between collection and allocation or remittance to the central government there were numerous opportunities for the dissipation of such revenues through official mismanagement, extravagance, or outright theft by the official or members of his staff. It was to overcome the depredations of these fiscal parasites that many of the early Ch'ing reforms in tax collection and assessment were introduced.

Centralization of Tax Accounting

At first glance there seems to be little to distinguish Ch'ing fiscal administration from that of its Chinese predecessors. The same taxes levied by the Ming and delineated in the *Comprehensive Books of Taxation and Services (Fu-i ch'üan-shu)* were adopted by the new government and made the basis of its own finances. The division of taxes into *ch'i-yün* and *ts'un-liu* and the relative shares allocated to central and local government were also a readily accepted legacy of the Ming. After nearly a century of war and rebellion, the most important measures undertaken by the Manchu conquerors were those aimed at promoting productivity and agricultural recovery. None of them involved any fundamental restructuring of the fiscal apparatus, but rather they employed traditional methods of expanding the tax base while relieving the tax burdens on the people. Land reclamation was encouraged by means of both tax exemptions and rewards of official rank to those who succeeded in resettling large numbers of people on barren land.[29] The court itself was careful to exercise austerity in its own expenditure. Imperial benevolence was manifested in frequent tax remissions. And, as the supreme sign of the new dynasty's good will and adherence to the dictates of traditional Chinese political economy, in the last decade of his reign the K'ang-hsi emperor paid tribute to the infinite fecundity of man and the finite area and productivity of land by freezing the head tax at the 1711 level.[30] Yet behind this façade of continuity there were taking place several important changes that set the stage for the fiscal crisis and the reforms of the Yung-cheng period.

If the fiscal system established by the Ming founder was characterized by decentralization and the substitution of informal for formal mechanisms of control, the system that evolved during the early Ch'ing was the opposite. The first generation of Chinese under Manchu rule witnessed the gradual development of a highly centralized system of tax administration and the evolution of a new, direct relationship between the taxpayer and the government.

As a first step, the Ch'ing founders attempted to resolve much of the chaos inherent in the Ming tax structure by placing all taxes delineated in the *Fu-i ch'üan-shu* under the direct control of the central government. Instead of having each ministry of the central government collect and manage its own revenues from the provinces, all central government funds were now to be supervised by the Board of Revenue.[31] Moreover, under the first Ch'ing emperor the Ming proliferation of tax categories was eased and large numbers of taxes were consolidated, with the result that the opportunities for corruption and the confusion they entailed were eliminated.[32] Further refinement was undertaken by K'ang-hsi, who ordered the simplification of *Fu-i ch'üan-shu* registration[33] and the elimination of tax categories for which there was no longer any basis in the Ch'ing economic structure.[34] All of these measures simplified the collection of taxes and helped eliminate some of the local idiosyncracies in the tax administration that had made central government supervision almost impossible.

Probably the most far-reaching innovation of the early Ch'ing fiscal system was the institution of "annual accounting" (*tsou-hsiao*). It is also the best example of the Manchus' more centralizing approach to government. Even before their entry into China, the Manchus had begun to investigate their own finances at the end of every year. However, the comprehensive system of fiscal auditing that eventually bore the name *tsou-hsiao chih-tu* was equally a product of the changes in fiscal administration carried out during the last years of the Ming and the first years of Ch'ing rule. Given the technology of the eighteenth century, only a tax system based mainly on cash payments, divided into relatively standardized and simple categories and collected and distributed through a clear and direct hierarchy of officials, could sustain detailed supervision of this type.

The basic parameters for annual accounting were established during the early years of the Shun-chih reign. In SC 3 (1646), the emperor ordered the Board of Revenue to investigate each category of taxes received by each yamen in the capital, with special attention to be given to how much the original Ming quotas had been and how this income was now received and allocated. At the same time, the Board was told to supervise similar investigations in the provinces. Their purpose was to find out the extent to which the people were still being burdened by surtaxes instituted to cover military costs in the late Ming, and, in a more general vein, to find out how much land was currently under cultivation, and how taxes on that land should be collected, remitted, and retained by local government.[35]

More than anything, the 1646 edict indicates how little the government knew about the practical working of its own fiscal administration. It was not until five years later that Metropolitan Censor Wei Hsiang-shu memorialized the emperor to request that the supervisory functions of the Board of Revenue be regularized through annual reports on finances from the provinces.[36]

> The expenditure of state taxes is controlled by the Board officials and income is controlled by the provincial financial commissioner. The amount of income is not clear. Therefore, the amount of expenditure is not clear. I request that starting in SC 8 (1651), the financial commissioner of each province, at the end of the year, calculate the taxes of the entire province and compile an itemized account to be presented to the governor, governor-general, and judicial commissioner for auditing. On the one hand the governor shall compile a routine memorial with the totals and send it along to the Emperor with a "yellow account" (*huang-ts'e*) for his perusal. Another "clear account" (*ch'ing-ts'e*) shall be compiled and sent to the yamen in the capital for auditing. In this way we can prevent duplicity on the part of the financial commissioners and also check on the irregularities of Board officials.

In SC 9 (1652), the practice of sending annual accounts of paid and unpaid taxes to the Board was approved.[37] Once the principle of annual Board audits was established, further legislation concentrated on refining the rules governing deadlines for reporting, items to be reported, responsibility for verification of accounts, and punishments for falsification and delays.

Some sense of the nature of these refinements can be obtained by examining several orders promulgated under the K'ang-hsi emperor. In KH 11 (1672), the emperor became concerned about the failure of officials to investigate discrepancies in accounts. He ordered that thenceforth, in the reports of the annual accounts (*tsou-hsiao ts'e*), the total taxes reported collected by the chou and hsien must correspond to the amounts found in the lists sent to the people to inform them of their tax obligations. Furthermore, the actual amounts collected, the original quotas, the financial commissioner's totals, and the detailed figures submitted by the chou and hsien had to tally.[38] Such data would seem to be a minimum requirement for accurate audit of provincial finances. That the emperor saw fit to issue an edict specifying their inclusion indicates that considerable confusion existed as to what information was required by the Board. Moreover, by requiring submission of accounts at each level of the administration, an attempt was clearly made to institute a system of checks to avoid embezzlement or fraud at any level.

This system of surveillance was further clarified in KH 28 (1689). At that time, regulations were established whereby a governor or governor-general would be punished for failure to memorialize deficits in the provincial treasury and to impeach the officials responsible. An edict was also issued requiring that the governor of each province personally inspect the provincial treasury each year at the time of the annual accounting. When there were no deficits, this fact was to be memorialized and commendations requested for the officials who had filled their quota. In addition, at the end of the year, each prefect was to compile an account of the items collected and approved for delayed collection in the *chou* and *hsien* under his jurisdiction, and investigate them personally. When cases of "collecting more and reporting less" (*cheng-to pao-shao*) were discovered, it was the duty of the prefect to report this immediately to his superior.[39] Responsibility for investigating other revenue stores was also codified. Taxes kept in the treasuries and granaries of the grain intendant and post intendant were to be inspected by the financial commissioner. Those stored in the various prefectural treasuries and granaries were the responsibility of their respective circuit intendants (*tao*). Where no deficit or arrears were found, the prefects were to be recommended to the governor, who would issue rewards to express encouragement.[40]

This allocation of supervisory responsibility was to take on particular importance when large-scale inquiries of deficits and arrears (*ch'ing-ch'a*) were undertaken later in the dynasty. Responsibility for making good shortages was placed on the official himself if the shortage had been reported by his superior at the time it occurred. However, in cases where shortages had not been reported, whether due to negligence or cover-ups, the supervisory official was also required to share in repayment (*fen-p'ei*) and was occasionally charged an additional fine at the rate of as much as ten times the original amount due.[41]

The primary focus of the annual accounting system was the *ti-*

ting ch'ien-liang, those taxes derived directly from levies on the population by head and from private land under cultivation. Not only was this the largest single source of central-government revenue, but its volume was fixed by quota and was therefore more easily controlled.[42] In addition, it was the one source of government revenue that was shared statutorily with the provinces in the form of "retained taxes." Inasmuch as the purpose of the *tsou-hsiao* system was to control both income and expenditure, the *ti-ting ch'ien-liang* was obviously given special attention. In response to a memorial in KH 7 (1668), the special nature of the land and head taxes in relation to the *tsou-hsiao* reports was clearly outlined.[43] All taxes collected by the chou and hsien but not emanating from the *ti-ting* were to be reported in the same manner used prior to the reform. These included the salt gabelle, duties on tea, customs duties, the reed-land tax, tribute grain, tribute presented by local aboriginal chiefs, miscellaneous duties, the pawnshop tax, contract tax, brokerage tax, taxes per head of livestock and mules, fines and payments to atone for crime, and so on.[44]

At the end of the year, the magistrate compiled detailed accounts of the taxes collected and those still outstanding in his chou or hsien. These accounts were then turned over to the financial commissioner, sometimes through an intermediary such as the prefect or circuit intendant. The financial commissioner himself drew up the four-column accounts for the whole province, listing the balance to be carried forward, new receipts, expenditures, and the present balance. In turn, he submitted a draft to the governor or governor-general, whose staff transcribed it in the form of a "yellow account" for the emperor and a "clear account" for the Board. These reports included a summary of how much *ti-ting ch'ien-liang* was collected, how much was paid and in arrears, how much was remitted to the capital and retained in the province, how much was transferred to the military, how much was used to buy local products for the capital, and how much was left over.[45]

This new system of auditing not only meant that provincial officials had to justify their accounts at the end of the year, but also gave the Board of Revenue authority over the way in which local revenues were used on a day-to-day basis. Although enforcement must have been difficult, the law now required that no local retained funds could be allocated without prior Board authorization. Even funds that had been so budgeted could not be disbursed until another report had been made indicating the exact amount that was required at the moment of allocation.[46] At the end of the year, the Board compared the local official's annual accounts against these "receipts" in the capital to make certain that all items of income and expenditure balanced, and that all expenditures had been approved in advance.[47] After an item-by-item audit, the Board would either accept the accounts (*chun*) or reject them (*po*) and return them to the governor for revision or clarification. Although the work of verification and compilation was carried out at lower levels of the provincial administration, culminating in the financial commissioner's report, the ultimate responsibility for promptness and accuracy again lay with the governor and governor-general. If a magistrate was found guilty of delaying his *tsou-hsiao* report, or of compiling confusing accounts designed to conceal fraud, he was to be impeached immediately by the governor or governor-general. If the latter failed to report irregularities perpetrated by their subordinates, or were lax in their supervision and failed to discover malfeasance that was later revealed, they were held jointly responsible.

In view of the large number of deficit cases uncovered in the first years of the Yung-cheng reign, the efficacy of this system of centralized control may be doubted. As we shall see, it was possible to evade careful scrutiny of accounts by bribing the Board officials and clerks. Moreover, the penalties for delays were minor and were prorated according to the length of the delay.[48] Sanctions for discrepancies were also light, ranging from demotion of one grade and transfer for a magistrate or prefect to a fine of one year's salary (*feng-yin*) for a commissioner or circuit intendant and six months' salary for a governor or governor-general.[49] This was not considered a great hardship, inasmuch as *feng-yin* was itself a token sum.[50] Moreover, during part of the K'ang-hsi period, official salaries were suspended to help pay the costs of pacification campaigns.[51] Even when they were granted, the salaries of officials and yamen staff were often arrogated in full or in part by the governor to pay for expenditures not covered by *ts'un-liu* funds, a practice euphemistically called *chüan-feng* or "contributions of salary."[52]

However ineffective this system of scrutiny may have been in the early years of the dynasty, it did establish a standard for local and provincial accountability in the area of public finance that was strengthened under later emperors. In particular, it marked a further refinement of the Ming system by placing supervision of both collection and expenditure under one agency. Not only did this contribute greatly to the centralization of fiscal authority, but it also enhanced the central government's interest in improving tax-collection and local-accounting procedures. The form of the *tsou-hsiao ts'e* itself can be seen as contributing to the development of local budgets. Moreover, without such a system, the investigation of deficits undertaken in the Yung-cheng period would have been impossible. Finally, by placing all legitimate income clearly under the control of the central government, the *tsou-hsiao* system of annual accounting also contributed to the crisis in local funding that led to the reorganization of provincial finances in the early eighteenth century.

Centralization of Tax Collection

The aim of the *tsou-hsiao* system of annual accounting was to prevent revenue loss resulting from official waste and corruption. However, the early Ch'ing government also devised methods to rectify the defects in the Ming fiscal apparatus that had prevented taxes from ever reaching the local and provincial coffers. Whereas the Ming had attempted to utilize local elites as instruments of government policy and had failed, the Ch'ing remained committed, until the nineteenth century, to the principle of a direct relationship between the government and the people. In the realm of tax administration this meant waging an unending campaign against both official and nonofficial intermediaries who took on the role of tax farmer, and creating an informed public that could both do without such middlemen and resist their efforts at control of tax collection.

The first step in this direction was taken as soon as the Manchus entered China. In part because the dynasty had not yet been able to compile its own editions of the *Fu-i ch'üan-shu*, the new rulers turned to the use of "easy-to-read lists" (*i-chih yu-tan*) to inform taxpayers of their annual rates. *Yu-tan* were not unknown in the Ming dynasty. However, the memorialists requesting the use of "easy-to-read lists" in 1644 placed a new emphasis on their effectiveness in cutting through the confusion of regulations, quotas, and tax rates as they appeared in the *Fu-i ch'üan-shu*. This was not intended as a mere stopgap, but as a way to improve tax collection in the long term by providing both officials and taxpayers with an easily understood enumeration of the actual amount of taxes each household owed.[53]

Whatever the hopes of its original formulators, the system of *i-chih yu-tan* failed as a panacea for China's fiscal ills. By KH 24 (1685) they were discontinued because officials and yamen runners were found to be using the costs of their production as a pretext to levy surcharges on the people.[54] In place of the defunct "easy-to-read lists," the emperor ordered all county-level administrative units to set up stone tablets in front of the yamen informing the people of the tax rates in the vicinity according to the *Fu-i ch'üan-shu*.[55] Unfortunately, this system once more left the peasantry prey to the machinations of middlemen, because few villagers made regular trips to the county seat where they could see these tablets. Even those who did undertake such a journey would still have to estimate their own personal liability and manage to insist on that amount in the face of the conflicting and often much larger claims of yamen runners and tax-collection clerks. Thus, the task facing government was twofold—to find a new way to inform the peasants of their individual tax liabilities and to free the taxpayer from those institutions that perpetrated the hold of middlemen over them.

The most culpable of such institutions was the old Ming *li-chia*. By the early Ch'ing this system of rotating responsibility for tax remittance had become little more than a vehicle through which local strongmen and bullies (*hao-lieh chien-kun*) took control of an area's taxes. Domination of the collection process by third parties fostered extortion. In some places the practice of levying surcharges through the *li-chia* was so well established that the methods used had even been given names. If all the *li* in a hsien shared in the annual payment of these fees it was called *juan-t'ai*. If, on the other hand, each *li* and *chia* took turns paying, it was called *ying-t'ai*.[56] Whatever the name, the result was the same: added burdens for the people and diminished revenues for the government.

The means devised to overcome these malpractices was the system of "rolling lists" (*kun-tan*). Unlike the "easy-to-read lists," "rolling lists" were not simply grafted on to the *li-chia*, but were meant to replace them. Under this new system, households were still grouped together in units called *li*. However, the Ming arrangement of households into artificial decimal units, regardless of physical proximity or social relationship, was abandoned. "In a single hsien, a *li* might have five households or ten households."[57] The basis for establishing these new units was that they be natural groupings of households whose relationships with each other went beyond tax collection. The kind of information provided on the "rolling lists" was also more extensive than the system they replaced. Under the name of each household in the *li* was clearly delineated the amount of land its members owned, how much tax was due on that land in silver and in kind, how much should be paid in the spring collection period, and how much should be paid in the fall. These payments were then further divided into ten installments and the amount due in each installment was also set out in detail.

The most important feature of the "rolling lists" was not what it was, but what it was not. It was not a system of collecting taxes. It was only a means of notifying the taxpayers of the taxes due. In the edict promulgating the use of "rolling lists," special emphasis was placed on informing the populace that each taxpayer was to wrap his own taxes and deposit them personally in the county tax chest. No one was permitted to act for the people in this regard, whether it be the old *li* headman, silversmiths, yamen personnel, or any other third party. The "rolling lists" would guarantee tax payments not by making one man responsible for delivery of everyone's taxes, but by making rotation of the list itself contingent upon each household's fulfilling its obligations to the government. The list containing all of the above-mentioned information would be issued to the first name and passed on in turn to the others. As the list came to each household it was to pay its individual tax. When one installment period was completed, the list was passed around again for the second period. If a taxpayer destroyed the list, did not pay in full, or failed to pass the list on to his neighbor, he as an individual was to be investigated, arrested, and severely punished.[58]

If taxpayers were to be responsible for wrapping and depositing their own taxes, in turn they had to be protected against false accusations of arrears. Under the system inherited from the Ming, chou and hsien magistrates entered the amount of tax received from each taxpayer on special receipts bearing the magistrate's official seal (*yin-p'iao*). Two copies were made for each payment. One was kept by the magistrate and one was given to the taxpayer as proof of payment. Abuses were common. Most often, on the pretext of needing the second copy to provide yamen runners with evidence when investigating and prompting payment of arrears, taxpayers were deprived of their own copies. Unscrupulous officials and clerks would then record the paid taxes as unpaid or would record payment at less than the amount actually collected.[59] The helpless taxpayer was left with no recourse but to pay his taxes a second time or produce a bribe in order to avoid being harassed by tax-prompting runners.

To solve this problem, "three-stub receipts" (*san-lien yin-p'iao*) were introduced. Each receipt had three sections. One was retained by the magistrate, one was turned over to the taxpayer as proof of payment, and one was kept by the yamen runners to compare with the other two in prompting payment of arrears (*ying-pi*).[60] It was hoped that the addition of one piece of paper would not only deprive the magistrate and his underlings of any pretext for withholding taxpayers' receipts, but would also ensure the magistrate's superiors of a record against which to compare the former's remittances to the capital.

Imperial Benevolence and Fiscal Administration

"Rolling lists" and "three-stub receipts" represented an important advance over the Ming system of tax assessment and collection. By placing the emphasis in tax collection on the individual household in a direct relationship with the government, these early Ch'ing reforms served as a local counterpart to the centralizing efforts within the bureaucracy manifested in the *tsou-hsiao* system of annual accounting. Yet, just as the latter was plagued by evasion and manipulation, so did "rolling lists" and "three-stub receipts" fail to wipe out tax farming and the oppression of the masses by rapacious yamen functionaries.

Seeing the problems facing them strictly in terms of tax evasion and bureaucratic corruption, late Ming and early Ch'ing reformers naturally sought to root out the sources of government shortages through refinements in the existing system of imperial finances. As important as these refinements were, they were all bureaucratic solutions to what were perceived as fundamentally bureaucratic problems. The weakness of such measures is epitomized in the case of the three-stub receipt. When, in the Yung-cheng period, this system was found inadequate in preventing official and clerical corruption, it was replaced by the four-stub receipt. But even a ten-stub receipt would not have solved the problems that gave rise to this corruption in the first place.

One source of difficulty was the laxity with which the government handled offenders. We have already seen that the sanctions accompanying the implementation of annual accounting were insufficient to dissuade the most determined officials from exceeding deadlines and tampering with their fiscal records. As will be seen, the incomplete state of most tax registers after the long period of dynastic transition also impeded the government's efforts at fiscal control.[61] The existence of such obstacles could only have contributed to the K'ang-hsi emperor's personal leniency as a ruler, a trait for which he was famous. For K'ang-hsi, gaining the confidence and support of the local elite and the overwhelmingly native Chinese bureaucracy was as pressing a task as increasing government revenues. Leniency, as a personal quality, may have suited the emperor's temperament, but in the early years of the dynasty its importance was clearly political.

Leniency was common in the handling of both of the traditionally recognized causes of government shortages. When the level of unpaid taxes rose too high, the K'ang-hsi emperor would simply declare a tax amnesty. For example, in KH 43 (1704) the emperor cancelled all the tax debts of the entire populations of Shansi and Shensi. In KH 50 (1711), he excused Chihli, Fengtien, Chekiang, Fukien, Kwangtung, Kwangsi, Szechuan, Yunnan, and Kweichow from 8,377,100 taels in land and head taxes. At the same time, in order to lessen the burdens on the people, the emperor cancelled accumulated arrears of more than 1,185,400 taels.[62]

Even in cases of obvious official corruption, K'ang-hsi seems to have been exceedingly hesitant to apply strict disciplinary sanctions. In 1685, the Director of Grain Transport memorialized on corrupt practices in the shipment of tribute grain to the capital. The Council of Ministers deliberated the case and recommended the impeachment and removal of the officials involved, but the emperor's edict on the affair advised instead that the guilty parties simply be given a stern warning against any future repetition of such activities. As malfeasance of the kind they were accused of had long since become common practice, it was, K'ang-hsi felt, unfair to single these men out for punishment. The emperor was equally lenient in the face of mounting official deficits. Despite regulations requiring officials to repay all deficits incurred during their terms in office, he ruled in a case in 1702 that such repayment was too difficult and asked that the Grand Secretariat find another solution to the problem.[63]

An excellent example of the more "benevolent" approach taken toward tax offenders during the K'ang-hsi period can be seen in the handling of so-called "hidden lands" (*yin-ti*). Hidden lands were the product of the widespread concealment of newly reclaimed land from the tax registers. Some of this concealment was perpetrated by individual peasants who reclaimed small plots and either deliberately or through ignorance of the law never reported them to the authorities. However, according to later investigators, much of the land was reported to the officials, who themselves collected the taxes and did not report these additions to the tax rolls to the central government.[64] Thus, the problem of hidden land can be seen as encompassing all of the defects in early Ch'ing fiscal administration: incomplete records, tax evasion, and official peculation.

In KH 51 (1712), an exchange of views took place that highlighted the contrasting approaches advocated on the issue of hidden land.[65] The debate developed over the poor progress being made by Szechuan province in restoring its tax income to that collected during the late Ming.[66] The original quota was 1,616,600 taels. However, by 1710 the most that could be wrung out of the province was 202,300 taels. Szechuan Governor Nien Keng-yao was appalled that after nearly seventy years of Ch'ing rule, revenues in the province had been raised to only a little over 10 percent of what they had once been. In part, he blamed officials who used the occasion of reporting new land for taxation (*shou-liang*) as a pretext to extort fees from the people. Consequently, the people often did not report reclaimed land.

Nien took a hard line on the problem. The only way to ensure increasing quotas was a strict policy of rewards and punishments. He suggested, therefore, that promotions be granted to all chou and hsien magistrates who could increase tax collection to 40 or 50 percent of the Ming quota. On the other hand, promotion would be blocked for those who could not reach at least 20 percent of the quota. Any official failing to collect even 10 percent of the taxes collected in the Ming would be demoted and transferred, and those showing no increase over present levels would be deprived of their rank and office.

A more moderate approach was advanced by the censor Tuan Hsi. Tuan pointed out that the main cause of Szechuan's low level of tax revenues was the depopulation that had occurred in the province during the uprisings of the late Ming. Even a diligent governor like Nien himself had been able to add only 26,000 taels to the tax rolls. Whereas Nien would claim that the wealth, in population and cultivated land, was there to be tapped if only the law gave him the weapons to do so, Tuan felt that such a policy would benefit only the corrupt. Virtuous officials would find these figures impossible to achieve and would be impeached. Unscrupulous officials seeking promotion would force the innocent to confess to hiding land they did not have in order to reach the magic numbers they needed. Even though Tuan's plan supported a thorough investigation of hidden land and omitted taxes (*yin-lou*)[67] and punishment of any official who used the process of reporting new land to engage in extortion, its main emphasis was moral exhortation. Raising Szechuan's quotas could be accomplished only by ordering officials to encourage the people wholeheartedly to report their land and by punishing those who evaded taxation. Nothing was said of those officials who succeeded in getting the people to declare the fruits of reclamation but who never passed this added income on to the state.

Needless to say, it was Tuan's method of gentle persuasion that was endorsed by K'ang-hsi. Benevolent rule was upheld, but hidden land, along with other forms of embezzlement and tax evasion, continued to be a problem long afterwards. Nevertheless, it was not simply laxity that led to the deficits discovered by Yung-cheng when he inherited the empire from his father. Had that been the case, the strengthening of sanctions and the tightening of official discipline imposed by Yung-cheng from his first day as emperor would have been enough to solve China's fiscal problems and the reforms of the 1720s would never have taken place. It was certainly with no more ambitious prescription in mind that the new emperor initiated his attack on the fiscal chaos that was his birthright. Once the campaign was launched, it disclosed weaknesses in the Ch'ing fiscal system that went far deeper than anything admitted by the formulae of the traditional political economy and would require far more fundamental changes than the patchwork refinements and exhortations to virtue so popular in the past.

2

INFORMAL
NETWORKS
OF FUNDING

SINCE THE DAYS WHEN FREE TRADERS AND MIS-
sionaries first insinuated themselves into Chinese society, Westerners have clung to an image of a China ruled by a corrupt bureaucracy in which the "squeeze" or bribe was the usual means of
achieving objectives. When the Yung-cheng emperor first took up
the reins of power, he also saw corruption as the root of his government's fiscal difficulties. Such an analysis made possible the
Westerners' sweeping denigration of the Chinese system of rule.
Ironically, for the Chinese the all too visible evidence of corruption
in their ranks facilitated uncritical acceptance of fiscal arrangements that had long since been removed from the administrative structure for which they were designed. If government deficits
and arrears were the result of evil deeds by evil men, all that was
needed was the intensification of moral exhortations and the punishment of the worst offenders. It was by these means that generations of Chinese reformers sought to restore the health and purity
of the system as a whole.

No one would deny that fiscal malpractices abounded in late-
imperial China. Nor would anyone deny that the chief victims of
these evil deeds were the common people. However, if we view
corruption strictly in terms of the venality of the ruling strata of
Chinese society, we miss the opportunity to understand why it

played such an important part in Chinese public life. Men who steal for personal gain exist in any social system. Far more pernicious were the conditions that made manipulation of the legal tax administration necessary for the very survival of the Chinese bureaucracy. Once such practices became established, it is not surprising that their more self-aggrandizing manifestations also multiplied.

Revenue Sharing in the Early Ch'ing

The early Ch'ing rulers were centralizers. Having entered China from outside its borders, they had little stake in local customs and little knowledge of local needs. When implementing policy they generally aimed at uniform application of the law (*hua-i*). When they adapted Ming institutions, they did so in such a way as to enhance the authority of the state. This is most striking in the area of fiscal administration. We have already seen the extent to which the Single Whip reforms of the late Ming contributed to the weakening of the fiscal bases of local government. The Manchus took over the framework of postreform finance and added to it refinements designed to strengthen further the control of the central government over all the resources of the empire. As a result, provincial and local administrations were left without adequate sources of income of their own. We can begin to understand the dilemma facing the official in the field by examining how tax revenues were distributed during the early Ch'ing.

Retained and Remitted Taxes

China's early-eighteenth-century fiscal crisis was not primarily a result of an inadequate appreciation of the taxable resources of the late-imperial economy. Taxation was moderate, but included a wide variety of direct and indirect levies. Besides the predominant land and head tax (*ti-ting ch'ien-liang*), paid largely in cash, several minor taxes in kind also persisted.[1] In addition, several provinces owed a quota of grain tribute (*ts'ao-liang*) in kind, shipped to the capital along the Grand Canal.[2] Miscellaneous indirect taxes (*tsa-shui*) without fixed quotas brought the government a share of local commercial profits. Taxes were levied on the sale of specific commodities such as tobacco, cotton, wine, pigs and other livestock, and goods being unloaded at transit points or for sale at local and regional markets. Real-estate transactions were recorded and taxed through the levy on title deeds, and retail establishments, pawnshops, and brokers were also subject to imposts and licensing.[3]

The most important sources of commercial revenues were the salt gabelle, the tea tax, and customs duties. Next to the land and head taxes, these constituted the largest portion of the central government's annual income.[4] Moreover, unlike the land and head tax, miscellaneous duties, and so on, which were collected by the regular county-level bureaucracy, each of these duties was generally managed by its own special administrative apparatus. The existence of special agencies to collect the salt, tea, and customs revenues strengthened the central government's control over these duties, though according to dynastic law all the above-mentioned taxes were the property of the central government. In documents pertaining to fiscal matters these taxes were often referred to collectively as the "primary revenues" or "regular taxes" (*cheng-hsiang*) to distinguish them from taxes or tribute of a more regional or sporadic nature and from surcharges levied on the regular tax quota itself.

Of all these taxes, only one was statutorily shared with the provincial and local governments. This was the land and head tax. In the *Comprehensive Books of Taxation and Services* for each province, the land-and-head-tax quota was divided into the amount to be retained for provincial use (*ts'un-liu*) and the amount to be remitted to the imperial capital (*ch'i-yün*). It is therefore on the basis of the retained land- and head-tax quotas that we must judge the adequacy of the Ch'ing system of revenue sharing. Table 2.1 presents the distribution of retained and remitted taxes in 1685. The retained tax quotas for Honan, Shansi, Shantung, Chihli, Kiangsi, Hupei, Hunan, and Chekiang are high because they include revenues sent directly to assist nearby provinces with small gross-tax receipts. Likewise, the high percentage of local revenues retained by provinces such as Szechuan and Yunnan was a reflection of their unusually low level of land-tax income and not any greater munificence in providing for their local administrative needs. Because these retained taxes underwent extensive redistribution, the most we can conclude from these figures is that an average of 21 percent of all land and head taxes was left in the provinces for local use.

Table 2.1   *Retained and Remitted* Ti-ting *Taxes in 1685*
(all figures are rounded off to the nearest tael of silver)

Province	Remitted tax quota	Retained tax quota	Tax total	Retained taxes as % of total
Kiangsu	2,836,593	1,141,923	3,978,516	28.7
Chihli	2,881,108	562,500	3,443,608	16.3
Shantung	2,504,209	687,206	3,191,415	21.5
Shansi	2,678,779	338,510	3,017,289	11.2
Chekiang	2,188,575	732,054	2,920,629	25.0
Honan	2,268,602	445,055	2,713,657	16.4
Kiangsi	1,525,637	434,918	1,960,555	22.2
Anhui	1,153,291	536,567	1,689,858	31.7
Shensi	1,277,096	298,656	1,575,752	18.9
Kwangtung	1,006,377	139,718	1,146,095	12.2
Fukien	866,448	203,405	1,069,853	19.0
Hupei	821,754	213,073	1,034,827	20.6
Hunan	487,419	150,575	637,994	23.6
Kwangsi	243,211	89,311	332,522	26.8
Kansu	105,969	105,123	211,092	49.7
Yunnan		174,818	174,818	100.0
Kweichow	61,692	1,524	63,216	2.4
Szechuan	12,461	29,535	41,996	70.3
Totals	22,919,221	6,284,471	29,203,692	21.5%

SOURCE: *Ta-ch'ing hui-tien,* Yung-cheng edition, *chüan* 32, *hu-pu* 10, *fu-i* 2, *ch'i-yün.*

This does not mean that *ts'un-liu* quotas were unalterable. As the total income from direct taxes increased, so did the amount left in the provinces.[5] In fact, the quotas of retained taxes were set annually, on the basis of estimates of salary and military-supply requirements submitted by the governor and governor-general of each province.[6] Thus, adjustments could be made to meet specific increases in anticipated expenses, such as wages for additional troops stationed in a province, or salary raises resulting from the upgrading of subordinate administrative units. There was also provision for emergencies. Additional assistance funds could be requested from neighboring provinces, and if these proved insufficient, salt-gabelle revenues or direct aid from the central government might also be obtained.[7]

Nevertheless, the flexibility of *ts'un-liu* funding was extremely limited. The definition of an emergency allowed only for such events as major natural disasters and military campaigns. Nothing was provided for the local authority confronted with pressing shortages in the course of day-to-day administration. Such confrontations were frequent, in part because the share of revenues left for local government was small. Equally important was the fact that these funds were available for specified uses only, and even then were strictly monitored by the newly created *tsou-hsiao* system of accounting.

The Poverty of Local Administration

The calculation that 21 percent of all land and head taxes were allocated at the local level masks a startling fact about *ts'un-liu* revenues. In reality, an overwhelming portion of these funds was not available for local expenses at all.

The uses to which retained taxes in the Ch'ing could be applied fell into three broad categories: military supply, the imperial post, and local expenses. Until recently it was possible only to attempt rough estimates of the relative weight given to each of these types of expenditure. However, with the opening of the Ming-Ch'ing Archives in Peking to foreign scholars we can now examine existing *tsou-hsiao* accounts to determine the precise manner in which local revenues were distributed during the late K'ang-hsi period.

The only complete *tsou-hsiao ts'e* containing the information we seek is a report on Shansi land and head taxes for the last year of the K'ang-hsi reign. This report is particularly valuable because it delineates, hsien by hsien, the amount of retained *ti-ting* taxes that was allocated to each of the categories for which local revenues were allocated. Most revealing in the Shansi statistics is the unexpectedly high proportion of retained revenues destined for military expenses. If we add to this the portion reserved for the upkeep of the imperial post stations, a responsibility exercised at both the county and provincial levels,[8] we find that over 84 percent of all land and head taxes left for local use were earmarked for expenses primarily of concern to the central government.[9]

The constraints on local finances become more apparent when we examine the kinds of expenditures covered by "local expenses." These were quite specific. Besides the government stipend for all ranking officials (*kuan-feng*), retained funds included wages for yamen runners (*i-shih*), ceremonial expenses (*ch'i-ssu*), student stipends (*ling-shan*), and charity for the orphaned, widowed, and poor (*ku-p'in*).[10] That these were fixed allocations based on the type of administrative unit is obvious from the narrow range of variation in the figures in the sixth column of table 2.3. If the size

Table 2.2 *Shansi Retained* Ti-ting *Taxes in 1722*

Total *ti-ting* taxes	Total retained *ti-ting* taxes	Retained *ti-ting* as a percentage of total *ti-ting*	Categories of expenditure as a percentage of total retained *ti-ting* taxes			
			Military supply	Imperial post	Local expenses	Local expenses as a percentage of total *ti-ting*
2,792,578 taels	848,947 taels	30.4	65.63	18.54	15.83	4.8

SOURCE: "Tsou-hsiao ti-ting ch'ien-liang shih wen-ts'e," *Nei-ko ta-k'u hsien-ts'un Ch'ing-tai han-wen huang ts'e*, no. 501.

Table 2.3 *Retained* Ti-ting *Taxes in Fifteen Chou and Hsien in Shansi Province in 1722 (in taels)*

County-level unit	Total *ti-ting* taxes	Total retained *ti-ting* taxes	Retained *ti-ting* as a percentage of total *ti-ting*	Retained *ti-ting* by category		Local expenses	Local expenses as a percentage of retained *ti-ting*
				Military supply	Imperial post		
Hsiang-ling	48,825	14,745	30.2	10,768	2,450	1,527	10.4
P'ing-lu	18,792	7,218	38.4	3,920	2,011	1,287	17.8
Ho-ching	37,024	8,694	23.5	4,598	2,351	1,745	20.1
Tai-ku	40,163	5,477	13.6	1,775	2,143	1,559	28.5
Chi-shan	51,232	11,120	21.7	7,491	2,375	1,254	11.3
Ting-hsiang	18,200	7,454	41.0	5,229	1,095	1,130	15.2
Chieh-chou	27,711	6,532	23.6	4,053	1,240	1,239	19.0
Ta-ning	6,102	3,735	61.2	2,488	169	1,078	28.9
Jui-cheng	36,031	8,108	22.5	4,369	2,032	1,707	21.0
Hsiang-ning	11,412	3,094	27.1	1,043	846	1,205	38.9
Ch'in-chou	16,260	6,324	38.9	3,787	1,120	1,417	22.4
Hsing	12,786	3,883	30.4	2,145	581	1,157	29.8
Wu-hsiang	14,769	5,246	35.5	4,470	—	776	14.3
Pao-te	4,790	1,968	41.1	610	172	1,186	60.3
T'un-liu	26,094	12,694	48.6	9,006	2,297	1,391	11.0

SOURCE: "Tsou-hsiao ti-ting ch'ien-liang shih wen-ts'e," *Nei-ko ta-k'u hsien-ts'un Ch'ing-tai han-wen huang-t'se*, no. 501. (Because space does not permit the listing of all the chou and hsien in the province, fifteen randomly selected county-level units are shown. Average retained taxes are slightly lower than the provincial average, which accounts for the slightly higher percentage retained for local expenses).

and complexity of an administrative unit was reflected in its total land- and head-tax revenues, the percentages of retained taxes allowed, as listed in the third and seventh columns, show that there was little relationship between funds allocated and the administrative needs of a chou or hsien. Larger county-level units, with greater population and productive capacity, kept a much smaller proportion of their gross output in taxes than did their more remote and backward neighbors.

These figures appear small to have served as the total administrative budget legally available to local governmental divisions. However, not even these sums were destined entirely for local use. For accounting purposes most of the retained taxes of the whole province were deducted at the county level.[11] Thus, the average of about 1,500 taels listed under local expenses in each chou and hsien also included its share of the expenses of all higher administrative units. After deducting their own allotment, most counties seem to have sent their portion of the prefecture's expenses directly to the prefectural seat.[12] The remaining taxes were then transmitted to the provincial financial commissioner, who completed the distribution of *ts'un-liu* revenues to higher levels of government.

Included in the third category of retained funds was also a vague item usually called miscellaneous expenses (*ching-fei tsa-chih*). Most of these funds were stored in the provincial treasury and were utilized for emergencies and minor outlays. In the event of a serious natural disaster, retained funds were used to provide famine relief. At times they were even used by one province to buy grain for relief of a neighboring province.[13] Early in the dynasty a portion of the regular taxes was allowed for the transportation of taxes to the capital (*chiao-chia*). In KH 2 (1663), transportation expenses were also extended to shipments of military-supply funds outside the province of origin.[14] On occasion, regular tax revenues were also made available for repairing granaries, opening mines, and other extraordinary expenses.[15]

The allocation of regular tax revenues for the above expenditures was clearly of benefit to the province as a whole. Except in the case of famine relief, local governments were affected less directly. The costs of provincial projects not paid for by central-government grants of regular taxes were often met by assessing a contribution from each chou and hsien magistrate. They in turn usually raised the necessary amount by levying surcharges on the local population. Thus, at the very least, the existence of ts'un-liu relieved the local administration of some of the burdens of added taxation. However, it still left provincial officials at all levels of the bureaucracy with considerable expenses for the everyday tasks of government.

Of course, Shansi cannot be taken as a microcosm of the whole empire. However, besides being the only province for which complete ts'un-liu data of this kind have been preserved, it does have the advantage of having been in the middle range of land- and head-tax quotas. Regional variations in retained revenue allocation did exist. Kiangsu province stands out in table 2.1 as retaining an unusually large portion of its regular taxes, and an examination of a tsou-hsiao ts'e for Soochow prefecture in KH 32 (1693) confirms this impression. (See table 2.4.) Not only did chou and hsien in Kiangsu receive special ts'un-liu funds for water conservancy, but the sums allocated for local expenses were also the highest in the empire. There are a number of possible explanations for this. Miyazaki Ichisada has shown that the number of statutory yamen runners in Soochow was extremely large.[16] This is not surprising, considering Kiangsu's role as the economic and tax-producing center of early Ch'ing China. Moreover, it is likely that the figures given for official stipends, runners' wages, ceremonial costs, charity, and miscellaneous expenses in Soochow included the contribution its subordinate units made to the various specialized agencies in the region, notably the imperial salt and silk administrations. Nevertheless, it does seem that officials in Soochow, and Kiangsu as a whole, may have been less pressed financially than were officials in other parts of China.[17]

If we were to seek a southern example to compare with that of Shansi in the north, Kiangsi is more representative. Here the problem lies in the failure of the annual accounts to separate out military supply in the enumeration of retained taxes. However, if we view "local expenses" as a percentage of total land- and head-tax revenues, they come to 6.8 percent, only slightly higher than Shansi's 4.8 percent. The similarity is even greater when we look at the breakdown of ts'un-liu by hsien. Taking as an example Chiu-chiang fu, a prosperous prefecture where we might expect retained revenues to be higher than average, we can see that the funds available for local expenses were only about 100 taels greater than in

Table 2.4 *Partial List of Retained Ti-ting Taxes in Soochow Prefecture in 1692 (in taels of silver)*

County-level unit	Total *ti-ting* taxes	Total retained *ti-ting* taxes	Retained *ti-ting* by category				Local expenses	Local expenses as a percentage of total *ti-ting*
			Water conservancy	Military supply	Imperial post		Local expenses	
T'ai-ts'ang chou	128,706	21,176	763	11,559	1,720		7,134	5.5
Ch'ang-chou hsien	205,113	32,968	1,521	16,069	4,592		10,786	5.2
Wu hsien	87,741	22,246	657	9,353	4,197		8,039	9.1
Wu-chiang hsien	205,136	39,212	1,275	21,921	7,532		8,484	4.1
Ch'ang-shou hsien	199,798	31,877	1,417	22,989	345		7,136	3.6
K'un-shan hsien	180,514	30,390	1,275	20,062	1,166		7,887	4.4
Chia-ting hsien	269,766	27,813	1,302	18,014	437		8,060	3.0

SOURCE: "Soochow fu-shu e-cheng ch'i-ts'un ti-ting pen-che ch'ien-liang . . . wan-ch'ien fen-shu wen-ts'e," *Nei-ko ta-k'u hsien-ts'un Ch'ing-tai han-wen huang-ts'e,* no. 572.

Table 2.5 *Kiangsi Retained Ti-ting Taxes in 1722 (in taels of silver)*

| Total *ti-ting* taxes | Local expenses | | | | | Total local expenses | Local expenses as a percentage of total *ti-ting* |
	Yamen expenses/ official salaries and runner wages	Student stipends	Charity	Imperial post			
1,979,410	124,194	4,197	7,566	108,171		135,957	6.8%

SOURCE: Kiangsi Governor P'ei Shuai-tu, "Hu-pu hsiang-hsia ti-ting min-t'un ch'i-ts'un ch'ien liang ping t'un-ting tsou-hsiao wen-ts'e," *Nei-ko ta-k'u hsien-ts'un Ch'ing-tai han-wen huang-ts'e*, no. 699.

Table 2.6 *Chiu-Chiang Prefecture, Kiangsi, Retained Ti-ting Taxes in 1723 (in taels of silver)*

| Hsien | Total ti-ting taxes | Local expenses | | | | Imperial post | Total local expenses | Local expenses as a percentage of total ti-ting |
		Yamen expenses/ official salaries and runner wages	Student stipends	Charity				
Te-hua	14,515	1,748	120	144		6,528	2,012	13.9%
Te-an	14,027	1,349	40	70		3,379	1,459	10.4%
Shui-ch'ang	11,141	1,229	40	40		732	1,309	11.7%
Hu-kou	18,669	2,202	40	24		1,507	2,266	12.1%
Peng-che	18,323	1,677	40	18		2,100	1,735	9.5%

SOURCE: *Tung-cheng pao-hsiao*, no. 2876, cover page missing. (The early portions of this *huang-ts'e*, listing total revenues for the province, are missing. However, by combining this *huang-ts'e* with the one for the preceding year (see table 2.5) we can get a fairly complete picture of Kiangsi taxes in the early 1720s).

Shansi. Moreover, here, too, the amount of a unit's retained revenues does not seem to rise as a function of the size or complexity of the hsien itself.

The Fiscal Demands on Local Government
Local-government Expenses

Even the most virtuous and frugal of local officials would have found it difficult to operate within the limits set by this system of revenue sharing. Although all *ts'un-liu* allocations included a category of official salaries, the amounts granted for this purpose were minuscule, comprising neither a living wage nor an administrative budget. Yet, as we have seen, along with runners' wages, these were almost the only funds legally available to civil officials for the purposes of local government.

One's salary as an official depended solely on the rank of one's post. Posts were divided into nine main grades, each containing two subgrades. (See table 2.7.) Runners' wages were considerably lower, averaging around six taels annually, although they could be as much as twelve taels for runners with highly specialized skills.[18] Inasmuch as the number of officials and statutory runners at any

Table 2.7 *Official Salary* (feng-yin) *Scale in the Ch'ing Dynasty*

Official rank	Salary (taels)	Type of official (sample)
1a	180	Grand secretary
1b	180	Governor-general
2a	155	Director of river conservancy
2b	155	Governor, financial commissioner
3a	130	Judicial commissioner
3b	130	Salt controller
4a	105	Grain intendant, circuit intendant, salt intendant
4b	105	Prefect, reader of the Grand Secretariat
5a	80	Subprefect (1st class), independent chou magistrate
5b	80	Assistant department director (six boards)
6a	60	Assistant reader of the Grand Secretariat
6b	60	Chou magistrate, subprefect (2nd class)
7a	45	Commissioner of records (judicial commissioner's office)
7b	45	Hsien magistrate
8a	40	Assistant hsien magistrate, hsien director of schools
8b	40	Hsien subdirector of schools
9a	33	Hsien registrar
9b	31	Sub-hsien magistrate

level of government was fairly constant, it is no wonder that throughout the empire, figures for local expenses in the *ts'un-liu* records were almost the same.

Because of the low level of local funding, all officials were urged to practice economy. However, the need to manifest one's rank in sumptuary display, as well as the need to support large entourages of relatives, servants, and disciples who accompanied officials to their posts, made real austerity impossible. Oertai, a prominent governor-general noted for his frugality, estimated that he required 6,000 taels annually for his living expenses alone.[19] Kansu Governor Hsü Jung calculated his living expenses at 5,000 taels of silver plus 405 piculs of grain, the latter being sent to him from his own family property.[20] The costs incurred by lower-ranking officials were undoubtedly less, but they could not have been met by the meager salaries provided by their *feng-yin*.

In addition to his own living expenses, every provincial official had a considerable staff to maintain. Because the quotas for yamen runners were set at a time when many administrative tasks were still carried out by the local population as corvée labor, the number of yamen runners for whom the government provided wages was never sufficient to meet the requirements of local administration. As the population grew and administrative responsibilities multiplied, most chou and hsien found that they needed extra staff. By the eighteenth century, An-yang hsien in Honan was spending over 1,700 taels per year on runners' wages alone, only a portion of which was allocated out of *ts'un-liu* revenues.[21]

Although at least some yamen runners received wages from the province's retained land and head taxes, no funds were provided to pay the large number of clerks employed by yamen at every level of government. A hsien in the early Ch'ing could have anywhere from several hundred to several thousand clerks.[22] Clerks were generally grouped into two alternating shifts, each confined to the yamen for ten days at a time, in order to insulate them from the public and lessen the chances for corruption while they conducted official business. During their confinement they had to be provided not only with the stationery and ink that were the tools of their trade, but also with food, water, firewood, lamp oil, and other necessities of life.[23] Most officials also retained a number of private secretaries (*mu-yu*) who were specialists in law, finance, and administration. Their high status and classical education merited salaries that were often greater than that which the government paid the official himself. A private secretary employed by a chou or hsien magistrate probably received around 100 taels a year. Salaries for private secretaries serving higher officials were considerably larger.[24] Despite the strain this clearly put on an official's finances, private secretaries were considered an indispensable part of one's administrative staff. Every magistrate could be expected to have at least two, and it was not unusual for a high official to have ten such men in his employ.

Wages, stationery, ink, fuel, food, and so on can be seen as constituting the "inner" expenses of the yamen, those raw materials that kept the administration functioning. However, the responsibilities and expenses of a provincial official did not stop at the yamen gate. Even before his arrival at a new post, an official could be expected to go into debt to pay the enormous costs of moving his family and staff to a distant assignment.[25] To this were added the costs of transportation, food, and lodging whenever he or his deputies left the yamen to tour the area under his jurisdiction.[26] The burden of transporting taxes within the province was shouldered by the unit collecting them, that is, the chou and hsien and the various agencies specializing in commercial taxes. Likewise, the costs of most official communications within the province were borne by the officials who sent them.[27] Government post stations maintained and manned with provincial ts'un-liu revenues did not exist to facilitate contact among local officials.

All of these expenses pale before what may be called the costs of physical maintenance of a province or county. Imperial gifts flowed into the provinces for the erection of Confucian temples, memorial arches, and plaques bearing facsimiles of the imperial calligraphy, but the emperor left largely to fate those structures upon which the practical welfare depended. The central government funded major flood-control projects, but the smaller dams, dikes, and irrigation projects of the seventeenth and early eighteenth centuries were built through local initiative, with local funds and local labor.[28] Similar means had to be found to repair yamen buildings, city walls, granaries, and bridges and roads that did not lie along major post routes. Even famine relief was frequently left to the devices of local officials whose legally available revenues provided them with scant means to aid the victims of disaster or to prevent such disasters in the future.[29]

The records of the Board of Revenue abound with accounts of officials who could not make ends meet and who were unlucky enough to get caught trying. Sometimes it was natural disaster that upset the delicate arrangements worked out at the local level to cover the costs of being a "parent official" to the people. The case of Ho Shih, a forty-one-year-old *chü-jen* from Chungking, was not unusual.[30] Ho was appointed magistrate of Yin hsien in Ningpo prefecture, Chekiang, in 1715, and for almost nine years had served in that post, seemingly without blemish. Then, in 1723, he was impeached for embezzling 7,882.6 taels in regular land and head taxes. According to Ho's own testimony, his troubles were the result of the poverty of the area he governed. Because this was a coastal hsien, agriculture was poor and many of the inhabitants made their living from fishing. To require them to pay their taxes in silver would have been a hardship, and so he allowed them to pay in the common local medium of exchange, copper cash. Yin hsien was so economically backward that in order to remit these taxes to the provincial capital, Ho had to send the copper cash to a nearby marketing town in another county to be converted to silver. His first impeachment occurred when, unexpectedly, the Ningpo prefect arrived to inspect his treasury and found that the 3,224.7 taels being converted were missing from the hsien.

Ho's inquisitors accepted his explanation regarding these funds, because they were restored as soon as his messenger returned. The magistrate's real problems began when he tried to deal with natural disasters affecting the area at the same time. In 1721, Yin hsien suffered bad harvests due to severe drought, and the next year was also hot and dry. The poor soil of this coastal region had never supported an early rice crop, and in 1722 the late rice crop was lost. Although he had requested a tax remission for the hsien, the shortage of food was so urgent that Ho took 2,217.9 taels of taxes due to be sent to the central government and bought rice from wealthy households in the hsien to try to stabilize rice prices. Unfortunately, many of the families under his jurisdiction were too impoverished to buy rice even at reduced prices. Therefore, he had each affected locality draw up a register of the very needy and offered direct loans of this rice at a rate of one peck (*tou*) per adult and five pints (*sheng*) per child. The cost of the rice was to be repaid by the recipients after the harvest the following year.

Later in the year, Ho became concerned about further rice shortages because the drying up of waterways had discouraged outside merchants from transporting rice into the hsien. He asked his superiors to urge merchants from Soochow to bring in cheaper rice and himself allocated 2,380 taels in land and head taxes to send a messenger to Soochow to make a direct purchase of 1,700 piculs of rice for sale in the hsien. Once again an untimely visit by the Ningpo prefect's representative led to impeachment for embezzlement, but because this rice was eventually sold and the money returned to the treasury, Ho was also excused for this indiscretion. In fact, Ho might have escaped prosecution altogether had these two years of drought not been followed by tidal waves in 1723 that made it impossible for the people to pay back the 2,217.9 taels worth of relief grain borrowed the previous year. As a result, the magistrate was forced to sell his personal property to reimburse the central government for relief services provided out of taxes that should have been remitted to Peking.[31]

The story of Magistrate Ho is only one of many examples of central-government failure to provide for even basic relief measures necessitated by natural disaster. Nevertheless, had Ho's manipulation of regular tax funds worked as originally planned, and had the Ningpo prefect not turned up just when Yin hsien funds were temporarily missing, he might have escaped censure altogether. More pressing was the expense for which a magistrate could expect no reimbursement, as was discovered by the Chü-ning hsien, Szechuan, magistrate Chuang Ch'eng-tsu.

Magistrate Chuang was probably not the most savory of characters to be found in the early Ch'ing bureaucracy. Among the numerous charges of official malfeasance leveled against him was that of collecting illegal surcharges (*chia-p'ai*).[32] Chuang was able to clear himself of part of the charge by showing that the silver in circulation in Chü-ning was only 70 to 80 percent pure, so that an additional weight had to be added to every tael of tax paid. However, he was still held responsible for levying an illegal surcharge of 10 percent on all taxes remitted in the hsien between the last month of KH 59 and the time of his impeachment in mid-YC 1. Chuang's explanation for his actions reads like a litany of expenditures left to badly underfunded local governments:

> The total surcharges I collected came to 2,167.1 taels. During these three years I allocated 320.4 taels for yamen runners' wages. To repair the tower over the city gate and the city wall I spent 238.43 taels. To repair the hsien prison I spent 126.035 taels. To build a charity school (*i-hsüeh*) I spent 148.78 taels. To repair the Confucian temple I spent 482.49 taels. To repair

the temple to the city god I spent 149.09 taels. To build
an alms house I spent 82.47 taels. To build an ever-
normal granary I spent 52.54 taels.[33]

In addition, Chuang disbursed 210.7 taels for construction of a
new stone bridge at Hsi-mei chen, 63.27 taels for repairs on the
large stone bridge outside the south gate of the hsien city, 39.31
taels for repairs on the temple to loyal officials, 24.6 taels for construction of a ferry at the city's lower pier, and 37.8 taels for the
wages of ferrymen. The total expenditure came to 2,168.66 taels,
a little over one tael having been "contributed" by the magistrate
himself. When the investigators pressed Chuang again, accusing
him of using these repairs as a pretext to levy surcharges, Chuang
pointed out that all of the above undertakings were the responsibility of a local official, even if funds were not provided for them:

> If you expected me to contribute my own money to
> repair them, I didn't have the means. If I had let them
> topple, this too would have meant shirking my duties.
> This is why I added a surcharge to the regular tax. This
> is really a case of using public funds to pay for public
> expenses (*i-kung wan-kung*). All the gentry and com-
> moners in the hsien know I haven't taken a bit for
> myself.[34]

The failure of the regular system of revenue sharing to provide
for such basic expenses as small-scale relief efforts, construction
and repairs of city edifices, and the hiring of sufficient runners to
man the hsien yamen left local officials little choice but to devise
other means for their provision. Of course, once such methods
were in force, it was easy to extend their use to personal gain.
However, whatever happened, the local official was unlikely to
emerge from his term in office completely unscathed. If he limited
his expenditures to those revenues allowed him in the provincial
ts'un-liu budget, the hsien would almost surely suffer and the magistrate would be impeached for dereliction of duties. If he did not
remain within his budget, he was open to impeachment for corruption and embezzlement, a charge that carried a penalty of banishment to the outer reaches of the empire. Even if the government
recognized that he had used unauthorized funds for public purposes, the responsible official would be forced to sell his worldly
goods to repay the amount he had improperly used.[35] The central
government made the task of local officials no less difficult by itself

placing irregular demands on the meager retained revenues of the provinces.

Higher-level Demands

The central government was entitled to almost 80 percent of all land and head taxes collected in the provinces. However, this did not prevent Peking from frequently denying local officials even their full share of ts'un-liu quotas. Sometimes this took the form of outright confiscation. During the war to suppress the Three Feudatories, military expenses were so high that most of the regular taxes designated for the provinces, including for a time the salaries and wages of officials and yamen runners, were appropriated by the court.[36] More often, deductions from ts'un-liu were the result of a regulation that required that the central government be sent its full ch'i-yün quota before local officials began to put aside their own retained share of tax revenues.[37] Since all chou and hsien experienced arrears because of poor harvests, ineffective administration, tax farming, or simple tax evasion, few officials escaped shortages in their operating funds. An official struggling to rejuvenate an administration plagued with arrears was doubly handicapped by loss of all or part of the funds allocated to support himself and the very yamen employees he used to collect taxes. One practice even made officials responsible for compensating the central government for portions of the tax quota that could not be collected because the land on which they were levied had become unproductive and the inhabitants had fled.[38] Thus, just at a time when additional funds might be needed for relief work, reclamation, or to deal with popular unrest, officials were expected to make deductions from their own salaries and that of their staff to fill the central government's coffers.

Direct encroachment on provincial retained revenues was not the central government's only contribution to local fiscal problems. The rigorous accounting procedures developed by the Ch'ing to ensure strict central-government supervision of local expenditures caused as much corruption as it prevented. The tsou-hsiao system of annual accounting required exact allocations for specific items of expenditure. Because many administrative expenses were budgeted years in advance, a certain amount of rigidity was built into the system. When budgeted funds proved insufficient, an official often had to advance funds from other sources.[39] Inasmuch as such advances were illegal, a chain reaction was often set in motion whereby an official borrowed from one category of expenditure after another to cover up his mounting shortages. A post could change hands many times before the discrepancy was discovered, by which time it might be impossible to trace the official originally responsible.

Another aspect of the annual accounting system that could cause difficulties for local officials was the Board price (pu-chia). The Board of Revenue established rates at which local officials could use regular tax revenues to purchase goods for shipment to the capital and pay for materials and labor for the military, water and road works, and post-station maintenance. When the market price was lower than the Board price, officials could net a profit from such purchases, but where the Board price was underrated or prices fluctuated greatly, the burden on officials could be enormous. In the imperial post service, the costs of horse feed and wages for the laborers who tended the horses varied considerably from place to place. It fell to the officials in each area to make up any discrepancies between the real costs and the funds budgeted for these expenses.[40] The same was true of many construction projects. Once a budget was set, the costs of materials could change, weather conditions could slow up work, and unforeseen engineering problems could emerge, but the original allocation usually remained unaltered. Cost overruns were so common that an official would arguably have been better off raising the necessary funds by contributions and illegal surcharges, rather than expose himself to charges of mismanagement of ts'un-liu appropriations.[41]

The provincial financial commissioner had access to greater ts'un-liu revenues than did individual local officials, but these were rarely granted to supplement the costs of local endeavors. Chou and hsien magistrates could borrow funds from the provincial treasury in the event that tax collection was postponed because of natural disaster. However, this procedure, known as chieh-kei, applied only to circumstances in which the magistrate was left without enough money to cover official salaries, runners' wages, and other fixed ts'un-liu expenses, especially those necessary to perform the seasonal sacrifices. Only rarely were emergency funds extended to local government for more tangible purposes, such as bridge and road construction. Even then, the financial commissioner was bound by the same regulations that governed all ts'un-liu expenditures. Estimates of costs had to be submitted and verified by the financial commissioner, and all allocations had to be approved by the Board of Revenue prior to disbursement.[42] The Board could, and often did, reject such proposals or reduce the allowed costs. The financial commissioner had little discretionary control over the retained revenues in his treasury, and along with the governor, was often held responsible for repayment of any funds the Board deemed to have been wrongly spent.

The Board of Revenue placed one further claim on local tax resources. A portion of the retained taxes of every jurisdiction in the empire was illegally shunted back to the Board in the process of reporting the annual accounts. Ostensibly this "Board fee" (pu-fei) was a voluntary contribution to cover the Board's own stationery and clerical costs. In reality no official could hope for approval of his accounts without it, and much could be overlooked if it was sent.[43] Inadequate funding of central-government administration thus combined with the weaknesses of the local fiscal base to undermine official discipline and the elaborate precautions taken by the court to prevent corruption and shortages in the taxes remitted to Peking.

The emergence of the practice of salary and wage contributions by officials (chüan-feng) is evidence of the dilemma facing provincial officials trying to balance the demands of provincial administration against the requirements of the fiscal system. At least by the late K'ang-hsi period, lower officials and yamen runners were routinely being forced by their governors and financial commissioners to remit to the provincial capital all or part of their salaries and wages granted by the central government.[44] A portion of these funds was used by the provincial leadership to pay for specific projects whose costs could not be met with regular ts'un-liu revenues. Honan Governor T'ien Wen-ching reported that when dredging of the Chia-lu River began in 1706, 29,000 taels were raised for the enterprise from the salaries and wages of local officials and runners.[45] A somewhat different case involved the distribution of rice gruel to famine victims in three prefectures of Shantung province during 1719–20. Over 117,000 piculs were drawn from the province's relief granaries at the time, all of which were replenished through contributions from the salaries and wages of the local bureaucracy.[46]

The most common justification for appropriating salaries and wages was to make up provincial deficits. The prevalence of this practice may have resulted from the apparent sanction it received from the throne. Because the chou and hsien were required to re-mit the central government's tax quota before deducting their own *ts'un-liu* allowances, the contribution of salaries and wages that came from the *ts'un-liu* was in a sense built into the fiscal system. This was reinforced in 1706 when the K'ang-hsi emperor repri-manded the Honan bureaucracy for reporting tax arrears that year amounting to over 400,000 taels. Clearly, the emperor did not view these shortages as arrears, and accused the Honan officials of falsifying their accounts in the hope of receiving a large tax remis-sion. If the shortages in Honan were, on the contrary, a product of bureaucratic incompetence, K'ang-hsi felt it only right that the of-ficials bear the burden of repayment from their own salaries and their underlings' wages.[47]

For provincial governors, *chüan-feng* was an invaluable tool for balancing provincial accounts, and the Board of Revenue was lib-eral in approving its use. Governor Chang Po-hsing received per-mission to use salaries and wages for the years 1710–12 to repay 150,000 taels of deficits in Kiangsu.[48] During his term as Yunnan financial commissioner, Li Wei reported that sizeable military ex-penditures which had not received Board approval were now being made up through *chüan-feng*.[49] Contributions of wages and sala-ries released high provincial officials from personal responsibility for repayment of certain deficits and as such overcame some of the rigidity built into the *tsou-hsiao* system of annual accounting. It did so, however, at the expense of local officials, who could ill af-ford yet another encroachment on their already meager legitimate resources.

The Informal System of Funding in the Early Ch'ing

Shortages were part of the life of every provincial official in late-imperial China. Yet, throughout the seventeenth and early-eighteenth centuries, rivers were dredged, city walls repaired, bridges built, and roads improved. Justice was administered and order maintained, the poor were given aid, and the greatest con-sumer of public revenues, the bureaucracy itself, continued to function unimpeded. By no means was China under the Manchus a welfare state, nor was it ruled by a particularly activist regime. Nevertheless, the government of early Ch'ing China operated at a level of achievement far beyond the capacity of the regular system of taxation and finance.

With all regular taxes the property of the central government, and revenue-sharing provisions grossly inadequate to meet local administrative needs, additional funds had to be found elsewhere. Donations from influential and wealthy families were of some assistance, as were the independent undertakings of prominent individuals and lineages. The total contribution from these sources, however, was small when compared with the myriad expenses local governments incurred each year. Nor did China have the benefit of great banking houses, which could have themselves developed as the underwriters of public finance. In the end, provincial officials in China had only two options: either siphon off funds allocated by the central government for other purposes or destined for remittance to the central government, or squeeze the necessary funds from the people in the tax-collection process or in the marketplace.

By the eighteenth century, there had evolved in China a complex informal system of funding local government that utilized both options. Operating parallel to, and in coordination with, the regular fiscal administration, it was informal only in that it was not part of the statutory system of revenue sharing. As such, the money and goods that entered this system were not subject to the control of any higher authority. Most of the methods used to acquire them were illegal, but the informal funding network was not simply corruption institutionalized on a national scale. Although many of those who participated in the network undoubtedly took advantage of it for personal gain, its existence was primarily a response to the failure of the late-imperial fiscal administration to provide officials with the means to carry out their duties. For at least a century the informal funding network filled this gap so well that many in government refused to acknowledge the existence of the problems that had brought it about in the first place.

The Magistrate

As the official closest to the people, the magistrate bore the main responsibility for funneling the wealth of the countryside into the coffers of local government. It was he who collected most of the empire's taxes, including the land and head tax. The magistrate was also the issuing agent for local merchant licenses and contract and deed certificates and was the collection agent for a number of commercial taxes. He compiled the tax and census registers, collected contributions from local wealthy households, and in some cases supervised the sale of salt, tea, and other government monopolies. As such, the official assigned to govern a chou or hsien was in a unique position to manipulate the legal tax structure in order to generate the extralegal revenues that allowed the massive Chinese bureaucracy to function.

Few magistrates engaged in overt extortion of large sums of money from the people. The methods used were more subtle, and the amount taken from any one source was usually small. The two most commonly employed means to acquire extra funds were the levying of surcharges (*chia-p'ai, ssu-p'ai, k'o-p'ai*) and "collecting more and reporting less" (*cheng-to pao-shao*).

Surcharges were not always levied surreptitiously. In the event of a beneficial government undertaking, especially an irrigation or dredging project, local people were frequently assessed a part of the costs according to the amount of land they owned.[50] Because the revenue from land and head taxes in Yunnan was low, the governor ordered all chou and hsien to collect a fixed surcharge on the regular tax to pay for government operating expenses. The rates for this surcharge, called *kung-chien*, were engraved in stone to prevent their collection from giving rise to further exactions.[51] Most chou and hsien collected a general surcharge in the form of wastage allowances. These allowances, called *hao-mi* in the case of tribute grain and *huo-hao* or *hao-hsien* in the case of taxes paid in silver, were originally instituted to cover any shortages resulting from rotting grain or losses in the value of silver when it was melted down into larger ingots for transport to the capital.[52] As we shall see, by the end of the seventeenth century, in some provinces, these surcharges had grown to as much as 50 percent or more of the original tax quota.

Several other means were used to levy surcharges without appearing to do so. One of the best-known methods was the manipulation of conversion rates.[53] Magistrates would allow the people the convenience of paying their taxes in copper coins instead of silver. However, the ratio of copper to silver would be set higher than the prevailing market rate. The official would then make a small profit when he converted the taxes back to silver. The same process was applied to the collection of tribute grain, allowing the people to pay in cash at a rate higher than the official would have to pay to buy the equivalent amount of grain. Similar results were obtained by employing weighted scales or oversized measures at the tax-collection points set up throughout the county. An ingenious combination of devices was used in the collection of tribute grain in parts of Kiangnan. During the K'ang-hsi period, magistrates engaged in a practice known as *chiu-k'ou*. For every picul of rice paid by the taxpayer, the magistrate issued a receipt for only nine pecks. In addition, the use of weighted scales meant that in the end the taxpayer was credited with only 80 percent of his actual remittance. When this practice was discovered and outlawed, a weighing fee (*tui-fei*) of 0.06 tael per picul was permitted. The chou and hsien promptly converted this payment to copper coins at a rate of 1,000 per tael. The price of copper coins in Kiangnan was quite high at the time, 1.2 to 1.3 taels per thousand. Moreover, as harvests had been good and the price of rice was low, the people continued, in effect, to pay the *chiu-k'ou*.[54]

In the process of collecting the land and head tax, several methods of exacting surcharges were also widespread. At the beginning of the tax-collection period, when the magistrate compiled the tax-collection registers listing the quota due from each taxpayer, he would secretly add a hundredth or a thousandth of a tael to the liabilities of each taxpayer. This practice was known as *fei-sa*. If the people were ignorant of the tax rates, as was often the case, it could be done with virtually no chance of detection. Although the amount added to the tax on each *mou* of land was minuscule, for an entire hsien, particularly if it was located in an area of high taxes and productivity, the yield from *fei-sa* alone could be as much as several thousand taels.[55]

When submitting his taxes in silver, a practice that was increasing during the late Ming and early Ch'ing, the taxpayer had to rely on the services of a silversmith. The latter weighed the silver and melted it down into ingots, applying his stamp as proof of the metal's purity. Some magistrates took advantage of this by requiring the people to go to "official silversmiths" (*kuan-chiang*) who set up shop in the vicinity of the chou or hsien yamen. If the taxpayer's silver did not bear the stamp of the official silversmith, he was not permitted to deposit it in the tax chest. The silversmiths usually took a fee of several hundredths of a tael for every tael of silver weighed and wrapped. In return for the magistrate's patronage, the silversmith would then send a portion of his fee to the yamen.[56]

Even after the taxpayer had returned home, secure in the knowledge that he had settled his accounts with the government, he was still not free from the magistrate's demands. On the pretext that there were deficiencies in the weight of the silver (*tuan-p'ing*) found when the taxpayer's tax envelope was opened, the magistrate would occasionally send a trusted runner or clerk to the countryside to force the taxpayer to make up the additional amount. The actual silver would be removed and a red tag attached to the empty envelope. On the tag a shortage of 0.03 or 0.04 tael might be recorded for every tael of taxes due. The silver having already been combined with the other taxes received by the yamen, the taxpayer could not demand that his own remittances be reweighed in his presence. He had no choice but to pay the increase. This practice, called "making up the weight of an empty envelope," could also result in hundreds or thousands of taels of additional income for the magistrate's yamen.[57]

The above techniques for acquiring additional revenues were carried out mainly at the expense of the taxpayer. When the method of "collecting more and reporting less" was utilized, the magistrate siphoned off silver and grain that should have gone into the regular tax network and funneled them instead into the informal system of funding. Although the common people might also suffer from this practice, the main victim was the central government.

When paying the land tax, it should be recalled, each individual taxpayer was required by law to deposit his wrapped tax silver in locked chests set up either at the hsien yamen or at other locations in the chou or hsien established for the convenience of the people. These chests were locked to prevent embezzlement prior to remittance to the capital. The taxes collected each day were entered in registers known as *liu-shui hung-pu*, and the taxpayer was given a receipt for the amount paid. Two other copies of the receipt were kept at the yamen for comparing with the taxes recorded in the *liu-shui hung-pu* and with the taxes actually found in the chests when they were opened. That these methods of cross-checking were taken seriously by provincial officials is testified to by the care they exercised to cover their tracks when taxes were "stolen." It was common for magistrates to take a portion of the taxes paid and report it to his superiors as unpaid (*wei-wan*). This was accomplished either by *fei-sa*, by the use of weighted scales, or by lifting whole packets of taxes from the chests by means of specially designed hooks.[58] The evidence of such malpractices was hidden by issuing receipts to the people which did not bear the official seal[59] or by writing one amount on the official receipt given the taxpayer and a smaller figure in the records kept by the yamen.[60]

These taxes were then reported as people's arrears (*min-ch'ien*). Because the sanctions against an official reporting arrears were less severe than those incurred for embezzlement or for having deficits, it was usually to the magistrate's advantage to appropriate regular taxes illegally rather than be found lacking in the funds with which to carry out his official duties.

Another closely related method used by magistrates to conceal deficit spending was the practice of "shifting funds" (*no-i*) and using newly collected taxes to cover up old shortages (*i-hsin yen-chiu*). When an official found himself short of funds he might delay reporting his annual accounts. Because the annual accounting (*tsou-hsiao*) by the governor was sent to the Board of Revenue no earlier than the fourth month of the following year, by the time the documents from the province had reached the Board and a Board response had been sent back to the province it was usually winter. By then, the magistrate would have begun collecting the taxes for the next year and could use a portion to pay the shortages amassed the year before.[61] This process was repeated year after year, setting in motion an endless cycle of deficits and concealment. The central government rarely received its full quota, and the magistrate could avoid being implicated in malfeasance before he was transferred.

When the magistrate did report people's arrears, whether real or fabricated, he could easily profit from the way in which arrears were collected. The central government being concerned only with recovering the total taxes not yet paid, it left the matter of who owed what to the individual magistrate. In order not to burden the taxpayers so heavily with back payments that they could not pay the new taxes due, arrears were generally collected in installments (*tai-cheng*) over a period of from eight to ten years. A fixed total was set for each year, but magistrates often pressed the people to pay more than their installment for a particular year. The magistrate could then keep the difference and would long be out of office before the people began to complain that they had already paid in full.[62]

In addition to the land and head tax, magistrates were also responsible for the collection of a number of commercial taxes called *tsa-shui*.[63] Although they were supposed to be remitted in full to the central government, most magistrates sent a fixed amount established by custom and retained the rest.[64] This was in part a hedge against fluctuations in the volume of market transactions. Magistrates feared that if they remitted a large quota for several years they would be accused of embezzlement at times when business was slow and *tsa-shui* revenues decreased. However, the amount retained by magistrates was often as great as, or greater than, the amount they remitted. For example, Yun-kuei Governor-general Kao Ch'i-cho reported that the regularly remitted quota of miscellaneous duties in Yunnan was about 14,700 taels. However, a prefect might have a surplus beyond the quota of between 2,000 and 6,000 taels. Likewise, the surplus collected by a chou or hsien usually ranged from 40 to as much as 600 taels.[65]

Land reclamation provided an excellent opportunity to manipulate the tax rolls in order to divert taxes from the regular tax network into the hands of chou and hsien magistrates. Hiding reclaimed land in order to keep it from inclusion in the *Fu-i chüan-shu* was not the only means available to profit from economic recovery and expansion.[66] In some instances, magistrates did report reclaimed land. According to the law, a taxpayer had from six to ten years, depending on whether wet or dry cultivation was being used, from the time his land was entered in the tax rolls to the time he actually began paying taxes (*sheng-k'o*). This was in recognition of the fact that land recently opened to cultivation required a number of years before it could reach full productivity. Magistrates took advantage of this regulation to begin tax collection immediately, and added these taxes to their other illegal revenues until the stipulated time to remit them to the central government was reached.[67]

Magistrates were also in a position to use imperial tax postponements and cancellations to their own benefit. When a suspension of taxation was declared, the chou and hsien would occasionally delay making the Board of Revenue's notification public and continue collecting taxes as before.[68] Some magistrates would even falsify reports of natural disasters in the area under their jurisdiction in the hope of receiving a tax remission for that year. Because productivity had not actually been affected, they would then be able to collect the exempted quota and keep it for other expenses.

In regions where the reed-land tax (*lu-k'o*) was levied, it was particularly easy to manipulate the tax quota.[69] In provinces such as Kiangsu, Kiangsi, and Hukwang, with sandy land along the banks of rivers that would not support the cultivation of food crops, the people planted reeds and paid taxes at a lower rate than on other types of land. Because this land directly abutted river beds, it was constantly being built up and washed away. In order to balance out losses to the reed-land tax quota when the land eroded, magistrates generally did not report new additions to such land. Taxes collected on the new land could then be added to the other sources of informal income at the magistrate's disposal. Some officials used this as an opportunity to exact bribes from those whose land had eroded before granting them a tax exemption and from those opening new reed land in return for keeping their land off the tax rolls.

At all levels of the official hierarchy, whenever funds were allocated or purchases made, various methods were used to "save" money from the officially available funds. No real revenues were generated in this way, but it enabled officials to circumvent the rigid system of accounting established in conjunction with the regular revenue-sharing system. This process was most important in providing informal funds for higher provincial officials, especially the financial commissioner, but magistrates were also able to exploit the local population by saving money in the procurement of supplies for the yamen and post stations. Some magistrates went so far as to commandeer supplies, granting no payment at all to the merchant, craftsman, or farmer who provided them.[70] In other cases, the people were paid an official price (*kuan-chia*) below the market price (*shih-chia*) of the goods or services.[71] In situations where magistrates made purchases of local products for the central government, they were allocated funds based on rates set by the Board of Revenue (*pu-chia*). Unlike the *kuan-chia* set by the local officials themselves, during the early Ch'ing this Board price was often higher than the rate at which magistrates could procure the required item. Moreover, because market scales usually weighed lighter than the scales issued by the Board for use in the official yamen, an additional discount was possible.[72] The funds saved in this manner were also added to the informal network.

A number of other irregular sources of funds were available to magistrates. All chou and hsien maintained one or more granaries to provide the people with relief in times of famine and in order to inject grain into the market to stabilize prices. The stores contained in these granaries were less easily measured by inspecting superior officials than were the contents of government treasuries. For this reason, some magistrates kept the silver obtained from sales of government grain instead of replenishing stocks at harvest time. Others accepted cash payment of the taxes and contributions by which the granaries were to be filled and never bought grain to fill them.[73]

Contributions from wealthy households to help finance government projects were a regular part of the legal system of government finance under the Ch'ing. Sometimes, however, officials oversubscribed donations for a particular project, saving the remainder of the funds for unrelated expenses. Magistrates were even known to force wealthy households to make contributions, assessing the amount they should provide in accordance with the amount of land recorded under their names in the tax registers.[74] Commoners making grain contributions in order to purchase an official degree were often charged an extra fee before they could receive the certification of their new rank.[75]

Like all officials, magistrates were also the recipients of numerous customary fees and gifts (*lou-kuei, kuei-li*), some of them from their clerks and runners. It is obvious that without the aid of clerks and runners the magistrate would not have been able to engage in many of the above practices. The necessity to acquire funds by illegal means lessened the magistrate's control over his own staff. If clerks and runners were instructed to tamper with the tax-collection process for the benefit of the local administration, they could equally do so to benefit themselves. Just as we cannot determine what portion of funds so acquired was pocketed by the magistrate and what portion was used for government business, it is impossible to determine the magnitude of clerk and runner engrossment. At least some of the funds they amassed by illegal means were used for their own legitimate stationery and travel expenses. However, the measures they employed to extract money from the people often worked against the interests of the magistrate and the government as a whole, and the fruits of their manipulation of the tax system were less likely to enter the nexus of funds used to operate the provincial administration. For this reason, the role of clerks and runners in the informal funding network more properly forms a part of our examination of those factors that obstructed the collection of taxes at the local level.[76]

High-ranking Provincial Officials

Few high-level provincial officials were involved directly in the process of collecting taxes from the general population. In order to operate their yamen, support their families, and perform the numerous public services for which they were responsible, they had to rely on transfers of funds from subordinate administrative units through the informal funding network. These transfers were of four main types: (1) revenues submitted directly to a superior official by a subordinate in the form of gifts and fees; (2) "surplus" from major specialized revenue-collecting agencies, namely the customs and salt administrations; (3) percentage deductions from taxes and goods remitted along the regular taxation network; and (4) funds skimmed off in the process of purchase and allocation.

Customary Fees

In the broad sense, the term customary fees (*lou-kuei*) may be applied to all illegally obtained revenues. In official correspondence denouncing corruption, this usage was fairly common. However, *lou-kuei* had a more limited meaning of fees and gifts sent on a regular basis by one member of the bureaucracy to another. The distinction is an important one, because it was primarily *lou-kuei* in its narrow sense that was ardently attacked by the Yung-cheng reformers.

All officials and functionaries, from the lowest assistant magistrate to the governor-general, periodically sent gifts of customarily established sums of silver to their superiors. These gifts were usually sent on the occasion of an official's birthday (*sheng-ch'en kuei-li*), or his arrival at a new post (*tao-jen ho-li*), when paying a visit to the official (*piao-li*), and at the time of the four major festivals of the lunar year (*chieh-li*).[77] These gifts could amount to a considerable sum, especially when the recipient was a high provincial official such as the governor or financial commissioner. In YC 2 (1724), the Liang-kuang governor-general confessed to having received 47,110 taels in *chieh-li* from his subordinates.[78] The total annual *chieh-li* sent to the Kwangsi governor was 12,400 taels. In addition, he received gifts upon arriving in office equivalent to the *chieh-li* for one season, and surplus from the unloading duty (*lo-ti shui*) collected in Kuei-lin, P'ing-le, Hsün-chou, and Wu-chou prefectures of 7,000 taels per year.[79] Shantung Governor Sai-leng-e reported that the former financial commissioner of that province had accepted 9,784 taels in gifts from the chou and hsien, and that the former educational commissioner had been the beneficiary of 3,204 taels from the same source.[80]

Even when the immediate source of *chieh-li* was an official above the chou and hsien level in the official hierarchy, it must be noted that the original source of all customary fees of this kind was the magistrate, and ultimately, the people. The magistrate sent customary fees of varying small amounts to every official in whose jurisdiction he was located. He sent *ts'ao-kuei* to the grain inten-dant[81] and *i-kuei* to the post intendant,[82] *chieh-li* to his prefect and circuit intendant, as well as the customary fees he remitted directly to the financial and judicial commissioners, the governor, and the governor-general. Likewise, all those officials above the magistrate consolidated the fees they accumulated from their subordinates and sent a portion to each of their superiors.

In addition to the fees sent to higher officials, subordinates usu-ally contributed to the operating costs of the yamen above them in the form of "food silver" (*fan-shih yin*) for the superior yamen's clerks. This practice probably grew out of the custom of sending a small sum whenever business was transacted with a superior yamen, to cover the food and stationery costs of the clerks who were confined to their offices while processing the documents or taxes sent by lower officials. Eventually these contributions be-came regularized, and commonly accompanied tax remittances as a fixed percentage of the quota.

The names applied to such fees varied from province to prov-ince. In Kwangtung the chou and hsien sent an extra 3 taels for every 100 taels remitted in taxes to the provincial treasury. Of this sum, 10 percent was deducted as *hsiao-fei yin* and used to pay the expenses of the treasury keepers (*k'u-ta-shih*), treasury clerks (*k'u-li-shu*), boatmen, cooks, messengers and runners, guards, and scale-keepers associated with the financial commissioner's yamen.[83] In Chihli, a customary fee called *hsiao-fan yin* of 4 taels per thousand was sent to the treasurers and treasury clerks when local taxes were transported to the provincial seat.[84] In the customs admin-istration, food silver was also collected in addition to the regular tax quota. For example, at the Huai customs an extra 16,404 taels was received in the form of *fan-shih yin* to pay the daily living ex-penses and stationery costs of the customs clerks and patrols. Part of this sum was also remitted to the superintendent of customs to cover his own living expenses and administrative costs.[85]

Besides the food silver for their own yamen, the governors and financial commissioners had to set aside customarily agreed-upon amounts of *fan-shih* for the clerks in the central-government of-fices with which they regularly transacted business. The judicial commissioner sent stationery and food money (*chih-pi fan-shih*) to the Board of Punishments. Governor Yang Wen-ch'ien reported that prior to the Yung-cheng reforms, the chou and hsien in Kwangtung annually remitted 6,042 taels for this purpose. These funds were used to cover the costs of remitting fines and confiscated property to the Board, and to provide food silver for the Board clerks and travel expenses for officials and runners on government business. Contributions from the province also paid the costs of compiling the records for the autumn assize of capital offenses and provided gifts of ink and stationery for prisoners.[86]

At the time of the annual accounting, the financial commissioners of every province remitted *fan-shih yin* to the Board of Revenue and the Office of Scrutiny of the Board of Revenue. Szechuan sent 1,300 taels for this purpose.[87] Honan-Shantung Governor-general Wang Shih-chün claimed that there was no fixed quota prior to 1728, but in that year it was established that 3,600 taels should be sent to the Board of Revenue and 600 taels to the Office of Scrutiny.[88] Moreover, when purchases in kind were made for the central-government storehouses, additional sums were allocated for the travel expenses of the officials escorting the shipment and for Board *fan-shih*. This so-called *pang-fei* could be quite large. For Honan's annual shipment of paints, fabrics, cattle tendons, and wax, the *pang-fei* averaged around 5,300 taels.[89]

Although lower officials contributed to the expenses of the clerical staff in their superiors' yamen, it was not uncommon for high officials to play a part in the selection of clerks in their own and subordinate yamen. In return they received "gifts" (*kuei-li*) from the clerks appointed. In effect, the clerks paid a fee for the purchase of their posts. Most of the existing evidence of this practice relates to Kwangtung province, where an intensive investigation was conducted as part of a high-level impeachment case. Other provinces, however, probably had similar customs enabling high officials to take advantage of the competition for government jobs to add to their own informal income.

In Kwangtung it was the local officials who posted the notices inviting local people to apply for vacancies in the ranks of low-level functionaries and clerks. Although they did the actual hiring, every appointment had to be approved by the financial commissioner. In his letter of authorization, the financial commissioner specified the amount of *kuei-li* he expected from the lucky candidate in accordance with the level of the post being filled. The fees demanded varied widely and the way in which this practice was carried out may have depended on who was financial commissioner at the time. In one report, dated YC 5 (1729), Liang-kuang Governor-general K'ung Yü-hsün testified that this fee could be as little as a few tenths or hundredths of a tael, but was known to rise as high as seventy or eighty taels for some positions. K'ung called the fee *hsin-hung* and said it served to purchase the red ink used to apply official seals to documents.[90] During an investigation of official corruption in Kwangtung, Yin Chi-shan reported that the amount of *kuei-li* generated in this manner really ranged from several tens to several hundreds of taels per applicant. The combined fees collected by the financial commissioner were divided monthly with the governor and governor-general and, according to Yin, were used to defray the costs of operating the yamen of all three officials.[91]

Kuei-li was particularly steep when appointments were made in the customs administration. These posts were highly coveted as they provided the clerk with access to a large amount of fees and graft in the collection of customs duties. Fu T'ai, when governor of Kwangtung, received 300 taels from each of the five clerks appointed to the Canton customs during his term.[92] The Huang-chiang customs clerk customarily paid 200 taels each to the financial commissioner, governor, and governor-general to purchase his post, because it was considered very lucrative and the term of office was long. Under investigation during the mid-1720s, Financial Commissioner Kuan Ta was accused of extorting 1,250 taels from a clerk newly appointed to this position. Of this, only 240 taels each, slightly more than the customary amount, was sent by Kuan to the governor and governor-general.[93]

Contributions from the Customs and Salt Administrations

Besides the various categories of *lou-kuei* sent by subordinate officials, a large portion of high provincial yamen expenses was offset by customary contributions from the customs and salt administrations operating within their territory. It was chiefly in this way that the provinces were able to tap the growing wealth of the commercial sector in the early Ch'ing period.

The income generated from customs duties was transferred to high provincial officials in two forms, customary fees (*shui-kuei*) and surplus (*ying-yü*). *Shui-kuei* was not unlike other customary fees. It was sent by a subordinate to a superior, often on special occasions, the annual remittance commonly being agreed upon in advance.[94] Sometimes these fees were sent by officials other than customs officials who were responsible for collecting specific duties. For example, the Shantung financial commissioner received 1,500 taels each year from the incense tax (*hsiang-shui*) collected by the magistrate of T'ai-an chou.[95] However, the largest portion was sent by officials in charge of customs-collection stations. In Fukien, after deductions were made to cover the costs of running the customs administration, the total income from customary fees was divided into four shares. Two shares were sent to the governor's yamen, one share was divided among the deputy customs inspectors, and one share was apportioned among the messengers and personal servants working in the customs administration.[96] The Canton customs was especially prosperous and produced an average of sixty thousand to seventy thousand taels annually in customary fees, which were also divided among those working in the customs stations and high government officials.[97] In Shantung the customs stations handled a far smaller volume of trade. Besides its regular tax quota of 7,540 taels, the Chiao-chou customs sent the governor 3,676 taels in *kuei-li yin* and Lai-yang sent 497 taels along with its 770-tael quota.[98] Sometimes the *lou-kuei* from customs was sent to a lower-ranking official with supervisory responsibilities for particular duties and he sent a portion to the governor and governor-general. Such was the case in Szechuan, where the judicial commissioner sent the governor-general 2,500 taels in salt and tea fees (*yen-ch'a kuei*) and the financial commissioner sent him 4,040 taels from the fees on exported rice (*liang-kuei*) and customs (*shui-kuei*).[99]

Where did the funds to pay these customary fees come from? For the most part they were derived from surcharges levied on merchants in addition to the regular tax. During an investigation of the customs station at the T'ung pass it was discovered that officials had long been in the habit of increasing the rates for duties established by the Board of Revenue. The Board had set the tax for a mule-load of thread or satin at 0.6 tael, but the customary practice was to charge 1.2 taels per load of thread and 1.4 taels per load of satin. On cotton goods the Board authorized a duty of 0.11 tael per load of finished cloth and 0.06 tael per load of raw cotton, but the actual rates of collection were 0.18 tael and 0.08 tael respectively.[100]

Sometimes *lou-kuei* was collected as an across-the-board percentage on regular duties. Special names were often applied to such fees, as in the case of the registration fee (*kua-hao*) and *tan-kuei* collected in Kwangtung[101] and that of the *tan-yin tsa-hsiang* found in the records of customs stations in Fukien.[102] In other instances, these fees were combined under the rubric of wastage allowances (*huo-hao, hao-hsien*), the same term used to describe land- and head-tax surcharges.[103]

Unauthorized fees might also be charged for vehicles and livestock passing through customs barriers. In Fengtien, customs inspectors exacted 0.16 tael for every small cart that arrived at their stations. Of this, 0.08 tael was sent to the metropolitan prefect, 0.02 tael went to the registrar, and the rest was divided among the prefecture's clerks as food money and to cover stationery costs. For a large cart the fee was doubled. Every year an average of 1,600 to 1,700 taels was collected from cart fees alone. A similar fee, 0.03 tael per head, was levied on pigs and sheep passing through the customs barriers.[104]

The Huai-an customs administration was particularly tenacious in exacting extra duties from merchants. Originally a 2-percent *huo-hao* was collected when merchants paid their regular duties. However, in 1725 it was reported that when the new inspector, Ching Yuan, came to office he eliminated the wastage allowance and set up five or six small customs barriers (*hsiao k'ou-tzu*) along the main transportation route. Whenever a merchant passed through one of the barriers he was required to obtain an inspection certificate (*yen-p'iao*), for which he paid a number of fees. If these surcharges, including inspection certificate cash (*yen-p'iao ch'ien*), stationery fees (*chih-pi ch'ien*), and food money (*fan-ch'ien*) were not paid, the merchant's boats were not allowed to proceed. The fees at each barrier were at least 0.13 or 0.14 tael per tael of regular duties, so that a merchant might end up paying almost double the legal customs tax before he reached his destination.[105]

Profits were also generated by levying duties on items not designated for taxation in the Board's regulations. By precedent, common people transporting small quantities of rice to large provincial markets were not taxed. However, at the Huai-an customs, a lone peasant carrying rice on his back would be detained until several others came along and their combined load equalled a whole picul. They would then be treated as a merchant convoy and ordered to pay the tax.[106] It was also the custom that silks that had been cut and made into clothes, even when carried by traveling merchants, were to be regarded as personal clothing and not subject to taxation. On the pretext that female clothing so transported had to be used clothing destined for resale, the Huai-an customs taxed all clothing, male or female, old or new. None of these revenues were reported to the central government, but were sent directly to the provincial coffers.[107]

The Canton customs was in a unique position to exploit profitmaking opportunities by levying special taxes on foreign trade.[108] Besides levies on the value of cargo (*shang-huo fen-t'ou*), customary fees were collected for opening the hatches, inspecting the hatches, and unloading cargo.[109] Compradors and interpreters also paid a public-expense fee (*kung-fei yin*) in return for monopoly privileges in supplying services to the foreigners. Those working for boats anchored at Whampoa paid between 40 and 100 taels and those residing in the provincial capital paid from 60 to 160 taels, depending on the size of the foreign vessel by which they were employed.[110] During the Yung-cheng period it was estimated that almost 70,000 taels were collected in this way, though by that time not all of the revenues were retained by the province.

An even more unusual levy was the so-called "people tax" (*jen-shui*). During this period, western traders were restricted to residence in Macao. In order to discourage them from traveling inland, the Kwangtung authorities, on their own initiative, imposed a charge of eighteen Mexican silver dollars on every westerner coming to Canton from Macao and an additional two Mexican silver dollars on those traveling from the provincial capital back to their base.[111]

Several other methods were used by customs officials to accumulate the revenues they shared with the provincial government as *shui-kuei*. These were quite similar to the practices of magistrates and other officials directly involved in tax collection. Customs stations in Kiangsi were found to be using scales to weigh tax silver that weighed heavier than those used in the financial commissioner's yamen. These heavy scales produced a "surplus from weighing" (*p'ing-yü*) of 3 taels for every 100 taels of duties collected.[112] At the Kan pass, the taxes collected on single articles, ranging from 0.05 to 1.5 taels, were simply not entered in the accounts.[113] Small bits of silver collected were also consolidated and retained for provincial use.[114]

By far the greatest volume of unreported customs duties fell into the category of surplus (*ying-yü*). Unlike *lou-kuei, ying-yü* was not the product of official and staff peculation, but of the growth of trade beyond the volume calculated when the government's customs quotas were originally established. As in the case of the surplus commercial taxes collected by magistrates, once the official quota was filled, the officials could amass large sums simply by continuing to collect the duties at the legal rate. Until the reforms of the Yung-cheng period, most of these surplus duties remained in the provinces, although it is difficult to determine what portion was transferred along the informal funding network and what portion was pocketed by officials directly engaged in customs administration.

We can get some idea of the amount of funds that were potentially available to assist in paying provincial expenses by examining the reports concerning *ying-yü* submitted during the reform period. In YC 11 (1733), the Lung-chiang and Hsi-hsin customs in Kiangnan reported a gross surplus of 78,900 taels beyond the regular quota of 152,000 taels.[115] Two years earlier the Fukien customs administration boasted a total surplus of 54,516 taels.[116] Kwangsi was granted 15,000 taels of customs surplus in 1727, but it was later discovered that the Wu-chou and Hsün-chou customs stations annually generated another 31,400 taels.[117]

Because these surplus funds were carefully hidden from the central government, we do not have accurate reports of their distribution through the informal funding network. We do know that a portion was utilized to cover the costs of wages and supplies, travel expenses, and stationery costs of the customs personnel. Some funds were undoubtedly pocketed by customs officials, as in the case of the official who reported 600 taels of surplus, only to have it revealed that there was an additional 2,100 taels, which he was ordered to return.[118] However, because the existence of large sums of *ying-yü* was known to financial commissioners and governors and they were later legally incorporated into those officials' administrative budgets, we can assume that at least a part of this provincial windfall reached these higher officials during the early Ch'ing, either as a direct remittance or as part of the *lou-kuei* sent to the provincial capital.

One of the most bountiful sources of revenues flowing into the informal funding network was the salt gabelle. Opportunities for profit were numerous, because officials were often intimately in-

volved not only in marketing salt but also in the process of manufacturing it. Because they owed their strong economic position to a
government-sponsored monopoly and relied on the government to
protect them against bandits and smugglers, salt merchants were
also a constant source of "voluntary contributions" (*le-chüan*) to
the provincial coffers.[119] Moreover, salt manufacture and marketing brought the merchants into contact with officials at all levels of
the bureaucracy. In part, this accounts for the fact that customary
fees from the salt administration, unlike customs fees, were not
confined to high-level officials.

There were three major sources of informal income from the salt
administration: (1) surplus income from the sale of salt, (2) *lou-
kuei* collected by officials and clerks employed in the salt administration, and (3) contributions from salt merchants on an annual
basis and for specific projects.

In China, salt was sold by specifically designated salt merchants.
Merchants were required to obtain salt certificates (*yen-yin*) by
payment of the gabelle (*yen-k'o*). Each certificate entitled the
bearer to sell a certain amount of salt in a specified area.[120] The
income from the sale of salt certificates was fixed by quota and remitted to the central government. However, the income from salt
sales was often not limited to the legal quota. Either through percentage fees on the sale of certificates or by allowing additional
sales of salt beyond the quota, the provinces were able to accumulate a salt-revenue surplus which was retained locally for public
expenses. In Ho-tung, the regular salt-gabelle quota was around
171,700 taels. Income from the sale of excess certificates was as
high as 104,300 taels.[121] The annual salt quota for Chen-chou prefecture in Hunan was 1,375 taels, but it was discovered that the
actual amount collected was about twice that figure.[122] In Yunnan
and Kwangsi, official participation in the actual marketing of salt
resulted in sales far beyond the limits set by the Board of Revenue.
Soon after the Yung-cheng emperor assumed the throne, a scandal
erupted in the Yunnan salt administration. According to Metropolitan Censor Chao Tien-tsui, the salt gabelle from the nine salt
wells in Yunnan yielded an annual quota of 168,145 taels. The
amount of salt to be sold in each chou, hsien and prefecture was
also fixed by quota. However, because the management of the salt
wells was in the hands of the provincial administration, the governor, governor-general, and salt intendant had authorized the production of extra salt and increased the quantity of salt sold in the

province's retail shops. This had resulted in sales of "private" salt far in excess of the official salt, the profits from which went to the central government. Even if the official salt went unsold, there was pressure on the shopkeepers to sell the governor and governor-general's "private" salt. In Yunnan this was possible because salt was not marketed by salt merchants but by runners and clerks deputed by the salt intendant.[123] In Kwangsi the salt was also transported and wholesaled by deputies of high provincial officials. For every sack (*pao*) of salt authorized for sale by the quota, an extra eighteen *chin* was added. This extra salt was called *p'ing-t'ou* and the proceeds from its sale, like the proceeds from the sale of private salt in Yunnan, were used for provincial expenses.[124]

It is difficult to determine the exact nature of the *lou-kuei* exacted by officials and runners employed in the salt administration. Nevertheless, references to the elimination of *lou-kuei* after the Yung-cheng reforms are fairly common.[125] Both *lou-kuei* and part of the surplus described above were used to defray the operating expenses of salt-administration personnel. During his term as superintendent of the Liang-huai salt administration, I-la-ch'i reported disbursing 12,485 taels in salt-customary fees for officials' salaries, runners' wages, banquets, awards to merchants, and for the relief of salt workers who were the victims of floods and other disasters. He also set aside 3,500 taels for his own daily living expenses and traveling costs, as well as 19,284 taels for the food money and stationery costs of his yamen's registrar, archivist, clerks, and runners.[126] The Shantung salt controller's yamen received 37,000 taels in *kuei-li*, from which similar expenditures were made.[127]

Besides being the conduit for income generated by the sale of salt, the salt merchants themselves sent customary fees called *yen-kuei* to provincial officials. The officials to whom *yen-kuei* was sent and the amount of the fees varied from province to province, but it would not be an exaggeration to say that almost every official from the hsien magistrate to the governor-general benefited from salt fees. In Kiangsi, for example, the governor's yamen was sent an annual *yen-kuei* quota of 16,000 taels. The financial commissioner received 3,000 taels, as did the judicial commissioner. The salt and post intendant had special responsibility for salt affairs and so received a total of 4,729 taels in gifts from salt merchants. The combined *yen-kuei* of the grain intendant, the Jao-chiu and Nan-kan circuit intendants, and the prefects and assistant prefects of five of Kiangsi's prefectures was 7,453 taels. In addition, the remaining prefectures and the chou and hsien also received an unspecified amount of *yen-kuei*.[128]

The customary fees sent by salt merchants to high provincial officials were often quite large. The total *yen-kuei* in Hukwang was 160,000 taels, most of which was remitted to its two provincial capitals.[129] The annual quota of the Chekiang governor and governor-general was over 25,000 taels.[130] In Yunnan, the governor-general was sent 17,000 taels annually, and the governor's share of *yen-kuei* was 60,000 taels. To this was added another 6,000 taels sent directly to the provincial seat from two of the province's salt wells.[131]

In addition to the customary fees paid on a regular basis, merchants were often called upon or volunteered to make contributions to supplement public expenses. Their wealth and their special debt to the government placed salt merchants in the forefront of commercially based philanthropy. This was especially true when their home areas were struck by natural disaster or required funds for a major construction project, or when the merchants themselves were the beneficiaries of extraordinary imperial favors. In Shensi, after the emperor increased the number of salt certificates that could be issued in that province, the salt merchants offered to contribute 5,000 taels annually to assist in defraying local administrative expenses.[132] When a similar increase in the amount of salt that could be sold for each certificate was granted in Kiangnan, the Liang-huai salt merchants petitioned to contribute 240,000 taels to the charity granary maintained by the salt administration in their region, as well as 80,000 taels to Governor Ko-er-t'ai to offset yamen expenses.[133] Several years later, these same merchants also contributed to the river-conservancy administration in Kiangsu to aid in the repair of embankments.[134]

Thus, the business of salt production and distribution played an extremely important role in supplying revenues for the informal funding network. As we shall see, even when other forms of *lou-kuei* were under violent attack during the period of the Yung-cheng reforms, it was very difficult for provincial officials to conceive of operating their yamen without *yen-kuei*.[135]

Percentage Deductions from Remitted Taxes

Just as magistrates levied surcharges when collecting taxes from the people, higher provincial officials who received local taxes collected a portion of their own operating expenses in the form of remittance fees from subordinates. The main recipient of these fees was, of course, the financial commissioner.

Remittance fees appear to have existed in every province, although once again the names given to such fees and the amounts collected varied greatly. For every 100 taels of taxes remitted by the chou and hsien in Kwangtung, an extra 3 taels was added. This three-percent surcharge was called *ta-p'ing yin*.[136] In Shantung, when the chou and hsien delivered their land and head taxes they sent *chieh-fei* to the financial commissioner. The amount ranged from 1.1 to 1.2 percent of the total tax quota, depending on the tax potential of the area. Along with this, a shipping fee (*yün-fei*) of five- or six-tenths of a tael was remitted to cover the costs of transporting the taxes to the Board in Peking. Any funds left over were funneled into the informal funding network.[137] Remittance fees were also charged when miscellaneous taxes were sent to the financial commissioner and when higher officials such as prefects and circuit intendants sent in fines and confiscated property.[138]

Both tax revenues and administrative expenses in Kiangsu were among the highest in the empire. The Suchow financial commissioner not only received an item called "food money accompanying the regular tax" (*sui-cheng fan-shih*), but also collected a 1.3-percent surcharge known as *tso-p'ing yin*, which was used to supplement the costs of remitting taxes to the capital and to offset expenses within the province itself.[139] Chang Tan-lin reported that during his predecessor's one and one-half years as financial commissioner these two fees alone produced a total of 76,143 taels that were made available for provincial public expenses.

In addition to the revenue accumulated through direct levies, most provinces were able to amass a small surplus when the taxes received from all the chou and hsien were melted down into large ingots for shipment to the imperial capital. This surplus was generally known as *p'ing-yü* or *ping-feng yin*. The silver added to the provincial coffers in this way could add up to as much as several thousand taels each year.[140]

Besides surcharges on the actual remittance of taxes, there was a wide range of possibilities for levying fees connected with the accounting and record-keeping functions of the provincial yamen. We have seen that all chou and hsien were expected to pay fees at the time of the annual accounting (*tsou-hsiao fei*). The methods used by financial commissioners in Kwangtung were not unlike those devised by officials in other provinces to extract additional revenues from their subordinates. When the grain collected from military-colony land was allocated to the military as rations (*ping-mi*) an inspection fee (*yen-pi yin*) of 0.03 tael per picul was sent to the financial commissioner.[141] When prefects and magistrates collected miscellaneous duties they had to obtain official "two-stub receipts" (*shuang-lien shui-tan*) from the financial commissioner on which to record income and issue proof of payment. For every 100 sheets he distributed to his subordinates, the financial commissioner collected a customary fee of three taels. A similar fee of five taels was exacted for every 100 sheets of contract paper (*ch'i-wei*) issued by the commissioner for use by the chou and hsien in recording land and property sales. Moreover, assessments totaling 6,000 taels were levied on subordinates at the time of the quinquennial census.[142]

Other high officials with revenue-collecting responsibilities were also privy to percentage deductions. For example, in Honan, the grain intendant received 14,568 taels per year in "public-expense silver" (*kung-yung yin*) from the chou and hsien when they sent in their tribute rice. When grain shipments were sent to the intendant for storage in provincial granaries an additional 1,456 taels was remitted as *sui-feng yin*, along with 1,720 taels of *kung-yung yin*.[143]

Once revenues transmitted by the chou and hsien and other subordinate administrative units reached officials such as the financial commissioner and grain intendant, they did not become their exclusive property. Rather, these tax-receiving yamen served as conduits in the flow of funds to even higher yamen. In Shantung, most of the funds received in the form of transportation fees (*chieh-fei, yün-fei*) and food money (*fan-yin*) were consolidated under the name of *fen-kuei* because they were shared (*fen*) by the financial commissioner, governor, and governor-general.[144] Likewise, the *ta-p'ing yin* deposited in the provincial treasury in Kwangtung was divided among the governor-general, governor, financial commissioner, and judicial commissioner.[145] Kiangning Financial Commissioner Chüeh-lo Shih-lin reported that he had received 12,900 taels in *sui-p'ing yin* from the chou and hsien in Kiangsu province, from which a fixed fee (*p'ing-kuei*) of 1,500 taels was sent to the governor-general and 2,700 taels was sent to the governor annually.[146]

These fees were small in comparison with the revenues derived from customary fees from subordinate officials and merchants.

Nevertheless, they were a source of much-needed funds during a period of transition when corvée labor was no longer available to undertake the transportation of taxes. The growth of these fees to provide a surplus to help defray the other administrative expenses of high provincial officials is just one instance of how the informal funding network adjusted to and utilized the existing fiscal system to supplement statutory appropriations.

Funds Skimmed Off in the Process of Purchase and Allocation

During the late-imperial period, tax collection in China became increasingly monetized. However, there were a number of items which, while collected in cash at the local level, had to be remitted in kind to the military or the central government. During periods of high productivity and low commodity prices, the reconversion of these taxes to staple produce afforded the provincial government an excellent opportunity to make a profit. This profit was commonly called *chieh-sheng yin* or "saved silver," and was viewed as a legitimate addition to the informal funds accruing to the financial commissioner's treasury.

Several examples of this practice may be cited for the Kiangnan region. In both Kiangsu and Anhui, many chou and hsien paid their tribute grain in cash instead of rice. In Anhui, a conversion rate was set at 1.3 taels per picul of rice. However, in a year of good harvests as little as 0.94 tael could buy a picul of high-quality white rice on the open market. At a saving of 0.36 tael per picul, Anhui Governor Ch'eng Yuan-chang reported a profit of over 7,000 taels.[147] A similar saving of 7,213 taels was reported by the Kiangning financial commissioner when tribute rice was purchased in Kiangsu.[148] Savings were also possible when purchases of beans were made for feed for the horses of banner forces stationed in the province. A particular strain of bean was required. Inasmuch as it was not produced locally, the taxpayers were permitted to pay at a rate of 1.2 taels per picul. When the market price was low, the purchase of these beans yielded a profit of almost 3,000 taels.[149]

Another source of savings from the regular tax quota closely related to *chieh-sheng yin* was a category of income called *p'ing-yü*. The use of the term *p'ing-yü* in this instance probably derived from the fact that this revenue was the result of differences between the weights used on yamen scales (*k'u-p'ing*) and those used in the marketplace (*shih-p'ing*). When supplies and taxes were disbursed to other agencies of government the financial commissioner normally used the scales he was issued by the Board of Revenue. Thus, at least in theory, all payments between yamen were calculated in standard weights and measures. However, when funds were disbursed to make purchases from the people, payment was made according to the scales in the markets.[150] The market scales in Kiangning were about 2 taels per hundred lighter than the treasury scales. Whenever purchases of goods for shipment to the capital or of materials for construction and repairs were made, this differential produced a saving from the Board price that was deposited in the financial commissioner's treasury.[151] During his term as financial commissioner, Chüeh-lo Shih-lin accumulated 2,675 taels in this way.[152]

P'ing-yü was a particularly common source of funds in the yamen of river-conservancy officials, grain intendants, and other medium-level provincial officials who made large purchases of supplies and materials from the province's share of regular taxes.[153] The Kiangnan superintendent of river conservancy reported that the old scales used in his yamen had been 1.8 taels heavier than the local market scales. These scales had in fact been below the Board standard weight, and the new weights sent by the Board of Revenue during his term in office yielded 2.5 taels more than those commonly in use among the people. Consequently, when the people paid money to the government, it was by yamen scales heavier than those in use in the marketplace. When they received payments from the government, it was invariably according to the lighter market scales. The provincial government profited at the expense of both the people and the central government, with neither really feeling the pinch.[154]

A remarkable characteristic of the informal funding network was the extent of the regularity with which it functioned. Both the paths of transmission and the types and amounts of fees and payments were standardized, and they were followed fairly consistently over decades despite numerous changes in official personnel. This was by no means the "catch as catch can" form of private aggrandizement that some contemporary critics and modern scholars have led us to expect. Nevertheless, however well this system functioned, it was bound to have adverse effects on government in the early Ch'ing.

Some of the methods used to raise funds for use within the provinces did not create any new income, but rather moved around taxes that were meant for other purposes. When a magistrate shifted revenues designated for the purchase of relief grain and used them to pay laborers repairing dikes, it was with the hope that famine would not recur while he was in office. His actions were not corrupt, in that the funds were put to beneficial use, but he did violate the administrative code which set rigid guidelines as to how the funds allotted to him were to be spent. Worse, the fact that his actions had to be taken in secret meant that the shortage in granary stores would probably not be discovered until flood or drought made the discovery too late.

From the central government's point of view, methods such as "collecting more and reporting less" and "using newly collected taxes to cover up old shortages" were especially insidious. By creating spurious arrears, they directly contributed to deficiencies in central-government coffers. Furthermore, because the deficits of officials were camouflaged as evasion by the taxpayers, retrieval of missing funds was made more difficult and an undue burden was placed upon the people.

Practices such as these accounted for many of the deficits in central-government treasuries discovered by the Yung-cheng emperor in 1723. However, the other side of the informal funding structure was also damaging to government finance. Whether transmitted as *lou-kuei*, as *p'ing-yü*, or as *fan-shih*, a large portion of the funds that made their way up the provincial hierarchy originated in one form or another as surcharges levied on the common people. When surcharges became too heavy, regular taxes went unpaid. When surcharges became accepted as a source of funds for legitimate expenses, it was easy to take a bit more to line one's own pockets. Because the informal funding network was parallel to, but not integrated with, the regular system of taxation and allocation, it fed on the statutory tax structure but lacked any formal means to check abuses by individual officials or to distribute more equitably the revenues accumulated. Inasmuch as almost all the sources for funding this network were illegal, even when officials were scrupulous in their appropriation of these revenues, their very acquisition presented a threat to both official discipline and the health of central-government finances.

The weakest link in the system was at the level of the chou and hsien. Although most magistrates received their positions from the Board of Civil Appointment, their greatest concern, once in office, was to keep in the good graces of their superiors in the provinces.

It was they who held the power to impeach a magistrate for infractions of the disciplinary code. But their willingness to do so was impeded by their dependence on the chou and hsien as a source of informal revenue. Under conditions where high provincial officials could operate their own yamen only with the aid of funds received from their subordinates, a symbiotic relationship developed that was based on bribery from below and coverups and favoritism from above. It was this convergence of interests that formed the backbone of the informal funding system and made it work. The county magistrate's treasury thus became the trough at which all other officials fed. The magistrate in turn was dependent on his runners and clerks to fill the trough with the bits and pieces of silver they extracted from the multitude of taxpayers. Fundamental reform of the regular system of revenue sharing might reduce the need for many of the fund-raising devices associated with the informal funding network, but the old and profitable habits it fostered among yamen underlings would be much harder to break.

In 1723, most of those in power still saw only the symptoms and not the disease. They thought that corruption was causing shortages and did not see that it was actually shortages that had necessitated corruption. Only when the Yung-cheng emperor launched his vigorous attack on the symptoms was the true nature of the illness gradually revealed.

3
THE RETURN OF
THE MELTAGE FEE
TO THE PUBLIC
COFFERS

THE INFORMAL FUNDING NETWORK WAS ONE OF THE
most telling manifestations of the contradictions inherent in the
traditional Chinese political economy. In its commitment to benevolent rule, the Ch'ing dynasty had doomed the Chinese people to
an uncertain existence, prey to the demands of officials, runners
and clerks, and numerous local power brokers who took advantage of the government's weak financial condition to act as middlemen in the taxation process. Only by recognizing the need for a
thorough reorganization of the revenue-sharing system could the
government hope to combat the evils of a corrupt bureaucracy. Yet
to do so would mean a rejection of some of the basic principles of
good government upon which the dynasty's legitimacy depended.

It was not ignorance that prevented a more rational approach to
local fiscal administration. Many of the reforms initiated in the
early Ch'ing were specifically designed to eliminate the most con-
spicuous abuses associated with the informal funding network.
Surcharges were prohibited as early as the first year of the Shun-
chih reign, and the K'ang-hsi emperor warned twice against their
collection, permitting the people to report officials who persisted
in this practice.[1] Needless to say, the practice continued, but the
aversion to high taxation was so strong that many in government
preferred to close their eyes to the evidence of surcharges rather

than admit their necessity and make them legal. The K'ang-hsi emperor himself stated that "If a magistrate collects a 10-percent meltage fee (*huo-hao*) and does not collect a bit more, he may be called a good official."[2] However, when Shen-kan Governor-general Nien Keng-yao took this opportunity to request the legalization of meltage fees, the emperor demurred. Nien pointed out that the level of illegal surcharges collected in his jurisdiction had reached as much as 40 or 50 percent of the regular tax quota. Inasmuch as magistrates obviously needed additional funds, he suggested that they be allowed to keep a portion of the current meltage fee to cover their yamen expenses and make up deficits. K'ang-hsi reminded Nien of the stiff penalties for the collection of "private exactions" (*ssu-p'ai*), but could offer no concrete solution to the problem.[3]

> This is basically a private matter. I once said to Ch'en Pin that a 10 percent meltage fee seemed tolerable. He felt this was a great benevolence, but I could not permit him to make my words public. Today, though Nien Keng-yao has sent a secret memorial, if I write a rescript it will have the same precedent-making effect as if I granted a request presented in a routine memorial. How can I bear the stigma of one who approves of surcharges?

K'ang-hsi could not deny the logic of Nien's request, but to say so would be to sanction the legalization of increased taxes and recognize the legitimate need for surcharges. Moreover, although his government did employ legal means to control the behavior of officials, the emperor's statements reflected a very narrow interpretation of Confucian principles of good administration. Thus, institutional change was not the ultimate solution to corruption. Only personal restraint on the part of moral officials would serve this purpose. It was for this reason that the emperor preferred to relegate the issue of surcharges to the private realm. This was also why the emperor could praise an official if he limited his "private exactions" to a minimal amount. What the emperor failed to confront was why a good official should have to collect any surcharges at all.

If K'ang-hsi's rejection of institutional reform was based on principle, there were many in the bureaucracy with a more immediate interest in concealing the magnitude of local need and local corruption. Magistrates often welcomed the insecurity of the informal funding network rather than risk the increased control by central-government officials that rationalization would entail.[4] For their part, the latter had little understanding of the administrative difficulties or fiscal requirements of their provincial subordinates. Anxieties over the health of their own treasuries caused them to underestimate local needs, and ignorance led them to suspect the motives of the few who did take up the cause of local fiscal reform.

Ironically, it was the informal funding network itself that was probably most responsible for the persistence of the fiscal inequities in response to which it had evolved. The real requirements of local administration were masked by the success with which informal methods provided local and provincial officials with additional revenues. Pleas for more funds for public business rang less true at court when one's predecessors seemed to fare perfectly well on what they had. More important, the techniques used within the informal funding system to raise revenues necessarily sabotaged the statutory checks on corruption and destroyed the utility of *tsuo-hsiao* accounts as an accurate reflection of local expenditure. Before fundamental reform could take place, the smokescreen created by the informal funding network had to be dispersed. One precondition for this was a new emperor whose approach to government was different from that of his father. A necessary catalyst was a new approach to the problem of government shortages that would leave local officials exposed, without the mechanisms of the informal funding network to hide behind.

The Attack on Government Deficits
Arrears and Deficits in the Early Ch'ing

Arrears and deficits were a chronic feature of Ch'ing fiscal administration. An important distinction existed between these two categories of government shortages. Strictly speaking, arrears (*min-ch'ien*) referred to shortages in tax receipts, the result of failure of officials to collect the tax quota in full. Deficits (*k'uei-k'ung*), on the other hand, applied specifically to discrepancies between the funds on hand in government treasuries or granaries and the amount that should have been there had all funds been disbursed according to government regulations. During different periods, emphasis was placed on alleviating shortages in one or the other of these two categories. In fact, deficits and arrears were intimately related. Real tax evasion naturally contributed to the fiscal insolvency of local officials, and the pressure on officials to cover the costs of government expenditures not provided by the regular funding network led officials and their staff to utilize a number of devices that camouflaged their deficits as arrears. The decision to wage a campaign against deficits or against arrears was often a reflection more of the central government's perceptions of who was more guilty of abuses, the people or the bureaucracy, than of evidence that could be culled from administrative records.

This is not to say that arrears and deficits were not distinct problems or that one or the other was not more central to financial difficulties in different places or at different times. Severe natural disaster always brought on a period of economic hardship for the people in the stricken area, which was usually reflected in tax arrears for a number of years thereafter. However, the traditional fiscal apparatus was fairly well prepared to meet such crises in the form of imperial tax exemptions and deferred payments (*liu-ti*). Certain areas, most notably Kiangnan, suffered from endemic arrears, in part as a result of tax resistance perpetrated by the large numbers of literati households with tax-exempt status in the region.[5] Measures designed to restrict the privileges of degree holders and reductions in the region's excessive tax quota were combined to bring the situation under control for a time.[6] Moreover, as we have seen, reforms in tax-collection procedures were introduced throughout the empire to reduce opportunities for interference by middlemen and peculation by yamen staff. Despite these efforts, arrears continued to exist, and when they became too great the usual solution was to declare a tax amnesty, wiping the slate clean or relieving the population of current obligations in order to allow them to catch up with debts long due.[7]

Deficits were a more enigmatic issue in the early Ch'ing. As we have seen, given the level of regular local funding, it was almost impossible for a provincial official to spend any time in office without incurring some deficits. Although the official position of the government was to discourage shortages and punish offenders, the actual record of prosecutions and impeachments points to a good deal of tolerance toward such malfeasance.[8] Many cases of deficits went unreported, and when missing funds were brought to the attention of the government, it was common practice to use the wages and salaries of all the officials in a province to pay them back.[9] As a result, some officials became complacent about balancing their accounts. Moreover, the practice of *feng-kung* contribu-

tions to make up shortages furthered government insolvency because these same funds were needed to offset the expenses that had
led to deficits in the first place.

The existence of large deficits in government treasuries during
the early Ch'ing did not grow out of a failure to institute statutory
controls on official behavior. Stringent regulations existed to ensure the meticulous monitoring of local-government income and
expenditure. Under the *tsou-hsiao* system of annual accounting,
officials were required to report all expenditures to the Board of
Revenue. Only after approval was given by the Board could an official disburse funds and declare their expenditure (*k'ai-hsiao*) in
his annual accounts. One could not simply report expenditures at
the end of the year. If an official had to appropriate more funds
than originally requested, or failed to request permission in advance to allocate funds for a particular purpose, he was acting
contrary to the regulations and could be impeached. Whether or
not the additional disbursements were legitimate, they were considered deficits and the guilty official was compelled to pay them
back.

Laws such as these were designed to forestall embezzlement, the
only recognized cause of deficits. Similar precautions were taken
when an official handed his office over to his successor (*chiao-tai*).
When an incumbent official left his post, he compiled an inventory
of all income, arrears, and taxes disbursed and actually on hand
and turned it over to the incoming official. The latter checked the
records and weighed the funds on hand to be sure they agreed with
the incumbent's inventory. Only after his successor had issued a
bond of guarantee testifying to the accuracy of his *chiao-tai* accounts was the outgoing official supposed to leave his post for
transfer or retirement. If discrepancies existed, the incoming official was to report them to the governor or governor-general, who
would impeach the outgoing official. The latter was then held responsible for the deficit and the new official was cleared of any
liability.

The operation of the informal funding network had a profound
effect on these two methods of fiscal scrutiny, rendering them useless in many cases. Oertai described the situation graphically when
he was Kiangsu financial commissioner.[10]

> Kiangsu's wealth is the greatest in the empire. Regard-
> ing previous items of deficits, those owed by the people
> are probably caused by disaster and famine, [but] those

owed by officials are in part caused by avarice. Investigating deeply into the cause, leniency (*tan-ku*) is really the source of avarice and following the old habits (*yin-hsün*) is the legacy of leniency. Given leniency and adherence to old habits, there are none who will not tend toward avarice. The high officials extort from their subordinates and the subordinates oppress the little people. When the income extorted [from the people] is insufficient to meet expenses, then they disburse treasury funds (*k'u-t'ang*, i.e., *cheng-hsiang* tax revenues) . . . The result is deficits. The chou and hsien are not necessarily all without scruples (*wu-liang*). In reality, sometimes unscrupulous governors, governors-general, commissioners, and circuit intendants are responsible.

In return for their heavy contribution to provincial expenses, magistrates were often protected against charges of amassing deficits. Only rarely did the high provincial officials impeach lower officials as part of the *tsou-hsiao* process. The early Yung-cheng investigations of official deficits uncovered hundreds of thousands of taels of deficits that had never been brought to the attention of the central government by the governors of the province at the time they occurred.[11] Moreover, to protect *themselves* from implication in these cover-ups, the governors had to subvert the *chiao-tai* process and force incoming officials to accept the accounts of their outgoing subordinates, deficits and all.[12] Most new officials were willing to do so because they knew that in all probability they too would incur deficits and would receive similar protection from prosecution.

Officials of the central government also participated in the subversion of the scrutiny system established during the first two reigns of the dynasty. Because Board officials were no more adequately provided with administrative expenses than were their colleagues in the provinces, the Boards participated in the informal funding network by accepting "Board fees" (*pu-fei*) whenever they had business with provincial officials.[13] This practice was particularly damaging in the case of fees that accompanied provincial annual accounts.

Although the accounts are clear and in order, if Board fees are not paid, they will be rejected on the grounds that the figures therein do not match those in the routine memorials [requesting prior Board approval for said expenditures] or on the pretext that the figures are a few taels off. As soon as the Board fees are paid, millions of taels may be wasted, but the *tsou-hsiao* accounts will still be approved. Sometimes [the accounts] will be rejected for an unimportant matter to preserve the pretense of rejecting accounts while the truth is covered up. Then when [the official concerned] replies, [the Board] will deliberate to approve his accounts. Officials in the capital and in the provinces conspire to steal and lie.[14]

Thus, even if an official had deficits his accounts were approved, so long as he paid the required fee to the Board of Revenue. The façade of fiscal scrutiny was maintained while deficits in the provinces grew year after year.

The Target Shifts

The focus of reform during the K'ang-hsi period was on arrears. This was reflected in efforts to improve tax prompting and in the liberal granting of tax remissions. The tendency to view fiscal problems primarily in terms of the failure of the people to pay their taxes in full handicapped officials seeking to rectify basic weaknesses within the regular tax system itself. In fact, if arrears really were the main problem, little *could* be done beyond exhorting officials to exert greater energy in tax collection or issuing exemptions and remissions. The latter measure, in effect, removed the problem by decreeing it out of existence.

This focus changed dramatically with the Yung-cheng emperor's ascent to the throne. His first policy initiative was to declare a frontal attack on the problem of government deficits and official and clerical peculation. Almost immediately after K'ang-hsi's death, the Yung-cheng emperor issued two edicts laying the blame for deficits not on the people but on the corrupt activities of officials and their clerks. In an edict to the Board of Revenue and Board of Works he first called for stricter auditing of provincial *cheng-hsiang* expenditures.[15]

Wealth is the means for accomplishing one's ends. The ancient rulers considered frugality the basis for abundance for the state and the people. Since taking the throne I have constantly worried about embezzlement of government treasury funds by clerks. Hereafter, these two Boards must carefully investigate all taxes in cash and in kind and the costs of materials and labor

in the annual accounts (*tsou-hsiao*) and compile and
memorialize them in a clear account (*ch'ing-ts'e*). They
may not report vague estimates. If there are those who
report less as more (i.e. in disbursing funds) or cheap
as expensive, or whose figures don't balance or who
make false estimates [of the costs of labor and materi-
als], when they are discovered, let the Board officials
[who approved their falsified accounts] be severely
punished along with them.

The emperor recognized that one way in which funds were diverted from the regular tax network to the informal network was by
manipulating the accounting of those projects for which regular
tax funds were provided. By holding the Board officials equally ac-
countable, Yung-cheng was also making clear his knowledge of
the Board's complicity in this process. As a check against collabo-
ration by the Board of Revenue in circumventing the *tsou-hsiao*
system, the emperor established a separate accounting office called
the Hui-k'ao fu. At the head of the Hui-k'ao fu, Yung-cheng
placed his most trusted officials in the central government—his fa-
vorite brother, Prince I; his uncle, Lungkodo; the Grand Secretary
Pai Huang; and the Censor Chu Shih. These four officials were
commissioned to handle all *tsou-hsiao* matters, no matter which
Board was involved. To assist them in their investigations, a separate yamen was established with a staff consisting of a Manchu
and a Chinese assistant department director (*lang-chung yuan-wai
lang*), three second-class board secretaries (*chu-shih*), and ten
clerks of the seventh to ninth rank (*pi-t'ieh-shih*).[16] By requiring
that all questionable annual accounts be investigated by this independent authority the emperor hoped to halt the practice of evading scrutiny by paying a fee to the Board of Revenue. Moreover,
the Hui-k'ao fu undertook to investigate the accounts of the Boards
themselves to help clear up deficits on the central-government level.
In YC 3 (1725), when the emperor was satisfied that the corruption in local and central finances had been brought under control,
the Hui-k'ao fu was disbanded and its duties returned to the jurisdiction of the Board of Revenue.

Yung-cheng's understanding of the vicious cycle of revenue manipulation and concealment was expressed even more vividly in
the second of these edicts.[17]

Since ancient times, regular taxes have been stored up
for the expenses of the military and the state. In times

of peace, [we] must cause the granaries and treasuries
to be full in order to be prepared and without cause
for worry. Recently there have been numerous circuit
intendants, prefects, and chou and hsien magistrates
in each province with tax deficits. The governors and
governors-general are well aware of this abuse, but
cover up for them until a time of extreme difficulty,
when they usually report embezzlement as "shifting
funds for public expenses." When ordered to set a time
limit for recovery [of the embezzled funds] they regard
them as ancient history and those who pay up in full
are few. Repayment is put off for years but the pretense
of recovering [deficits] remains. In the end there is no
one who can be held responsible (ch'üan-wu-cho-lo).
New officials are forced by their superior officials to
accept the handing over of their predecessors' accounts
(chiao-tai). Although [these accounts] contain deficits,
[an incoming official's] fear of the power of high officials compels him to accept them. Moreover, in imita-
tion of [his superior's corruption] he will use [the fact
that his superior allowed the previous incumbent to
amass deficits] to intimidate his superior and will of
necessity get [his superior's] protection for wrongdo-
ings so that he may embezzle as he pleases. This in turn
leads to even worse deficits. I calculate that this was the
cause of several hundreds of thousands of taels of deficits in the Shantung financial commissioner's treasury.
How could this all be the result of shifting funds for
public expenses (yin-kung no-i)? Now, although [offi-
cials in Shantung] are using feng-kung to make up the
deficits, in reality they cannot but take [the needed
funds] from the people, adding on surcharges beyond
the tax quota. If this is the case in Shantung, [the situa-
tion] in other provinces can be imagined. When the
flesh and blood of the common people is used to rectify
[the deficits] of the officials, how can there not be
hardship in the countryside? I am deeply concerned
about these abuses.

The emperor's first impulse was to combat corruption by instituting a general audit of all provincial treasuries similar to the
type used in earlier reigns to ferret out gentry tax evaders. However, his recognition of the extent to which these practices were
imbedded in the fabric of local government prompted him to leniency. Rather than create conflicts between the central government and the provinces by sending imperial commissioners to pry
into local affairs, he ordered the governors and governors-general

to investigate the deficits of their own subordinates. No one would be punished for having shortages in his yamen treasury or for having failed to detect such shortages in those of his underlings, but all deficits would have to be repaid within three years. Moreover, officials were warned against trying to settle their accounts with the government by extorting from the common people or further falsifying local records.

Thus began the Yung-cheng emperor's crusade against corruption. All government deficits were to be cleared within three years. Thereafter, anyone whose treasury exhibited shortages would be severely punished. This was a policy marked by stern determination, but it promised little originality in the management of the empire's fiscal affairs. What ruler in Chinese history would not have liked to wipe the slate clean, so that moral government under his own leadership could be given a fresh start? The emperor's hard line on official peculation precluded any consideration of the difficulties faced by the bureaucrat in the field. On the contrary, his equally strong commitment to the protection of the people from the excessive demands of the county tax collector magnified the problems of local officials. At least during the first few months of his reign, Yung-cheng continued to view with skepticism claims that missing funds were "shifted for public expenses," and held to the conviction that deficits could have resulted only from the embezzlement of local revenues.

Therefore, it is not surprising that on the inaugural day of his own reign period, Yung-cheng categorically refused permission to use *huo-hao* to make up deficits in the manner suggested by Nien Keng-yao and others during his father's reign. Instead, he took advantage of this auspicious occasion to deliver a series of traditional exhortations to officials at each level of the bureaucracy to behave virtuously in their assigned duties. In his edict to chou and hsien magistrates he linked the pursuit of moral conduct directly to the issue of deficits.[18]

> As for taxes, they are especially important. The smallest grain of rice represents the blood and sweat of the people. Increase the taxes by one *fen* [0.01 tael] and you increase the burden on the people by one *fen*. Decrease them by one *fen* and the people receive one *fen* of grace. In the past there were those who requested to add *huo-hao* temporarily [to the people's taxes] in order to make up deficits in the public treasury. The late emperor issued an edict in court disapproving the re-

quest and all the officials heard it. Now the *huo-hao* of the chou and hsien is being increased with impunity and is viewed as a fixed precedent. How can the people bear it? Henceforth it must be prohibited. If it is discovered and [the official is] impeached by his superior or impeached by a censor, he must be severely punished and certainly cannot be treated leniently. If one wants to clear up the source of deficits, there is no better [way] than frugality and upright conduct. If one is frugal there will be no lack of funds for expenses. If one is upright in conduct, one cannot be [drawn into misdoings] by one's superior.

It is impossible to determine whether the emperor's stance during these first few months was dictated by the exigencies of filial piety, hesitancy to offend the sensibilities of officials who had risen in the bureaucracy under his father, or a genuine belief that the real source of difficulty lay in official corruption and not in the fiscal system itself. What we do know is that Yung-cheng's commitment to clearing deficits remained firm, but his approach to the problem was soon to change.

Who is Responsible? Who Shall Pay?

The emperor's decision not to penalize officials for deficits incurred prior to the Yung-cheng reign was a shrewd one. Within weeks of his edict, reports of shortages began pouring into the capital as officials attempted to demonstrate their zeal and struggled to rid themselves of the burden of deceit and manipulation that deficits demanded. The missing funds uncovered during the three-year grace period totalled millions of taels. Unraveling the tangle of accounting devices used to disguise fiscal insolvency was an onerous task. However, the real challenge lay in transforming acknowledged shortages and fictitious reserves into tangible stores of silver and grain.

For those deficits that did have to be repaid, primary responsibility fell on the chou and hsien magistrates and on financial commissioners. In cases where these officials did not have the resources to compensate the central government and the governor had failed to report the debts at the time they were incurred, the latter was held jointly responsible for repayment.[19] High provincial officials were also held responsible when expenditures had been made without prior approval or funds had been shifted from one category to pay for expenses in another.[20] In cases where an official was no longer in the post in which he incurred his deficit, the amount of the shortage was supposed to be retrieved by voluntary or forced sale of the official's personal property, both at his new post and at his ancestral home.[21]

On paper, such an allocation of responsibility promised the speedy retrieval of all outstanding revenues. As the investigations proceeded, however, it became increasingly obvious that it would require more than an imperial fiat to succeed in eliminating deficits and the corruption that had brought them about. Not only was there no consensus regarding either the causes of deficits or the way to prevent them in the future, but it soon also became apparent that a large number of deficits existed for which it was impossible to assign responsibility.

The one source of deficits widely acknowledged by both provincial and central-government officials was mismanagement of granary stores.[22] Scattered throughout the provinces, government granaries were, by nature, more difficult to inspect than treasuries and were equally prey to manipulation. It was not uncommon for officials short of silver in their treasuries to sell off grain as a source of additional revenues. In some places, public grain contributions were diverted immediately to other uses and never stored as a safeguard against famine or high grain prices. When they were set aside for disaster relief, it was often in the form of an equivalent sum of silver. Not only did this result in shortages when grain was needed promptly for relief, but the conversion rate at which the silver was stored was frequently below the current market price of grain.[23] Even the most scrupulous magistrate could find himself without the statutory stocks of grain because loans made to the people in bad times were often never repaid.[24]

Far more controversial was the issue of treasury deficits. Most central-government officials felt that shortages in provincial- and local-government supplies of silver were the result of embezzlement. Therefore, their contributions to the debate were usually in the form of suggestions for more stringent oversight of provincial financial transactions.[25] In particular, they decried the shifting of funds for public expenses (yin-kung no-i). Under this rubric were included all instances in which local officials used funds designated for one purpose to pay for something else, even if those funds were originally intended for remittance to the central government. Implicit in the condemnation of such practices was the belief that shortages at the local level were the result of official extravagance and not real need.[26] In no case was it accepted that either inadequate revenue allocations to local government or heavy demands for funds from superiors were responsible for the discrepancies in local accounts.[27]

The recommendations of central-government officials tended to deflect attention away from the causes to the symptoms of the disease that infected the Chinese fiscal system. They cannot be blamed for ignoring the real problems faced by local officials trying to fulfill their administrative duties. Many central officials had no experience in local government and their present positions excused them from the practical tasks of clearing the deficits that already existed. Even censors, whose role it was to oversee the activities of officials in the field, spent little time in the provinces. However, as reports began filtering in from provincial officials themselves, a very different picture of the problem began to emerge.

A frequent claim was that deficits in treasury stores were actually the result of arrears on the part of the taxpayers. Particularly in Kiangnan, the tax quotas were often too large for a single official to handle. The likelihood that an official assigned to such a post would be dismissed for failure to collect his taxes in full was great. When a new official came to replace him, he would not only be responsible for collecting the taxes for that year, but would also have to dun the arrears accumulated under his predecessor. In order to avoid removal himself, the new official would have to shift regular taxes (*cheng-hsiang*) designated for other purposes to cover the taxes he was unable to collect.[28] Eventually the shortage would be discovered, but by that time the manipulation of tax records would have hidden all evidence that the deficit was once "people's arrears." Even in remote and tax-poor provinces such as Kwangsi, tax resistance and embezzlement by tax farmers could force magistrates to take such measures to prevent impeachment.[29] In fact, so common was this problem that in some provinces Prince I and the Board of Revenue ordered a special investigation to determine whether any of the deficits attributed to official peculation could be traced to nonpayment by the taxpayers.[30]

The central government was less sympathetic toward officials who reported that their deficits had resulted from legitimate expenditure. Scores of officials memorialized having allocated funds for necessary purchases not provided for under the regular revenue-sharing system. In most cases they were in support of the military, maintenance of public security, and construction of public works. All of these areas were of vital concern to the central government, as well as the local jurisdiction. Nevertheless, once the deficits were discovered, the funds had to be reimbursed, either by the official who had authorized the expenditure or by remanding the wages and salaries of all the low-level officials and functionaries in the province.[31]

Although the responsibility for the repayment of deficits was supposed to fall on the official who had incurred them, it was not always possible to determine who that person was. This was particularly true when shortages appeared in the financial commissioner's treasury. The manipulation of accounts that was the product of the informal funding system had its greatest impact at the provincial level. With well-placed gifts, a lower official could avoid impeachment for failure to fulfill his tax quota. At the same time, governors and governors-general frequently borrowed funds which the financial commissioner would be forced to cover up. Since even expenditures for public purposes were illegal if not authorized by the central government, high provincial officials had a powerful incentive to make the accounts of the financial commissioner's treasury as difficult as possible to understand.[32] This became vividly clear when the Board of Punishments attempted to clear up a case of deficits in the Hupei provincial treasury.[33]

From the beginning, the Board's interrogation of high-level Hupei officials did not promise a speedy solution to the disappearance of funds placed in their care. After much cajoling, the former governor-general, Man-pi, admitted that 100,000 taels had been missing from the treasury during his term of office. This, he claimed, had been repaid out of his own income from *huo-hao* and customary fees and that of the governor and financial commissioner. However, when questioned on this subject, the present financial commissioner, Chang Sheng-pi, reported that the funds had not been made up at all. Instead, the shortage had been camouflaged by Hsü Ta-ting, who had been appointed to replace the financial commissioner in whose term the deficit had arisen. In order to hide the fact that 100,000 taels could not be accounted for, Hsü had ostensibly fabricated allocations of 60,000 taels to make up a shortage in the funds set aside to purchase copper and 40,000 taels of *feng-kung yin* to purchase horses for the military. Chang Sheng-pi had then been forced to go along with this deception when he took office.

If the investigators thought they now had the truth, they were once again thrown into confusion by the testimony of the original financial commissioner, Chang Wen-ts'an. According to him, the money involved was not 100,000 taels, but 150,000 taels. Moreover, it was not a deficit, but the result of people's arrears. Nevertheless, as the official in charge of fulfilling the province's tax quota, Chang Wen-ts'an had personally undertaken to make up the funds, some of which dated back to the period before he had taken office. With money obtained from the sale of considerable family property, several loans, remittances from servants and treasury officers implicated in the case, and a grant of 20,000 taels of *huo-hao* from the governor and governor-general, Chang claimed to have been able to replace the entire amount in one year.

Who was really to blame? Certainly, after so much tampering, the records of the Hupei provincial treasury would yield few clues. Moreover, more than 100,000 taels were still missing. Presumably, these funds would end up like so many others for which responsibility was indeterminate. Such deficits were usually classified as *wu-cho chih-k'uan*. Their very existence was a clear indication of the laxity with which shortages in government treasuries had been handled under previous administrations. Time and again, officials trying to clear up the accounts in local and provincial yamen bemoaned the passage of years and often decades during which deficits had been allowed to grow unchecked and unreported. In some cases the official originally responsible for the shortages was long dead.[34] Even if he was still alive, his personal and family property was often insufficient to make up deficits that could amount to thousands or tens of thousands of taels.[35] The web of deception that had grown up around the system of turning over accounts created many cases of disputed responsibility. The position taken by officials in the field was that the original official should make good any shortages that arose during his term of office, even if he had already left government service. However, fearing delays in repayment and complications resulting from attempts to retrieve funds from outside the province in question, Prince I and the Board of Revenue held to a strict interpretation of the dynastic statutes. Once an official had issued a bond of guarantee stating that all revenues placed in his charge were present and accounted for, it was his responsibility to rectify any discrepancies that might later be uncovered. If an incoming official had signed such a bond knowing that his predecessor's accounts were not in order, it could only have been in hope of some future illicit gain.[36] In effect, this ruling made officials now holding a post exclusively responsible for the repayment of the deficits of all their predecessors who had not been impeached, except in cases where evidence existed that they had filed a report and had been coerced into accepting the *chiao-tai* of the outgoing incumbent.

Needless to say, the local officials at the time of the deficit investigations balked at having such a huge financial burden placed on their shoulders.[37] However, their resistance to paying for the crimes of others constituted only one of the obstacles confronting officials trying to replenish provincial silver stores. Retrieval of missing funds by confiscation of the guilty party's family property was a slow process and involved one province in what amounted to litigation in another province. Officials in the guilty official's home province had their own deficits to worry about and were usually unenthusiastic about engaging in the tedious process of uncovering a person's assets and selling them, especially when the proceeds would be sent elsewhere. Moreover, when the guilty party was an official who held higher office than the magistrate or prefect in charge of his case, it was often extremely difficult for the latter to treat him with the severity that was usually necessary.[38] When responsibility for deficits that had not been reported, or which had arisen out of unauthorized expenditures at the provincial level, devolved upon one or two high officials, the sums were often so great that there was no realistic expectation that they could be repaid swiftly. Finally, in the case of *wu-cho* deficits, responsibility for repayment could not even be assigned.

Under these circumstances, many provincial officials turned once again to the system of informal funding. On the level of the chou and hsien, magistrates often forced the people to pay surtaxes to make up their deficits.[39] Some higher officials continued to rely on contributions of wages and salaries from their subordinates (*chüan-feng*).[40] Because *feng-kung* was still a major source of funding for provincial expenses, and deficits usually far exceeded the funds these wages and salaries made available, most provinces also relied on contributions of officials' customary gifts and fees to make up shortages in the provincial treasury.[41]

It was at this point that the Yung-cheng emperor dealt the decisive blow to local fiscal administration as it had functioned for several years. In the process of investigating deficits, the emperor became increasingly convinced that the demands placed on lower officials by their superiors were one of the major factors leading to shortages in *cheng-hsiang* funds. Therefore, in an edict to all governors and governors-general, he issued a ban on contributions of wages and salaries. At the same time, he issued an edict ordering that steps be taken to eliminate the sending and receiving of *lou-kuei*.[42] It might have been possible for officials to ignore the emperor's instructions and secretly continue to rely on these two sources of funds in daily transactions to cover expenses for which *cheng-hsiang* revenues had not been provided. However, when repayment of deficits was being handled directly by the Board of Revenue, it was impossible to camouflage the source of such huge sums. The hands of provincial officials were tied. A new solution, both to the problem of repayment of deficits and to that of preventing similar shortages in the future, had to be found.

The Reform of Local Fiscal Administration: Huo-hao kuei-kung

The crisis generated by the emperor's ban on *feng-kung* and *lou-kuei* contributions once again focused official attention on the richest of all informal sources of revenue. References to *huo-hao*, or meltage fees, appear as early as the Sung dynasty.[43] However, their importance as a form of tax surcharge is associated with the increasing monetization of the Chinese economy in the late Ming. Technically, the meltage fee was a charge added to regular tax remittances to compensate for the inevitable loss of silver that resulted when taxes were melted down into large ingots for transporting to the central government. Loss of silver also occurred because of the difference between the quality of silver received from taxpayers and the standard fineness required of taxes sent to the capital. Although the actual loss was rarely more than 1 or 2 percent, the proportion of meltage fees levied on land and head taxes increased steadily from the late Ming until the eighteenth century.[44] At the same time, the term *huo-hao* came to describe almost any general percentage surcharge for which no other special term existed.

The amorphous nature of meltage fees and their diminished connection with actual silver depreciation led to their immediate ban by the new Manchu rulers of China.[45] This proscription was continued under K'ang-hsi, who was not incorrect in equating *huo-hao* with the unauthorized appropriation of the people's resources through the informal funding system.[46] Under the K'ang-hsi emperor, laws were promulgated permitting commoners to report officials who collected taxes beyond the quota and specifying punishments for superior officials who covered up for subordinates who exacted *huo-hao*.[47] Nevertheless, the magistrates' need for funds for daily living expenses and the wages of servants, clerks, and runners compelled officials to recognize the need to collect at least some extra revenue in the form of *huo-hao*. As we have seen, even K'ang-hsi had to concede that an official who demanded only 10 percent above the tax quota could still be recommended as a good administrator.[48] *Huo-hao* therefore came to occupy an ambiguous position as both an illegal surcharge and a source of funds increasingly viewed as the private property of the chou and hsien bureaucracy. Notwithstanding frequent exhortations to high provincial officials urging them to supervise their subordinates and eliminate abuses in tax collection, *huo-hao* continued to be collected and rates continued to rise.

Once alternative means to eliminate deficits were obstructed by the emperor's ban on *lou-kuei* and salary contributions, several characteristics of *huo-hao* made it an obvious choice. As an openly declared percentage of regular taxes, *huo-hao* escaped the stigma of more deviously contrived methods of milking the common people through falsification of records, tampering with weights and measures, and extortion. Moreover, because the collection of *huo-hao* could be integrated into the system of "wrapping and depositing one's own taxes," officials would not be forced to rely on the complicity of clerks and runners to defraud the taxpayer. Integration of *huo-hao* into the legal fiscal administration would therefore not undermine the taxpayer's direct dealings with the state, a principle central to Ch'ing administrative ideology. The collection of *huo-hao*, although generally viewed as a form of peculation, had always been tied to real levels of local revenue and government fiscal requirements. Areas with large gross tax receipts customarily levied *huo-hao* at considerably lower rates than areas with very small tax receipts. This put a greater burden on the taxpayers in the agriculturally depressed parts of the empire, but guaranteed all magistrates comparable funds for at least a portion of their administrative expenses. Perhaps even more important to officials at the time was the fact that as a strictly local levy, *huo-hao* was not associated with bribery. Although revenues from *huo-hao* contributed to the pool of funds sent to higher officials in the guise of *lou-kuei*, it was not linked directly to the concealment of official malfeasance that critics of local fiscal administration saw as the main cause of deficits.

It was probably such considerations that had prompted officials such as Nien Keng-yao to recommend the legalization of *huo-hao* to clear deficits in the past. However, if the return of the meltage fee to the public coffers (*huo-hao kuei-kung*) had been simply a program to eradicate government debts, it would deserve little more than a footnote in the annals of Chinese fiscal administration. The great achievement of officials seeking a solution to the immediate issue of debt repayment was their attempt, for the first time in late-imperial history, to attack the causes of deficits. Their efforts gave rise to a complete reorganization of local-government finance, in which *huo-hao* would play the pivotal role.

From Desperation to Innovation

Government toleration of salary contributions and *lou-kuei* had been founded on a monumental fallacy. Because these funds appeared to come out of the officials' own pockets, they were rarely associated with increased taxation imposed on the common people. On the other hand, *huo-hao*, the source of much of the *lou-kuei* that circulated within the bureaucracy, was nothing more than an illegal surcharge, a deplorable evil. The Yung-cheng emperor's attack on salary contributions and *lou-kuei* was aimed at improving state finances by rehabilitating official discipline and morale. How was it, then, that after decades of resisting such a step, the Ch'ing dynasty legalized the collection of *huo-hao* and transformed it into the basis for the rationalization of government funding at the local level? *Huo-hao kuei-kung* violated the supreme taboo, that against high taxes. How was the emperor able to implement a policy which to many Chinese officials appeared to sacrifice the people's livelihood for the sake of state finances?

The manner in which *huo-hao kuei-kung* became public policy bears some resemblance to the way in which the Single-Whip reforms were implemented in the late Ming. Initiative appeared to be local, transmitted to the central government by the governors and financial commissioners of individual provinces. No general order or legislation was enacted requiring empire-wide implementation, and when it was carried out, each province took into consideration local differences in establishing rates and methods of collection and remittance. However, beneath the surface a crucial difference existed in the mediating and guiding role played by the emperor during the Ch'ing reform. In part, this was the result of the emperor's dynamic personality and personal commitment to fiscal reform, which we have already seen demonstrated in his attack on deficits. Closely related to these factors was the institution of a new communication device, the secret palace-memorial system, in this same period.[49]

One persistent theme in late imperial Chinese history was the devolution of imperial control over the bureaucracy and the decision-making process. In the routine memorial system, or *t'i-pen chih-tu*, the correspondence of local officials passed through the offices of the Grand Secretariat, which not only selected those memorials that were deserving of the emperor's attention but drafted possible responses from which the emperor could choose his rescript. At times, this system enabled the central bureaucracy to manipulate policy by screening the information available to the emperor. It also produced a situation in which weak emperors could evade all responsibility for government decisions. In a political system where decision-making authority was ambiguous, this greatly limited the possibility for innovation, particularly that emanating from the provincial level. Moreover, it obstructed rationalizing reforms for which a major prerequisite is the most complete possible information about conditions as they really are.

Beginning in the last years of the K'ang-hsi reign, a second memorial system was instituted. Its full development was realized under the Yung-cheng emperor. This secret palace-memorial system, or *tsou-che chih-tu*, made possible unmediated communication between the emperor and his officials in the field. The existing central-government organs were completely by-passed and correspondence by this route was guaranteed total confidentiality. Because all high officials knew that all other high officials had the same privilege of secret communication with the emperor, the latter was assured of honest reporting from his subordinates. Their reports were for the emperor alone, hence officials could express their opinions and present their ideas freely, without fear of censure from their peers in the central government or of accusation that they were spurning widely held values. Moreover, the emperor, who composed most of his rescripts himself, was in a position to experiment with new ideas without the formal sanction that adhered to any imperial statement made in response to a *t'i-*

pen.[50] Through private communications of this kind the emperor could also help mold official opinions and actions by means of subtle suggestions and criticisms while preserving provincial autonomy in areas where he felt it important. Thus, through the secret memorial system, both imperial and provincial decision-making power were greatly enhanced. One of the most notable examples of this may be found in the implementation of the *huo-hao kuei-kung* reforms.

Among many high provincial officials the prospect that their main avenues of funding would be cut off inspired panic rather than creativity. Some governors and financial commissioners even nurtured the hope that a persuasive argument could win exemption from the ban applied elsewhere. Kiangsi Governor P'ei Shuai-tu boasted that he had eliminated all customary gifts previously sent to his own yamen and that of the commissioners, circuit intendents, and prefects. However, his virtuous display of compliance with the emperor's wishes did not prevent him from receiving 12,000 taels in fees from the grain intendant and the financial commissioner. P'ei realized that his role as a Confucian administrator was to set a good example for those beneath him. To accept such fees would encourage his subordinates to do the same. Yet without some informal source of funding, neither he nor the financial commissioner would be able to operate their yamen.[51]

Whereas P'ei sought imperial sanction for his continued acceptance of *lou-kuei*, other officials attempted to circumvent the prohibition of contributions of *feng-kung*. Liang-kuang Governor-general K'ung Yü-hsün feared that without contributions of *feng-kung* the provincial government would be forced to farm out purchases of materials and supplies to the individual chou and hsien. This could only result in the latter making up the costs by levying surcharges on the people. Interpreting the emperor's ban as a demonstration of concern for poorly paid officers and staff on the lowest rungs of the official hierarchy, K'ung proposed that Kwangtung continue to appropriate official salaries, but only those of officials of magisterial rank and above.[52] Along the same lines, Chekiang Governor Huang Shu-lin proposed solving the problem of *wu-cho* deficits in his province by using contributions of *feng-kung* collected during the period before the imperial ban was issued.[53]

In each of the above cases the emperor's rescript was noncommittal. On the one hand, he reiterated his concern that the collection of fees and salary contributions be terminated. On the other, he promised that the pleas of officials who really found themselves in financial straits would not go unheeded. Although only a few were aware of it at the time, Yung-cheng himself was becoming convinced that no provincial official could survive on the revenues legally made available to him by the state. Communicating with them through secret palace memorials, he allowed a small number of officials to experiment with the use of *huo-hao* to make up deficits and provide a more stable source of income for provincial administration.

The earliest evidence of a plan to use *huo-hao* for public expenses appears in a memorial from Hukwang Governor-general Yang Tsung-jen. Even before Yung-cheng issued his edict prohibiting the contribution of *feng-kung*, Yang expressed his fear that if lower officials were deprived of their salaries they would have no choice but to extort funds from the people. However, if no provision was made for provincial expenses, the costs of government projects would inevitably fall on the magistrates, who in turn would pass them on to the taxpayer. In order to solve this problem, Yang proposed that the chou and hsien be allowed to collect *huo-hao* at a rate of 10 percent. Of this, 20 percent would be sent to the financial commissioner for provincial expenses, 10 percent would be sent to the Board of Revenue to cover losses in the regular taxes remitted (*yü-p'ing*), and 70 percent would be retained by the chou and hsien to meet their own administrative costs. The emperor's response to Yang's plan was extremely enthusiastic. He called it "completely correct and without a flaw," but warned Yang to be cautious in carrying it out.[54]

At the same time that Yang Tsung-jen was implementing his plan in Hunan and Hupei, Shansi Governor No-min was formulating the scheme that would eventually become the model for the whole empire. No-min's original memorials have not survived. However, Shansi Financial Commissioner Kao Ch'eng-ling reported two years later that in a memorial dated YC 1, 5, 13, No-min requested that the rate of collection for *huo-hao* in Shansi be standardized at 20 percent. Inasmuch as nowhere in the province was the rate lower than 20 percent, this meant an immediate saving for many of Shansi's taxpayers. The governor then estimated that the total *huo-hao* for the province would be approximately 500,000 taels. Of this, 300,000 taels were to be set aside for officials' expenses and for the public expenses of the whole province. The remaining 200,000 taels would be deducted annually to make up *wu-cho* deficits.[55]

Although they receive no mention in the official accounts of the *huo-hao kuei-kung* reforms, other provinces were also initiating programs utilizing this new method of funding. After receiving an ambiguous response to his own proposal to continue the use of salary contributions for public expenses, Chihli Governor Li Wei-chün memorialized the emperor, advocating limited use of *huo-hao* for this purpose.[56] Shantung Governor Huang Ping began to investigate the collection of *huo-hao* in his province as early as the end of YC 1 (1723).[57] His efforts to control rates of collection as a prelude to their use in deficit repayment was reported to the emperor early the next year.[58] However, an elaborate scheme for sharing *huo-hao* on a provincial basis was already being attempted at this time. According to Wu Lung-yuan, who passed through Shantung's Yen-chou prefecture on his way to proctor the examinations in Kiangnan, the rate of *huo-hao* collection in Shantung had been fixed at 15 percent of the regular tax. For every tael of tax collected in Yen-chou an additional 0.03 tael was put aside for transportation expenses, 0.01 tael for the prefect, 0.007 tael for the Yen-ning circuit intendant, and 0.005 tael for the judicial commissioner. The remaining 0.098 tael (65.3 percent of the total *huo-hao*) was being used to make up deficits. Once all the deficits were paid in full, the chou and hsien would be permitted to deduct an additional 0.03 tael for themselves, the remainder being allocated for public expenses.[59] Surviving documentation makes it impossible to determine whether the situation observed by Wu Lung-yuan was typical of all administrative units in the province. Nevertheless, it is clear that some form of *huo-hao kuei-kung* was being practiced quite early in Shantung.

The same may be said of neighboring Honan. Toward the end of YC 1, Honan Governor Shih Wen-cho toyed with the idea of using the *huo-hao* of the whole province to make up *wu-cho* deficits. The bans on *lou-kuei* and salary contributions were not yet in effect, but Honan's *feng-kung* was already completely committed to military-supply costs and dike repairs. However, Shih still shared the common view that *huo-hao* was the exclusive property of the chou and hsien magistrates, and at this point felt it was unfair to require magistrates without deficits to contribute to the repayment of deficits for those who did have them.[60] Instead, he decided to continue the use of *lou-kuei* to make up these shortages.

By the new year, *lou-kuei* was no longer a permissible remedy for government shortages and Shih proceeded to present the emperor with a detailed proposal for the use of *huo-hao* to clear deficits and furnish local officials with funds for their expenses. Governor Shih's plan made no attempt to alter the existing rates of *huo-hao* collection, rates which at the time varied between those paid by the gentry and those paid by commoners. He estimated that the average rate was about 13 percent. Given Honan's annual land- and head-tax quota of approximately 3,600,000 taels, this would provide the province with around 400,000 taels of *huo-hao* each year. From this total, each official would be granted personal expenses, as well as public expenses, and funds would be set aside for advance payments (*p'ei-chih*, probably to cover unexpected costs that would be paid back from the *cheng-hsiang* after approval was received from the Board of Revenue). Once the above were deducted, Shih calculated that between 150,000 and 160,000 taels would be left over to make up deficits and pay for provincial-level expenses.[61]

The emperor's reply to Shih Wen-cho's memorial is very revealing. Unlike the noncommittal responses he made to officials who tried to bend the rules and continue the use of funds from the informal network, Yung-cheng's rescript openly praised Shih's plan. The emperor told him that this memorial could not be compared with the vague mutterings in his previous memorials. Yung-cheng pointed out that a high provincial official's duty lay precisely in this kind of thorough attention to fiscal matters. Only by calculating total available funds and determining how much was needed to make up deficits and to pay for officials' personal and public expenses could the smooth functioning of government be assured. Platitudes about morality and good government were not enough. "If one speaks in imprecise and confused generalities, uttering phrases such as 'taxes are important,' then what one says amounts to empty words on paper. What practical [result] does it have?"[62]

What differentiated Shih's and others' discussions of *huo-hao* reform from previous proposals to clean up government was their focus on rectifying the dysfunctional aspects of the regular system of revenue sharing. In every case, *huo-hao* was recommended not only as a temporary means to repay deficits, but as a long-term source of official living and administrative expenses. The idea that virtue in administration was the product of factors other than the moral qualities of the men in office was not a new one. At least as early as the late K'ang-hsi reign, memorials on good government referred to the need to nourish virtue (*yang-lien*) by assuring officials adequate income. As we have seen, however, most officials in the central government persisted in the belief that the Ch'ing dynasty had already achieved this ideal through existing fiscal arrangements. It was not until the Yung-cheng period that the term *yang-lien* was applied to funds designated specifically to provide provincial officials with a substantial and autonomous source of revenue.

In the middle of the first year of the Yung-cheng reign, Shih I-chih wrote a memorial linking deficits to the insatiable demand for funds imposed by provincial governors and governors-general on their subordinates. These high officials made a great show at being virtuous (*chiao-lien*), but even when they claimed to have eliminated *lou-kuei* and *huo-hao* in their jurisdictions, the amount they continued to extort was great. Shih's observations did not come as a revelation to the emperor, but his remedy reflected the sentiments of a growing number of practical reformers in the field. Shih felt that the reason corruption continued unabated was that the expenses of officials exceeded their share of legal tax revenues. No individual could possess the personal resources necessary to run a whole province. Rather than warning against greed, Shih proposed that the best way to eliminate the pretense of virtue and make it a reality was to liberalize these high officials' sources of *yang-lien*. Therefore, he requested that the emperor issue an edict to all the governors and governors-general in the empire to calculate the amount of *huo-hao*, *chieh-li*, salt, post, customs, and tribute administration fees for their provinces and present a list of them to the emperor. The emperor would then calculate the amounts and items that could be retained on the basis of the size and remoteness of the province and the harm and benefit pertaining to the collection of each kind of fee. Those funds approved by the emperor would be a source of *yang-lien* for the governor and governor-general, and all other informal sources of income would be eliminated.[63]

The emperor did not issue such an edict at this time, but the concept of a regular source of *yang-lien* was integrated into most of the plans for *huo-hao kuei-kung* presented to the emperor. The term was used by Shih Wen-cho, Yang Tsung-jen, and No-min in their memorials to refer to the funds they proposed to set aside from *huo-hao* for provincial officials' expenses. Their initial proposals were rather vague in this regard and it remained for specific procedures to be established for determining who would receive *yang-lien*, what amounts would be given each official, and how the new funds would be distributed.

The catalyst for this final stage of fiscal rationalization was introduced in Shansi late in YC 1. Governor No-min and Financial Commissioner T'ien Wen-ching decided to require that the chou and hsien magistrates remit their *huo-hao* in its entirety to the province's financial commissioner. The latter would then calculate the amount of public-expense funds and *yang-lien* to be issued to each official yamen. In all the previously memorialized plans the magistrates were allowed to deduct their own expenses from the *huo-hao* collected, remitting only that amount that was allocated for higher levels of government and to repay deficits. As we shall see, it was this innovation that really distinguished *huo-hao kuei-kung* from plans that merely coopted previously illegal levies into the regular network for the purpose of paying up deficits.

Reactions to Reform

Criticism of the new fiscal practices began to appear during the early part of YC 2. Experiments with *huo-hao kuei-kung* not having been publicized through official channels, most of those who commented on the reforms at this time were central-government officials who had been sent to proctor examinations in provinces where the reforms were being tested.

One of the main targets of these early critics was the newly proposed requirement that chou and hsien magistrates remit all of their quota of *huo-hao* to the provincial treasury. Censor Wang Chih-lin was not averse to the legalization of *huo-hao* or its use to provide provincial officials with *yang-lien*. He did object to the waste in resources that transportation to the provincial capital and back to the local administrative units would entail.[64] Others were not so sanguine. Lo Ch'i-ch'ang, who witnessed the reforms in action while proctoring the examinations in Honan, expressed unqualified opposition to the remittance of *huo-hao*. During his travels, Lo had heard that in Chihli, Shantung, Shansi, Shensi, and Honan the governors and financial commissioners had demanded that all *huo-hao* collected on the land and head tax be deposited in the provincial treasury in preparation for expenses incurred in carrying out public business. In return for their sacrifice the chou and hsien magistrates were given *yang-lien*. The amount allocated varied with the size of the jurisdiction, ranging from 600 to 1,000 taels per year. Although this may have solved the fiscal problems of high government officials, Lo reported that the magistrates were now complaining about inadequate funding from *yang-lien*.[65]

Criticism was also leveled against the reforms by officials who felt that the issue of reform could not be divorced from Confucian principles of rule. A number of officials feared that legalization of *huo-hao* would result in higher taxes. If *huo-hao* were drawn upon to make up deficits, magistrates would use this as a pretext to increase the rates at which this surcharge was collected. One such critic invoked the ancient precept that stressed the rule of men over the rule of law (*yu chih-jen, wu chih-fa*). If the emperor truly wished to solve the problem of deficits, he would be best advised to abandon these administrative schemes and concentrate on choosing virtuous men for the posts of governor and governor-general.[66]

Probably the most famous opponent of *huo-hao kuei-kung* was Shen Chin-ssu. Best known as a philosopher and devoted follower of the Chu Hsi school, Shen's critique of the reforms also reflected a concern for the preservation of Confucian moral values. Unlike many other central-government officials, Shen had had a distinguished career as a local magistrate, a fact that added credence to his evaluation of the new policies. In 1723 the new emperor appointed Shen to the post of director in the Board of Civil Appointments, and in 1724 Shen was sent to proctor the examinations in Shantung.[67] Shen also feared that the legalization of *huo-hao* would encourage official avarice and lead to heavier tax burdens on the people. However, his main concern at this time was the effect that *huo-hao kuei-kung* as a method of making up deficits would have on official morale.

In his memorial, Shen pointed out that not all deficits were the same. He felt that the governors and financial commissioners in each province should be ordered to undertake a general audit of all deficits. The deficits should then be divided into four categories: (1) those that were the result of an edict ordering officials to make public contributions (*kung-chüan*) for construction or other projects; (2) those that were the result of funds being used on the official's own initiative for projects of benefit to the whole province; (3) those in which one official was taking the responsibility for deficits left by a former official; and (4) those that were the result of embezzlement or shifting of funds by the incumbent official himself. Shen insisted that in cases where funds were embezzled by the incumbent himself, repayment should be made by that official and should be accompanied by severe punishment. In cases where an edict was issued to contribute funds the officials should be exempted entirely from repayment. He agreed that where an official was being held responsible for funds used for province-wide expenses or for deficits left by his predecessor, it was not fair to make him use his own wealth to make up the shortage. Nevertheless, Shen persisted in the belief that *huo-hao* was a strictly local source of funds. To use *huo-hao* to make up any but the official's own deficits would still be equivalent to confiscating his personal resources.

According to Shen, the desire of the reformers to restock their treasuries had led them to overlook the importance of moral factors in governing the empire. Even if an official had good cause to have accumulated deficits, the very fact that his accounts were not clean was a blot on his integrity and a sign that he did not know how to economize. Shen was convinced that, if such an official were left in office, not only would he fail to repay his previous deficits, but he would surely run up new ones in the future. The result could only bring more harm to the people and increase levies of *huo-hao*. Therefore, he recommended that any official with deficits be removed from office and another official be appointed in his place. The latter could then record the exact size of the deficit in the jurisdiction and calculate how much should be paid back each year from collection of *huo-hao*. Moreover, *huo-hao* rates would be fixed at no more than 10 percent of the regular tax quota, and any official exceeding this amount would be impeached for avarice (*t'an-wu*) and severely punished.[68]

The implication of Shen Chin-ssu's remarks was that, although the policy was not ideal, it was permissible to legalize the collection of a limited amount of *huo-hao* for the express purpose of repaying deficits. This was because the harm caused by deficits to official morality was greater than the potential damage caused by legitimizing *huo-hao*. However, collection could be sanctioned for only a specified time period and would be controlled by having a yearly quota calculated and remitted for deficit repayment. Given his conclusion that, even in extenuating circumstances, deficits were a sign of moral depravity, it is not surprising that Shen made no mention of using *huo-hao* to rationalize provincial expenditure.

Not all the reactions to the new policies were negative. Some central-government officials were impressed with the reforms and urged the emperor to make improvements in their implementation. One such proposal came from Board of Punishments Vice-president Chang Ch'ing-tu, who was sent to proctor the examinations in Hunan. As we have already seen, in that province magistrates collected a uniform percentage of *huo-hao*, deducting their own share at the source. Chiang suggested that the chou and hsien continue to collect *huo-hao* at a rate of 10 percent, but that they be ordered to remit it in full along with their regular taxes. The governor and governor-general could then calculate allocation on the basis of each administrative unit's location and the complexity of its government business. In this way an official's *yang-lien* would reflect his needs and not just the size of the tax quota in his area.[69] Chang probably did not know that his was precisely the method being introduced in Shansi and Honan, a method others did not find so appealing.

Backlash in Honan

Much of the initial reaction against *huo-hao kuei-kung* was prompted by a genuine concern that Confucian principles of benevolent rule not be violated. However, concern for personal gain also motivated the reluctance of many officials to abandon the informal funding system. It is no accident that the magistrate's right to control *huo-hao* became the rallying cry of *huo-hao kuei-kung*'s most fervent critics. As long as *huo-hao* remained illegal and its collection unregulated, it could provide the magistrate and his superiors with a lucrative source of personal income. Even among those for whom profit was not an issue, the idea of supervised collection and allocation of meltage fees raised the spectre of new shortages at the local level. Only several years of successful implementation could dispel this fear. Consequently, the physical remittance of *huo-hao* to the provincial coffers became the main target of resistance to the reforms in the provinces where they were actually being implemented. By the summer of 1724, opposition to the theory of *huo-hao kuei-kung* was translated into opposition to the practice of *huo-hao kuei-kung*.

In Shansi this was manifested in the refusal of a number of magistrates to remit their *huo-hao* to the provincial treasury.[70] Rapid impeachment of the recalcitrant minority soon brought the situation under control, and as a result, the reforms received little adverse publicity. In Honan, magistrates also sought to forestall the remittance of *huo-hao*, but here they did so by joining forces with officials in the capital to discredit one of the earliest proponents of the reforms, the newly appointed Honan financial commissioner, T'ien Wen-ching. Requests for T'ien's impeachment and the simultaneous outbreak of gentry resistance to another of T'ien's policies focused the attention of officialdom on *huo-hao kuei-kung* and prompted the emperor's first public intervention on behalf of the reforms.

T'ien typified the kind of energetic, practical administrators who were selected for high provincial posts by the Yung-cheng emperor. Like the other officials instrumental in Yung-cheng's campaign to improve local government, T'ien had entered the bureaucracy by the irregular route.[71] His rise to prominence was a direct result of imperial patronage.[72] T'ien Wen-ching began his career as an assistant magistrate in 1684 and in twenty years of government service rose no higher than the rank of magistrate of an independent chou. In 1708 he was transferred to Peking and held several middle-level positions. During the last years of the K'ang-hsi reign, however, T'ien seems to have developed a close relationship with the prince who was soon to become the new emperor,[73] and throughout his reign Yung-cheng referred to T'ien as one of his three most trusted officials.[74]

T'ien's relationship with the Yung-cheng emperor was based in part on a common approach to administrative affairs. In their public lives, both men demonstrated a deep commitment to the aim of improving the institutions through which virtue could be revealed in government. Though reviled in his own day, T'ien was one of the great exemplars of *ching-shih* activism in office, and many of his memorials were republished in the nineteenth century. The minister and the ruler also shared an intense distrust of scholar-officials and the cliques that were often formed among successful examination candidates.[75] This may explain their readiness to blame many of the problems inherent in Ch'ing fiscal administrations on favoritism and cover-ups among provincial officials. T'ien's long tenure in local government led him to place value on practical experience and not on the effete book learning of Confucian degree holders. He consistently emphasized administrative expertise in his evaluations of his subordinates and may have been responsible for the introduction of a system of official apprenticeship (*shih-yung kuan*) adopted during the Yung-cheng period.[76]

Moreover, T'ien's own writings on administrative matters were published by the government as part of its efforts to train local officials.[77]

Although we do not know whether T'ien Wen-ching was promoted to high provincial office with the specific purpose of advancing the cause of *huo-hao* reform, he was clearly an ideal vehicle.[78] T'ien was sixty-two years old when he was rescued from obscurity and sent to Shansi as financial commissioner. As he himself often stated, he was too old to let career concerns influence his actions in office. As a Chinese bannerman without local ties or literati interests, his loyalty was to the emperor alone. T'ien's intimacy with Yung-cheng and his confidence that he was carrying out the emperor's desires contributed to his single-minded pursuit of reform.[79] Nevertheless, his lack of tact made him one of the least popular of provincial officials. It is not surprising, therefore, that early resistance to the new policies came to focus on the person of T'ien Wen-ching.

Once the concept of the return of the meltage fee to the public coffers was established in Shansi, T'ien was transferred to the post of financial commissioner in Honan. Just as his arrival in Shansi marked the beginning of a systematic use of *huo-hao* to finance local government, T'ien's move to Honan was immediately reflected in changes in fiscal administration there. As we have seen, it was early in YC 2 that Governor Shih Wen-cho decided to use *huo-hao* to make up deficits and provide officials with a stable source of operating funds. With T'ien as his second in command, this was accomplished by means of full remittance of *huo-hao* to the provincial treasury.

Lo Ch'i-ch'ang's criticism of this method of local funding was soon echoed in a barrage of memorials calling for T'ien's removal from office. According to his impeachers, under T'ien's leadership "not a 'cent' is given to the chou and hsien." As a result, "the officials are poor and the people are experiencing hardship."[80]

Shih Wen-cho responded to these accusations by pointing out that in return for sending their *huo-hao* to the provincial capital, all officials in Honan now received *yang-lien* as well as additional funds for public expenses. Because the magistrates were no longer called upon to provide their superiors with gifts and fees or submit to unscheduled calls for contributions to public expenses, their financial situation was now much better than before.[81] T'ien's own reply was even more emphatic in its insistence on the importance of full remittance of *huo-hao*. If *huo-hao* was deposited in locked chests along with the regular tax and sent in full to the financial commissioner, the magistrate would have no incentive to increase the demands he made on the people. Only in this way could high provincial officials ensure a steady flow of funds for all provincial expenses and halt the escalation of surcharges imposed on the taxpayer.[82]

Yung-cheng had no personal doubts as to T'ien's integrity, but his reply to T'ien's memorial clearly reflects the experimental nature of the reforms at this point and the caution with which officials had to proceed in carrying them out.[83]

> Now that I see your explanation, although it is clear, you and the Governor seem to have managed this inappropriately, arousing suspicion and hate. Even more incredible, there are those who say this action of yours is worse than accepting bribes. Your hearts do not harbor such things, but in your actions there is perhaps a little to lead people to suspect that you do. Be careful to examine yourself, act fairly, and be flexible. You cannot let people have the slightest excuse to make trouble.

The trouble that Yung-cheng feared was not long in coming. By early July, 1724, T'ien's efforts to reform local finance were being linked to the oppression of the masses in the execution of public works. Within a short time the interests of local gentry and of opponents of *huo-hao kuei-kung* were joined in a scandal that could have brought an end to the rationalization of fiscal administration.

The incident that precipitated this crisis was the result of extensive dike repairs being undertaken in Honan. To ensure the success of the project, local effort had been enlisted to supply labor and materials. According to denunciations of T'ien's policies, the financial commissioner, by forcing the magistrates to send all their *huo-hao* to the provincial treasury, had left them no choice but to confiscate straw from the common people and compel them to transport it to the construction sites. In addition, despite the Ch'ing abandonment of corvée labor, both gentry and commoners were being conscripted to work on the dikes.[84]

In fact, the situation in Honan was somewhat different from that described. Large numbers of peasants were transporting straw to the construction sites, but only because the government was offering a good price that would probably drop once the new harvest was in. However, the real target of T'ien's opponents was the government's assessment of labor service on the dikes. In order to hasten completion of the project before the onset of the rainy season, T'ien had authorized the chou and hsien to apportion the necessary number of workers among the people on the basis of land holdings. One man was to be provided for every 150–200 *mou* of land owned. Each laborer would then be paid a wage calculated according to the amount and difficulty of the work he accomplished. Clearly, the assessment of labor on the dikes was aimed at the wealthier inhabitants of the local community, for few peasants owned this much land. T'ien himself acknowledged that those who would fill the quota were gentry households with large holdings and few adult males. As a result, "(the gentry will) hire poor people to work on the river for them. So apart from their wages, these people will also get paid by the rich to substitute for them. This is a case of the landless poor getting a means of livelihood, not a case of burdening the people."[85]

Not everyone judged the situation as T'ien did. Before the month was over, 100 Honan *sheng-yuan*, *chü-jen*, and *chin-shih* had staged a protest against the labor assessment. Blocking the reentry of the Feng-ch'iu magistrate into the hsien city, they presented a series of demands aimed at halting the government's employment of hired labor on the dikes. However, their most important grievance was the government's failure to distinguish between gentry and commoners in taxation and assessment of labor service. Vigorous efforts to calm the protestors failed, and in late July lower-gentry discontent reached its climax in a boycott by all but twenty-three of the students enrolled to sit for the hsien examinations.[86]

The examination boycott was taken very seriously by the Yung-cheng emperor. Refusal to take the examinations was one of the few outlets available to the literati to express their displeasure with the government. In effect, such an act challenged the dynasty's right to rule. Despite efforts by the Honan educational commissioner and other high officials to gloss over the affair, the emperor insisted that the leaders be arrested, and in a secret rescript to T'ien Wen-ching, suggested that one or two be executed as an antidote to this kind of wicked behavior.[87]

T'ien Wen-ching was also worried about the implications of the boycott. Throughout the ensuing month and a half, protest over the labor assessments continued to be linked to dissatisfaction with *huo-hao kuei-kung*. Some of T'ien's own subordinates joined in the outcry against remittance of *huo-hao* to the provincial treasury, charging T'ien with using this innovation to line his own pockets.[88] T'ien's anxiety was expressed in the growing defensiveness of his memorials, which sought again and again to show that *huo-hao kuei-kung* was a measure designed to end corruption and not contribute to it. The financial commissioner's fear that he had perhaps gone too far in the interest of reform was partially assuaged by the assurances the emperor appended to his memorials. Time and time again Yung-cheng urged him to ignore the hatred that his zeal had engendered.[89] In the emperor's own words, T'ien was "one of those who really understands my wishes and I trust you to do your best."[90]

The emperor's rescripts must have been comforting to this ageing bureaucrat, but Yung-cheng's greatest expression of support for reform came in actions, not words. Three months after these protests took place, T'ien Wen-ching was promoted to the post of governor of Honan.[91] Of even greater significance, at the height of the conflict over reform in that province, Yung-cheng chose to make his support of the new policies public by presenting the Shansi version of *huo-hao kuei-kung* for the approval of the court.

From Experimentation to Empire-wide Implementation

Prior to the summer of 1724, discussion of *huo-hao kuei-kung* had taken place exclusively through the medium of secret palace memorials. For the first year and a half of his reign, the Yung-cheng emperor had been content to allow these officials in the provinces to examine local conditions and present plans for the solution of the fiscal crisis independent of any coercive action from above. Perhaps because of his recognition of the divergence of attitudes and interests between officials serving in the provinces and those in the central government, Yung-cheng preferred to grant provincial officials considerable autonomy in fiscal matters throughout his reign. During the early months of *huo-hao* experimentation, no edicts were issued on the subject beyond a reiteration of the ban on official extortion of gifts from one's subordinates.[92] In his rescripts to the secret memorials of those who had put forth solutions to the deficit problem, he had encouraged those whose ideas coincided with his own, but had not advocated any specific course of action.

In mid-July the emperor decided to press the issue of *huo-hao kuei-kung* by having Shansi Governor No-min request its implementation in a memorial to the Grand Secretariat.[93] Opposition to the reforms was mounting. In particular, magistrates in the field were gaining allies in their fight against loss of control over informal revenues. Yung-cheng could have avoided intervening in the controversy, but only by risking the abandonment of the reforms where they had already been carried out. Perhaps he felt that a demonstration of his own support for the new policies, however veiled, would force court officials to consider the merits of No-min's plan. If so, he was soon disappointed. Rejection of No-min's request was swift and unanimous.[94]

Only two individual responses to No-min's memorial have survived. Shen Chin-ssu, who had already expressed reservations regarding the use of *huo-hao* to make up deficits, offered new grounds for opposing legalization of this surcharge. In particular, he feared that by converting a surcharge which until now had had no fixed quota to a tax remitted to the provincial treasury, officials would come to regard *huo-hao* as a regular tax (*cheng-hsiang*). In Shen's view, this would inevitably lead to additional levies of *huo-hao* in order to compensate for that which the magistrates were forced to send elsewhere. The result would only be hardship for the common people.[95]

An equally emphatic condemnation was put forward by Ch'a Ssu-t'ing.[96] Ch'a felt that *huo-hao* should not be legalized, but was willing to concede that it might be necessary to do as a temporary expedient for the purpose of clearing deficits. However, his greatest concern was the lack of any provision for Board supervision of *huo-hao* revenues in No-min's plan.[97] As a remedy, he proposed that the financial commissioner of each province compile an account of the amount of *huo-hao* that could be collected each year and the amounts of the deficits that had to be repaid. On the basis of this information, a schedule of repayment could be drawn up and the Board could monitor the use of *huo-hao* by comparing the amount collected against the amount of deficits reimbursed. Knowledge of each province's capacity to clear its debts would then allow the Board to set a definite time for the completion of the task, after which remittance of *huo-hao* could be terminated.

Ch'a clearly had little faith in the moral qualities of most provincial officials, a fact that led him to oppose any plan to use *huo-hao* to pay for provincial and local public expenses. Not only would this interfere with the repayment of deficits; it would also provide officials with the opportunity to embezzle government funds. Once again the issue of Board scrutiny of provincial fiscal affairs was crucial to Ch'a's objections. As presented by No-min, *huo-hao* allocations for public expenses would not be subject to Board approval and would not be reported in the annual accounts (*tsou-hsiao*). If officials were able to embezzle millions of taels from the *cheng-hsiang* that was reported in the annual accounts, Ch'a could imagine only too well what would happen if the provinces were allowed to collect funds over which they alone had control.

The apprehensions expressed by these two men were valid and would continue to worry supporters of rational local funding for many years. The system of informal funding that was now threatened had grown out of the inability of the bureaucracy to cope with the tension between centralization and the need for local autonomy, and that between a belief in low taxation and the fiscal requirements of local government. The official response of the Grand Secretariat to No-min's memorial reflected their unwillingness to tamper with a system that had worked so well, albeit by masking these tensions and encouraging a double standard of morality in official life.

The Grand Secretariat's deliberations were published in the *Peking Gazette* (*T'i-ch'ao*). Although the original text no longer exists, we can reconstruct their argument in the detailed rebuttal offered by the new Shansi financial commissioner, Kao Ch'eng-ling.

Kao Ch'eng-ling's memorial was one of the most convincing defenses of *huo-hao kuei-kung* written during this period.[98] Kao began by attacking the basic misconception that *huo-hao* was the exclusive property of the chou and hsien. The key to his argument was the classical premise that all the land in the empire belonged to the monarch. The greatness of the kingly way (*wang-tao*) being rooted in human feelings (*jen-ch'ing*), the regular taxes are used to supply the state's expenses, whereas *huo-hao* is used to nourish virtuous officials. "Ruling men and feeding men are intimately connected." In other words, an official can be a good administrator only if he himself has the means to live. Although *huo-hao* is the people's money, it is also the dynasty's wealth, because all land belongs to the king. Therefore, according to Kao, the emperor, in his sympathy for his officials, decided to supplement the regular salary of *all* officials, including governors, commissioners, circuit intendants, and prefects. These funds were not established for the sake of the chou and hsien alone.

Kao asserted that if, as the Grand Secretaries stated, *hao-hsien* belongs to the chou and hsien and should not be remitted to their superiors, then they do not understand that there is an intimate relationship between *hao-hsien* and customary gifts (*chieh-li*). If *hao-hsien* is not remitted to the high officials, then their subordinates must send them *chieh-li*. Under these circumstances the lower officials weigh the power and influence of the governors, governors-general, commissioners, prefects, circuit intendants, and *t'ing* officials, and determine the amount of *chieh-li* to send them accordingly. Gifts are given on the occasion of the Dragon Boat Festival, Mid-Autumn Festival, New Year's, and birthdays. These are called "the four-festivals gifts." To the four-festivals gifts must be added gifts when paying a visit to the superior official (*piao-li*). To the gifts on paying a visit must be added gifts of local products (*t'u-i*). To the gifts of local products must be added gifts of seasonal delicacies (*shih-hsien*). Lower officials send gifts to ingratiate themselves with their superiors. Once they have established a dependency relationship they can intimidate their superior to the point that they can do as they please with no fear of reprisal. Superiors crave the gifts of their subordinates and therefore cover up for them and say nothing when they are involved in malfeasance. Moral integrity is damaged and the official code of conduct is destroyed. The exploitation of the people and the deficits in the state treasury are a result of this.

Kao then anticipated the rebuttal of moralists by pointing out that banning gift-giving and selecting virtuous officials would not solve the problem. Even if *chieh-li* were prohibited, unscrupulous officials would find a way to defraud and give license to their insatiable demands. Even if there were those who were content with a simple life and wanted to break off the exchange of gifts, high yamen officials would have no other source of funds. They would have to do their jobs without salary while the chou and hsien peacefully enjoyed large profits. Who, Kao asked, could bear that?

For the above reasons, Kao advocated that the *huo-hao* of the chou and hsien be remitted to the provincial treasury. The high provincial officials would redistribute it, using everyone's *huo-hao* to supply everyone's *yang-lien*. This, Kao assured the opposition, was in fulfillment of both heavenly principle (*t'ien-li*) and human feelings and was not prohibited by the law of the empire. He stressed that when *huo-hao* was remitted, if the whole province incurred unavoidable public expenses, they could be allocated as needed without recourse to assessments on the chou and hsien (*fen-p'ai*). If the high officials did not have to levy assessments, then the chou and hsien would not have a pretext to extort from the villages. In this way, remitting *huo-hao* could also eliminate private surcharges (*ssu-p'ai*). Thus Kao sought to transform the very policy that K'ang-hsi refused to endorse for fear of being accused of approving *ssu-p'ai* into a major force against *ssu-p'ai*.

Kao then defended the reforms against accusations that it would burden the taxpayers. He showed that in the case of Shansi province the *huo-hao* in each chou and hsien had been investigated and reduced so that the rates of collection were now half as much as they had been in the past. Moreover, in keeping with the emperor's edict on tax arrears, collection was being carried out in installments over a period of three years so as to ease the people's ability to pay. Against arguments that a fixed *huo-hao* quota would lead to higher taxes, Kao pointed out that only by fixing the rate of collection could the people know how much tax they should pay and protect themselves against officials who collected taxes in any way they pleased. He linked the fixing of *huo-hao* rates with the practice of having the individual taxpayer deposit his own taxes in locked chests and reiterated that because the chests were locked and the rates fixed, the chou and hsien could not interfere. Therefore, as T'ien Wen-ching had earlier emphasized, magistrates would have no incentive to collect more than the quota. He also assuaged the fears of those who wondered what would happen to *huo-hao* collections in famine years by stating, sarcastically, that one did not have to be a sage to know that when the regular taxes could not be paid in full, neither would the *huo-hao*.

To those who complained that reductions in the amount of *huo-hao* retained by the magistrates would leave them with too small a sum for their expenses, Kao also had a riposte. On the one hand, if the share of funds received by the chou and hsien now seemed diminished it should be remembered that they would also save on expenses, because they no longer had to send *chieh-li* to their superiors and no longer had to find their own sources for public expenses. Kao felt that if officials followed the regulations and refrained from bringing large entourages to their posts, and practiced frugality and virtue, then their *yang-lien*, coupled with miscellaneous duties (*tsa-shui*) and surplus, would be more than enough for their food and clothing. In any case in Shansi, besides their *yang-lien*, chou and hsien officials also received funds for transportation and smelting taxes, and additional fodder for post horses beyond the Board quota. Busy chou and hsien at much-traveled crossroads were given over 2,000 taels in *yang-lien*, and that of even the simple and out-of-the-way chou and hsien was not a mere three *fen* per tael, as claimed by some critics.

Kao finished his memorial by assuring the opposition that using *huo-hao* to make up deficits did not constitute giving officials with deficits a free ride at the expense of their more virtuous peers. In Shansi the policy was still to impeach officials with deficits and retrieve the missing funds from their office and family property before declaring them *wu-cho* and repaying them with *huo-hao*.

Kao conceded that good government depended on men and not laws. In the final analysis there would be no way for him to guarantee that there would not be unscrupulous officials who would abuse the remitting of *huo-hao* to profit themselves. Nevertheless, he requested that the emperor order the governor and governor-general of each province to follow Governor No-min's memorial to carry out *huo-hao kuei-kung*. At the end of each year they could then calculate the amount of *huo-hao* collected, and on the last day of the year memorialize in a *t'i-pen* how much was disbursed for *yang-lien*, how much was allocated for public expenses, and how much was retained to make up deficits. In Kao's words, "under the emperor's scrutiny, who would dare embezzle?"

Armed with Kao Ch'eng-ling's penetrating analysis, Yung-cheng again submitted the idea of *huo-hao kuei-kung* to the court. This time he extended discussion to the Censorate and the Council of Ministers and Princes, which included the top echelon of all the Boards. He cautioned them to deliberate calmly, fairly, and justly or heads literally would roll. In case opinions were split, the emperor granted permission to present two or even three opinions.[99]

Yung-cheng may have hoped that by expanding the arena of debate he would be presented with a mandate to implement the reforms. There could be no doubt in the minds of the officials asked to comment that the emperor favored this measure. Therefore, it is no surprise that the court submitted an endorsement of the plan. However, as the emperor's reply to their memorial shows, it was an endorsement with grave reservations that reflected the persistent differences between the emperor and his ministers on fiscal organization.[100]

Originally *huo-hao* should not exist. However, the expenses and *yang-lien* of the whole province must come from it. *Huo-hao* has been collected for many years, but the chou and hsien magistrates still levy additional surcharges and embezzle state funds. Deficits amount to over several thousand taels [in each administrative unit]. The reason is that the magistrates send gifts from this money to their superiors and the superiors demand all their daily expenses from the magistrates. . . . Thus, magistrates have an excuse to satisfy their own greed and their superiors, because they too are involved in wrongdoing, tolerate the situation. These long-standing abuses must be eliminated. Would it not be better for the superiors to appropriate *huo-hao* to support the magistrates rather than having the chou and hsien save *huo-hao* to support the superior officials?

You memorialized to set a quota for each subordinate's *huo-hao*. But I think in each province there are large and small chou and hsien, places with high and low tax quotas. Where a chou or hsien is large and its taxes are great, if you collect *huo-hao* [at a low rate] it will be enough. But this will not be so in a small chou or hsien with few taxes. Only by not setting a quota can more funds be raised to handle situations of extreme need. On the other hand, if one year a locale's affairs are few and simple, *huo-hao* can then be reduced. . . . If one sets a quota, in the future it will become an established quota. It will only rise and never decrease. So we cannot set quotas for *huo-hao*.

As for your suggestion that we should let the magistrate deduct the funds he should receive and not remit it to be allocated back to him: Now when the chou and hsien magistrates collect taxes, the people wrap the money themselves and throw it in the locked chest. If, when the time comes, all the responsible officials open the chests together and examine the contents, and the huo-hao and the regular taxes are remitted together, not a bit can go into their own pockets. Then the magistrates will all know there is no benefit to themselves in collecting exorbitant *huo-hao*. In that case who will be willing to collect extra huo-hao? On the one hand *huo-hao* will be used to furnish *yang-lien* for all the high and low officials. On the other hand, by using it to make up deficits it will be beneficial to the state finances. If you let the magistrates take out the amount they should receive, they definitely will exact more surcharges beyond their quota and burden the people. [An even more pressing reason is] if you have it all sent to the provincial governor there will be obvious evidence [of how much has been collected and disbursed]. But if it is deducted in the chou and hsien, it will be very hard to verify who is greedy and who is not. This is why the magistrates cannot deduct their *hsien-yü*.

You also said Governor No-min is incorruptible and very able and that Financial Commissioner Kao Ch'eng-ling's character is very good. You therefore suggested that these two be allowed to wholeheartedly deliberate and test their proposal in Shansi first. This is particularly impermissible. In the world, things either can be carried out or they cannot be carried out. If something can be carried out it can be carried out in the whole empire. If it [is a wrong policy], then it should not even be tried out first in Shansi. It is the same as in the treatment of an illness. If you try every medicine, one at a time, rarely will you get a cure. Thus, I cannot bear for you to use Shansi as an experimental province. Are you trying to say that in the whole empire no other governors or financial commissioners can compare with No-min and Kao Ch'eng-ling. Are these two alone capable of implementing [such a policy]?

You also said that sending the *huo-hao* to the provincial treasury is not a method which can be carried out for a long time. I think whenever a law is promulgated there is no guarantee that it will never incur abuses. In the past we have had the rule of men and not the rule of law. However, the development of civil or military administration depends on one's policy. If the person [whose strategy it is] remains, the policy will develop. Laws must change to suit the situation. For example, if a person is sick you give him medicine according to the disease and you stop the medicine as soon as the disease is cured. Thus, now to remit the *huo-hao* is a policy to fit the situation of the present time. In the future, when the deficits are made up and the treasuries are full and officials all know how to be incorrupt, then we will not have to send up [the *huo-hao*] and the [amounts collected] can also be reduced.

Are your deliberations for the benefit of the state finances? Are they for the good of the people? They are only for the good of the magistrates. You think the magistrates have their problems, but the high officials have their problems too. Your arguments must be fair and impartial. Furthermore, the court and the people

are one body. If the state finances are sufficient, then, if
the people encounter a bad year, there will be enough
to furnish them with relief. The people need not worry
that there is not enough. This is why clearing the deficits is beneficial to the state's finances and to the
people.

Foremost in the emperor's mind was the problem of eliminating
corruption by rationalizing the local fiscal base. Yung-cheng located the source of local fiscal instability in the irregular funding
practices of provincial officials and not in the inability or unwillingness of the people to pay taxes. More important, he recognized that the problem resulted from the inadequacy of regular fiscal arrangements on the local level. Although he acknowledged
that *huo-hao* had its origins as an illegal surcharge, he now felt
that its collection was essential to supply officials with *yang-lien*
and provincial administrative expenses.

Traditional Chinese political economy, with its emphasis on low
tax rates, carried with it an implicit injunction against raising the
tax burden of the people. As we have seen in K'ang-hsi's rescript to
Nien Keng-yao, the late emperor feared that raising taxes by legalizing *huo-hao* would be viewed as a sign of bad government. In
traditional historiography, the three tax rises at the end of the
Ming were seen as primary causes of the downfall of the dynasty.
Rather than recognize the need for expanded revenues as population and services performed by the government increased, most
rulers closed their eyes to the informal funding network, thereby
giving tacit approval to corruption. The results were as Yung-
cheng described them in his edict. Now, for the first time, in place
of exhortations to virtue, Yung-cheng hoped to supply the practical prerequisites for good government—a regular and sufficient
source of provincial funds, administered through the provincial
treasury, but with enough local autonomy to guarantee the flexibility demanded by changing local needs.

As for the method of implementing *huo-hao kuei-kung*, Yung-
cheng clearly favored complete remittance of chou and hsien *huo-
hao* to the provincial treasury. The arguments he presented in
favor of this method were precisely those made earlier by T'ien
Wen-ching and Kao Ch'eng-ling. However, complete remittance
was a measure designed for the sole purpose of curbing corruption
and should not be confused with other aspects of the reform.
Many later officials interpreted Yung-cheng's remarks—that in the

future when deficits were made up, the treasuries full, and official morale had been restored, remittance would no longer be necessary and *huo-hao* rates could be reduced—to mean that *huo-hao kuei-kung* was a temporary expedient to be eliminated as soon as possible. This was a complete misunderstanding. What Yung-cheng meant was that once deficits were eliminated and efficient management restored to local finance, not as much *huo-hao* would be needed. Once rational financing had become the rule it would no longer be necessary to require complete remittance to guard against official peculation. However, the use of *huo-hao* to supply officials with *yang-lien* and public expenses was a policy of lasting benefit to the state and to the people.

Yung-cheng's rejection of the suggestion that *huo-hao kuei-kung* be carried out first in Shansi was not a rejection of the experimental approach, but rather an indication that he felt that the experiments prior to this point had been successful. The court could not have been ignorant of the fact that in addition to Shansi, remittance of *huo-hao* was already in effect in Hupei, Honan, Shantung, and Chihli. It is likely that the emperor saw their recommendation as an attempt not to experiment with the policy but to curtail its use in those places where it was already being carried out. By now, the emperor was ready to see the reforms extended throughout the empire.

Even more revealing was the fact that the emperor chastised the court for its reliance on virtuous officials to carry out the reforms. Implicit in the court's remarks was the Confucian interdiction against *fa*, laws or methods. Yung-cheng's confidence in the primacy of methods was expressed in his insistence that if a policy is good it can be carried out everywhere and if it is bad it should not be carried out at all. What had virtuous officials to do with the issue? The emperor recognized that all laws contained within them the potential for being violated. However, in his own words, "the development of civil or military administration depends on one's policy." In a subtle reinterpretation of the adage that good government relies on the rule of men over the rule of law, the emperor stated that what was important was not the virtue of men (for Yung-cheng had grave doubts about the virtue of most men in public office), but the policies they put forth. With new men, new policies could be implemented to benefit the country and the people. Moreover, as the circumstances of both change, so must the laws. Thus, here as elsewhere, the Yung-cheng emperor freed himself from the constraints of tradition to govern in the best way he saw fit.

The policy of *huo-hao kuei-kung* was not without its own philosophical underpinnings. Concern for the people's livelihood was a fundamental principle of both Confucianism and what Abe Takeo has called "Manchu benevolence."[101] Although on the surface the reforms of the Yung-cheng period appeared to raise taxes, in practice the emperor saw them as a means to lower the gross burden on the people by eliminating all other surcharges. Whereas proponents of Confucian statecraft placed their faith in the morality of the scholar in office and at home to promote the general welfare, early Manchu rulers harbored a deep distrust of the degree-holding elite. It was this distrust that prompted the Ch'ing reduction of gentry tax exemptions, as well as Yung-cheng's expansion of the number of non-degree holders in office.[102] The emperor felt that court opposition to *huo-hao kuei-kung* reflected an exclusive concern for the profits that a magistrate could gain by milking the people of their taxes. This abuse of office holding as a source of personal wealth violated the major tenet of Manchu benevolence or what Frederic Wakeman has labelled Manchu paternalism—the unity of national welfare and people's welfare. This concept was expressed in Dorgon's compact (*yüeh*) with the Chinese people when he first entered Peking in 1644.[103] Inherent in the statements of both Dorgon and Yung-cheng was a belief that the corruption of Han officials was the main threat to an almost sacred bond between the dynasty and the people. Moreover, this bond was the foundation for the prosperity of all the inhabitants of the realm.

Embodied in Yung-cheng's fiscal program was a bold challenge to the vested interests of the Han scholar-gentry. Therefore, although his edict was an unqualified endorsement of the *huo-hao kuei-kung* reforms, the emperor still felt it necessary to proceed with caution. In the face of only grudging acquiescence on the part of officials in the central government and growing opposition on the part of many officials and gentry in the provinces, Yung-cheng was forced to leave the implementation of *huo-hao kuei-kung* to the discretion of the individual governors and governors-general in the provinces. Once again, the palace-memorial system provided the vehicle to ensure that discretion should be exercised in the way the emperor intended.

4
FISCAL
RATIONALIZATION
AND LOCAL
ADAPTATION

THE YUNG-CHENG EMPEROR'S ENDORSEMENT OF *huo-hao kuei-kung* was the first step toward its implementation throughout the empire. A firm advocate of change, the emperor also recognized that reform of this magnitude could not successfully be accomplished by fiat. Relying on the principle of "adapting one's policies to the time and the place," Yung-cheng left the details of implementation to the governors, governors-general, and financial commissioners of each province. Moreover, the emperor was acutely aware of the conflicts that might arise between provincial and central-government officials on the issue of local financing. He therefore insisted that the funds made available by the reforms remain under the exclusive jurisdiction and supervision of the province in which they originated. During the first decade, the accounting of these provincial funds was completely divorced from the *tsou-hsiao* system used to regulate the principal taxes. However, as in the formative period discussed in the preceding chapter, the emperor lent a guiding hand through the mechanism of the secret palace-memorial system. By placing men whose approach to government he trusted in the highest provincial posts, and by privately chastising those whose methods he found at odds with the spirit of the reforms, only rarely did Yung-cheng have to exercise his role as supreme arbiter of administrative policy.

Finding a Model

Because no precise regulations were established at the outset to govern the implementation of the *huo-hao kuei-kung* reforms, some confusion surrounded its early stages. In particular, the provinces differed considerably in the speed with which they moved to institute the new structures for local financing. Resistance, less overt than before the emperor's edict, was also present, though it soon became clear that the method of implementation formulated in Honan and Shansi was to be considered the model for reform. Limitations imposed by differences in local resources, topography, and spending requirements did lead to variations in each province's adaptation to this ideal. However, despite the large amount of local autonomy granted in carrying out these reforms, the differences that emerged between provinces were primarily ones of degree. Moreover, unlike the reforms in tax collection and registration undertaken in the late Ming and early Ch'ing, the fiscal reorganization during the Yung-cheng period was under the strong direction of the governors and financial commissioners from the beginning, so that variations *within* provinces were minimal. Before turning to the problems encountered by individual provinces and their solutions, let us first examine the major structural elements common to all provinces and the principles that guided their implementation.

Behind all the structural innovations encompassed by the *huo-hao* reforms was the principle of "using public funds to carry out public business" (*i-kung wei-kung*). On the surface, such a statement seems quite simplistic. However, in the light of our analysis of the previous funding system, it implies several very important advances in fiscal thinking. First, a distinction was made between tax revenues belonging to the state and those belonging to the province. The *kung* referred to in this phrase must be understood to mean provincial as well as public. Under the reforms a new category of taxes was created, which was generated in and used by the province itself. Taxes of this kind, emanating primarily from *huo-hao*, but including other types of levies, were called *kung-hsiang*. This term was used to distinguish them from *cheng-hsiang* taxes paid to the state and used to meet expenses considered to be the responsibility of the central government.

Secondly, *i-kung wei-kung* was a confirmation of the need to provide the administrative units at each level of provincial government with their own legitimate sources of income to carry out their business. As we saw in the preceding chapters, even before the Yung-cheng period there was allusion to an ideal of funding adequate to meet an official's expenses and discourage recourse to peculation. Discussion of this kind, however, was almost always couched in very personal terms. Most often an official who feared encroachment on his informal funding sources would claim that items such as *huo-hao* or *lou-kuei* were necessary to permit him to "nourish his virtue" (*yang-lien*). In fact, the virtue nourished by such means was tenuous at best. Because no attempt was made to calculate the actual expenses incurred by officials at various levels of the administration, the funds required to nourish his virtue were determined by the official himself, a decision tempered only by what the people providing those funds were willing to tolerate. Inasmuch as neither the official's personal expenses, nor most administrative and service costs were provided for through legitimate government channels, no distinction was made between public and private means or ends in the operation of the official yamen. *Huo-hao kuei-kung* was thus most of all an effort to eliminate corruption by setting limits on any official's access to funds and by providing him with enough public funds so that he would no longer have a pretext to levy additional surcharges or extort additional *lou-kuei* from his subordinates. Thus, the term *kung* signified not only a distinction between central and provincial funds, but heralded a strong attack on the privatization of fiscal affairs as carried out under the informal funding network. This separation of public and private was also manifested in the way funds were allocated, differentiating for the first time between an official's private costs and the expenses incurred in governing his area.

The notion of using public funds to pay for public expenses manifested itself in another way. Because officials were to be granted funds from the provincial treasury, the intricate network of personal relationships upon which the informal funding system revolved would be eliminated. An official's expenses would be based on a rational determination of local needs rather than on a particular man's skill at milking those under his jurisdiction. Funds would accrue to the office and to the locale, not to the man. Even in those few instances where funds which had previously been *lou-kuei* were returned to the public coffers rather than being eliminated, they became impersonal levies, and could no longer be relied upon to provide the donor with special considerations. Thus, salt fees once negotiated with, and paid personally to, the governor became just one of a number of levies which entered the pool of funds in the provincial treasury to be disbursed throughout the province. Likewise, the funds sent by the chou and hsien magistrates to their superiors became regular, fixed remittances and could no longer be seen as buying them protection from scrutiny over their activities in office.

A final corollary of using public funds for public expenses was an expanded view of the government's responsibility for public projects. With the *huo-hao kuei-kung* reforms, a vast amount of funds that had previously been diverted to the pockets of local officials was now made available for public purposes. Government resources could now be applied not only to the limited number of large projects and military undertakings provided by the central government's grants of regular taxes, but to smaller, more localized projects which previously had been neglected or financed through irregular tax levies and contributions.

The two main structural innovations introduced during the *huo-hao kuei-kung* reforms were "nourishing virtue silver" (*yang-lien yin*) and "public-expense silver" (*kung-fei yin*). Putting aside for the moment the sources of these funds, we can see that the division of provincial resources into these two categories provided both a fixed-base allocation for each level of government and a more elastic, project-oriented fund under the supervision of the provincial governor and financial commissioner. This system of financing was designed to suit the requirements of a bureaucracy in which administrative costs were fairly stable and service expenditures were often temporary, large, and unexpected.

Yang-lien yin has been translated as "supplemental salaries."[1] This designation is useful in calling attention to the huge increase that *yang-lien yin* represented over the emoluments granted officials from the regular tax revenues.[2] However, the term salary tends to connote a separation between public and private income that may be misleading in the context of Chinese imperial political economy. A more useful distinction is that between "inner" and "outer."

A provincial official both lived and worked in his yamen. While in office there was nothing he did that did not pertain to his capacity as an official. Individual temperament might lead to differences in consumption, but a higher level of what we would call personal living standards was expected of an official at the upper level of government than of one at the lower level. The entourage he brought with him to office would be larger, as would the staff he required to help him govern. Although the yamen itself was divided into inner quarters that housed the official's family, personal servants, and secretaries, and an outer section in which government business was conducted, all who worked and lived within this august compound, by virtue of their service to the official, were vital to his functions as an agent of government. This is clearly so in the case of private secretaries who, although hired by the official himself, functioned in much the same way as a modern administrative assistant does in the United States. However, even a personal servant might assist in the conduct of official business when a trusted agent was necessary. Thus, just as previously there was no provision of funds for any of the diverse activities within the yamen (besides wages for a limited number of yamen runners), the total allocation of *yang-lien yin* was seen as providing for all yamen activities. It was used for the personal living expenses of the official and his family and salaries for the staff, as well as for more clearly administrative expenses associated with stationery costs, routine government procedures, tax collection, catching criminals, and so on.

These "inner" expenses may be contrasted with those costs incurred for defense, or in the provision of funds for construction projects or services of benefit to the local population and the provincial government. The latter, including wall and bridge repairs, granary construction, waterworks, and the like, were "outer" expenses, and, as we shall see, were paid for out of the second category of funds, the *kung-fei yin*.

The first problem faced by those carrying out the reforms was to determine the amount of *yang-lien yin* for each official and how the officials were to receive their share. These issues went to the very heart of the reforms. As we have seen, two approaches had been tried during the period before Yung-cheng's edict calling for empire-wide implementation. In both Honan and Hupei, funding by means of customary fees and gifts was banned and in its place the governor of each of the two provinces sanctioned the collection of a flat percentage charge on all land and head taxes. This charge, called *huo-hao*, was then to be used to provide officials with *yang-lien yin* and *kung-fei yin* and to make up *wu-cho* deficits.

The Hupei Model

The rudimentary *huo-hao* remittance scheme first proposed by Hupei Governor Yang Tsung-i in mid-1723 was refined during the next year and extended to include Hunan. This new plan was designed not merely as a temporary device for eliminating deficits, but as a lasting system for providing officials at many levels of government with *yang-lien yin*. By the middle of 1724 the rate of collection of *huo-hao* was set at 10 percent. Thus, for every tael of regular taxes (*cheng-hsiang*) collected, an additional 0.1 tael was appended for provincial expenses. For every 0.1 tael of *huo-hao* the chou and hsien received from the taxpayers, 0.068 tael was remitted to provide funds for their superiors. Allocation of this 0.068 tael was broken down as follows: 0.015 tael for the financial commissioner's *yang-lien*, 0.004 tael for the *yang-lien* of that chou or hsien's circuit intendant, 0.01 tael for its prefect, 0.003 tael for its subprefect (*t'ung-chih*), and 0.03 tael for *kung-fei*. The remaining 0.032 tael was retained by the chou or hsien magistrate for his own *yang-lien*. Those chou and hsien with taxes of 5,000 taels or less were exempt from remittance because their total *huo-hao* would be 500 taels or less.[3]

This system was a great advance over the informal funding network it superseded. However, it contained a number of disadvantages that led the emperor to bypass it as a test case when presenting the reforms to the court. In fact, an examination of the weaknesses in the Hupei method can serve to underline some of the major objectives of the reforms as they were finally formulated in Honan.

First, the Hupei plan was not equitable in its distribution of funds. An official was not granted a fixed amount of *yang-lien yin* based on need, but rather received a percentage of the taxes collected in his area. Because the taxes collected by the chou and hsien ranged from several thousand to tens of thousands of taels, some magistrates would be left with only a few hundred taels whereas others would enjoy several thousand. Moreover, by allowing those areas with a tax quota of 5,000 taels or less to retain all of their *huo-hao*, a chou or hsien with 4,900 taels of taxes would retain 490 taels, but a chou or hsien with 5,100 taels of taxes would have to share its *huo-hao* in the same way as a very wealthy area, leaving the magistrate with only 164 taels with which to operate his yamen. Inasmuch as tax collection was one of the most important and demanding functions of local government, and a high tax quota often did signify that an area was "busy" in other respects as well, it is not unreasonable that some officials favored granting *yang-lien yin* as a percentage of taxes collected. It is also true, however, that poorer areas were in need of far more funds than they could generate internally. Their inhabitants were less likely to be able to contribute to projects such as water-conservancy works, and because many poorer areas were located in remote or mountainous regions they often had a higher incidence of banditry and incurred greater costs for the transportation of goods and taxes and for travel on official business.

The second weakness of the Hupei plan lay in its method of *yang-lien* distribution. Higher officials continued to receive their own operating expenses in the form of small contributions directly from the chou and hsien. This not only was less convenient than receiving one's funds in a lump sum, but also invited a reversion to the kinds of extortion and blackmail that had been rampant under the informal funding system. In addition, because the magistrate collected the *huo-hao* and deducted his own share before remitting the share designated for his superiors, there was no institutional check to prevent him from collecting more than he was supposed to. In effect, the fiscal management of the entire province was diffused in the hands of scores of magistrates. Under these conditions the potential for rational supervision of local finances at the provincial level was small indeed.

A final weakness of the Hupei plan was its failure to provide any *yang-lien yin* at all for a number of provincial officials, most obviously the governor and governor-general. Neither were provisions made for the grain, post, and salt intendants and the educational commissioner. On a lower level, *yang-lien* was allocated for the subprefects but not for the assistant prefects (*t'ung-pan*), who, as Examiner Chuang Ch'ing-tu pointed out, had many expenses connected with their responsibility for the tribute grain.[4] A number of other officials were excluded from the original reforms everywhere, and we shall discuss provision of *yang-lien* for them later.

The Honan Model

The second approach to the allocation of *yang-lien* is best represented by the method instituted in Honan under the guidance of Financial Commissioner T'ien Wen-ching.[5] Prior to T'ien's arrival in Honan, Governor Shih Wen-cho had already issued an injunction against the collection and remittance of customary fees to high government officials.[6] In addition, the collection of a fixed percentage of *huo-hao* was legitimated. However, until T'ien Wen-ching's arrival, the focus of attention was on using *huo-hao* to clear up *wu-cho* deficits, and the regulations governing the use of these new funds for *yang-lien yin* and public expenses were vague.

In a memorial dated the third month of Yung-cheng 2 (1724), Governor Shih declared that all *huo-hao* from the chou and hsien would be remitted to the public coffers, in other words, to the financial commissioner's treasury. Although high officials would no longer have *kuei-li* and chou and hsien officials would no longer have *huo-hao*, all officials of the rank of hsien magistrate and above would now be granted *yang-lien yin* in sufficient amounts to meet their expenses. In this way, officials could perform their duties without concern about their finances.

Total *huo-hao* revenues at a rate of 10 percent of the land and head tax were estimated at 400,000 taels. On the basis of this figure the following schedule of fixed *yang-lien* allowances was formulated:[7]

Education commissioner	4,000 taels
Financial commissioner	24,000 taels
Judicial commissioner	10,000 taels
K'ai-Kuei circuit	10,000 taels
Yellow River circuit	4,000 taels
Nan-Ju circuit	3,000 taels
K'ai-feng prefect	4,000 taels
The 7 other prefects	3,000 taels each
	(21,000 taels)
1 assistant prefect with military jurisdiction	1,000 taels
5 first-class subprefects	800 taels each
	(4,000 taels)
10 second-class subprefects	600 taels each
	(6,000 taels)
Magistrates of Ju-chou and Hsiang-fu hsien	2,000 taels each
	(4,000 taels)

43 other magistrates of large-ranked chou and hsien	1,000 taels each (43,000 taels)
50 magistrates of medium-ranked chou and hsien	800 taels each (40,000 taels)
12 magistrates of small-ranked chou and hsien	600 taels each (7,200 taels)

Total: 185,200 taels

In addition, Shih requested *yang-lien* for the governor based on the amount of funds that that office used to receive under the old system, approximately 30,000 taels.

Besides paying for each official's *yang-lien*, Shih stated that *huo-hao* would also be used to provide for the public expenses of the whole province as well as to supplement certain fixed local costs such as the purchasing of fodder for post horses and goods sent to the capital, the travel expenses of officials sent to the chou and hsien to supervise the opening of the tax envelopes, the travel expenses of messengers on official business, and the transportation expenses incurred by the chou and hsien in remitting their taxes. The total annual expenditure of *huo-hao* for *yang-lien* and public expenses was estimated at 245,000 taels, leaving about 150,000 taels to make up deficits and repay funds borrowed from the regular tax for such purposes as buying additional tribute grain.[8]

The emperor commended Governor Shih on his plan, adding a note of satisfaction that Honan was now following the method first implemented in Shansi under Governor No-min. Interestingly, the only criticism Yung-cheng offered was that the *yang-lien* of certain chou and hsien might not be large enough. He suggested that after all the deficits were cleared, *yang-lien* rates be reevaluated,[9] confirming the view that the emperor did not see *huo-hao kuei-kung* simply as a temporary expedient to overcome the deficit crisis.

The Honan plan represented a considerable improvement over the method of implementation utilized in Hupei. All *huo-hao* was remitted to the provincial treasury for redistribution in the form of *yang-lien* and *kung-fei* allowances. Coupled with the practice of sending officers from outside the chou and hsien to supervise the opening of the tax chests, this marked a great step forward in the control of surcharges and corruption on the lowest levels of administration. As T'ien Wen-ching pointed out, because magistrates kept none of the land and head taxes they collected, they no longer had any incentive to collect at rates beyond the legal quota.[10] Moreover, as all officials received their *yang-lien* in quarterly installments, directly from the financial commissioner,[11] they were relieved of both the inconvenience and stress of receiving their operating expenses in dribs and drabs from their subordinates. In addition, *yang-lien* was given first priority in allocating *huo-hao*, so that officials were guaranteed receipt of their expense fund regardless of difficulties arising from natural disasters, arrears, or high provincial-level expenditures. By divorcing funding concerns from the relationship between officials and their supervisors, the Honan system eliminated at least one of the sources of extortion and favoritism characteristic of financing under the informal funding network.

A second advantage of the Honan method of distributing *yang-lien* was that it provided a more equitable allocation of funds based on need and not on rank or the tax income of a particular area. This too was made possible because all the *huo-hao* in the province was pooled and reallocated in fixed amounts. The attention given to need is illustrated particularly in the case of magistrates' *yang-lien*. The chou and hsien were divided into three ranks based on the degree of public business in the area, location at important crossroads, and distance from the provincial capital, and *yang-lien* was granted accordingly. Circuit intendants were given larger stipends in view of the extensive travel their jobs entailed. This in turn relieved the chou and hsien of the responsibility for housing, feeding, and providing transportation for supervisory officials' tours of inspection. The K'ai-feng circuit intendant and prefect were given additional funds reflecting the added burdens placed on officials in the capital precincts. The high *yang-lien* granted the financial commissioner is particularly noteworthy, not only as a manifestation of the increased prestige and power of that post in the Ch'ing, but because it specifically included added provisions for the financial commissioner's yamen's *kung-fei*. This *kung-fei* was in response to the expanded accounting responsibilities that the implementation of *huo-hao kuei-kung* would entail.[12]

It should be noted that as conceived in Honan, *yang-lien* was not meant to cover all the expenses that an official would incur in office. At the very least, besides those expenses customarily viewed as a provincial responsibility, such as river works and major construction projects, the chou and hsien were to be provided with additional funds to cover travel and transport costs and the costs of tribute goods and post-horse feed. All of these expenses had previously been major drains on local resources.[13]

Finally, the Honan plan was more comprehensive in its provision of *yang-lien* for all officials at the level of magistrate and above. Later, *yang-lien* would be extended to lower officials, with Honan once again taking the lead. From the start, *yang-lien* rates were not considered immutable. Not only could the more flexible funds stored in the provincial treasury as *kung-fei* be drawn upon to increase *yang-lien* allocations, but, as we shall see, new sources of funds could be earmarked for provincial use now that the concept of "return to the public coffers" (*kuei-kung*) had received the imperial blessing.

The methods of implementation used by the remaining provinces combined elements of both the Honan and Hupei plans. Professor Abe Takeo, in his pioneering work on *huo-hao*, divided the methods of remittance that appeared in the course of the reforms into three categories: total remittance, remittance of most *huo-hao*, and remittance of little *huo-hao*.[14] Total remittance followed the method first utilized in Honan and Shansi. The *huo-hao* was collected by the chou and hsien at a fixed rate and sent in full to the financial commissioner for allocation in the form of fixed *yang-lien* allowances and flexible public-expense disbursements. In the second form, *huo-hao* and *yang-lien* rates were also fixed, but the chou and hsien were permitted to deduct their own *yang-lien* before remitting their *huo-hao* to the financial commissioner. Other provincial officials then received their *yang-lien* directly from the provincial treasury. The last category most closely parallels the method first utilized in Hupei. The chou and hsien collected their fixed rate of *huo-hao* but remitted only that portion designated for provincial *kung-fei*. They retained their own *yang-lien* and were responsible for distributing any *yang-lien* due higher officials to the officials individually. Table 4.1 summarizes the methods of implementation used and how they changed during the course of the Yung-cheng reign. It should be noted that throughout this period there was a definite trend toward closer conformity with the Shansi-Honan model.

In the remainder of this chapter we examine the reforms as they were carried out in each province and the problems encountered which led to local variations. In chapter 5 we then discuss some of

Table 4.1   *Implementation Dates of* Huo-hao kuei-kung

Province	Complete remittance	Partial remittance	Little remittance
Anhui	1729		
Chekiang	1727		1724
Chihli	1729		1723
Fengtien		1729	
Fukien		1730	
Honan	1724		
Hukwang	1728		1723
Kiangsi	1729	1728	
Kiangsu	1728		
Kwangtung		1726	1724
Kweichow	1725		
Shansi	1723		
Shantung	1730	1724	
Shensi	1725	1723	
Szechuan	1727		
Yunnan	1725		

the major themes and continuities underlying local variations and evaluate the implementation of the reforms in general.

Suiting One's Policies to the Time and the Place

Part of the appeal of *huo-hao kuei-kung* was its simplicity. The legalization of one surcharge would provide provincial officials with a predictable and reliable source of funds for all local-government expenses not covered by the regular system of revenue sharing. Because *huo-hao* was levied on the preexisting land and head tax, it required no new bureaucracy to administer its collection and entailed little additional effort to compile registers and accounts. Likewise, it could be integrated into the system in which the individual wrapped and deposited his own taxes, diminishing the magistrates' reliance on corrupt yamen runners and clerks and enabling the government to notify the taxpayer of the precise amount of *huo-hao* due. Because it did not consist of taxes of diverse origin, budgeting allocation of *huo-hao* income was a relatively easy task and left little room for manipulation by officials seeking to profit from the new system of funding.

The successful implementation of such a system was predicated on several conditions. Most important was the existence of a large land- and head-tax quota. If the agricultural productivity of a province was small, even a very high percentage charge on the regular tax would yield inadequate revenues to provide for all of its administrative needs. Moreover, resort to high surcharges would risk arousing discontent among the local population. The second requirement was that the land and head tax be readily collectable. If tax evasion or arrears were endemic, then even a high quota on which to base *huo-hao* levies would not guarantee local officials a stable source of income from year to year.

For these reasons, *huo-hao kuei-kung*, as originally formulated, was most successful in a few provinces in north China where experimentation had already been under way prior to the summer of 1724. In Shansi, Honan, and Chihli annual *cheng-hsiang* tax quotas all exceeded 3 million taels. Shensi's more modest quota was offset by a somewhat smaller bureaucracy and a lower level of necessary government services.[15] Equally important, most taxes in these four provinces were collected from independent, small-holding peasants. Land tenancy was not unknown in the north, but played a far smaller role in the rural economy there than in the south. In addition, the earlier reforms in land-tax collection had proceeded further in the north, and the relative similarity in land quality and the slower progress of commercial agriculture made tax rates and collection more uniform than in China's major rice-producing provinces. The rapid surrender of much of north China's bureaucracy to the Manchu conquerers also provided the Ch'ing with intact land and tax registers for that region, whereas prolonged resistance and the flight of local officials left southern yamen records woefully incomplete. For decades, southern-gentry opposition to Manchu rule continued to be expressed in the form of tax evasion, and even where remedied by legal means, this greatly impaired the efficiency of local tax-collection efforts.[16] Differences in land tenure and the existence of large concentrations of wealth may also account for the greater power exercised by the elite in south China. Although the Honan examination boycott of 1724 caused the dynasty considerable embarrassment, the gentry of Feng-ch'iu were unable to rally sustained support for their cause.[17] Whereas gentry interference in tax collection and involvement in tax farming was a constant theme in south China, in the north it is rarely mentioned prior to the nineteenth century. Floods and drought always threatened, but the imperial system of tax remissions could respond with exemptions and postponements so that arrears were far less common than in the south, where both tax resistance and submagisterial corruption presented serious obstacles to reform.

The problems posed by the structure of society beyond the north China plain delayed implementation of *huo-hao kuei-kung* in many provinces for several years. Differences in tax base, tenancy relationships, commercial activity, and the structure of local power led to the evolution of different patterns of reform. In agriculturally underdeveloped provinces such as Yunnan, Kweichow, Kwangsi, and Kansu, land- and head-tax quotas which totalled less than the *huo-hao* of more advanced provinces were inescapable barriers to the adoption of the Honan model. Only by the creative use of local commercial and mining revenues were these provinces able to provide adequate income for local government.

However, backwardness was not the only obstacle to reform. The high tax quotas of provinces along the southeast coast were not simply a reflection of higher agricultural productivity. *Cheng-hsiang* tax rates were themselves higher in the south, a fact which militated against the *huo-hao* levies of 13 to 20 percent that were common in the north. Thus, despite their greater wealth, several southern provinces consumed an inordinately large portion of their total revenues on *yang-lien*, leaving little for productive provincial expenditure. (See table 4.2.) What remained was often wiped out by shortages incurred in the process of tax collection or coopted by the central government in the form of Board fees and military expenses. Here, too, revenues from commercial duties and surplus income from government monopolies came to play a part in ensuring the successful implementation of the reforms. Of equal importance was the central government's own efforts to rescue the reforms by providing grants to supplement provincial budgets and by relieving some of the burden of defense responsibilities formerly relegated to *kung-hsiang*.

The adaptation of the original Honan model that was achieved in each of these provinces attests to the remarkable flexibility permitted by "provincial management of provincial revenues." By the end of the Yung-cheng reign, every province in China had implemented its own variation of the original theme of local fiscal rationalization, making use of its own particular resources and satisfying its own special needs.

Table 4.2 *Distribution of* Yang-lien *and* Kung-fei *in Selected Provinces During the* Yung-cheng *Period*

	Rate of *huo-hao*	Amount allocated to *yang-lien* (in taels)	Amount allocated to *kung-fei* (in taels)	Percentage of *huo-hao* allocated to *yang-lien*
Shansi	10–20%	110,513	93,042	54
Honan	10%	215,200	184,800	54
Chihli	13%[a]	179,960	128,227	58
Shensi	20%	177,393	126,135	58
Szechuan	30%[b]	99,414	656[c]	99
Fengtien	10%	15,459[d]	30–36,000[d]	100
Shantung	18%[e]	200,000	140,000[c]	58
Kiangsu	10%	184,300	157,600[c]	54
Kiangsi	10%	162,760[f]	60,608[c]	73
Anhui	10%	108,100	90,173[c]	55
Fukien	14%	133,559[f]	74,732[c]	64
Hupei	10%	91,400	20,439[c]	81
Kweichow	15%	44,700	16,194[c]	73

SOURCES: KCT 20208, Shansi Financial Commissioner Kao Ch'eng-ling, YC 3,2,8; KCTYCCTC, Honan Governor Shih Wen-cho, YC 2,3,3; CPYC, Acting Chihli Governor Yang K'un, no date; KCT 0686, Yueh Chung-ch'i and Hsi Lin, YC 6,5,7; KCT 0448, Shensi Governor-general Yueh Chung-ch'i and Szechuan Governor Hsien Te, YC 5,9,4; CPYC, Acting Fengtien Metropolitan Prefect Wang Ch'ao-en, YC 7,6,4; KCT 2493, Fengtien Metropolitan Prefect Yang Ch'ao-tseng, YC 10,8,3; KCT 17111, Shantung Financial Commissioner Chang Pao, YC 4,4,5; KCT 19634, Acting Suchow Governor Wang-chi, no date; KCT 10983, Li Lan, YC 7,2; KCT 15061, Acting Kiangsi Governor Hsieh Min, YC 7,11,9; KCT 8630, Anhui Governor Wei T'ing-chen, YC 7,1,10; KCT 19111, Prince I, no date; KCT 16570, no name, no date; KCT 13735, 13738, 13741, Acting Kweichow Governor Shih-li-ha, YC 3,8,3.

NOTE: Data on Kansu, Chekiang, Hunan, and Kwangtung are insufficient.

[a] Approximate.
[b] Later lowered to 25%.
[c] Supplemented by non-*huo-hao* income.
[d] Almost entirely from non-*huo-hao* income.
[e] Later lowered to 16%.
[f] Includes later additions for minor officials.

The Sweet Smell of Surplus: Huo-hao kuei-kung in North China

The most striking manifestation of *huo-hao kuei-kung*'s success was the appearance, within a few years of its inception, of large surpluses in provincial revenues. After years of struggling with deficits, provincial officials in north China found themselves with more money than they knew how to spend.

The most dramatic reversal of provincial fiscal fortunes occurred in Honan. Here, Governor T'ien Wen-ching's careful control of corruption combined with a large and relatively easily collected tax quota to produce an accumulated surplus that reached as much as 600,000 taels.[18] Because the repayment of deficits had also meant replenishing granary stores, T'ien first applied this windfall to the construction and repair of granaries throughout the province.[19] Cautious lest a natural disaster occasionally prevent the collection of taxes in full, the governor set the remainder aside as a cushion for the future. At the emperor's urging, a portion of these idle funds was put to more immediate use. Public expenditure for the repair of city walls, temple and public-building construction, and famine relief were substantially increased, as was the *yang-lien* of those officials whose posts brought them into closest contact with the people.[20] As a result, the long-neglected physical substructure of the province was greatly improved and low-level officials in Honan became among the highest paid in the empire.

As a major proponent of the *huo-hao kuei-kung* reforms, T'ien Wen-ching was convinced of the link between adequate salaries and the ability of officials to carry out their responsibilities honestly and efficiently. Therefore, he moved next to utilize his province's large surplus income to provide *yang-lien* for officials below the rank of magistrate. These so-called minor officials performed duties that brought them into constant touch with the people. Many were charged with catching criminals and with supervising the *pao-chia* organizations of the local populace, and they were frequently sent on missions outside the chou or hsien capital, all of which involved heavy expenses that should not have to be passed on to the local population. T'ien first offered this proposal in 1725, but was turned down by the emperor on the ground that other provinces might not have enough funds to follow Honan's example.[21] That Yung-cheng approved the governor's plan three years later was an indication not only of the success of the reforms in Honan, but also of the emperor's growing confidence that other provinces would soon be able to reward their minor officials in the same way.[22] This innovation provided assistant and submagistrates of independent chou an annual *yang-lien* of 120 taels and jail wardens and assistant and submagistrates of regular chou and hsien 80 taels, at a cost to the province of 10,600 taels per year.[23]

The above increases in *huo-hao* expenditure do not seem to have seriously decreased Honan's provincial surplus. In 1739, Honan still had uncommitted revenues in excess of 400,000 taels.

As we shall see, by the beginning of the Ch'ien-lung reign, officials in other provinces where the reforms were not as successful in providing for all provincial expenses began to eye Honan's abundant treasury stores with envy, an envy that was to undermine Yung-cheng's principle that the *huo-hao* revenues of a particular province were to be its inalienable property.[24]

Honan was not alone in producing a surplus of *huo-hao* revenues. By the end of the Yung-cheng reign, similar successes could be claimed by Shansi, Shensi, and Chihli as well.[25] Like Honan, they achieved their success without having to resort to significant infusions of funds in addition to *huo-hao*. In this respect, they constituted the only provinces in which *huo-hao kuei-kung* functioned in the manner envisioned at its inception. Nevertheless, even in these provinces the implementation of the reforms did not proceed without problems.

Although Shansi had been the test case for the introduction of *huo-hao kuei-kung*, officials there were never able to enforce compliance to a fixed rate of *huo-hao*. Under Governor No-min the rate of 20 percent that was established seems to have served more as a guideline than as a definite quota.[26] His successor, Chueh-lo Shih-lin, lowered the rate to 13 percent as the provincial debt was gradually paid off. However, even then the rate continued to range in practice from 14 to 20 percent.[27] Despite this lack of uniformity, the reforms do appear to have held magistrates to a maximum levy of 20 percent. In at least one instance where this limit was exceeded, the magistrate, Wang Meng-hsiung, was criticized by the people of his county and a special investigating team was able to force him to lower his rate to 17 percent.[28]

Violations of a standard rate of *huo-hao* was less troublesome than magisterial resistance to the reforms. In some counties, magistrates remained wary of the province's promise of funds for local projects and continued to collect surcharges on an ad hoc basis.[29] In others, magistrates resisted remittance of their *huo-hao* to the provincial coffers.[30] In the first year of the reforms, this cost the province 60,000 taels of its almost 500,000-tael *huo-hao* quota.

Many of these problems were alleviated when Chueh-lo Shih-lin took over as governor in 1727. Following a thorough investigation of provincial revenue management over the preceding five years, he established strict guidelines to prevent excessive expenditure.[31] For expenses of a relatively predictable nature, quotas were set. (See table 4.3.) This marked an important step in the rationalization of

Table 4.3   *Allocation of* Huo-hao *in Shansi*

	Taels
Funds deposited to make up deficits	200,000
Yang-lien for each official	110,513
Miscellaneous expenses for construction and other purposes in the chou and hsien	10,158
Costs of transporting taxes and melting tax silver into large ingots	3,018
Fodder for post horses beyond the quota provided by *cheng-hsiang*	8,766
Public expenses for the whole province	71,100
Total expenditures	403,555

SOURCE: KCT 20208, Shansi Financial Commissioner Kao Ch'eng-ling, YC 3,2,8.

provincial financing. Whereas earlier in the reforms the only effort at accounting had been to add up the funds expended and saved each year, as the reforms began to be accepted by all officials and remittances became more reliable the governor was able to budget allocations for the coming year, based on accurate information on spending and a consistent flow of silver into the provincial treasury. Nevertheless, there was still a great deal of flexibility in these allocations in that the ultimate decision to disburse funds still remained the responsibility of the provincial governor.

Chihli and Shensi also suffered from initial confusion in the implementation of the reforms. It was not until YC 7 (1729) that Chihli instituted a standard 13-percent rate of collection and complete remittance to the provincial coffers.[32] Although a modified version of direct remittance had been introduced in Shensi by Governor-general Nien Kung-yao, his successor, Yueh Chung-ch'i, discovered that little effort had been made to hold magistrates to the rate established at that time, a more generous 20 percent.[33] Indeed, under Nien, local officials had been permitted to increase or decrease their *huo-hao* levies in response to the size of the deficits incurred in their chou and hsien, a policy that differed little from the common practice prior to the reforms.[34]

The haphazard management of *huo-hao* in Chihli and Shensi was rectified with the help of vigorous provincial leadership appointed later in the Yung-cheng reign. Enforcement of direct remittance of *huo-hao* to the provincial coffers ended most of the problems stemming from excessive exactions from the taxpayers.

In Shensi, Yueh Chung-ch'i took the added precaution of ordering the accepted rates of *huo-hao* posted in every city and village, in the belief that an informed public was the best defense against official malfeasance. New regulation scales were issued to every chou and hsien to prevent the use of weighted balances to manipulate tax rates, and village headmen were instructed to report any magistrate accused by the people of overcharging.[35]

In all four northern provinces, a little over half the provincial revenues were earmarked for allocation as *yang-lien*. This left a sizable allowance for those expenses designated as *kung-fei* or public expenses. In Honan, Shensi, and Shansi, officials received special allowances of *kung-fei* in addition to those funds set aside for the public expenses of the whole province. We are fortunate to have a complete list of the expenditures made from Shensi's *kung-fei* in YC 4 (1726). From this we can see that *kung-fei yin* did indeed pay for expenses of a provincial nature, including repairs to yamen buildings, watchtowers, examination halls, transportation costs of officials on provincial business, city repairs, and special purchases and expenses incurred by high-level provincial officials. (See table 4.4.) Governor Yueh pointed out that some of these

---

Table 4.4   *Shensi* Huo-hao *Allocations in 1726*

	Taels
Yang-lien, chou and hsien *kung-fei*, and wages for yamen clerks	177,393
Production of inscriptions in the imperial hand for Ch'ang-an and Hsien-ning hsien	39
Costs of transporting Nien Keng-yao's confiscated property to the Board (including mules and sedan chairs, and the escorting officials' travel expenses)	2,606
Supplementary travel expenses for imperial commissioners sent to Ch'ang-an and Hsien-ning hsien	761
Materials, grain, and labor costs for additions to the provincial granary	2,000
To Ch'ang-an hsien for hire of sedan-chair carriers to transport Sai-en-hei's son and for travel expenses for the subprefect, military officer, and jail warden escorting him to Peking	269
To Hsien-ning and Ch'ang-an hsien to hire mules for the imperial commissioners' trip back to Peking	750
For the Sian Tartar general's seal and his office staff's stationery expenses	120
To Hsien-ning and Ch'ang-an hsien for travel expenses of widows from the Sian garrison returning to Peking	542
To Hsien-ning and Ch'ang-an hsien for repair of the Ssu-ch'eng gate tower	853

Table 4.4 (continued)

	Taels
To Hsien-ning and Ch'ang-an hsien for repairs to banner offices, additions to the offices of the Tartar general, and repairs to the lieutenant-general's sedan-chair parasol	1,300
Rewards to soldiers accompanying Yueh Chung-ch'i on an inspection tour of the frontier	2,000
To Hsien-ning and Ch'ang-an hsien for annual support of the Kuang-jen ssu Lama[a]	391
To Hsien-ning and Ch'ang-an hsien for support of the Taoist Li Pu-ch'i, ordered by the emperor to Nan-shan[b]	72
Food money to the Boards of War and Revenue accompanying KH 60 to YC 3 annual accounts	13,580
To the treasury ironmonger (k'u-tzu t'ieh-chang)	417
Extra twelve days yang-lien	467
To Ch'ang-an and Hsien-ning hsien for mules sent by the Ministry for Barbarian Affairs as a gift to the tribute mission from Tibet[a]	188
To Ch'ang-an and Hsien-ning hsien for candles and incense for the Kuang-jen ssu Lama[a]	40
To Sian prefecture for repairs to the examination hall and construction of additional cubicles[c]	3,122
To the Manchu army prefect of Sian (Ch'ing-chün t'ung-chih) to supplement the costs of the military examinations[d]	498
To the T'ung-chou submagistrate and the Ch'an hsien jailor for travel expenses while escorting former Financial Commissioner Sa-mu-ha to Peking[e]	80
To the Hsün-yang hsien jailor, Lo-yang hsien jailor, and the inspector of post stations to travel to Sha-kua chou to supervise construction projects[e]	429
To the Sian registrar to escort the former Sian prefect to Peking[e]	44
To the Ho-yang hsien jailor for escorting a censor to Peking[e]	39
To expectant hsien magistrate T'u K'ai for travel expenses to Sha-kua hsien to assist on construction projects[e]	43
To Ch'ang-an and Hsien-ning hsien to buy land for charity graveyards	240
To Ch'ang-an and Hsien-ning hsien to repair buildings and sewers in the Manchu city	65
To two former officials without means to return home	11
Travel expenses for a censor returning to Peking[f]	600
To Ch'ang-an and Hsien-ning hsien for river dredging	860
Total	209,819

SOURCE: KCT 0686, Yueh Chung-ch'i and Hsi-lin, YC 6,5,7.

[a] Previously paid for from contributions of feng-kung.

[b] Disallowed because Li was sent to Nan-shan in exile.

[c] Previously paid for from surplus commercial duties.

[d] Previously paid for from surcharges on the land and head tax on military-colony land.

[e] Granted because minor officials were not yet given yang-lien.

[f] By order of the emperor.

costs would previously have been raised through levies on the villages in the areas where projects were being carried out. By dividing the expenses among all the people in the province, the inhabitants of frontier areas and areas with a high concentration of official yamen were thus given a measure of much-appreciated relief.[36]

Only Chihli appears to have had inadequate funds for public expenses. A large portion of its *kung-fei* was initially remitted to the Board of Revenue in the form of fees that the province had to pay when submitting its taxes.[37] This was partially remedied by the absorption into the provincial budget of 7,000 taels in weighing fees previously paid at tax-collection time to the officers and clerks in charge of the provincial treasury.[38] However, in the following year this added revenue was more than offset by the allocation of over 8,600 taels to provide minor officials with *yang-lien*. It was not until YC 12 (1734) that Chihli was able to join the other northern provinces in providing local officials with public-expense allowances as well as much-needed increases in their *yang-lien*.[39] This was accomplished without an increase in *huo-hao* as a result of a decrease in the fees demanded of the province by the Board.[40]

The success of the reforms in these four provinces demonstrated without question that the rationalization of local-government finances was an attainable goal. However, only creative adaptation of the original model would enable this success to be translated to the majority of provinces beyond the north China plain.

Overcoming Backwardness: Huo-hao kuei-kung on the Periphery

Unlike the flat, fertile north China plain where *huo-hao kuei-kung* was first conceived, China's southern and western frontiers were largely mountainous regions which, in the early eighteenth century, contributed little to the fiscal resources of the state. Large areas of the border provinces were occupied by aboriginal peoples whose integration into the mainstream of Chinese life had barely begun. Even Szechuan, which is now one of the most populous and agriculturally productive provinces in China, suffered in the early Ch'ing from the devastation of land and inhabitants that was the legacy of Chang Hsien-chung's war against the last rulers of the Ming. Only Kwangtung could boast a land- and head-tax quota comparable to those found in southeast and central China. However, poor inland communications made direct remittance of *huo-hao* to the provincial treasury impractical.[41] Elsewhere on the frontiers of the empire, inadequate revenues combined with rugged terrain to necessitate a completely new approach to the reforms mandated by *huo-hao kuei-kung*.

Szechuan was the only border province to attempt to follow the Honan model in implementing the rationalization of local-government finance. This was not an easy task. In YC 5 (1727), when Shensi-Szechuan Governor-general Yueh Chung-ch'i sought to apply the lessons learned in Shensi to his more southerly jurisdiction, he found that the latter yielded an annual regular tax quota of only 333,567 taels.[42] In order to generate sufficient *huo-hao* to supply every official in the province with *yang-lien*, the rate of collection was set at an unprecedented 30 percent. In this manner, the taxpayers generated an extra 100,070 taels for provincial use. However, because Szechuan's *yang-lien* quota consumed 99,414 taels (see table 4.5), little was left for expenses of a more general kind. To remedy this, Yueh and the Szechuan governor, Hsien Te, proposed the continuation of an informal levy known as *pang-t'ieh kung-shih*, formerly collected illegally from the villages to supplement the costs of running the local yamen.[43]

Table 4.5 *Szechuan* Yang-lien *Quotas*

	Taels
Governor-general	3,330
Governor	6,660
Financial commissioner	10,024
4 circuit intendants (1,500 taels each)	6,000
8 Prefects:	
Ch'eng-tu, Chungking (very busy) (2,400 taels each)	4,800
Lung-an fu (remote and simple)	1,600
Remaining 5 fu (2,000 taels each)	10,000
10 assistant and subprefects (400 taels each)	4,000
1 assistant prefect with military jurisdiction	add 200
2 ranking secretaries in the governor's yamen (*pi-t'ieh-shih*)	
(600 taels each)	1,200
10 magistrates of busiest chou and hsien (600 taels each)	6,000
22 magistrates of next busiest chou and hsien	
(500 taels each)	11,000
83 magistrates of remote chou and hsien (400 taels each)	33,200
Add 200 taels to *yang-lien* of 7 chou and hsien newly raised to status	
of independent chou	1,400
Total	99,414

SOURCE: KCT 0448, Shensi Governor-general Yueh Chung-ch'i and Szechuan Governor Hsien Te, YC 5,9,4.

Such a high rate of *huo-hao* was not desirable. Even the officials responsible for its introduction declared their intention to lower it as soon as land reclamation had sufficiently increased the tax base. The emperor himself expressed displeasure at the way *huo-hao kuei-kung* had been accomplished, but decided to grant approval pending a thorough survey of the taxable land in the province. In the meantime, Yueh once again turned to an informed public as a safeguard against further exactions. Signs were posted in all towns and at major crossroads notifying the public of the new rates and of their right to report any official guilty of exceeding them.

By the summer of 1729 the land survey was under way. Behind this investigation of taxable land in Szechuan was the assumption that far more land had been returned to cultivation than was indicated in existing county records. Indeed, as we have seen, as long ago as the K'ang-hsi reign, some officials had suspected the people of Szechuan of scheming to keep their land off the government's tax rolls. Therefore, it should have come as no surprise when the people of Wan hsien seized upon the arrival of the land-survey team in their vicinity to protest against the government's taxation policies. What had not been expected was that the heavy rates of *pang-tieh* now collected in concert with *huo-hao* would become the focus of popular discontent. Convinced that the real target was the land survey itself, Governor Hsien removed the inept censor heading the team in Wan hsien and dispatched a more-experienced investigator in his stead. The disturbance was quickly brought under control and the governor felt vindicated in his assessment of the crisis.[44]

The connection between the land survey and anger over *huo-hao* and *pang-tieh* was not as tenuous as portrayed by Hsien Te. So long as a substantial portion of Szechuan's reclaimed land was hidden from government scrutiny, some segments of the population were probably quite willing to tolerate high levels of extra-quota fees. During the K'ang-hsi period, Nien Keng-yao had reported that Szechuanese taxpayers were supporting a level of surcharges as high as 50 percent of the regular tax. However, the prospect of accurate tax registration and high *huo-hao* was too much for the local inhabitants to bear. Soon after the Wan hsien protest, the taxpayers of Szechuan found an ally in the governor of neighboring Kweichow province. In an impassioned memorial to the emperor, Chang Kuang-ssu reported that whereas in his tax-poor province *huo-hao* was only 20 percent of the regular tax, in Szechuan, the combination of *huo-hao* and *pang-t'ieh* raised the additional liability in some places to an outrageous 55 percent. Chang felt this could not be justified once the present land survey had augmented Szechuan's tax rolls, and he suggested that the *huo-hao* rate be lowered to match that in Kweichow. If this was insufficient to provide for all the province's needs, then magistrates could be authorized to collect a *pang-t'ieh* of no more than 5 percent.[45]

Governor Hsien was not averse to such a plan, but intended to await the completion of the land survey before making any adjustments in existing rates. However, Chang Kuang-ssu's plea on behalf of the Szechuan people was soon echoed in an imperial audience by a prefect newly arrived in the capital from a term in Szechuan. As a result, early in 1730 Hsien received notification from the Board of Revenue to lower Szechuan's *huo-hao* and eliminate *pang-t'ieh*.[46]

The governor reluctantly complied with the order, but in subsequent communications with the Board he expressed concern that the levels of revenue generated by the new 25-percent *huo-hao* would be insufficient to meet Szechuan's administrative needs. Although the Board claimed that it had not meant *huo-hao* to be lowered until the new quotas for regular taxes were in effect, it could not sanction a rise in the rates so soon after a cut had been announced. Instead it recommended the temporary continuation of *pang-t'ieh* levies and proposed that discussions regarding further adjustments be held after the new land registers were compiled.[47] For his part, the emperor attributed the mishandling of the affair to the incorrect referral of *huo-hao* matters to the Board of Revenue.[48] The confusion created in Szechuan only strengthened Yung-cheng's conviction that provincial funding had to be kept independent of Board supervision.

The problems encountered in implementing *huo-hao kuei-kung* in Szechuan served to underscore the difficulties entailed in rationalizing local-government finance in provinces where land- and head-tax revenues were small. In the end it was commercial taxes, in the form of surplus duties on tea and salt, that salvaged the reforms in Szechuan and saved the populace from the reinstitution of *pang-t'ieh*.[49]

The availability of surplus revenues from the taxation of commerce and government-run industries was the key to the successful implementation of the *huo-hao kuei-kung* reforms in each of the other provinces of the northern and southwestern frontier as well.

In Kansu, Governor Hsü Jung estimated that he would require 79,740 taels to pay for the *yang-lien* and public expenses of the officials in his province.[50] Even at a rate of 30 percent, *huo-hao* would not yield sufficient revenues on the basis of the 254,000 or so taels Kansu collected annually in regular taxes.[51] In order to supplement the income from *huo-hao*, Hsü incorporated into the provincial budget some 20,000 taels of surplus duties from the frontier trade (*shui-hsien*) and 11,900 taels of customary fees sent to the governor each winter by merchants applying for licenses to do business.[52] These additions to the provincial coffers were still insufficient to provide Kansu with the level of funding found elsewhere in the north. Therefore, in YC 7 (1729), the governor appealed to the emperor to allow some of Shensi's surplus *huo-hao* to be transferred to Kansu.[53] Although the alienation of *huo-hao* from one province to another was generally not permitted, the fact that Shensi and Kansu had long been administered as a unit made an exception possible in this case.[54]

Perched at the northern and southernmost extremes of China, Fengtien and Kwangsi were handicapped by the lowest *huo-hao* quotas in the realm. In Fengtien, a land and head tax of only 34,592 taels initially inhibited any efforts to institute *huo-hao kuei-kung*. However, in 1729 Yung-cheng ordered the provision of *yang-lien* for all officials not previously covered by the reforms. Even allowing for much lower levels of *yang-lien* than allocated elsewhere,[55] the funds available from *huo-hao* were clearly insufficient to cover all expenses incurred by Fengtien's bureaucratic personnel. Extra revenues from the cart-license fee levied when merchants and commoners carried goods over the border into China proper helped augment the *yang-lien* of the metropolitan prefect and provided wages and stationery expenses for the clerks in several other yamen.[56] However, annual income in Fengtien was still too small to permit the allocation of any funds for public expenses.

This problem was remedied by the emperor in YC 10 (1732). On the condition that it not interfere with the collection of the regular commercial-tax quota, Yung-cheng allowed Fengtien's officials to levy a 30 percent surcharge on goods carried by merchants through the Shan-hai pass separating China from Manchuria. It was calculated that this impost could yield between 30,000 and 36,000 taels annually. Revenues derived from this source were immediately applied to the costs of compiling the prefectural gazetteer, paying laborers at the customs stations and guarding dikes, and repairing public ferries and roads leading to the Fengtien capital.[57]

In Kwangsi a low regular-tax quota was exacerbated by the 2-percent rate of *huo-hao* established by Li Fu when he was governor of this remote province. Only 6,000 taels could be returned to the public coffers each year, all of which was set aside for emergencies affecting the whole province.[58] Nevertheless, later governors were able to tap enough surplus revenues from maritime customs duties, excess commercial duties, and surplus income from government-owned copper mines to pay all officials *yang-lien* and *kung-fei* and supplement the costs of suppressing an uprising by the province's Miao minority in the latter part of the Yung-cheng reign.[59]

Yunnan and Kweichow provide the best evidence of the flexibility with which the reforms could be carried out in areas with unfavorable economic conditions. With their large, unassimilated aborigine populations and land- and head-tax quotas of only 172,525 taels and 66,661 taels respectively,[60] neither could rely on *huo-hao* alone to meet the expenses of a developing border region. Nevertheless, by making use of income from commercial taxation and the rich mining resources within their jurisdiction, even these two remote provinces were able to show a fair level of success in joining the agricultural heartland in the task of fiscal reform.

Available data concerning the implementation of *huo-hao kuei-kung* is more complete for Kweichow than it is for Yunnan. We do know, however, that as early as YC 1 (1723), officials in Yunnan were considering ways to provide funds for provincial expenses. One of the richest sources was Yunnan's numerous copper mines. Although taxes on copper production were the sole property of the central government,[61] provincial control over copper extraction and marketing yielded a sizable income for local use.

By the early part of the Yung-cheng reign, the Ch'ing government was beginning to look favorably upon private operation of mineral extraction.[62] However, lack of capital and poor labor productivity still discouraged large-scale merchant investment in such enterprises.[63] Miners were considered shiftless and unruly, and honest and efficient managers were also difficult to find. Transportation posed another problem. Ores had to be carried from the mines by teams of pack animals driven by aborigine tribesmen who alone had sufficient knowledge of Yunnan's rugged terrain. Risk of loss was great. If they were attacked by bandits or their animals collapsed under their burden, the porters would simply abandon the copper and flee. Some no doubt themselves stole the load they were hired to carry. Even the disposal of this essential commodity posed problems. The market in copper was extremely erratic, necessitating the warehousing of bulky ores for several years at a time, only to see the entire stock sold out in a matter of months when demand suddenly increased.[64] As a result, government still dominated the mining industry in the southwest.

Despite these difficulties, Yunnan was able to net a profit of 20,000 taels from its copper mines, all of which was used to supplement the province's meager income from *huo-hao*.[65] Looking forward to the day when most mines would be privately run, provincial officials also proposed a fee of 20 percent of the output of such enterprises as an additional contribution to the provincial coffers.

Copper was not the only commercial source Yunnan tapped to enhance the funds available for public expenses. Salt fees traditionally sent by merchants to the governor and governor-general generated more than 64,000 taels for *yang-lien* and *kung-fei*. Government operation of the salt wells themselves yielded another 65,721 taels after remittance of imperial salt quotas and the payment of wages and expenses at the wells.[66] Provincial officials also expressed hopes of considerable profits from the management of Yunnan's developing silver-mining industry.[67]

Given the low land- and head-tax quota and the availability of such large sums of nonagricultural surplus income, it is not surprising that Yunnan's high officials first responded to the *huo-hao kuei-kung* reforms by instituting a system of limited remittance to the provincial treasury. Whereas revenues from salt and mining were used to pay for provincial-level projects and the *yang-lien* of high-ranking officials, the chou and hsien were allowed to retain their own *huo-hao* to cover local expenses. Middle-level officials, such as prefects, and some chou and hsien magistrates obtained the greater portion of their expenses from surplus commercial duties above the small quotas due the central government.[68]

The emperor was not pleased with this system, perhaps because it amounted to little more than the legalization of existing patterns of funding under the informal network. In early YC 3 (1725) he issued an edict instructing the officials in both Yunnan and Kweichow to account for all revenues available from *huo-hao*, surplus duties, mining, and rents on imperial lands in preparation for their remittance in full to the provincial coffers. Once the total resources available in each province were known, their high officials were to allocate *yang-lien* for every post from governor to magistrate, calculated on the basis of remoteness from the provincial capital and the level of official business involved.[69]

We do not know how these funds were ultimately allocated in Yunnan, but we do have remarkably detailed accounts of how Kweichow's income was derived and the manner in which it was redistributed after the reforms. Table 4.6 shows that of the 60,894 taels returned to the provincial coffers in Kweichow, only 18 percent, or 10,792 taels, were derived directly from *huo-hao* on the land and head tax. Even if we include the income from surcharges on levies of rice and beans, the total revenues from traditional agricultural sources were only 33 percent of Kweichow's provincial funds under the new system.

The fact that most of Kweichow's provincial revenues were obtained from commercial sources and a grant of rents from imperial lands argues strongly against claims that the *huo-hao kuei-kung* reforms were a central-government ploy to extract an even greater portion of the extra-quota income collected by the provinces. By approving the accounts submitted by governors such as Shih-li-ha, the emperor was actually confirming the right of provinces to a

---

Table 4.6 *Analysis of Kweichow Provincial Revenues*

1. *Land and head tax huo-hao:*
   Rates vary from 10% to 20% for total 11,330 taels. Now decided on a uniform 15% for a total 10,792 taels.
2. *Huo-hao on autumn grain levies in rice and beans:*
   Total after deductions for spoilage in 16,588 piculs. At an average market price of 0.55 tael there is a surplus of about 9,123 taels.
3. *Rents from imperial estates and educational lands:*
   After deductions for courier substation soldiers' wages, allowances to *sheng-yuan*, relief for poor students and impoverished people, there is a surplus of 1,600 piculs. At 0.55 tael per picul this yields 880 taels. There is also surplus from rents on imperial lands totaling 1,090 piculs, yielding a total of 599 taels.
4. Surplus from above sources of officials who will not get *yang-lien*, including assistant prefects and magistrates, totaling 3,640 taels.
5. *Revenues from salt- and miscellaneous-duties surplus:*
   See table 4.7. Total estimated annual income, 35,860 taels.
   Total: 60,894 taels.

SOURCES: KCT 13736, KCT 13735, Acting Kweichow Governor Shih-li-ha, YC 3,8,3.

Table 4.7 *Kweichow Revenues from Salt- and Miscellaneous-Duties Surpluses*

Place	Salt quota	Duties quota	Total actual revenues	Total sent to government	Runners' wages	Approximate Surplus
			Taels			
Kuei-yang fu	2,906	2,611	9,000	5,517	120	3,360
An-shun fu	244	2,391	5,330	2,635	120	2,570
P'u-an chou	389	1,202	3,000	1,591	100	1,310
Chen-yüan fu	328	3,091	7,240	3,419	120	3,700
Wei-ning chou	243	97	7,000	340	120	6,540
Yung-ning chou	—	1,030	2,530	1,030	100	1,400
Ta-ting chou	111	119	1,610	230	80	1,300
P'ing-yüan chou	72	115	1,700	187	80	1,430
Ch'ien-hsi chou	288	98	2,800	386	80	2,330
Pi-chien hsien	306	264	5,500	570	100	4,830
Yung-ning hsien	310	93	4,200	403	100	3,690
Ch'ing-chen hsien	712	29	1,920	741	80	1,100
Ssu-nan fu	448	—	2,200	448	80	1,670
T'ung-jen fu	174	498	800	negligible surplus after quota and wages		
Shih-ch'ien fu	141	Do not collect enough annually to meet the quota				
Hsiu-wen hsien		689	1,200	689	80	430
K'ai chou	—	75	Annually collect just enough for quota			
P'u-an hsien	216					200
An-nan hsien	72	Do not collect enough annually to meet the quota				
Totals			56,030			35,860

portion of the customs and salt revenues originating within their borders. It is clear that the emperor's concern was not to commandeer additional income for the central government, but to ensure that each province had the means to carry out the rational management of local finances with the same success that was possible in areas with reliable, high land-tax receipts. This is particularly striking when we realize that 64 percent of Kweichow's estimated annual income from salt and commercial taxes was now to be retained by the province for its own use.

Even with the addition of funds from imperial-lands, salt, and miscellaneous duties, Kweichow's provincial revenues were barely enough to meet all its fixed costs. (See table 4.8.) A comparison with *yang-lien* statistics for other provinces shows that an official in Kweichow received several hundred taels less than that of an average official of the same rank in other, wealthier provinces. (See table 4.9.) Moreover, only 1,190 taels remained to meet the elastic public expenses of the province, such as yamen and road repairs and water-conservancy projects.

Table 4.8   *Kweichow Annual Public Expenses*

	Taels
Seasonal gifts (appear to be to the emperor)	220
"Food money" to the Board when reporting the annual accounts	1,200
Travel expenses to send the annual accounts	40
"Food money" to the Board of Punishments at the time of the autumn assizes	240
"Food money" to the Board at time taxes are shipped to the capital	400
Transportation expenses for mercury shipments to capital	66
Supplemental funds for Honan and Hupei post stations	900
Travel expenses when submitting the governor-general's annual accounts	120
Governor's yamen clerks' stipends	132
Annual year-end rewards to soldiers and functionaries in the provincial capital	1,500
Governor's yamen expenses: supplies for military drill, cannon, firearms, powder; daily-use items; salaries for private secretaries	8,500
Stationery costs:	
Governor-general's yamen	830
Governor's yamen	856
Yang-lien (see table 4.9)	44,700
Total	59,704

SOURCES: KCT 13735, 13738, 13741, Acting Kweichow Governor Shih-li-ha, YC 3,8,3.

Table 4.9   Yang-lien *Quotas for Kweichow Province*

	Taels	
Educational commissioner	2,000	
Financial commissioner	4,500	
Judicial commissioner	3,000	
Kuei-tung circuit intendant	2,000	
Kuei-hsi circuit intendant	1,800	
Kuei-yang prefect	1,300	
Wei-ning and 2 other prefects	1,100 =	3,300 total
P'ing-yueh and 2 other prefects	1,000 =	3,000 total
Ssu-nan and 4 other prefects	800 =	4,000 total
Kuei-yang subprefect	500	
The Cheng-ta garrison subprefect and Kuei-yang assistant subprefect	400 =	800 total
Wei-ning assistant subprefect	300	
11 large chou magistrates	600 =	6,600 total
K'ai-chou magistrate	400	
Nan-lung t'ing assistant subprefect	500	
Kuei-chu hsien magistrate	700	
4 medium hsien magistrates	500 =	2,000 total
20 other hsien magistrates	400 =	8,000 total
Total		44,700

SOURCE: KCT 13741, Acting Kweichow Governor Shih-li-ha, YC 3,8,3.

Events of the next few years placed intolerable strains on Kwei-chow's already tight finances. Jurisdictional reorganization made Yung-ning hsien a part of Szechuan province, resulting in a loss of over 3,600 taels in duty surpluses. In addition, Tsun-i prefecture was transferred to Szechuan and five other hsien were made a part of Hunan province. At the same time, several new prefectures and chou were created in areas previously under aborigine rule, increasing the province's burden of *yang-lien* and public expenses.[70] A further budgeting problem resulted from the fact that so much of Kweichow's income depended on surplus revenues from the salt and customs administration. Both of these sources were highly variable, depending on the volume of trade during a given year. The estimates of salt and duty surpluses used by Shih-li-ha in drawing up the Kweichow budget were those of the year before the reforms were implemented. Income in later years did not always reach the levels of the first few years of the Yung-cheng reign. During the intervening period it was often necessary to reduce the *yang-lien* of all officials by as much as 10 percent to make up for unforeseeable losses in revenues.[71] As a result of all these circumstances, Kweichow province was faced with a shortage of approximately 20,000 taels by YC 8 (1730).

In order to solve this problem and provide *yang-lien* for newly created posts and for miscellaneous officials, Governor Chang Kuang-ssu devised a novel plan that would enable the province to profit from its rich mining resources, as Yunnan had done earlier in the dynasty.[72] Within its borders Kweichow had mines at Nan-lung fu and Wei-ning chou that produced a form of lead known as *wo-ch'ien*. Because Yunnan had opened a mint and needed lead for its smelting factory, these Kweichow mines had been placed under its jurisdiction. By 1730, the Lo-p'ing mines in Yunnan were producing sufficient lead for Yunnan's needs and the lead that had earlier been sent from Kweichow was lying idle. To remedy this, the officials in Yunnan had memorialized to borrow funds from their provincial treasury to buy up the surplus lead and ship it to Hangchow for sale. For every 100 *chin* of lead shipped north, they netted one tael, after deducting the purchase price and transportation costs. The profits were deposited in Yunnan's public-expense fund.

According to Governor Chang, Kweichow was now undertaking to establish its own smelting operation and requested that all produce from the mines within its territory be placed once again under Kweichow's control. The province would use the lead to supply its own smelting facilities and dispose of any surplus after central-government production quotas were filled in the same manner as Yunnan. He estimated that Kweichow would be able to purchase the entire surplus from the lead mines, 4 to 5 million *chin* annually. In addition, 700,000 *chin* would be collected by the province in the form of taxes. Because the smelting factories would be able to handle only about 160,000 *chin* when they first opened, the remaining lead from taxes could also be sold. Calculating a net profit of 1.5 taels per 100 *chin*, Kweichow could obtain between 50,000 and 60,000 taels in additional income per year. Governor Chang requested the emperor's permission to keep this sum to make up the shortages in the current provincial budget and to provide 28,200 taels to increase the *yang-lien* granted to each official and allocate *yang-lien* for miscellaneous minor officials and newly created posts along the Miao border. This would leave as much as 11,800 taels for those cost-elastic projects previously neglected under the administration of Shih-li-ha.

Only one obstacle stood in the way of this plan. Whereas Yunnan had advanced the initial capital for its own merchandising experiment from surplus funds in the provincial treasury, Kweichow's treasury was already suffering a deficit. Therefore, Chang also requested to borrow from the 100,000 taels set aside by the central government for land-reclamation projects within Kweichow's border regions. Originally these funds had been designated to provide working capital for Han Chinese opening new land to cultivation. However, Chang claimed that most of the land was actually being reclaimed by Miao who were supplying their own tools and labor and had not requested public assistance. Chang proposed to borrow 60,000 taels from this fund. This could then be repaid over a period of three years out of the profits from the sale and shipment of lead. The emperor's only comment on Chang's memorial was to question whether educational officials would be provided with *yang-lien*, hence it may be assumed that this plan was indeed carried out.

The use of government entrepreneurship to increase provincial revenues in Yunnan and Kweichow was an extremely important step in the development of Chinese fiscal policy. Although the projects undertaken entailed merchandising endeavors and not manufacturing *per se*, they may have set a precedent for the provincial enterprises established during the nineteenth century. Although government monopolies were as old as the imperial system itself, this was the first time that provinces engaged in profit-making projects for the sole purpose of providing funds for their own provincial coffers. The existence of surplus revenues in the Yunnan treasury with which the province could initiate its own lead-merchandising scheme indicates that the reforms in that province, aided by income from copper mining and salt production, were a success. With Kweichow's own leap into the arena of provincial entrepreneurship, that tax-poor province, too, was able to join the agriculturally rich provinces to the north in providing a steady and secure source of income for its officials and to carry out public works.

The absorption of surplus salt, customs, and miscellaneous commercial tax revenues into the budgets of these border provinces also demonstrates that what mattered most in the implementation of the *huo-hao kuei-kung* reforms was the changes that they made possible in the operation of local-government finance. *Huo-hao* as the vehicle for these changes was only secondary. Moreover, because most of these funds belonged by statute to the central government, it is clear that the emperor's commitment to fiscal rationalization outweighed even the desire to augment central-treasury reserves.

Commercial duties played an important part in the funding of provincial government in the provinces along China's eastern seaboard as well. However, here in the economic heartland of China, even more overt grants of aid from the central government were necessary to offset the obstacles presented by tax evasion and the heavy demands placed on provincial resources.

Poverty Amidst Riches:
Huo-hao kuei-kung in Shantung and the Southeast

For the first time in imperial history, the fiscal reforms of the Yung-cheng period addressed the problem of inadequate funding of local government. As such, they provided the Chinese bureaucracy with a powerful weapon against corruption within its own ranks. However, *huo-hao kuei-kung* could not alter the structure of local society. In those provinces where the influence of the local elite was strong, the proponents of reform met their most intractable adversaries. Rationalization of local-government finances threatened to break the control that members of the gentry exercised over magistrates by releasing them from their dependence on tax farmers for revenues beyond the legal quota. In addition, *huo-hao kuei-kung* meant the equalization of surtaxes, ending the lower rates enjoyed by the privileged strata of the rural population.[73] In many parts of China, yamen clerks, local gentry, and village strongmen waged a quiet but unrelenting war against fiscal rationalization in the form of slander campaigns and, even more damaging, outright resistance to the payment of taxes.

Shantung province provides an excellent example of the problems confronted by officials in an environment where their authority over the tax-collection process was incomplete. Although it was a north-China province with a large tax base, Shantung was not able to emulate the Honan model of reform until the last years of the Yung-cheng reign. The policy first instituted in Shantung set the rate of *huo-hao* at 18 percent. On a regular tax quota of approximately 3 million taels, this yielded an annual income of about 540,000 taels. Of this, 200,000 taels were set aside to make up deficits, another 200,000 taels were used to provide officials with *yang-lien*, and the remaining 140,000 taels were appropriated for the public expenses of the whole province.[74] On the surface, at least, Shantung seemed well on its way to matching the performance of Honan, Shansi, and Shensi in the effective implementation of reform.

However, the policy of remittance established in Shantung set it apart from its fellow provinces to the west. The chou and hsien deducted their own *yang-lien* before sending their *huo-hao* to the provincial capital. Higher officials received their *yang-lien* directly from the financial commissioner, but this was almost the only revenue he controlled. Of the 140,000 taels designated for provincial public expenses, the chou and hsien were also permitted to retain 120,000 taels to cover their own *kung-fei* and the costs of remitting their taxes to the provincial treasury.[75] Consequently, only 20,000 taels were left for construction projects and famine relief administered for the province as a whole.

This policy undermined the efficacy of the reforms in several ways. Just as T'ien Wen-ching predicted, magistrates, when left to deduct a portion of their *huo-hao* revenues themselves, tended to persist in the collection of illegal surcharges (*ssu-p'ai*). Some magistrates were so determined to acquire this additional income that the people were forced to pay the illegal fees before remitting their regular taxes. When the burden became too great and the regular quota went unfilled, the magistrates simply reported a high level of people's arrears (*min-ch'ien*).[76] Because *huo-hao* was remitted along with regular quota, deficits in the *cheng-hsiang* also meant deficits in the *huo-hao* revenues sent to the provincial treasury. According to the original plan, it was anticipated that Shantung would be able to repay all her previous deficits by YC 4 (1726).[77] By YC 6 (1728), however, the combination of old deficits that had not yet been repaid and new deficits incurred since the reforms went into effect brought Shantung's total outstanding tax payments to an astonishing 2 million taels.[78]

Shantung's total tax quota was among the highest in the empire. Yet despite the ample revenues that an 18-percent *huo-hao* should have yielded, the problems encountered in collecting these taxes forced Shantung's officials to turn to additional sources of funds beyond the land and head tax. Unlike the other provinces in north China where an added incentive to engage in corruption was eliminated by banning most customary fees and gifts, Shantung province integrated many of these former informal levies into her revised fiscal system. A continual debate was carried on among provincial officials over which of these sources were legitimate and which should be eliminated. As a result, not only is it impossible for us to determine the annual income from these alternative sources, but even officials at the time were unable to predict their revenues for any given year.[79]

In YC 6 (1728), the emperor appointed Honan Governor T'ien Wen-ching governor-general of Honan-Shantung, a post created especially for him. T'ien's most important task in this capacity was to use the techniques developed in Honan to clean up the administration of his new jurisdiction.

T'ien Wen-ching attributed Shantung's fiscal difficulties directly to the strength of the local elite of the province. Unlike Honan, Shantung was plagued by vestiges of the outlawed *li-chia* system, under the guise of which influential members of the local community, often with the aid of hired thugs, collected the land and head tax at several times the legal rate.[80] In some parts of the province, magistrates had completely abdicated their responsibility for tax collection in return for a guaranteed share of the booty wrenched by these petty tax farmers from the common people. Although this corrupt alliance was a product of the days when the informal funding system was the only means available for financing local administration, the networks of power it supported in the countryside made both magistrates and their extrabureaucratic cohorts almost impossible to control.

True to the principles he espoused in Honan, T'ien first moved to institute complete remittance of *huo-hao* to the public coffers as a check on the manipulation of tax income. Impartial inspectors were appointed to examine the locked chests set up to receive the payments of landowners and relieve them from dependence on tax farmers. At the same time, strict measures were implemented to prevent high officials from encouraging low-level graft by demanding gifts and fees from their subordinates.[81] Nevertheless, gentry resistance to the new policies remained formidable and, as in Honan, was often aimed directly at the person of the governor-general. When the emperor ordered T'ien to visit Shantung in 1729 to investigate a case of corruption, his detractors leaped at the opportunity to discredit him in the eyes of the public he sought to release from their control. His admonitions to the local bureaucracy to clean up fiscal malpractices and carry out reform were met with rumors that T'ien had come on a mission to raise people's taxes and had even issued a new bamboo measuring rod inches shorter than the one normally used as a standard in assessing the size of the people's land holdings.[82]

Efforts to disparage *huo-hao kuei-kung* by linking it to augmentation of the peasants' tax burden was a common ploy during the early years of the reforms. However, the persistence of T'ien's adversaries was sufficient to cause him to postpone complete remittance of *huo-hao* to the provincial coffers. Unable to duplicate his performance in Honan, the governor-general had to be content with prohibiting the extra fees collected by magistrates and lowering the rate at which *huo-hao* was levied to 16 percent.[83] Moreover, instead of allowing the chou and hsien to retain a percentage of their *huo-hao* as public expenses, Governor Fei Chin-wu ordered that the amount of *kung-fei* deducted by each magistrate be calculated according to need and that transportation expenses (*chieh-fei*) be allocated on the basis of an area's remoteness from the provincial capital. In mid-1730, Financial Commissioner Sun Kuo-erh finally moved to complete the process by requesting that *huo-hao* be remitted to the provincial treasury in full and that the magistrates receive their *yang-lien* as a grant from the financial commissioner.[84]

Although the refinement of *huo-hao kuei-kung* in Shantung had required almost seven years to achieve, officials in that province had begun as early as the first year of the Yung-cheng reign to confront the problem of corruption in their midst. In the provinces of Kiangnan and the southeast coast, officials were much slower to respond to the emperor's invitation to reform.

Kiangsu, with the highest land- and head-tax quota in the empire, had the unique distinction of being the only province expressly denied the emperor's permission to carry out *huo-hao kuei-kung*. It was not until YC 4 (1726) that the governor thought to broach the subject. Even then, his main concern was to find a source of revenue to reimburse provincial deficits. However, it was not the high level of deficits in Kiangsu that made Yung-cheng reluctant to permit its experimentation with his reforms. Those deficits had reached 2 million taels by 1726,[85] but were no worse than the deficits already recorded in Shantung. More important were the province's 8,810,000 taels in arrears, a figure in excess of the combined arrears of all the other provinces in the empire.[86] Although the emperor had sanctioned the repayment of these outstanding taxes in manageable installments, magistrates had proven themselves incapable of retrieving more than 100,000 taels per year.[87]

The remarkable inability of Kiangsu's officialdom to meet its tax quotas was a reflection of fiscal corruption and disorganization that went far beyond that uncovered in Shantung. Early in his reign, Yung-cheng had begun to receive reports of irregularities in Kiangsu's tax rolls, the widespread contracting of tax payments, and various practices utilized by clerks and members of the gentry to disguise landownership and redistribute tax liabilities to their own profit.[88] Until these malpractices could be investigated and brought to a halt, any efforts at reform of local funding would be in vain. Chronic arrears would preclude the collection and remittance of adequate supplies of *huo-hao*. Furthermore, without regularization of the methods of taxation it would be impossible even to tell how much of the enormous arrears in the province was really the result of nonpayment by the people and how much was already lining the pockets of officials and their staff. If the latter could circumvent payment of over 8 million taels in taxes owed the central government, far better controls would be necessary to guarantee remittance of *huo-hao* quotas to the provincial coffers.

In order to clear the way for reform here and elsewhere in Kiangnan, Yung-cheng first decreed a thorough investigation of the region's arrears and tax-collection procedures. (See chapter 6.)

Only when this investigation was well under way was permission granted to undertake *huo-hao kuei-kung*.

The task of implementation was aided by the appointment of Kiangsu's financial commissioner as governor. Ch'en Shih-hsia had previously served in Honan and Chihli and had had considerable experience with the reforms. After a brief dispute with his replacement as financial commissioner over the method of remittance to be used, Ch'en's plan for complete remittance to the provincial treasury was promulgated in 1728.[89] A 10-percent rate of *huo-hao* was levied on all land and head taxes and on several smaller levies traditionally sent to the grain, river, post, and salt intendents.[90] An initial schedule of *yang-lien* quotas was submitted to the emperor by Ch'en Shih-hsia just prior to his retirement from his post. The emperor's criticism of these rates was integrated into the final schedule outlined in table 4.10. Except for the *yang-lien* of the financial and judicial commissioners, which the emperor judged to be too high, the salaries of almost every official were revised upwards in the final list. Practices in other provinces were also influential in determining the manner in which *yang-lien* was ultimately distributed. For example, originally no provision had been made for the fourteen subprefects and assistant subprefects in charge of river conservancy. The governor later decided to follow the precedent set in Honan and Shantung where *yang-lien* was granted to these low-level functionaries in order to free them from the necessity to overreport construction costs on waterworks as a means of acquiring funds for their yamen and travel expenses.[91] In addition, the *yang-lien* of Kiangsu's chou and hsien magistrates was raised to match that of the better-funded provinces. A fund for local public expenses called *pei-kung yin* was also established, from which each chou and hsien was allocated an additional 200 to 600 taels annually.

Kiangsu's total tax quota at the time the reforms were introduced was 3,719,000 taels. Of this sum, 2,271,000 taels were remitted directly to the financial commissioner, yielding 272,100 taels of *huo-hao*. Another 997,800 taels were sent to the grain, river, post, and salt intendants. They were allowed to retain 30 percent of the *huo-hao* derived from these taxes to make up the silver content of the taxes they sent to the central government. The remaining 69,800 taels were also forwarded to the financial commissioner. Kiangsu thus had a total of 341,900 taels with which to pay all *yang-lien* and public expenses.

Table 4.10   *Kiangsu* Yang-lien *Quotas*

	Taels
Governor-general	6,000
Governor	12,000
Hsün-ch'a	1,200
Ch'ing-ch'a censor	1,000
Educational commissioner	1,500
Department director (assigned to supervise water conservancy)	1,000
Financial commissioner	10,000
Judicial commissioner	8,000
Kiang-chen, Su-sung, and Huai-yang circuit intendants (2,500 taels each)	7,500
Kiang-ning and Suchow prefects (3,000 taels each)	6,000
Sung-kiang, Chen-kiang, Ch'ang-chou, Huai-an, and Yang-chou prefects (2,000 taels each)	10,000
7 subprefects (500 taels each)	3,500
8 assistant subprefects (400 taels each)	3,200
9 subprefects in charge of river conservancy (500 taels each)	4,500
5 assistant subprefects in charge of river conservancy (400 taels each)	2,000
66 chou and hsien *yang-lien* plus allowances for public expenses (*pei-kung yin*) (1,200 to 2,400 taels each)	103,900
Travel expenses for low-ranking officials	3,000
Total	184,300

SOURCE: KCT 19634, Acting Suchow Governor Wang Chi, no date.

Despite its large tax quota, Kiangsu had less income available for provincial expenses than did provinces with comparable quotas in the north. Table 4.11 shows the fixed expenses of the province in a typical year. Over 80 percent of these funds were spent in fulfilling obligations to the central government or to subsidize projects paid for out of *cheng-hsiang*. After allocations were made for fixed expenses, Kiangsu had only 36,000 taels for the elastic expenses of the province itself. This could hardly cover the costs of city-wall, road, embankment, and garrison repairs encountered by provincial officials each year. Moreover, this sum might not be available when the need arose. Even after the implementation of the reforms, tax arrears continued to cost the province an average of 70,000 taels in *huo-hao* per year.

In order to provide a reliable fund for provincial expenses, Governor Yin-chi-shan requested in 1731 that customary fees remitted by Liang-huai salt merchants to the salt controller be incorporated into the provincial budget. These so-called *yen-kuei yin-fei* totaled over 100,000 taels annually. With them, Kiangsu was able to guarantee the availability of funds for repairs and also joined the prov-

Table 4.11   *Kiangsu Fixed Public Expenses*

	Taels
Supplementary funds for warship repairs	50,000
Pu-p'ing for taxes remitted to the capital [a]	40,000
Supplementary funds to purchase dyes and pewter sent to the capital	11,512
Supplementary funds for the purchase of frame lumber (*chia-mu*) and wages for sailors manning lifeboats	1,523
Stationery for accounts sent to the Boards	4,980
Stationery, gunpowder, stipends for clerks and runners in governor-general's yamen (remainder paid by Kiangsi and Anhui)	1,773
Stationery, gunpowder, stipends for clerks and runners in governor's yamen	4,343
Firewood and other supplies for Kiang-ning and Suchow silk manufactory	1,346
Wages for scribes in the Hsün-ch'a's yamen	108
Financial commissioner's stationery	1,179
Superintendent of military posts' soldiers' wages, rations, accounting costs, etc.	2,742
Annual repairs of the Kiang-ning city wall	500
Ch'ung-ming gunpowder expenses	1,358
Total	121,364

SOURCE: KCT 19634, Acting Suchow Governor Wang Chi, no date.

[a] Funds used to bring the silver content of taxes remitted by the people up to the standard required by the Board of Revenue.

inces in the north in providing most minor officials with *yang-lien*.[92]

Official confusion and lack of initiative could be just as important a deterrent to reform as tax arrears and fiscal corruption. Under the informal funding network, high officials in Kiangsi were the beneficiaries of a source of income not affected by Yung-cheng's proscription against the acceptance of customary fees.[93] Along with the regular tax, each hsien in the province remitted an additional 0.0175 tael per tael, known as *p'ing-fei*. On an average annual tax quota of 1,500,000 taels, this yielded over 26,000 taels, which was distributed among the governor, governor-general, and financial commissioner, and used for both yamen and public expenses. Magistrates were allowed to collect *huo-hao* to cover their own expenses, leaving little incentive for high or low officials to lobby for its return to the public coffers.

When a plan for remittance of the meltage fee was finally devised for Kiangsi in YC 7 (1729), it contained the most unwieldy system of *yang-lien* allocation to be proposed by any province. Those hsien with a total regular tax quota of 9,000 taels or less were not required to remit any of their *huo-hao*. Those with between 10,000 and 60,000 taels were to remit 61 percent. Those with even higher tax quotas were to remit as much as 70 percent of their *huo-hao*, keeping the rest as *yang-lien*. The *yang-lien* of higher officials was calculated as a percentage of the *huo-hao* collected by the magistrates within their jurisdiction, deducting an amount equivalent to any salt fees each might receive.[94]

The emperor's reaction to this scheme was not enthusiastic, and he immediately suggested that it be reconsidered to make *yang-lien* quotas more closely reflect the real fiscal needs of the local administrative units. What he received in reply was almost comical. Instead of determining quotas for groups of hsien on the basis of their remoteness from the capital and the complexity of their public business, the financial commissioner simply revised the percentages of *huo-hao* to be retained, calculated the amount they would yield in each place and converted that amount into a fixed quota. The *yang-lien* figures obtained in this manner were so diverse that it clearly would be impossible to enforce provincial supervision of county accounts.[95] The *yang-lien* of higher officials followed a similar pattern. (See table 4.12.) Once again the emperor admon-

Table 4.12 *Kiangsi* Yang-lien *Before and After Equalization*

Office	Taels	
	Before	After
Governor-general	4,400	6,200
Governor	8,800	7,000
Financial commissioner	8,547	8,500
Judicial commissioner	5,762	6,000
Grain intendant	3,262	3,500
Post and salt intendant	1,968*	3,000
Jao-chiu circuit intendant	1,608	2,000
Kan-nan circuit intendant	1,568	2,000
Nan-ch'ang prefect	2,763	2,400
Nan-ch'ang subprefect	1,105	600
Nan-ch'ang assistant subprefect	2,096	600
Jui-chou prefect	1,267	1,400
Jui-chou subprefect	647	600
Jui-chou assistant subprefect	503	600
Yuan-chou prefect	1,298	1,400
Yuan-chou subprefect	659	600
Lin-chiang prefect	1,562	1,400
Lin-chiang assistant subprefect	819	600
Chi-an prefect	3,074	2,000
Chi-an subprefect	1,229	600
Chi-an assistant subprefect	1,359	600

Table 4.12   (*continued*)

Office	Taels	
	Before	After
Fu-chou prefect	2,474	1,600
Fu-chou assistant subprefect	688	600
Chien-ch'ang prefect	1,403	1,400
Chien-ch'ang subprefect	641	600
Chien-ch'ang assistant subprefect	323	600
Kuang-hsin prefect	1,494	1,600
Kuang-hsin subprefect	597	600
Kuang-hsin assistant subprefect	412	600
Jao-chou prefect	2,187	1,800
Jao-chou subprefect	874	600
Jao-chou assistant subprefect	1,014	600
Nan-k'ang prefect	1,285	1,400
Nan-k'ang subprefect	654	600
Nan-k'ang assistant subprefect	331	600
Chiu-chiang prefect	1,383	1,600
Chiu-chiang subprefect	633	600
Nan-an prefect	1,285	1,400
Nan-an subprefect	594	600
Kan-chou prefect	1,450	2,000
Kan-chou subprefect	580	600
Kan-chou assistant subprefect	600	600
Nan-ch'ang hsien magistrate		1,600
Hsin-chien hsien magistrate		1,400
Magistrates of 24 large and busy hsien	**	28,000[a]
Magistrates of 26 medium hsien	**	26,000[b]
Magistrates of 25 small hsien	**	20,000[c]
14 military officers in charge of transport	none	3,360[d]
14 military officers without transport responsibilities	none	1,400[e]
Totals	154,800	154,760

SOURCES: KCT 10983, Li Lan, YC 7,2; KCT 15061, Acting Kiangsi Governor Hsieh Min, YC 7,11,9.

  * Plus salt fees of 1,929 taels.
  ** Vary as a percentage of regular taxes.
  [a] 1,200 taels each.
  [b] 1,000 taels each.
  [c] 800 taels each.
  [d] 240 taels each.
  [e] 100 taels each.

ished Kiangsi's high officials to compile a schedule of salaries that would both be equitable and discourage embezzlement and fraud. The result of these new deliberations was a system of complete remittance of *huo-hao*, collected at a rate of 10 percent of the regular tax. Most magistrates, and many prefectural officials as well, enjoyed an increase in *yang-lien* under the new plan. Twenty-eight military officials were granted *yang-lien* for the first time. And all of this was accomplished at a saving to the province of forty taels.[96]

The emperor's influence was also an important factor in the outcome of the reforms in Anhui. Here, complete remittance at a rate of 10 percent was proposed from the start. However, in Anhui it was not *yang-lien* quotas but the allocation of *kung-fei* that caused confusion among provincial officials. Governor Wei T'ing-chen's provisional budget appears in table 4.13. Those items marked with an asterisk were rejected by the emperor as unwarranted. If we compare the items that the emperor questioned with those he left standing, we can see that he approved funding for all administrative expenses, including stationery costs, clerk and runner

Table 4.13 *Anhui Provincial Budget Proposed by Wei T'ing-chen*

Fixed expenses:	Taels
* Entertainment and travel expenses of governor's yamen	120
* Funds to governor-general's yamen for supervision of repair projects	96
Stipends, stationery, and firewood for clerks and runners of governor-general's yamen	1,630
* Costs of composing clean copies of governor-general's memorials	200
Stationery for the Tartar general's yamen and wages for his standard bearers and bodyguards	300
Wages for the Tartar general's *tsao-i*	180
* "Inspection funds" for the Tartar general and governor-general	140
* Brocade clothing for *wei* runners	27
Stationery expenses incurred during the compilation of reports on regimental and garrison rations by the staff of the governor and governor-general	242
Stipends for clerks of the governor's yamen	1,200
(add in an interlocutory month)	100
Wages for runners of the governor's yamen	973
Red ink, paper, cloth wrappers, and boxes for composing and remitting governor's memorials	510
Stationery and food fees sent by the governor's yamen to the northern and southern superintendents of military posts	166
Public-expense funds (*kung-fei yin*) sent by the governor to the superintendents of military posts	400
* Funds to the governor's yamen for the supervision of annual repair projects	120
Expenses incurred by the governor's yamen in compiling the annual accounting of horse-grazing lands	60
Triennial contribution of the governor's yamen to the purchase of piles for river-conservancy projects	375
Wages for the governor-general's standard bearers	224
Paper and red ink for the educational commissioner's yamen and stipends for clerks and runners on missions on his behalf	1,188

Table 4.13 *(continued)*

Fixed expenses:	Taels
Wages for copyists and runners of the censor's yamen	120
Annual accounting (*tsou-hsiao*) fees to the Board of Revenue and Department of Scrutiny	4,700
Annual food money (*fan-shih*) to the Board of Punishments	1,800
Transport fees to the Boards	90
Supplementary funds for the Kiangnan civil and military examinations (allocated once every six years)	6,000
Wages for Kiangnan post soldiers	1,000
* Annual funds for the repair of the capital wall	500
Contribution to Kiangnan's support of lamas	183
Remittance costs for the transport of taxes from the financial commissioner's treasury to the Board	20,000[a]
Remittance costs for the transport of taxes from the grain intendant's yamen to the Board	4,000
* Supplemental funds to purchase goods for remittance to the capital when market prices exceed funds allocated by the Board	20,000[a]
Customary fees (*piao-chien yin*) sent to the financial commissioner's yamen on each of the major festivals of the lunar year	140
Wages for clerks of the financial commissioner's yamen	1,200
Paper for compilation of registers by the financial commissioner's staff	960
Remittance costs for the transport of taxes from the post intendant's yamen to the Board	2,200
Total	71,144
Yang-lien quotas:	
Governor-general	6,000
Governor	8,000
Educational commissioner	1,500
2 *hsün-ch'a* (1,200 taels each)	2,400
Financial commissioner	8,000
Judicial commissioner	6,000
Grain intendant	3,000
Post intendant	3,000
Feng-yang circuit intendant	2,000
7 prefects (2,000 taels each)	14,000
7 subprefects (300 taels each)	2,100
7 assistant subprefects (300 taels each)	2,100
Magistrates of 9 large chou and hsien (1,000 taels each)	9,000
Magistrates of 30 medium chou and hsien (800 taels each)	24,000
Magistrates of 21 small chou and hsien (600 taels each)	12,600
11 *wei* officials (400 taels each)	4,400
Total	108,100
Grand total, *yang-lien* and *kung-fei*	179,244

SOURCE: KCT 8630, Anhui Governor Wei T'ing-chen, YC 7,1,10.
* Disallowed.
[a] Approximate.

wages, and so on. What he did not sanction was thinly veiled compensation for revenues which previously would have been obtained as customary gifts and fees. Among these were gifts received from subordinates when a high official was engaged in supervision of government projects, and gifts in kind, such as annual contributions of brocades to the governor's yamen. Moreover, the cost of entertainment and travel was considered part of the expenses covered by an official's *yang-lien*. Additional compensation for what amounted to fulfillment of one's duties was not compatible with Yung-cheng's conception of the *huo-hao kuei-kung* reforms.

Nor did good intentions and an understanding of the reform process guarantee the successful implementation of *huo-hao kuei-kung*. In Chekiang it was excessive zeal that created difficulties in the management of local finances. Chekiang's *huo-hao* levies had traditionally ranged between 5 and 8 percent. These low rates were due in part to the many different fees from the salt administration and commercial duties that were available to the province's bureaucrats.[97] However, when Huang Shu-lin came to office as governor in early YC 2 (1724), he not only followed the emperor's instructions and banned the collection of customary fees but also lowered the rate of *huo-hao* to a uniform 5 percent.[98] Subsequent officials found the income from *huo-hao* inadequate for their needs, a predicament aggravated by the cumulative arrears that prevailed throughout the region. With only 130,000 taels from which to allocate *yang-lien* and *kung-fei*, Huang's successors begged for special permission to continue the arrogation of *feng-kung* contributions banned by Yung-cheng the previous year. Unable to persuade the emperor of the justice of their cause, the governor and financial commissioner resigned themselves to implementation of *huo-hao kuei-kung* on a very limited basis. Chou and hsien officials continued to collect *huo-hao* at a rate of 5 percent. Three percent was retained for their own use and the remaining 2 percent was remitted to the financial commissioner's treasury for projects of benefit to the whole province.[99] No attempt was made to provide *yang-lien* for higher officials, who continued to receive customary fees from salt merchants.[100]

It was not until Li Wei, one of Yung-cheng's three most trusted officials, was appointed Chekiang governor in 1727 that order was brought to the implementation of the reforms in that province. However, the full credit cannot go to Li Wei. Even with the administrative skill and integrity that the emperor clearly felt he would bring to his post, Li could not create funds where none existed. As his predecessor, Shih Wen-cho, had once remarked, trying to use *huo-hao* to manage all of Chekiang's expenses was like trying to cook a meal without any rice (*wu-mi chih-ch'iu*).[101] Rather, it was the emperor himself who brought to Chekiang the opportunity for rational fiscal administration.

The instrument of the emperor's largesse was an edict issued in the winter of YC 5 (1727). In it he bestowed two favors upon the people of Chekiang. In order to relieve the burden of taxes, an important factor in the generation of arrears, Yung-cheng reduced the so-called excessive tax quotas (*fu-liang*) of Chia-hsing and Hu-chou prefectures.[102] This, of course, lowered even further the basic tax upon which Chekiang's already meager *huo-hao* was levied. Therefore, the emperor also granted Chekiang the extraordinary privilege of keeping for its own use 5 percent of the *cheng-hsiang* quota usually remitted to the central government by the nine prefectures not affected by the tax reduction. In effect, Chekiang's *huo-hao* was raised to 10 percent without any additional imposition on the people. An extra 100,000 taels was made available, with only one condition for its use—that it be part of a program of complete remittance and contribute to the equitable determination of *yang-lien* to all officials in the province.[103]

Yung-cheng's gift to Chekiang enabled the province to eliminate customary fees and allocate *yang-lien* on the basis of need. Moreover, for the first time, the province was endowed with enough funds to repay its deficits, subsidize repairs to warships, and defray the costs of disaster relief, water conservancy, and other emergencies that might arise.[104]

Indeed, it was only by means of imperial gifts and the absorption of revenues not generated from the land and head tax that many provinces in the southeast were able to cope with shortages in the funds available for public expenses. Kiangsi's lower *cheng-hsiang* quota yielded far less *huo-hao* than was available in Kiangsu or Chekiang. However, a smaller tax quota did not signal a smaller bureaucracy, and Kiangsi's officials required almost as much for *yang-lien* as the other two. In addition, more than half of Kiangsi's public-expense funds were drained out of the province in the form of Board fees and costs incurred in transporting tribute and taxes to the imperial capital. (See table 4.14.) *Huo-hao* alone could not provide for all of the province's needs. Fortunately, officials in Kiangsi had access to various commercial sources, which

Table 4.14 *Kiangsi Public Expenses*

	Taels
Fees to Board of Revenue	32,000
Fees when sending the annual accounts	3,527
Fees to Board of Punishments	1,200
Fees to Board of Revenue when reporting annual accounts of military rations	500
Fees to Board of Revenue when reporting annual accounts of tribute grain	500
Fees to Board of War when reporting annual accounts of post stations	1,300
Transport expenses for the above	62
Transport expenses for shipments of dyes to the capital	1,500
Transport expenses for shipments of sandalwood to the capital	200
Board fees when sending shipments of ramie to the capital	181
Travel expenses of the tribute grain controller	660
Tribute grain controller's expenses when reporting post soldiers' accounts	250
Governor-general's yamen expenses:	
clerks' and runners' wages	1,571
stationery	700
gunpowder	200
Governor's yamen expenses:	
clerks' and runners' wages	2,899
stationery	500
pen-hsiang yin	130
Judicial commissioner's yamen expenses:	
clerks' and runners' wages	636
stationery	224
expenses for the autumn assize	338
Stipends for the superintendents of military posts and post soldiers' wages	2,726
Salt and tea money for the alms house (*p'u-chi t'ang*) in the provincial capital	300
Repairs and additions to the provincial examination halls	1,300
Supplementary funds for the *yang-lien* of submagisterial officials (partly covered by salt fees)	8,000
Financial commissioner's yamen, clerks' wages	800
Total	62,204

Source: KCT 15061, Kiangsi Governor Hsieh Min, YC 7,11,9.

substantially increased their discretionary income. Several tens of thousands of taels were accumulated each year from salt fees and surplus revenues from the Chiu-chiang and Kan-chou customs.[105] The province was also able to set aside a few thousand taels each year from the sum the central government allocated to cover the costs of shipping taxes to the capital or as assistance to other provinces.[106] Concern that Kiangsi might still suffer from want of funds for public expenses and *yang-lien* for minor officials prompted the Board of Revenue to consider a special grant of regular tax funds in this province as well. Therefore, in YC 8 (1730), Kiangsi was permitted to retain part of its deed tax (*t'ien-fang ch'i-shui*) and surplus income from the unloading tax (*lo-ti shui*).[107] The Board's generosity did not end there. In the following year, a surplus appeared in the province's annual report of *huo-hao* income and expenditure, submitted to the emperor in a secret palace memorial.[108] Most of the unspent funds were attributed to *huo-hao* saved from "food money" (*hao-hsien fan-shih chih-sheng yin*). Inasmuch as such fees generally designated extra payments made to cover the Board's administrative costs, it is likely that a substantial portion of Kiangsi's obligation to this agency of the central government was waived in the interest of local fiscal stability. By YC 11 (1733) this had meant a cumulative saving to the province of approximately 112,800 taels.[109]

Officials in Fukien were not able to circumvent their fiscal difficulties with comparable ease. Fukien's *cheng-hsiang* quota was the lowest in the southeast. Even at a rate of 14 percent, *huo-hao* produced only as much income as some provinces spent on *yang-lien* alone.[110] After a brief flirtation with a system of little remittance, the emperor's obvious disapproval impelled Fukien's officials to establish quotas for *yang-lien*, but of necessity they fell far below the standards enjoyed elsewhere in the region.

Fukien's problems were compounded by its own obligations to the central government. These were in the form not of Board fees but of expenditures for coastal defense. Fukien was a major outpost for China's maritime forces and bore a large share of the responsibility for military provisions and the construction and repair of warships.[111] So critical to the empire's security were these charges against Fukien's treasury stores that it was the only province compelled to vary its allocations of *yang-lien* year by year, according to what remained after the allocation of *kung-fei*.

Once again, the intervention of the central government was crucial in rescuing the province from financial disaster. In 1729 an annual grant of 11,320 taels in surplus commercial duties and bridge tolls was recommended by the Board of Revenue. In addition, Fukien was allowed to retain 30,739 taels in revenues from imperial lands in Taiwan.[112] These funds enabled the province to improve its *yang-lien* quotas (see table 4.15) and provide salaries for minor officials below the rank of magistrate. More important were

Table 4.15 *Revisions in Fukien's* Yang-lien *Quotas*

Office	Taels			
	Original yang-lien	Increase	New yang-lien	Total
Governor-general	7,000	9,000	16,000	16,000
Governor	7,000	5,000	12,000	12,000
Financial commissioner	6,000	4,000	10,000	10,000
Judicial commissioner	4,000	2,000	6,000	6,000
Imperial commissioner for regulating customs	3,000	1,000	4,000	4,000
4 circuit intendants	1,500*	500*	2,000*	8,000
Fuchou prefect	2,400	600	3,000	3,000
Ch'üan-chou and Chang-chou prefects	2,000*	400*	2,400*	4,800
Hsing-hua, Yen-p'ing, and Chien-ning prefects	1,800*	200*	2,000*	6,000
Shao-wu and T'ing-chou prefects	1,500*	300*	1,800*	3,600
24 subprefects and T'ing officials	300*	200*	500*	12,000
Min hsien and Hou-kuan hsien magistrates	1,300*	300*	1,600*	3,200
5 busy hsien magistrates	1,000*	200*	1,200*	5,000
15 next busiest hsien magistrates	800*	200*	1,000*	15,000
14 medium hsien magistrates	600*	200*	800*	11,200
21 simple chou and hsien	500*	100*	600*	12,000
Total new yang-lien quota				132,400

SOURCE: KCT 19111, Prince I, no date.
* Each.

the Board's efforts to release Fukien public-expense funds for the province's own use. Convinced that the construction and repair of warships and military barracks and other defense-related projects was too great a drain on Fukien's meager resources, the Board instructed the governor and governor-general to submit a routine memorial on all such expenditures so that they might be reimbursed from *cheng-hsiang*.[113]

Even this degree of Board magnanimity was insufficient to relieve Fukien of all its fiscal woes. Like Kiangnan, it had a long history of politically as well as economically motivated tax evasion. Few comments on Fukien by its nonnative administrators lacked references to the province's scheming and unruly population, a reflection as much of current tensions as of Fukien's historic role as the last bastion of armed resistance to the Manchu regime. Although the impact of arrears on *huo-hao* revenues was often a matter of acrimonious debate among Fukien's officials, it was generally recognized that approximately 30 percent of the province's land- and head-tax quota was outstanding every year.[114] Some of the deficiency this created was offset by the repayment of past arrears, but even the most conservative estimates assumed an irretrievable loss to the province of almost 20,000 taels of *huo-hao* annually. In mid-1730 the emperor discovered that his grant to Chekiang exceeded its needs by precisely this amount, and an annual subsidy of 20,000 taels per year was transferred from Chekiang to Fukien.[115]

The efforts of the Yung-cheng emperor to guarantee the fiscal health of each province and the successful implementation of the *huo-hao kuei-kung* reforms even extended to the allocation of direct cash grants of central-government revenues to areas judged to have special funding needs. The precedent for such gifts was set early in his reign, when Wan-p'ing and Ta-hsing hsien in Chihli were presented with 10,000 taels each in recognition of the additional responsibilities entailed by their proximity to the metropolitan capital. In YC 8 (1730) the emperor broadened the scope of these grants to provide one-time allocations of between 200,000 and 300,000 taels to regions throughout the empire having unusually high costs due to military expenditure.[116] Although Kiangsu, Kiangsi, and Anhui were not militarily sensitive areas, their importance from an economic and political point of view induced Yung-cheng to authorize grants of 100,000 taels to each to provide for emergencies and guard against the delays that might occur if money had to be requisitioned from the central government in times of urgent need.[117]

By the end of the Yung-cheng reign, the legitimation of a single surcharge on all land and head taxes had evolved into a complex program, adapted to the unique fiscal requirements of each province in a large and varied imperial state. Customary fees had been brought under control, and commercial and industrial revenues had been openly enlisted into the service of local government. Even a portion of the central government's own tax quota had been diverted to provincial coffers in the interests of fiscal reform. Problems still remained, and in the ensuing decades their resolution would more than once test the viability of the new fiscal order. Nevertheless, when the third Ch'ing emperor died, a system of rational local finance could stand as one of his greatest bequests to his successor and to his subjects.

5
LOCAL VARIATIONS AND UNDERLYING PRINCIPLES

TOGETHER, THE DEVELOPMENT OF THE PALACE-memorial system and the operations of local finance under the *huo-hao kuei-kung* reforms reflect an important transformation in the structure of decision making during the early Ch'ing. Both were manifestations of the Yung-cheng emperor's efforts to manipulate the lines of official communication in order to by-pass the organs of central bureaucratic decision making and establish a direct link between the emperor and his representatives in the provinces. The purposes of this realignment of power were twofold. On the one hand, it allowed the emperor far more initiative and control than had been enjoyed by any previous Ch'ing emperor. More important, however, was the creativity that this change in the power structure permitted in the reform of administration. Without Yung-cheng's strengthening of the palace-memorial system, from an occasional avenue of information on crop and weather conditions to an institutionalized link between emperor and official for the reporting of all aspects of local affairs, the *huo-hao kuei-kung* reforms could never have taken place.

Information transmitted in secret palace memorials first alerted Yung-cheng to the real fiscal instability of local administrative units. It was in his replies to palace memorials that the emperor was able to orchestrate personally the direction of reform. Despite court opposition to the ideas embodied in No-min's and Kao Ch'eng-ling's memorials, the palace-memorial system made it possible for the reforms to spread throughout the empire without the interference and the potential obstruction of central-government bureaucrats, whose administrative philosophy was far more conservative than that of the emperor or his trusted officials in the field. The variations in local adaptation of the reforms and the ambiguities in the system of reporting and accountability utilized must be viewed in this light.

The Yung-cheng emperor was concerned that provincial autonomy in managing *huo-hao* funds be maintained in order to ensure the flexibility necessary for effective administration of local government. For this reason he was determined to prevent the Board of Revenue from imposing the item-by-item supervision over *huo-hao* accounts that it exercised in auditing regular taxes. However, the emperor's instigation of changes in certain provincial reform proposals shows that he was not content to leave implementation entirely up to the provinces themselves. Why, then, did the emperor not simply issue an edict declaring a uniform pattern for reform in all provinces? First, Yung-cheng firmly believed in the principle of "suiting one's policies to the time and place."[1] To assume that the specific mechanisms for provincial funding appropriate to a province with high land-tax revenues and relatively little commercial income, such as Shansi, would be effective in a place where agricultural production was limited and resources from mining played a major role in taxation, such as Yunnan, would have been disastrous. The only way to ensure the success of a plan for legalized and rationalized local finance adapted to the particular needs of individual provinces was to allow the provinces to develop their own plans for reform. At the same time, by using the palace-memorial system to advise provincial leaders as they designed their reform proposals, the emperor could guarantee that despite local differences, each province would adhere to the basic goals of *huo-hao kuei-kung*.

We are now privy to many of the secret exchanges by which the emperor and the provincial bureaucracies worked out the formula that we call the return of the meltage fee to the public coffers. However, to officials at the time, particularly those in the central government, it is likely that the emperor's guiding role was far less apparent. Moreover, Yung-cheng himself was often deliberately noncommittal, leaving the day-to-day decisions in the hands of the officials at the top of the provincial hierarchy. This strategy was designed not only to encourage provincial officials to take a greater role in local fiscal decision making, but to deflect from the emperor's own person the responsibility for any subsequent failure of the reforms. By appearing not to have a personal stake in the decisions made in connection with the implementation of the reforms, Yung-cheng could step in and initiate changes if they were necessary, without seeming to contradict his own orders. It was for this same reason that the original proposal for reform was introduced as a "grass roots" plan from the Shansi bureaucracy and not in the form of an imperial edict.

From our previous descriptions of the *huo-hao kuei-kung* reforms we can see that differences in economic resources, regular tax obligations and even the commitment of local officials to reform led to variations in the timing and structure of local fiscal reorganization. The emperor's own insistence on local initiative and planning in order to retain some of the flexibility inherent in the informal funding system might lead us to view the reforms as lacking a unifying set of principles, regulations, and goals. In fact, nothing could be farther from the truth. Local accommodations were made in the items of revenue included in local fiscal planning, and variations did exist in the proportions of *huo-hao* set aside for *yang-lien* and provincial expenditures. Implementation was delayed in a number of places and not every province adopted the same method of *huo-hao* remittance. An examination of the reforms as a whole, however, indicates a strong unifying conception embodied in principles and regulations which, though not always promulgated in the form of administrative statutes, were nevertheless known and followed by officials in every province. It is to these general guidelines and an assessment of the reforms that we now turn.

Public-expense Funds

Public Expenses and the Central Government

One of the most important concepts implicit in the *huo-hao kuei-kung* reforms was that provincial and local administrative units should have their own regular sources of funds, provided from clearly defined tax sources and immune to exactions either from the central government or higher administrative units within the province itself. Such funds came to be known as *kung-hsiang*. Items for which they were spent were usually called *kung-yung* or *kung-shih*. *Kung-hsiang* revenues allocated for *kung-shih* were known as *kung-fei*.[2]

Provincial and local revenues were designated as *kung-hsiang* in part to distinguish them from the *cheng-hsiang* under the control of the central government. This distinction was important not only to avoid the much-feared conversion of provincial-expense revenues into regular taxes, but also to demarcate central and provincial responsibilities in financing projects on the local level. The *huo-hao kuei-kung* reforms were not, as it is sometimes assumed, devised to relieve the central government of those fiscal responsibilities that it had previously assumed in the provinces. Examination of the scattered evidence of *cheng-hsiang* allocation in the provinces shows that, to the contrary, the share of local expenses borne by the central government probably increased during this period, as part of a comprehensive drive to eliminate deficits by providing mechanisms to guarantee local solvency.

Nor did the existence of a regular source of provincial revenue lead the central government to abdicate its primary responsibility for the more costly outlays connected with military security. To the contrary, the demise of the informal funding system stimulated a greater consciousness of the need to prevent such expenditures from burdening the common people. A dispute that arose in Kansu between Shen-kan Governor-general Ch'a-lang-a and Kansu Governor Hsü Jung illustrates this point. In order to meet urgent demands for military supplies in his province, Hsü Jung had ordered the accelerated collection of taxes in arrears. Resistance by the province's taxpayers prompted Ch'a-lang-a to file a complaint with the Board of Revenue against his overly zealous subordinate. In his recommendations to the emperor on this matter, Board President Prince I condemned Hsü's actions and set forth the government's position on funding for military campaigns. "If there is a shortage of funds for military expenses and provisions, the appropriate measure is to request, in a *t'i-pen*, that the central government allocate additional funds."[3]

The 1720s and 1730s were a period of heightened central-government awareness of its role in funding major relief and construction projects. Yung-cheng's condemnation of officials who solicited *feng-kung* contributions for disaster relief was in part a reflection of his commitment to the use of *cheng-hsiang* for this purpose.[4] Likewise, when reviewing Fukien's allocations of *huo-hao*, Prince I was disturbed at the extent to which that province was using its own funds for expenditures that were rightly the responsibility of the central government. He therefore ordered the governor and governor-general to pay for expenses such as warship construction and the erection of military barracks out of *cheng-hsiang* and to report such allocations to the Board of Revenue in a routine memorial.[5]

Soon after the Yung-cheng emperor's death, the question of the role of the central government in paying for public-works projects was raised again. The issue was not whether the government should pay for such projects in the provinces, but whether the practice of assessing contributions from the local population to pay for construction projects should be allowed at all. In a memorial to the new emperor, President of the Board of Works Lai-pao and other Board members pointed out that it was the usual practice for the Board of Works to allocate *cheng-hsiang* funds for projects such as river conservancy (*ho-fang*) and the construction of dikes (*t'i-an*), city walls (*ch'eng-yuan*), floodgates, and embankments (*cha-pa*). However, in Chihli, Shantung, Kiangnan, and Szechuan officials occasionally paid for these items out of special levies on the people's landholdings. A list of the projects for which such levies had been authorized was enclosed to assist the emperor in deciding whether this exception to the rules governing fiscal responsibility should be allowed in the future.[6] In advising the emperor, the members of the Board clearly favored banning these so-called contributions and placing full responsibility for major allocations on the central government. Their arguments were truly in the spirit of the *huo-hao kuei-kung* reforms, for although they recognized that many such contributions were made voluntarily, out of a sense of public-mindedness, the Board feared that any fiscal policy based on irregular contributions would invite extortionary exactions from the local population by higher officials.[7]

Concern that *cheng-hsiang* revenues be readily available to meet the central government's obligations in the provinces even led to changes in the method of storage and distribution of regular tax funds. Steps had already been taken in this direction during the late K'ang-hsi period, when "surplus" central-government revenues were placed in treasuries in Manchuria, as well as in those of each Manchu general-in-chief, garrison commander, and brigade general.[8] The transfer of these funds out of the imperial capital to depositories in the provinces was designed to facilitate funding in case of a military emergency. However, the later expansion of this policy to include civilian treasuries was a result of the government's desire to avoid delays in the allocation of *cheng-hsiang* revenues that might lead to a greater burdening of the common taxpayer. In YC 5 (1727) it was decided to distribute additional funds to the provinces of China proper, to be stored in provincial treasuries. The provinces were classified in three groups, each receiving between 100,000 and 200,000 taels. In CL 41 (1776) the quotas of stored revenues were increased.[9] These funds were in addition to the quotas of retained taxes (*ts'un-liu*) deducted by each province from the regular taxes remitted to the capital each year, and represented total deposits, not an annual deduction. Unlike *ts'un-liu* funds, these deposits were still the property of the central government, set aside for emergency expenses in the provinces. Deposit in the provincial treasuries was designed to avoid the costs and delays involved in transporting silver to the provinces when it was needed for an emergency.[10] Expenditure was probably much more closely scrutinized than were funds allocated to the provinces directly, and appropriation without authority (*shan-tung*) was punishable by beheading.

In addition to the funds stored in the provincial treasuries, the Yung-cheng emperor also initiated a policy of depositing central-government revenues in lower-level treasuries. At first no quota was set for the amounts to be stored, but in YC 8 (1730) these deposits were regularized. The amounts to be stored in prefectural, chou, and hsien treasuries were divided into four grades, ranging from 100,000 to 300,000 taels.[11] Central-government funds distributed among local administrative units in this manner were known as *fen-ch'u chih-k'uan*.[12]

The central government's concern for the efficient allocation of *cheng-hsiang* revenues was an outgrowth of the attention focused on local finance during the *huo-hao kuei-kung* reforms. The principle that public projects should be paid for out of public funds, duly collected and budgeted for such purposes, forced the central government to reevaluate its own proper contribution to the administration of the provinces. Rather than encouraging the central government to encroach on local funds, the reforms seem to have served to highlight the respective responsibilities of each level of the government. The funds designated as *kung-hsiang* were meant to be used for quite different purposes than *cheng-hsiang* and the methods of controlling, reporting, and allocating these funds were indicative of their unique nature.

Relieving the Burdens on the People

One of the main purposes of the *huo-hao kuei-kung* reforms was to relieve the local population of the burden of indiscriminate surcharges previously levied on the pretext of supporting local administration. By simply providing officials, runners, and clerks with adequate living expenses, it was assumed that the motivation for much of the corruption associated with the tax-collection process would be eliminated. More specifically, the provision of *yang-lien* led to the abandonment of many fees that were not extortionary but had been crucial to the operation of the informal funding system.

One striking example concerns fees previously levied to support provincial education commissioners. These men were charged with the duty of supervising both the hsien- and provincial-level examinations in their provinces and with monitoring the education and behavior of degree-holders and government students. Educational commissioners were among the officials whose hidden expenses were high and whose frequent travel brought them into constant contact with the local administration. In most provinces it was the responsibility of the magistrates to provide for the education commissioner's expenses, as well as the costs of administering the examinations.[13] This was usually accomplished by demanding fees from the inhabitants of the chou or hsien. In Shensi this fee was called *k'ao-p'eng kung-yin* and was collected from the people at the time that the examinations were administered in their jurisdiction. In Szechuan the education commissioner's costs were met by gifts of ceremonial presents (*chih-i*), usually of three or four taels each, sent to the commissioner by students taking the examinations. With the institution of *yang-lien* for the education commissioner these fees were banned and at least one extra burden was lifted from the shoulders of the local population.

We have already noted the central government's commitment to the provision of funds for major public-works projects in the provinces. However, minor projects remained the responsibility of the provincial governments themselves. In the past, despite the statutory elimination of corvée labor, it was often necessary to call upon the local people to contribute both the labor and supplies for these projects. The availability of *kung-hsiang* revenues enabled provincial officials to carry out on a cash basis most transactions involved in local construction and administration.

In Kwangtung province, for example, repairs on garrison buildings and watchtowers had previously been handled by apportioning the responsibilities for the supply of labor and materials among the local inhabitants. The governor-general was naturally worried that such levies would place inordinate demands on the people's resources. But he had more practical concerns as well. The equal division of labor services among the people was an inefficient way to carry out repairs. Corvée labor on military projects aroused tensions between the soldiers and the people, and the people's lack of specialized skills led to inferior workmanship and costly delays. Procurement of supplies by means of popular "contributions" also gave clerks and runners too great an opportunity for extortion. The governor-general therefore requested permission to follow the precedent already set in Shantung (and, in fact, in many other provinces as well) of allocating the funds for repairs from the *kung-hsiang*.[14] The emperor's response to Governor-general Shi Yü-lin's request indicates that the use of *huo-hao* funds for public projects was widespread and implicit in the original intent of the reforms.[15] "Public expense funds exist expressly for you to use in the province for this purpose. What reason would there be not to carry out a plan such as this one, of such benefit to the soldiers and to the people? Deliberate and carry it out."

An examination of the sample budgets submitted by the provinces to the emperor[16] shows that funds were invariably set aside for repairs and minor construction projects such as that mentioned above. Thus, many of the surcharges to which the people were subjected under the guise of contributions for public works were eliminated. Moreover, by prohibiting the contribution of officials' and runners' salaries and wages for construction projects, the reforms eliminated one of the main pretexts for levying nonspecific surcharges as well.

The Allocation of Kung-fei

The term *kung-fei*, as we have seen, referred to all funds collected by the province that were not remitted to the central government as regular taxes or distributed to individual officials in the

form of *yang-lien*. The manner in which these funds were budgeted and disbursed varied from province to province. However,
allocation can be divided into four general categories: allowances
given to chou- and hsien-level officials to cover "outside" expenses,
allowances granted to high officials to cover the cost of yamen operations, funds set aside in the provincial treasury for local- and
provincial-level irregular and emergency expenses, and funds set
aside to cover the fees and expenses incurred in sending taxes,
goods, and reports to the central government.

Kung-fei Allowances to Chou and Hsien Officials

As we have seen, the portion of *huo-hao* revenues allocated to
chou and hsien magistrates in the form of *yang-lien* was to be used
for the official's living expenses and for the costs of operating his
own yamen. Expenses incurred outside the yamen, most notably
for famine relief and for construction projects, were not expected
to be covered by the official's *yang-lien*.

In at least some provinces, a separate allowance was granted to
the chou and hsien for the public expenses in the magistrate's jurisdiction. The separate allocation of *kung-fei* to chou and hsien
magistrates in Shantung was instituted as early as YC 3 (1725). Of
the total annual receipts of *huo-hao* in that province, 140,000
taels were budgeted for the public expenses of the whole province.
However, in accordance with Shantung's policy of partial remittance of *huo-hao*, chou and hsien magistrates were allowed to retain 22 percent of their total *huo-hao* income for their own *kung-
fei* and the costs of remitting taxes to the financial commissioner.[17]
This was beyond the *yang-lien* allocated to them by the financial
commissioner. Thus, of the total funds set aside in that province
for public expenses, 120,000 taels were retained by the chou and
hsien themselves and only 20,000 taels were deposited in the provincial treasury for the expenses of the province as a whole.[18]

The magnitude of chou and hsien public-expense allowances in
Shantung was unusual. In general, *kung-fei* allocations to lower-
level administrative units were small and seen as supplementing
yang-lien and providing for emergencies. Beyond this, it would be
the responsibility of the province to handle major expenditures.
For example, when the governor of Kansu decided to increase the
very low rate of *yang-lien* payments in that province, magistrates,
who were receiving a uniform payment of 600 taels in *yang-lien*

per year, were given differentiated *kung-fei* allowances as well. These allowances were based on the complexity of public business in their jurisdictions and ranged from an additional 600 taels for the Lanchow magistrate to 360 taels for medium chou and hsien and 160 taels for out-of-the-way chou and hsien.[19] It was also the practice to grant separate allowances of *kung-fei* to the chou and hsien in Shensi. We have no evidence of the size of these allocations. However, Shensi Governor Chang Pao stated that "chou and hsien officials are each given public expenses besides *yang-lien*, on the basis of the complexity or simplicity of [official business] in their locale."[20] Although *yang-lien* and *kung-fei* were listed together in the provincial budget submitted to the emperor,[21] the fact that they were viewed as separate items is underscored by the provision that officials holding concurrent posts be given only half the *yang-lien* of the second post but receive the full allotment of *kung-fei* for both posts.[22] Inasmuch as *yang-lien* was used for an official's personal expenses and the internal operations of his yamen, he would not need as much *yang-lien* as two officials holding two different posts. However, the "outer" expenses of hsien would not decrease during a temporary vacancy in the magistrate's office.[23]

The same motivation seems to have been at work in the decision to grant *kung-fei* to chou and hsien officials in Chihli province. Sometime after YC 7 (1729), a tutor in the Imperial Academy named Ts'ui Chi memorialized regarding the need to provide magistrates with special funds for emergency expenditures.[24] Ts'ui pointed out that unexpected matters occasionally arose on the local level for which funds were needed immediately. If the chou and hsien had already collected the taxes in their areas, they normally would transfer these regular taxes for emergency use. If, however, there were no newly collected taxes to transfer, or the official feared impeachment for the transfer of funds, he would usually borrow the necessary funds from saltshops, pawnshops, or rich households, or exact a temporary levy from the people. These borrowed funds were called *ling-pi*. After the emergency had been resolved (and presumably the funds to meet the emergency had been allocated by the provincial government), the borrowed funds were returned. However, sometimes less than the original amount was returned or a long period of time was allowed to elapse before restitution was made. As a result, both the people and the merchants were burdened. Moreover, Ts'ui was convinced that "treacherous merchants and wealthy and powerful households" were using this situation to coerce officials into alliances for their own benefit.

Ts'ui sought to rectify this situation by calling on a precedent set by the emperor in YC 7. "Shifting funds" had led to chronic deficits in Ta-hsing hsien and Wang-p'ing hsien in Chihli's Shun-te prefecture. In order to relieve the fiscal pressures on these two hsien, both of which lay within the precincts of the imperial capital, Yung-cheng had granted 10,000 taels to each to be stored in the hsien treasury and used in the event of an emergency. The magistrates could report the allocation to the metropolitan prefect and issue the necessary funds without waiting for the latter's approval. After the emergency had passed, the funds would be returned to the hsien coffers so that a balance of 10,000 taels would always be on hand.[25]

Although he recognized that other chou and hsien did not require the reserve of funds granted to Ta-hsing and Wan-p'ing, Ts'ui felt that the problem of shifting funds and borrowing from the people was a serious one throughout the empire. He therefore requested that the emperor order each governor and governor-general to rank his subordinate chou and hsien according to the complexity of government business and allocate to them a portion of the *huo-hao*, unloading tax, property-deed tax and so on that was remitted to the province for public expenses. Ts'ui suggested that the busiest areas, situated at the crossroads of major transportation routes, might receive 1,000 taels. The next busiest could be given between 500 and 800 taels. The simplest, according to Ts'ui, need not receive any emergency funds at all.

Because the emperor did not issue a rescript to Ts'ui's memorial, it is difficult to know how Yung-cheng reacted to this suggestion, or whether widespread publicity was given to Ts'ui's views. It is clear, however, that even after the reforms, officials at various levels of the government continued to be concerned that magistrates would not have enough funds to carry out public business without some supplement beyond their original *yang-lien* quotas.

In YC 12 (1734), Chihli Governor-general Li Wei addressed himself directly to the problem of shifting funds at the chou and hsien level. When the *huo-hao kuei-kung* reforms were originally implemented in Chihli, many chou and hsien had been granted a reduced level of *yang-lien* because it was assumed that they would continue to receive a portion of surplus revenues and customary fees (*hsien-yü lou-kuei*) from the post stations within their territories. In the course of the reform movement in Chihli, these fees were also eliminated, resulting in shortages in the affected chou and hsien. In the YC 12 *huo-hao* report to the emperor, Governor-general Li proposed *yang-lien* increases in those areas to bring their *yang-lien* into line with the rest of the province.[26]

The governor-general did not stop there. Li Wei also pointed out that in Chihli many magistrates continued the practice of advancing funds for public business (*yin-kung p'ei-to*). In order to pay for non-yamen expenses, magistrates were also forced occasionally to contribute funds from their *yang-lien*. To remedy this problem, Li requested that each magistrate be allowed to retain "silver for carrying out public business" (*pan-kung yin-liang*) based on the complexity of public business associated with his post.[27] By requesting a special fund for chou and hsien public expenses, Li once again affirmed the principle of the separation of *yang-lien* from "outside" expenses.

It is not clear whether other provinces made separate allocations of *kung-fei* directly to the chou and hsien. For example, the Shansi budget submitted by Kao Ch'eng-lin in YC 3 (1725) indicates that 10,158 taels were set aside for miscellaneous construction and other costs incurred by the chou and hsien.[28] However, it is not possible to determine from this document whether the funds were sent to the magistrates along with their *yang-lien* or were kept in the provincial treasury in anticipation of annual requests for construction funds by local governments.

The mere fact that we do not have direct references to chou and hsien *kung-fei* allowances outside of Chihli, Shensi, Szechuan, and Shantung does not mean that they did not exist. The gazetteer of An-yang hsien in northern Honan contains a detailed discussion of the various local expenditures that were previously met through the collection of irregular surcharges. According to the authors of the gazetteer, once the policy of *huo-hao kuei-kung* was implemented, all of these items were subsumed under a single *huo-hao* surcharge of 15 percent of the hsien's annual regular taxes.[29] If we assume that all emoluments listed for ranking officials and teachers in Confucian schools, student stipends, sacrificial expenses, and alms for the widowed and poor were paid for from retained *cheng-hsiang* taxes (*ts'un-liu*), the hsien still required 6,171.78 taels in *huo-hao* allocations to pay for normal yamen operating expenses and "outside" costs incurred by the hsien administration. It is likely, therefore, that a sizable allowance was granted to the hsien beyond the magistrate's own *yang-lien*. If this was the case in Honan, it may also have been true of other provinces for which documentation has not survived.

Kung-fei to Higher Provincial Officials

In almost every province for which a provincial budget still exists, there is evidence that high-level officials were granted regular funds beyond their *yang-lien* quotas. In most cases, these funds took the form of special allocations to cover the costs of stationery and clerical wages. Usually they were budgeted separately and may have been thought of as elements of provincial public expenses, because these grants did not extend to officials below the rank of financial commissioner.

In Anhui province, the proposed budget submitted in YC 7 (1729) by Governor Wei T'ing-chen[30] included provisions for separate payment of the wages of runners and clerks in the offices of the governor-general, governor, Tartar general and financial commissioner, as well as wages for the standard-bearers and bodyguards attached to the Tartar general and governor-general. Certain stationery costs in the governor's, governor-general's, and financial commissioner's yamen were also paid for with provincial funds. Even the educational commissioner was provided with stationery costs, and stipends were made available for the clerks and runners in his yamen when they were sent outside the provincial capital on missions.[31]

The Kiangsu budget was not as generous as Anhui's in providing for the expenses of all high officials. It did, however, include substantial funds for stationery, gunpowder, and clerical wages for both the governor's and the governor-general's yamen. The only specific grant made to the financial commissioner was for stationery expenses.[32] In Kiangsi, similar allocations were provided for the governor and governor-general, in addition to which the financial commissioner and judicial commissioner were given wages for their clerks and runners. The latter was also allowed a special fund to cover his statutory expenses.[33] Specially budgeted *kung-fei* in Kweichow seems to have been limited to the offices of the governor and governor-general. Although the province contributed only toward the stationery expenses of the governor-general's yamen, provisions made for the governor's yamen included stationery supplies, clerical salaries, military supplies, firewood and lamp oil, and salaries for his private secretaries.[34] At least part of these extraordinary allocations may be accounted for by the fact that at the time this budget was drawn up, no measures had yet been taken to provide the governor with *yang-lien*.[35]

Both the amount of *yang-lien* granted to high provincial officials and the existence of special allowances of *kung-fei* to cover yamen costs indicate that considerable care was taken to ensure the fiscal solvency of officials residing in the provincial capital. This, of course, reflected the great expenses incurred in posts which had the responsibility of managing the affairs of the whole province. However, it also cannot be ignored that the original critique of deficits and corruption, out of which the reforms grew, placed a large part of the blame on high officials. If the government was to guarantee that high officials took their duty of supervising the fiscal behavior of their subordinates seriously, it was imperative that these same officials be completely removed from financial dependence on the chou and hsien.[36]

The Kung-fei of the Whole Province

Every province had a special category of revenue stored in the provincial treasury for the purpose of meeting provincial public expenses. This silver reserve is best viewed as a kind of provincial discretionary fund. In every province but Fukien, the amount of *huo-hao* revenues to be deposited in this fund was determined not by a calculation of annual expenditure requirements, but on the basis of the surplus available after the deduction of official *yang-lien* and other fixed expenses.[37]

The logic of such a system becomes apparent when we examine the kinds of projects that were paid for from the provincial public-expense fund. The reports of Governor T'ien Wen-ching to the emperor present a representative sample of *kung-hsiang* expenditures in Honan province. In 1725, *huo-hao* funds were used to buy a plaque for a state-sponsored temple. Cash was also lent to poor peasants whose land had been inundated by sand after severe floods, so that they could buy water buffalo to assist in plowing under the sandy soil. In addition, 8,000 taels were allocated to improve the military camps in the province.[38] In 1727, 612 taels were used to buy eight government boats to outfit a ferry crossing at a strategic communications point, and an unspecified amount was issued to rebuild a temple.[39] A grant of 2,000 taels was given to the Nan-ju circuit intendant to aid in flood relief in Ku-shih hsien, an area frequently affected by floods and small-scale bandit activity.[40]

In response to imperial criticism of the size of Honan's *huo-hao* surplus, several major projects were initiated in 1729. To pay for the repair of city walls, 65,550 taels were disbursed to nineteen chou and hsien. These funds were earmarked to cover the costs of both labor and materials. Another 5,836 taels were allocated to build 2,400 new examination cubicles to provide for the growing numbers of students coming to the capital to take the provincial examinations. Over 4,700 taels were used to construct a new jail for the judicial commissioner's yamen.[41] Finally, 6,750 taels were spent to repair Honan's granaries, making it possible for the chou and hsien to replace existing buildings made of straw and mud with new facilities constructed of brick.[42] In 1730, *huo-hao* funds were allocated to update and revise the provincial gazetteer.[43] Moreover, a project to repair city walls was undertaken again in 1731, this time focusing on replacing walls that had been made of mud with more durable brick structures.[44]

The situation in Honan was not exceptional. In discussions of provincial budgets submitted to the emperor, memorialists frequently mention appropriations for famine relief, river works, construction projects, and military procurement as falling into the category of provincial public expenses. In provinces where the chou and hsien officials were given separate *kung-fei* allowances, it is likely that some of the more distinctly local projects would have been handled without provincial-level intervention. However, in places like Honan, where *huo-hao* funds were more tightly controlled at the provincial level, magistrates generally had to petition for *kung-hsiang* funds, as was the case in Ku-shih hsien's appeal for famine relief. The reforms resulted in the transfer of much of the provincial surplus from the local to the provincial level, reducing the discretionary fiscal power of the magistrate. This loss of initiative on the local level was somewhat offset by the fact that control over large public-expense funds made it possible for the provincial government to initiate projects that individual chou and hsien might not have undertaken. Moreover, as in the case of city-wall building or the large-scale construction of examination halls, economies of scale in the purchase of materials were made possible that would not have existed if projects were carried out on a piece-meal or strictly local basis, as in the past.

In the absence of detailed yearly accounts of provincial *huo-hao* expenditures, it is difficult to determine whether the benefits of *kung-hsiang* funds were distributed equitably among subordinate administrative units. For the few expenditures we do know about in Honan, it seems that *huo-hao* funds were indeed dispensed liberally throughout the province. In the case of city-wall and granary construction, poorer areas were probably the most affected, because the emphasis was placed on upgrading construction that had earlier been undertaken with poor materials. However, there was a constant danger that concentration of the provincial surplus in the capital could result in a disproportionate allocation of funds to those chou and hsien within the capital environs. This seems to have been the case in Shensi province's 1726 budget,[45] and it may reflect the fact that other chou and hsien in the province were given separate *kung-fei* allowances.

The institution of a provincial discretionary fund was in keeping with the demands of a political economy that required flexibility at all levels. Whereas administrative expenses were viewed as permanent, the expenses covered by provincial *kung-fei* were seen as temporary, often arising without warning and necessitating large outlays of money. Although floods or drought occurred frequently in many parts of China, no one could predict where or when they would strike next. On the other hand, projects such as city-wall construction or the building of charity cemeteries might be necessary only once in a generation. Upon completion of such structures, maintenance was usually turned over to local authorities. Therefore, it would not make sense for the provincial government to establish permanent bureaus of wall repair, with their own staff and budget. Where continuous funding was necessary, as in the case of boat construction in Fukien, or periodic dike maintenance throughout the empire, separate budgetary categories were established.

This is not to say that projects of the kind described above were carried out on an entirely ad hoc basis. Supervision of a particular undertaking was generally assigned to a permanent staff, headed by a nearby prefect or a circuit intendant[46] and including expectant officials who used the opportunity to practice and demonstrate their administrative skills.[47] Before allocations were made, estimates of material and labor costs were submitted by officials at the site.[48] These estimates were subject to approval by the governor and, if central-government funds were involved, by the Board of Revenue as well.[49] Officials in charge of a project were under constraints of time as well as money, as deadlines were usually set for completion in order to avoid delays and corruption.[50] If a project took more than one year, accounts were submitted annually to ensure that the funds were not being wasted and that the final report would not result in huge cost overruns. At the completion of the project, a final account of expenses was submitted and any surplus funds were returned to the provincial *kung-hsiang.*[51]

Payments to the Central Government

One final category of *kung-hsiang* expenditures should be mentioned—funds spent in fulfillment of provincial obligations to the central government. It has been stressed that the *huo-hao kuei-kung* reforms were not an attempt by the central government to appropriate a larger portion of the local government surplus. Nevertheless, aside from those funds used to repay deficits, a part of the provincial *kung-hsiang,* and in some places a sizable part, did go directly or indirectly to the central government. It should be kept in mind that all of these expenditures would have been made whether or not the reforms had been implemented. *Huo-hao kuei-kung* had the effect of transforming what had been informal fees paid personally by high provincial officials into fixed allocations disbursed from the *kung-hsiang* of the whole province. Another burden was thus lifted from the shoulders of the governors, governors-general, and commissioners, reducing their own need to exact bribes and fees from their subordinates.

Payments to the central government fell into three broad categories: fees to central-government boards when submitting taxes or accounts, transportation fees for the shipment of those taxes and accounts, and costs of supplementing the Board allocations for the purchase of goods sent to the capital. Although we have direct evidence of such payments for only six provinces, it is reasonable to assume that some provision of this kind was made in every province. This is particularly so since the *yang-lien* of central-government officials was eventually budgeted from such provincial remittances.

The size of the allocations to the central government appears to have depended on the customary fees originally sent to the boards, the province's responsibilities in providing goods for the capital, and the size of its tax quota. The portion of the provincial budget devoted to such costs in the Kiangnan region was particularly high. Of a total of 71,144 taels allocated for public expenses in Anhui, over 50,000 taels were spent for purposes of no benefit to the province. These included fees to the Board of Revenue and its Board of Scrutiny at the time of the annual accounting, *fan-shih* to the Board of Punishments, the costs of remitting taxes to the Board, and supplemental funds for the purchase of goods costing more than the Board price.[52]

In Kiangsu, approximately 56,000 taels were set aside to pay expenses incurred in the remittance of taxes and to supplement the costs of dyes and pewter sent to the capital.[53] However, inasmuch as that province's total *kung-fei* budget was considerably larger than Anhui's, payments to the central government did not cut as deeply into the Kiangsu surplus. This could not be said of Kiangsi, where almost half of the fixed public expenses of 62,204 taels were allocated for Board fees and the transport of regular taxes and shipments of goods to the capital in Peking.[54] Chihli, as the site of the imperial capital, bore a particularly large responsibility for Board expenses in the form of remittance fees. If data for 1729 are typical, that province also spent about as much on Board fees as it did for all other provincial public expenses.[55] These figures, of course, refer only to the fixed allocations in each province. Because all four provinces had surplus *huo-hao* and *kung-fei* which could be used as a discretionary provincial fund, the proportion of provincial revenues siphoned off by the central government, although high, was not as enormous as it first appears.

Outside these two regions, allocations of Board fees were probably considerably lower. Particularly in newly developing areas with low agricultural productivity, the central government was hesitant to make unreasonable demands on local resources. Of the 79,740 taels spent by Kansu province for *yang-lien* and public expenses, only 2,000 taels were sent to the Board of Revenues and Punishments in the form of clerical fees.[56] Similarly, Kweichow spent only slightly more than 2,200 taels for this purpose.[57]

Accounting and Accountability

The manner in which officials reported *huo-hao* income and expenditure to the central government provides an excellent example of the Yung-cheng emperor's reliance on personal authority in dealing with the provincial bureaucracy. Just as the decisions leading up to the adoption of *huo-hao kuei-kung* were taken outside the normal bureaucratic channels of communications, so the emperor divorced the day-to-day administration of the new provincial funds from routine scrutiny by the Boards. The collection and allocation of regular taxes were subject to rigorous Board surveillance throughout the *tsou-hsiao* system of annual accounting. However, provincial authorities were specifically instructed not to report their *huo-hao* income to the Boards, but only to inform the emperor of their decisions via secret palace memorials.[58]

All deliberations concerning rates of collection, distribution of funds in the form of *yang-lien* or *kung-fei*, methods of remittance, and so on were undertaken by the provincial governors, governors-general, and financial commissioners. Although there is no record of the deliberations themselves, formal input from the lower levels of government probably was minimal, confined to requests for grants of aid for specific projects. Once the basic plan for *huo-hao* reform was established in a province, the governor or financial commissioner was required only to submit an annual report to the emperor in the form of a yellow register (*huang-ts'e*) similar to those submitted to the emperor for regular taxes.[59] These yellow registers merely listed total funds, following the format of the four-column account. In this manner the emperor was kept informed of the aggregate income and expenditures in a province, leaving the details of disbursement to the provincial authorities themselves.

Occasionally a more elaborate report of expenditures was made, particularly when a change in official personnel in the provincial capital took place.[60] These reports were similar to the *chiao-tai* reports submitted as evidence of proper management of regular tax funds when an official left office. In the case of both yellow registers and the more irregular end-of-term reports, the emperor usually returned the memorial without comment or with a simple "noted" (*lan*) appended to the end of the account.

The implications of this arrangement were twofold. On the one hand, the Yung-cheng emperor displayed his continuing concern for the fiscal independence of the provincial governments. If the *huo-hao kuei-kung* reforms were to succeed, the provincial governments had to be assured the same flexibility in allocating funds that had been possible under the informal funding system. If the finances of the provincial treasury were subject to the same item-by-item scrutiny that was applied to the disbursement of *cheng-hsiang* funds, it would have been impossible for the provinces to respond quickly to emergencies or react to changing local conditions. The emperor acknowledged that he could not know the conditions within the provinces in the same way that a local official could. It was therefore logical to leave the details of *huo-hao* expenditure to these men.

Yung-cheng also seems to have had a special antipathy toward the interference of court officials in local fiscal affairs. During the debates surrounding the implementation of the reforms, the conservatism of officials within the capital bureaucracy, who were divorced from the daily operations of local administration, became readily apparent. Although the emperor was quick to shift the personnel holding the highest offices in the provinces, filling these crucial posts with men whose integrity and administrative philosophy he could trust, it was far more difficult to alter the composition of the central bureaucracy. Many of these men were holdovers from his father's reign, and their approach to local finance reflected the K'ang-hsi emperor's reluctance to tamper with the balance of fiscal power by legalizing *huo-hao*. Moreover, the emperor may have felt that these men, who had viewed deficits only in terms of corruption, and had failed to recognize the real shortage of funds on the provincial and local level, would not have been sympathetic to the spending needs of provincial administration.

The emperor did give the governors and financial commissioners broad discretionary powers in the allocation of provincial funds. In fact, there is reason to believe that he was willing to tolerate far more local independence than even the officials themselves recognized. The yellow registers of annual accounts were the only reports specifically required of officials by the emperor. Yet the emperor was constantly being barraged by reports ranging from those of the *chiao-tai* type mentioned above to two- or three-line notifications whenever a large sum of money was allocated for any purpose. These reports are symptomatic of a form of bureaucratic paranoia common among officials during the Ch'ing period. Even when given authority in allocating provincial funds, high provincial officials felt the need to report their actions to the emperor. In all probability, they hoped to cover themselves in case their successors questioned the way in which funds were handled during their tenure. This fear grew out of the heavy emphasis placed on an official's handling of tax matters in his career evaluations. Consequently, even though *huo-hao* revenues were not subject to the same sanctions and review that were applied to regular taxes, the association between the mishandling of taxes and impeachment seems to have been too ingrained in the officials' collective psyche to allow them to exercise their autonomy in such matters.

In contrast to the often compulsive reporting by high provincial officials themselves was the emperor's own responses to these reports. When the emperor chose to issue any rescript to a memorial on the handling of *huo-hao* funds it was usually to urge the memorialist to take greater responsibility for decision-making himself. Sometimes he simply stated that he was leaving the decision up to the memorialist, as in the case of a report by the governor and governor-general of Kwangtung regarding allocations of *yang-lien* for submagisterial-level officials.[61] More often the emperor simply indicated that he would not interfere in local fiscal affairs by stating that he took no interest in memorials of this kind,[62] or that his habit was merely to glance at such memorials and nothing more.[63] Occasionally, Yung-cheng even displayed some exasperation when officials continued to request imperial approval for decisions that should have been their own. After a long memorial from the Kiangsi governor requesting raises in certain officials' *yang-lien* allowances, the emperor wrote in an extremely informal style, "Okay, if it should be raised then raise it."[64]

This is not to say that the management of *huo-hao* revenues was completely unsupervised. Notwithstanding his protestations to the contrary, the emperor did keep a close watch over the management of provincial finances through the palace-memorial system. As we have seen in the discussion of the implementation of the reforms, Yung-cheng was not averse to criticizing the manner in which a governor was handling the remittance, allocation, or disbursement of *huo-hao* revenues. The emperor also played a major role in guaranteeing that allocations were equitable and served the goal of redistributing the resources of a province where they were needed. Moreover, as the only agent privy to knowledge of the reforms in every province, the emperor also played an integrative role, informing officials as to how the reforms were being carried out elsewhere and ensuring that there were no undue discrepancies in the rates of *yang-lien* being paid to officials of comparable rank and responsibilities in different provinces.[65] Thus, although the actual management and allocation of *yang-lien* was in the hands of the governor and financial commissioner, these funds were still ritually attributed to the emperor as the ultimate source of all revenues and laws in the empire. Even when an official decided on his own *yang-lien*, it was not uncommon to send a memorial thanking the emperor for his magnanimity in granting the official this new source of funds.[66]

The emperor's occasional intervention in provincial financial affairs was not intended as an encroachment on provincial authority.

In view of the structure of authority in the Ch'ing legal system, it played an important function in strengthening the power of the provincial leadership as well as enabling the emperor to check abuses in the exercise of that leadership. But without the assignment of some general supervisory functions to the Board of Revenue, the provincial authorities had no means to enforce their control over the funds emanating from the local level. Because *huo-hao* revenues were not integrated into the regular Board of Revenue statutes, the provinces were allowed a far greater degree of autonomy in handling *huo-hao* than they had in handling *cheng-hsiang*. This assured considerable flexibility in the allocation of funds. However, it had one serious drawback, which had its roots in the dual nature of the Ch'ing legal system. Judicial cases involving crimes committed by commoners could be tried and adjudged at all levels of the bureaucracy. Although appeals could be made to the court and the emperor, provincial officials did not require central-government intervention in handling most cases. The same was not true when crimes involved misconduct in office. In such cases, although the official's superior in the provinces could recommend sanctions, the decision to apply sanctions against an official lay with the Boards and the emperor. Moreover, impeachable crimes had to be defined in the statutes of the various Boards, which taken together constituted a code of official discipline. In order to preserve provincial fiscal autonomy, *huo-hao* matters had not been integrated into the official code, hence corruption or recalcitrance in the implementation of *huo-hao kuei-kung* could not be dealt with through the usual channels used in cases of violation of the disciplinary code. High officials had only one way to deal with malfeasance in the newly created *huo-hao kuei-kung* system, which was to report the malfeasance directly to the emperor in a secret palace memorial and request that special sanctions be applied against the official involved.

Once deficits were paid up, as pointed out in chapter 4, magistrates in Shansi were reluctant to continue remitting *huo-hao* to the provincial treasury. This problem was not limited to Shansi province alone. In YC 10, Hupei Governor Wang Shih-chün sought imperial guidance in handling a similar problem in his province. Between YC 1 and YC 3, twelve hsien magistrates failed to remit a total of 4,232 taels of *huo-hao* to the provincial treasury. Although the amount was small, these cases were indicative of the difficulties encountered in trying to control *huo-hao* revenues. The governor had clear authority to impeach a subordinate and demand that he repay *cheng-hsiang* deficits, but he did not know if he could do the same in the case of deficits in the *kung-hsiang*.[67] The emperor assured Wang that deficits in the provincial public-expense fund were an even more serious matter than shortages in *cheng-hsiang* revenues, and advised against leniency in dealing with these magistrates. Stern procedures for retrieving the funds were therefore set in motion, procedures which the governor probably would not have invoked without the authorization of the emperor.

The Yung-cheng emperor's extraordinary attention to the details of everyday administration is well known. Even a cursory examination of the thousands of memorials bearing his voluminous personal comments provides convincing evidence of his care and understanding in supervising local-government affairs. In his effort to bypass normal bureaucratic channels and deal with local fiscal matters through direct communications with provincial officials, Yung-cheng had no choice but to handle personally the numerous memorials received at his quarters every day. There is evidence, however, that the emperor did not shoulder the entire burden himself. The few extant disposition slips submitted to the emperor on local fiscal matters by Prince I, in his capacity as President of the Board of Revenue, indicate that occasionally the emperor did turn to his most trusted fiscal advisors in deciding provincial fiscal issues. Even though secret palace memorials were to be viewed only by the emperor and the memorialist, Yung-cheng did sometimes show *tsou-che* concerning *huo-hao* and *yang-lien* matters to the Board of Revenue. Furthermore, these secret palace memorials were, in rare instances, even copied and kept in the Board's files.[68] Nevertheless, the Board only acted in an advisory capacity when reviewing these memorials and did not have the same powers of scrutiny that it exercised in the acceptance or rejection of *cheng-hsiang* accounts.

In YC 9 (1731), the system of reporting was modified to include additional input by the Board of Revenue. According to a Board communiqué, all governors and governors-general were ordered to inform the Board of any increases made in *yang-lien* quotas. The Board would then deliberate whether or not the proposed increases should be approved, and their recommendation would be sent to the emperor. The Board also indicated that it would inspect the accounts of *huo-hao* funds spent and saved when they were reported annually to the emperor.[69] This does not appear to have been an order requiring provincial officials to report their annual *huo-hao* accounts in a routine *tsou-hsiao tse*, but rather was an announcement of the Board's intention to continue its practice of informally advising the emperor on the accounts submitted as secret palace memorials. It was not until the Ch'ien-lung reign that the real discretionary powers of the provincial government in the management of local finances were encroached upon by the central government.

Yang-lien
Changes in Yang-lien Allocations

The *yang-lien* rates established in the early years of the Yung-cheng reign were not viewed as static quotas. Throughout the first decade of the reforms there were numerous instances of *yang-lien* being increased and occasionally diminished in order to meet the needs of officials in the field. Sometimes these increases were in the form of across-the-board raises for all officials in a province. At other times an increase was granted to an individual official whose expenses were agreed to be larger than the funds provided when *huo-hao kuei-kung* was first implemented in his province. Often the original deliberation to raise *yang-lien* came from the provincial officials themselves, but a change in rates could be called for by the emperor and, after 1731, at the instigation of the Board of Revenue in its advisory capacity.

The most striking across-the-board raises in *yang-lien* occurred in Fukien and in Honan. The rates of *yang-lien* originally formulated in Fukien were considerably lower than those for comparable posts in other provinces in central China. This was the result of both the low rate of *huo-hao* collected in that province and the high proportion of provincial funds that had to be allocated for administration and defense. As we have seen in chapter 4, the emperor was concerned that allocations of *yang-lien* in Fukien would be insufficient and ordered that surplus revenues from official lands and miscellaneous commercial taxes be used to compensate for shortages in provincial funds. Over 40,000 taels were required to bring Fukien's *yang-lien* rates into line with the needs of local officials.[70] When the surplus revenues granted by the emperor proved inadequate to meet all the costs of *yang-lien* and *kung-fei*, an additional grant of 20,000 taels was made to the Fukien treasury from *cheng-hsiang* revenues disbursed by imperial decree to Chekiang province.[71]

The circumstances leading to increases in Honan's *yang-lien* were the opposite of those found in Fukien. The success of the *huo-hao kuei-kung* reforms in Honan was reflected in an ever-increasing surplus in the provincial treasury. In 1728 the emperor reacted to this accumulation of revenues by ordering Honan Governor T'ien Wen-ching to devise ways to spend more of the provincial income for the benefit of the people and administration. T'ien responded by suggesting increases in the *yang-lien* quotas disbursed to lower-level officials. The governor felt that the 3,000 taels annually allocated to each circuit intendant was adequate. He did, however, ask for an increase of 400 taels for chou and hsien magistrates and 300 taels for independent chou magistrates. This raised the *yang-lien* as follows: independent chou magistrates to 1,800 taels, large chou and hsien to 1,400 taels, medium chou and hsien to 1,200 taels, and small hsien to 1,000 taels.[72]

There are also numerous examples of *yang-lien* rates being increased for individual posts. Such raises were generally proposed by the provincial governor or financial commissioner. In YC 5 (1727), Li Wei requested that the Chekiang educational commissioner's *yang-lien* be raised from 1,000 taels to 2,500 taels.[73] In YC 9 (1731), Kiangsi Governor Hsieh Min proposed that several border hsien and small hsien with large populations of "tent people" be reclassified as medium and large hsien and their *yang-lien* raised accordingly.[74] These changes were made in recognition of the difficulty entailed in controlling border areas and in preventing the people from fleeing into neighboring provinces to evade taxation. The grain and post intendants in Kiangsi had originally been in charge only of tribute grain and post and salt affairs. During the Yung-cheng period, however, each was given jurisdiction over three prefectures and was made responsible for all judicial matters in their respective subordinate chou and hsien. As a result, both intendants were faced with greatly increased travel expenses and the costs of hiring additional private secretaries expert in local administrative and legal issues. Therefore a raise in *yang-lien* was also requested for them.[75]

Changes in the remittance of customary fees could also give rise to modifications in the allocation of *yang-lien*. When the reform first went into effect, the director-general of water conservancy

(*Tsung-ho*) received contributions from salt merchants which constituted the major portion of his *yang-lien*. When these contributions were eliminated, the director-general was left with only a small grant from merchants and surplus silver from the river treasury, totaling around 5,000 taels. This was not enough to cover the costs of travel to inspect construction sites, assisting the governor, rewarding soldiers attached to the river administration, hiring private secretaries, and so on. Therefore, a request was made that a raise in *yang-lien* be granted for this post.[76] The elimination of fees as a means to support river administration and the substitution of increased *yang-lien* also reflected the gradual trend toward greater fiscal rationalization in local administration.

Officials sometimes requested raises in *yang-lien* for their own posts. In YC 6 (1728), the Hupei financial commissioner complained that the approximately 11,600 taels he received for *yang-lien* and operating expenses were too little in view of the high costs of remitting accounts to the Board and the numerous private secretaries and servants needed to man the province's top financial yamen. Hsü Ting claimed that because of the inadequacy of the funds provided in the provincial budget, he had been forced to rely on assistance from his father to cover his official expenses. This would not have been at all unusual under the prereform system of financing. Moreover, the usual response of emperors to claims such as Hsü's would have been an admonition to exercise greater frugality in his personal and official life. That Hsü Ting's own fears of such a reply proved unfounded is testimony to the transformation of the concept of fiscal responsibility after the reforms. Instead of chastising Hsü for excessive expenditures, Yung-cheng praised the plan to raise his *yang-lien* and stated that it had never been the policy of the dynasty to require an official's family to support him financially in the fulfillment of his administrative duties.[77]

By the end of the Yung-cheng period, officials were sometimes quite militant in insisting upon their right to receive adequate *yang-lien*. Szechuan Governor-general Huang T'ing-kuei was particularly angry about the way in which his request for a raise in *yang-lien* was handled after authority to judge such requests was extended to the court. Huang memorialized that the Szechuan governor-general's *yang-lien* was only 6,000 taels and requested that it be augmented by 4,000 taels. He received a reply from the Grand Secretaries Chang T'ing-hu and Chiang T'ing-hsi by court letter. Enclosed was an imperial edict which stated that the sum of

6,000 taels was really insufficient. However, since Huang was concurrently in charge of the post of provincial commander-in-chief, the edict ordered the grand secretaries to inquire whether or not Huang received *yang-lien* for that second post, and expressed anger that he had failed to mention this additional *yang-lien* in his memorial.[78]

Huang devoted an entire page of his rejoinder to insisting that he was not attempting to profit personally from his official responsibilities, pointing out that the post of provincial commander-in-chief carried no *yang-lien*, but only about 2,800 taels a year from emoluments and military rations. Huang stated that he had already run into shortages and had been forced to shift funds and to borrow 1,000 taels from the governor, which he had not yet been able to repay. Moreover, much of the funds from his military command had gone to pay for two military expeditions to Liang-shan, to reward soldiers, and to hire laborers and coolies. Finally, Huang complained that although the duties of the governor-general were the most numerous, the governor received 19,000 taels annually in *yang-lien* and the financial commissioner received 10,000 taels. He thereupon closed his memorial by doubling his original request to 20,000 taels per year for the governor-general's *yang-lien*, a request which the emperor acknowledged and accepted with a simple response of "noted."[79]

In general, the emperor left the determination of *yang-lien* rates to the provincial officials themselves. When he did intervene, it was most often when *yang-lien* was being established for a post for the first time. In such cases the emperor acted as an advocate for the official concerned to ensure that the *yang-lien* decided on was sufficient for his needs. For example, when the Anhui, Kiangsu, and Kiangsi governors were consulted to provide *yang-lien* for the Liang-chiang governor-general, it was suggested that the total contribution from the three provinces be 14,000 taels. Yung-cheng felt that this would not be enough and hinted that 20,000 taels would be a more appropriate figure.[80] Imperial intervention was also instrumental in guaranteeing adequate *yang-lien* for the Hunan governor. When Financial Commissioner Chu Kang suggested that the governor be granted a quarterly allowance of 1,000 taels, for an annual *yang-lien* of 4,000 taels, the emperor replied:[81]

> How can 1,000 taels be enough for the governor's needs? Previously, when Pu-lan-t'ai memorialized to

sell his family property [in order to finance his admin-
istration] I sent a rescript vehemently stating that this
was not right. When the new governor takes office, you
should discuss adequate *yang-lien* [with him]. Your
present stance makes you appear to be offering a pretense of virtue. I do not make it a principle to have
high provincial officials perform their duties on an
empty stomach [i.e., without adequate compensation].
As Hunan Financial Commissioner these last few years
you understand the situation thoroughly. . . . Handle
matters fairly.

In rare instances an official requested that his *yang-lien* be lowered. In YC 11 (1733), the Shansi governor reported that the new
acting judicial commissioner had spent only 7,000 taels of his annual 10,000-tael *yang-lien*. He therefore requested that the extra
3,000 taels be returned to the provincial public-expense fund.[82]
This, however, was reduction in that individual's *yang-lien* and
probably did not mean a revaluation of the *yang-lien* quotas for all
future judicial commissioners in the province. The only instance
where the downward adjustment of *yang-lien* might have had an
institutional impact was T'ien Wen-ching's refusal to accept additional *yang-lien* when he was elevated from the post of Honan
governor to that of Honan-Shantung governor-general.[83] However,
this post was created expressly for T'ien and was eliminated soon
after his death.

Extension of Yang-lien

The trend toward fiscal rationalization was not reflected merely
in increased *yang-lien* for posts where the original quota had
proven inadequate. As the reforms became established, the number of officials to whom it was granted was also extended to include all the ranking civil officials in the provinces. We have already seen how the omission of *yang-lien* for the governor and
governor-general of several provinces was quickly rectified.[84] In
many provinces it was several years before *yang-lien* was provided
for education commissioners. This was because they frequently had
an informal source of funds that was considered legitimate and
served as a substitute for *yang-lien*. In general, these funds were
linked to the administration of the civil-service examinations. For
example, whenever the education commissioner in Shensi went to
an area to hold the lower examinations, gifts were supplied by the

chou and hsien whose residents were among those attending the examination. These gifts were called *k'ao-p'eng kung-ying* or contributions of supplies to the examination hall, but were really obtained by levying surcharges on the local populace.[85] In Hupei the education commissioner received his funds from the sale of the examination booklets used by students to write their answers. For each set, a fee of two or three taels above the cost of the paper was charged, yielding as much as 6,000 taels per year.[86] These sources of funds were so widely accepted that in YC 5 (1727), when the Kwangtung education commissioner, Yang Erh-te, requested an increase in his *yang-lien*, the governor memorialized that the request should not be granted, because it was expected that the education commissioner would be provided with funds by the chou and hsien in which he conducted the examinations.[87]

The emperor left it up to the individual provinces to decide whether or not to grant *yang-lien* to education commissioners. On the whole he felt that to grant them four or five thousand taels a year was appropriate.[88] Moreover, Yung-cheng hoped that providing them with *yang-lien* would be an incentive to greater diligence in the execution of their duties.[89] The reason the emperor did not insist on the suspension of contributions for the support of these officials and the institution of empire-wide *yang-lien* payments for education commissioners may be traced to his fear that some officials would nevertheless continue to exact fees for holding the examinations. Because this fee was paid directly by those involved in the examinations, it was not something that could be easily stopped by applying official sanctions. There was no way to ensure that such a widely accepted practice could indeed be eliminated by fiat.[90] Despite the emperor's lack of leadership in this matter, efforts were made eventually in several provinces that had relied on informal funding practices to bring the funding of education commissioners into the mainstream of the reforms.[91]

When the *huo-hao kuei-kung* reforms were originally formulated, *yang-lien* was provided only for civil officials of the rank of magistrate and above. Those officials closest to the people, including assistant magistrates and the numerous officials attached to the main administrative yamen, such as registrars, jailors, education officers, and other minor officials of the eighth, ninth, and unclassified rank (*tso-tsa*) were not included in the new system of funding. The reasons for this omission were twofold. On the one hand, officers below the rank of magistrate were not considered part of the main body of the bureaucracy. Often these posts were filled by people who had not passed the highest levels of the examination system or who had obtained their rank by purchase. Except in rare instances, they were not eligible for promotion to higher positions, and although holding office, they were viewed by the rest of officialdom as not far removed from the clerks and runners below them. Moreover, they did not command the sort of multifunctional yamen found at higher levels in the bureaucracy and were not seen as requiring the extensive staff found under officials of higher rank. Economic constraints also played a part in their exclusion from the *yang-lien* rolls. During the early years of the reforms, there was a constant fear that *huo-hao* revenues would not be sufficient to cover all the costs of provincial administration. To include these low-level functionaries in the ranks of officials supplied with *yang-lien* might have been judged to be an inordinate burden on provincial resources.

This proposition is confirmed by the Yung-cheng emperor's response to the first attempt to bring minor officials into the *yang-lien* budget. Honan Governor T'ien Wen-ching first proposed providing *yang-lien* for low-level functionaries early in YC 3 (1725). He pointed out that these officials had important duties and were constantly being sent out on government missions. Their material rewards were meager, however, and their rank low, providing little incentive for them to abide by the official disciplinary code. T'ien, who himself had risen from the rank of assistant hsien magistrate, felt that many of the men in such posts were extremely talented, and he proposed that if the emperor extended his benevolence to them by granting them *yang-lien*, they naturally would respond by displaying more virtue and devotion in the execution of their duties.[92]

The emperor was not as confident as T'ien of the efficacy of such a policy. Although once again insisting that all such decisions were up to the governors and governors-general, Yung-cheng accepted the popular notion that very few of these low officials were really distinguished civil servants. The extraordinary few who were could be rewarded under a recent imperial act of grace that permitted their recommendation for promotion to higher rank. Rather than grant *yang-lien* to these lowly subordinates, the emperor felt it would be better to increase the *yang-lien* of the magistrates so as to enable them to improve the general level of administration throughout the chou and hsien. Yung-cheng's real concern, however, was reflected in the last lines of his rescript:[93]

> In this instance I have unavoidably been overly severe. You should weigh the situation further and not immediately take my words for the truth. . . . I am even more concerned that this matter does not concern Honan province alone. If there are provinces whose *huo-hao* is insufficient, where will they find the funds to spread this benevolence? You must think further about this point.

In other words, the emperor was concerned that by allowing low-level officials in Honan to receive *yang-lien* he would appear to be favoring the officials of one province over the others. Local differences in the application of the reforms were permissible so long as the general structure of fiscal management remained fairly uniform throughout the empire. Honan's surplus could not be used to provide its officials with benefits that other provinces could not match. So long as it was unclear whether other provinces would be able to follow suit, it was not advisable to allow Honan alone to take the reforms this major step further, no matter what the benefits would be in eliminating local corruption and rationalizing local fiscal management.

By the beginning of YC 6 (1728), it was becoming apparent that the reforms were a success and that adequate funds could probably be found to allow every province to extend its *yang-lien* budget to include all officials. Early in the year, T'ien Wen-ching once again proposed that low-level officials be provided with *yang-lien*. The real intention of such a move, to eliminate corruption on the lowest levels of the bureaucracy, was made clear by T'ien's concession that officials who were not in direct contact with the people need not be considered for *yang-lien*. However, such officials as assistant and subassistant prefects and magistrates and registrars, whose role in supervising and investigating local affairs brought them into close daily contact with the people, would be given *yang-lien* of between 80 and 120 taels.[94] This time the emperor found T'ien Wen-ching's proposal both fair and appropriate and told him to carry it out.

Concern about the continued acceptance of customary fees despite the institution of *yang-lien* was instrumental in the decision to extend this new dimension of the reforms beyond Honan province. In mid-1728, T'ien Wen-ching was promoted to the rank of governor-general of Honan and Shantung. One of his first acts as governor-general was to expose the continued use of customary fees as a means of funding in Shantung. T'ien's report prompted an edict by the emperor that was to result in the extension of *yang-lien* to all officials in the provinces as the most effective means to eliminate forever these corrupt and unregulated exchanges of funds.

In his edict of the eighth month of YC 6, the emperor acknowledged that some officials continued to receive *lou-kuei* regardless of the fact that they had already been granted *yang-lien*. This was to be deplored. Yung-cheng ordered the governors and governors-general of each province to investigate their subordinates one by one and report on their activities in a secret palace memorial. The emperor still felt that the solution to this problem was to ensure that every official had adequate *yang-lien*. Therefore, he also ordered the governors and governors-general to find out if there were any officials under them who had not yet been granted *yang-lien* and to extend it to them. At the same time Yung-cheng publicly endorsed the complete remittance of *huo-hao* to the financial commissioner and public redistribution of funds from the provincial treasury.[95]

One of the first provinces to respond to the emperor's edict was Hunan. The edict prompted Hunan to switch from partial to complete remittance of *huo-hao* according to the Shansi-Honan model. Officials in Hunan also used this opportunity to calculate *yang-lien* for minor officials within the yamen at all levels of the provincial bureaucracy. Following the principles set down by T'ien Wen-ching, these new grants of *yang-lien* were made only to officials who came into close contact with the people or who frequently were sent outside the yamen on official missions. Among those included were the secretaries in the financial and judicial commissioners' yamen (*li-men*, *cho-mo*), treasury keepers, jail wardens, registrars, and assistant chou and hsien magistrates.[96] Hunan's *huo-hao* revenues were not as large as Honan's; this accounts for the lower rates at which *yang-lien* was granted to these officials. Nevertheless, the province was able to supplement the cost of these additions to the provincial budget with the return to the public coffers of 8,000 taels in salt fees formerly sent to the grain intendant.[97]

Not every province was so quick to comply with the intent of the emperor's edict. In many instances, attempts were made to increase the existing *yang-lien* quotas or provide funds only for higher officials who had not been previously included in the provincial budget. It was in such cases that Prince I and the Board of Revenue began to exercise the initiative that eventually may have led to their greater authority in advising on *yang-lien* matters. For example, in YC 7 (1729) Chihli Governor-general Yang K'un sent the emperor a recapitulation of the deliberations conducted in that province to provide each official with adequate and fair *yang-lien*. Prince I and the Board found the amounts agreed upon to be generally appropriate and recommended that the emperor order him to allocate the *yang-lien* as suggested and turn the original accounting report over to the Board. Although these deliberations provided *yang-lien* for independent and regular chou subassistant magistrates, no attempt was made to provide *yang-lien* for officials of the rank of assistant hsien magistrate and below. In view of the fact that almost 80,000 taels still remained in the Chihli treasury after some 220,000 taels were disbursed as *yang-lien*, the Board recommended that the remaining low officials be provided with *yang-lien* ranging from several tens of taels to around 100 taels apiece.[98]

The emperor quickly reacted to the Board recommendation and ordered Yang K'un to reconsider *yang-lien* for minor officials. Yang consulted the financial commissioner and submitted a yellow register to the emperor listing possible rates of *yang-lien* for the officials in question. Surprisingly, the emperor responded that the rates seemed somewhat high and that he feared they would be too great a drain on provincial resources. Once again, Yung-cheng took the administration of Honan's finances under T'ien Wen-ching as a model and told Yang that he might inquire secretly as to the amounts these officials were granted in that province.[99] In the meantime, Yang K'un was replaced as governor-general by Metropolitan Censor T'ang Chih-yü. T'ang resubmitted a reduced *yang-lien* schedule that would cost the province slightly over 8,600 taels annually for minor officials, leaving the province a surplus for public expenses of over 30,000 taels.[100] These new rates were submitted to the emperor in the form of a yellow register and to the Board of Revenue in the form of a clear account (*ch'ing-ts'e*), indicating the increasing role being assumed by the Board in *yang-lien* matters.

Yang-lien for minor officials was such a novel concept that many provinces took years to carry it out. Occasionally delays were due to disputes over the amount of *yang-lien* that should be provided. In Kwangtung the provincial leadership readily acceded to the idea of providing *yang-lien* for these officials. However, differing interpretations of the purpose of salaries led to disagreement over acceptable rates. Both the governor-general and the acting governor regarded these new grants of *yang-lien* as token payments, along the lines of the emoluments granted officials by the emperor in the form of *feng-yin*. Therefore, they proposed simply to supply each official with funds from *huo-hao* equivalent to their *feng-yin* quota, thus doubling their salaries.[101] The financial commissioner disagreed with this method, pointing out that *yang-lien* was not intended merely to pay for an official's personal expenses, but also to cover the costs of yamen administration and missions outside the yamen. If this plan were followed, the officials would have enough to support their families, but nothing more.[102] The emperor left the decision up to the provincial authorities, who eventually came around to the financial commissioner's point of view. As a result, *yang-lien* for lower officials was set at between 60 and 80 taels, a decision that added 17,520 taels in new fixed expenses to the already strained Kwangtung provincial budget. The funds for the additional *yang-lien* grants were provided by surplus revenues from Kwangtung's commercial licensing tax (*shui-ch'i hsien-yü yin*).[103]

In view of the number of people involved, it is not surprising that ranking officials were hesitant to allocate large quotas for minor officials' *yang-lien*. In Kwangtung alone there were 255 officials for whom *yang-lien* was added. The largest categories were jail wardens (78) and subdistrict magistrates (126).[104] This latter figure is of particular interest because it shows that in at least some hsien, not only was there an assistant magistrate, but there must have been more than one subdistrict magistrate below him, bringing the administration far closer to the people than has generally been recognized. By providing such officials with sufficient administrative funds, the government was clearly taking an important step in the direction of eliminating illegal surcharges and extortion.

The control and elimination of corruption at the lowest levels of the administration seems to have been foremost in the minds of provincial officials as they sought to find the funds to furnish minor officials with *yang-lien*. As each province reported its deliberations to the emperor, several concerns expressed by the Kiangnan governor-general and Anhui governor were echoed repeatedly. Anhui had originally failed to provide *yang-lien* for its minor officials because there was not enough *huo-hao* in the provincial treasury. It was common knowledge that because these functionaries had no means to pay for their administrative expenses they exacted money from the villagers in their areas (*ssu-ch'u li-hsia*) and engaged in the practice of handling litigation for the people without official authorization (*shan-shou min-ssu*).[105] In YC 10 (1732), it was discovered that in Anhui salt fees of approximately 30,000 taels were being sent to high and low yamen in the province. With the approval of the grand secretariat and the emperor, Governor-general Kao Ch'i-cho and Governor-general Li Wei decided to return these funds to the provincial treasury to be used for provincial public expenses. As a result, they were able to allocate 50 taels apiece to the 163 minor officials in closest contact with the people, in the hope of eliminating the illegal methods utilized to support local administration.[106] In fact, in many provinces it was the cooptation of former *lou-kuei* and surplus commercial and customs revenues that made the extension of *yang-lien* and the success of *huo-hao kuei-kung* possible.

Lou-kuei after the Reforms

In chapter 2 we examined the informal funding network by which local government was financed before the *huo-hao kuei-kung* reforms. What became of these various items of "saved funds," bribes, customary fees and so on, once officials were provided with regular salaries and public expenses? Contrary to our expectations, not all of these funding sources were declared illegal and eliminated from the provincial budget. Some continued to be collected, but rather than entering private pockets in the form of graft, they were sent to the provincial treasury to "supplement public expenses" (*ch'ung-kung*). It was not mere expediency that allowed the Yung-cheng reformers to retain some of the irregular sources of income that had flowed into the informal funding network and reject others. In order to understand how these decisions were made, we must examine the values that lay behind the late-imperial conception of bureaucratic corruption.

Throughout China's imperial history, low taxation was viewed as a fundamental prerequisite of benevolent rule. During the early

Ch'ing this was linked to a vision of relatively static agricultural productivity which reached its ultimate expression in the K'ang-hsi emperor's ban on future increases in the head tax to match China's growing population (*yung-pu chia-fu*).[107] Although this proscription did not debar the government from extracting additional revenues from increased productivity on the land, especially that resulting from land reclamation,[108] it did prevent any increases in the legal rate of taxation on lands already entered in the tax rolls. K'ang-hsi recognized the need of local officials for supplementary income, but deemed it safer to allow them to collect it illegally than to condone a rise in the land tax. The risk of diminished central-government control over the behavior of local officials was far outweighed by the possible damage such an action would inflict on the emperor's credibility as a benevolent ruler. At a time when tax resistance was rampant and an alien dynasty was attempting to establish its legitimacy as the rulers of the Chinese people, presentation of the imperial image took precedence over matters of practical governance.

Such a position was possible so long as the "state finances" (*kuo-chi*) and "people's livelihood" (*min-sheng*) were not too adversely affected. When the illegal diversion of funds itself became a threat to both the *kuo-chi* and the *min-sheng*, it became necessary to rectify the existing fiscal system, even if it meant raising taxes and tarnishing the emperor's personal reputation.

If we view the Yung-cheng-period reforms as an effort to readjust the fiscal administration of the empire in order to protect the *kuo-chi* and *min-sheng*, the selective elimination and incorporation of elements of the informal funding network becomes more comprehensible. Two types of funds within the informal funding system were strictly banned during the reforms—private levies on the people (*ssu-p'ai*) and customary fees exchanged between officials (*lou-kuei*). The former were seen as instrumental in depleting the resources of the common people and as a primary cause of arrears in regular tax collections. The latter, by draining the funds available to lower officials, were viewed as a major cause of deficits in provincial treasuries. By fostering informal links of patronage, it was the main obstacle to bureaucratic discipline and morale. Moreover, when these forms of graft interacted, they tended to reinforce each other. Increased demands for customary fees forced lower officials to step up their collections of surcharges from the people. In order to protect themselves from disciplinary action as a result of the arrears and deficits caused by these illegal diversions of funds, officials were increasingly willing to pay off their superiors in the form of *lou-kuei*. It was for these reasons that *ssu-p'ai* and *lou-kuei* were the primary targets of the reforms, and it was to eliminate the need for such fees and surcharges that rational and legal funding on the local level was established.

Even before the reforms were instituted the emperor issued an unequivocal ban on surcharges and customary fees. Once the reforms were in effect, Yung-cheng continued to warn officials against such exactions. In his edict calling for the extension of *yang-lien* payments to all officials not previously provided for in provincial budgets, he again decried the collection of customary fees and specifically linked *yang-lien* to the elimination of these illegal practices.[109] Even the large-scale general audit of Kiangnan tax arrears undertaken in YC 7 (see chapter 6) was in part a response to irregularities in local tax-collection practices that defied the ban on surcharges and interfered with the well-being of the *kuo-chi* and *min-sheng*.

However, a number of items within the informal funding network continued to be collected after the reforms. In fact, our knowledge of many categories of funds within the network depends on reports to the emperor when these funds were returned to the provincial coffers to supplement public expenses. Surplus from the purchase of rice, materials for construction, and so on was considered a legitimate source of public funds. For example, taxes formerly levied in kind to provide local granaries with rice or to fulfill central-government quotas of tribute rice were commuted to cash payments at fixed rates. Inasmuch as the market price necessary to buy the rice for these purposes fluctuated greatly, any profits that accrued to the local government as a result were not viewed as having been taken from the central government or the people. Officials in Fukien were able to generate over 5,000 taels from the surplus "rice price" (*mi-chia*).[110] Similar surpluses, arising from the purchase and sale of stabilization rice, were reported in Shantung.[111] There, the financial commissioner also reported an average annual surplus of 3,000 taels in tribute-grain taxes that were also returned to the public treasury.[112] In contrast to windfall profits from the purchase of goods, the accumulation of funds through the use of improperly balanced scales was considered corrupt, because it entailed collecting more than the legal quota from the people. Whenever possible, this practice was eliminated, and in some instances new scales were issued to provincial yamen.[113]

Salt Fees

The most important of all the informal funds coopted by the provinces during the reforms were salt fees (*yen-kuei*). Almost every province depended to some extent on fixed periodic payments made by salt merchants to supplement the revenues in the provincial treasury.[114] Generally, these fees were paid to individual officials. In addition, in salt-producing provinces such as Yunnan, officials received surplus revenues from productive salt wells and surplus profits from the sale of salt within the province.[115] Following the emperor's proscription against the acceptance of customary fees, there was considerable confusion as to whether salt fees were to be included in the ban. Many officials, fearing prosecution for the acceptance of salt fees, immediately memorialized the emperor to demonstrate that they had used the funds derived from salt fees for public purposes. For example, Shantung Governor Huang Ping reported that during his six years as a judicial commissioner he had received a total of 30,000 taels in the form of "customary gifts from salt merchants" (*yen-shang kuei-li*). During that period he had used these funds to establish charity schools in each of the six prefectures in the province, to institute stipends for students and to pay teachers' salaries, to supply aid to families of deceased officials without the means to return to their home provinces, to aid starving refugees, to help repair bridges, buildings, and roads, to build charity cemeteries, and to help clothe and feed prisoners. In addition, in the spring of KH 60 (1721), when salt bandits appeared in the province, Huang claimed to have used part of his salt fees to send extra soldiers and police to assist in their capture.[116]

Despite their fears of imperial sanctions, officials did not move as quickly to curtail the collection of salt fees as they had in the case of surcharges levied on the common people. On the one hand, fees from the salt administration, as a source of revenue for high provincial officials, were too important to be eliminated without some consideration. Moreover, fees from salt merchants, and from merchants in general, were not viewed in the same light as fees exacted from the people. Whereas the productivity of the land was seen as finite, so that additional exactions by local officials would of necessity mean less available income for either the central government or the people, the salt industry was expanding and could accommodate additional demands for revenue without too much harm to the merchants and with virtually no drain from the revenues due the central government. Even more important, the salt merchants from whom these fees were derived obtained their wealth by the emperor's grace in their participation in an official monopoly. Therefore, it was considered natural that they should want to repay this favor by contributing to the well-being of the area in which they did business.

In fact, the main argument offered by officials in favor of the continued acceptance of salt-merchant fees and contributions was that they were given voluntarily and therefore were not to be compared with forced levies on the common people.[117] The case of a group of Ho-tung salt merchants was typical. In YC 3 (1725), 100,000 new salt licenses were issued in Shensi province. The salt merchants of the region benefited enormously from the opportunity for increased sales, and in YC 6 (1728) they volunteered to contribute 5,000 taels annually to the public expenses of the province. According to the merchants themselves, they made such an offer not only because they profited from the increased issue of salt licenses, but because the dynasty itself had brought such prosperity to the land that the population was increasing and the demand for salt was constantly rising.[118]

One merchant, Chang Hung-yü, felt that his life had been particularly touched by imperial grace and wished to contribute an additional 2,000 taels annually beyond that being proffered by the merchant group. Chang stated that his grandfather had been the first in his family to go into the business of selling salt. Chang and his father inherited this business from his grandfather. At first they were just small merchants doing business in the countryside. There were no contract merchants at the time to transport and sell the salt. After he had transported the salt from the well, he did not even have exclusive rights over its sale. Now, Chang said, he was in charge of all salt licenses for Honan's T'ang hsien. His license quota was 4,787 yin. As the population of T'ang hsien increased and harvests continued to be reaped in abundance year after year, he was able to sell all his quota and an excess quota (yü-yin) as well.[119] Chang offered to repay the government for his own success by contributing part of his profits to the public fund. It is important to note that it was only after the Board of Revenue was satisfied that the 7,000 taels these merchants wished to contribute were indeed "excess profits" resulting from the sale of additional salt licenses that they granted the merchants' request.[120]

From the above example we can see that the government was not unconcerned about the merchants' own welfare. Often, when salt fees continued to provide a source of provincial income, the amount paid by the salt merchants was reduced from the level common under the informal funding system. In the Ho-tung salt administration, more than 100,000 taels had previously been collected from salt merchants both to supplement public expenses and to help pay officials' *yang-lien* and the wages of clerks, runners, and patrol soldiers. This sum was considered excessive and was lowered under the supervision of the salt controller.[121] In Hukwang, the level of *yen-kuei* was reduced from 160,000 taels to slightly over 30,000 taels.[122] Similar, if not as drastic, reductions were also made in Chihli and Shantung.[123] Lack of evidence does not mean that reductions were not made elsewhere. However, whether or not the fees were lowered in every province, the method of remittance and management of these funds was probably altered everywhere in accordance with the funding guidelines established during the Yung-cheng reforms. It was these changes that had the greatest impact on local fiscal administration.

Prior to the *huo-hao kuei-kung* reforms, salt fees were sent by the merchants directly to the officials in whose jurisdiction they did business. Additional fees were also sent by groups of merchants to high provincial officials residing in the provincial capital. After the institution of *yang-lien* it was felt that officials had adequate funds for their own administrative expenses. Moreover, because the provinces now had public-expense funds in the provincial treasuries, the chou and hsien would no longer need supplemental funds with which to make contributions to provincial construction projects (*kung-chüan*). Therefore, salt merchants were instructed to remit their *yen-kuei* directly to the provincial coffers, either by sending them to the financial commissioner or by submitting them to the provincial salt controller, who would handle their transfer to the provincial capital.[124] Moreover, the rate at which salt fees were remitted was now fixed and no longer depended on the whim of the official to whom they were sent.

Salt fees and surplus revenues were used for various purposes, some of which were of special benefit to the salt merchants. The *huo-hao kuei-kung* reforms encouraged the integration into the regular chain of bureaucratic command services that previously had been provided through the informal funding network. For example, Acting Liang-huai Salt Controller I-la-chi reported that under the old system the salt controller sent agents to the dikes at T'ai-chou and Kao-yu chou and to the north bridge at Yangchow to inspect the boats delivering salt. Each of the three agents was sent *lou-kuei* by the salt merchants, providing them with an annual income of some 6,000 taels each. According to I-la-chi, these funds all ended up in the pockets of the three agents. These agents being yamen runners who received a fixed wage already adequate to support their families, I-la-chi did not feel it was appropriate for them to pocket fees from the salt merchants as well. Moreover, the embankments and bridges already had official deputies (*wei-kuan*) assigned to them, so it was unnecessary to send additional yamen servants to inspect the unloading process.[125]

I-la-chi discontinued the deputation of the three yamen runners. However, he did not eliminate the *lou-kuei* customarily sent to them. The salt controller reasoned that the elimination of this 6,000 taels would mean only a small increase in the profits of individual salt merchants, whereas it represented a valuable addition to the operating expenses of the official yamen. Instead he proposed to continue its collection to cover the costs of patrol and seizure of smuggled salt. This would not only serve the interests of the merchants in controlling illegal competition in the sale of salt, but would relieve the merchants of the need to supply the government with irregular levies of supplemental aid.

Under this new system of patrol, officials, runners, and yamen servants would be posted at strategic places along the salt-transportation route. A registrar, archivist, and saltwatcher from the salt controller's yamen would be used. Inasmuch as these officers already had salaries, no additional expenses would be incurred through their participation in the patrols. In addition, five low-ranking officers, including four probationary officials (*shih-yung kuan*), would also be assigned to this duty. I-la-chi estimated that it would require 400 taels per month, or 5,000 taels annually, to pay additional official salaries and to hire the necessary patrol boats and runners. The remaining 1,000 taels would then be saved and be available if it became necessary to set up additional patrols.[126] In this way the supervision of salt transport and sale would be systematically integrated into the regular control functions of yamen officials. At the same time, the funding of these services would be rationalized and it would no longer be necessary to levy additional duties on the salt merchants, thus eliminating the pretext for random extortion by yamen personnel.

Customary fees from salt merchants were also used to pay for the wages and salaries of officials, clerks, and runners within the salt administration. The wages and salaries of officials and runners allowed by quota in the regulations of the Board of Revenue were deducted from the salt gabelle in much the same way that civil officials deducted their wages and salaries from the regular land and head tax. As in the case of the regular administrative apparatus, however, these allowances never covered the full costs of clerical wages, stationery, and supernumerary runners. Therefore, after the reforms the salt administration itself continued to collect a fixed amount of customary fees to cover its own administrative expenses.[127] These fees were also used for social services such as banquets to honor leading salt merchants and to provide relief for salt-producing households that were victims of flood and other natural disasters.[128]

Of course, salt fees, once returned to the public coffers, were not used exclusively for services pertaining to the salt administration itself. In many provinces they provided an important supplement to the revenues derived from the land and head tax. In particular, when the decree was issued calling for the allocation of *yang-lien* for minor officials, many provinces were compelled to turn to salt and customs administration *lou-kuei* for the needed funds.[129] Salt fees also constituted an important part of the provincial surplus and were often used for such elastic expenses as the purchase of relief grain and the provision of welfare for famine victims.

Surplus from Customs and Commercial Duties

Determining the contribution of customs and commercial duties to the provincial coffers is far more difficult than assessing the impact of salt fees. By their very nature, customs revenues were more variable than other taxes, and throughout the late-imperial period control of these sources of income presented a challenge to the administrative skills of both the central and local governments. Because of the extreme fluctuations in customs revenues in any given year and at any particular collection point, logic would seem to dictate a policy of full remittance without setting specific quotas.

However, it was this very elasticity that compelled governments in the late-imperial period to set quotas for customs revenues fully recognizing that the quotas had little relationship to actual income.

A number of factors influenced the volume of trade at a particular customs station. Natural phenomena frequently disrupted commercial activity. The customs quota for the Lin-ch'ing station in Shantung was established during the Ming dynasty. However, spring flooding and winter freezing tended to limit the use of the Wen and Wei rivers leading to this customs station. Moreover, in the summer and fall, when ships were able to travel, the sluices were often closed on the route south, causing a backup of merchant ships and bringing transport to a standstill.[130] Therefore, merchants preferred either to unload their goods from the south and carry them by cart for the remainder of the trip north[131] or to bypass the Lin-ch'ing stop on the Grand Canal route and pass through Chi-ning and Tung-ch'ang instead.[132] By the Yung-cheng period, only ships carrying grain from Honan and Shantung on route to Tientsin continued to pass through the Lin-ch'ing station. A particularly good harvest in Shantung and Honan, however, coupled with natural disaster in the chou and hsien on the border between Chihli and Shantung, could stimulate a continuous stream of merchants plying the route through Lin-ch'ing. This was the case during one year in the late Yung-cheng period, with the result that instead of falling short of its quota, the Lin-ch'ing station had surplus customs revenue of more than 40,000 taels.[133]

In areas where trading was generally brisk, late rains and a poor harvest could reduce merchant activity by half, with disastrous results for individual customs stations.[134] Even when harvests were good throughout the empire, price differentials between regions could completely upset the flow of the staples trade. The Huai-an customs station relied largely on the bean trade moving south for its revenues. In 1727 and 1728, harvests in Kiangnan were extremely good and prices fell. As a result, merchants could not be induced to come to Kiangnan to trade in beans, and customs quotas at Huai-an could not be met.[135]

The flow of trade could also be affected by imperial policy, often in ways not anticipated when a decree was promulgated. The Yangtze River trade between Szechuan and Kiangsu relied largely on ships carrying textiles upriver to Szechuan and saffron and rice downriver to Kiangsu. About 50 to 60 percent of the taxes collected at the K'uei pass derived from these items. When the number of ships carrying cloth and saffron began to decrease, the K'uei superintendent of customs, Mu-ko-te-pu, investigated the matter and found that the reason lay in the emperor's prohibition against carrying Szechuan rice across its borders. According to the testimony of long-distance merchants, in the past all bolts of cloth shipped to Szechuan were collected at Chungking prefecture for sale to the villagers in the surrounding countryside. Rice was the main medium of exchange used to purchase the cloth. Since the prohibition against carrying rice out of the province had become effective, merchants were unwilling to trade for rice but demanded their payment in silver. Consequently, the cloth piled up unsold and less new cloth was moved into Szechuan, resulting in serious losses in customs revenues.[136]

Given the unpredictability of those revenues, a dual system of remittances was established to guarantee minimum revenues to the central government and to allow enough flexibility to ensure that at least some of the income collected beyond the quota was also sent to coffers in the imperial capital. The regular quota (*cheng-e*) was sent to the Board of Revenue quarterly. Collections beyond this quota were accumulated in the course of the year and remitted annually in a lump sum to the Imperial Household treasury.[137] These excess revenues, called *ying-yü*, varied from year to year and were not considered in an official's evaluation of performance in office. This arrangement was designed to protect merchants from excessive exactions by officials competing to surpass their predecessor's collection record,[138] besides providing a source of income for imperial coffers. Because one's career did not depend on accurate accounting of *ying-yü* income, a large portion of excess customs revenues was never reported to the central government and ended up in the pockets of local officials, runners, and clerks connected with the customs administration.[139]

In conjunction with the reforms in the collection and distribution of land- and head-tax revenues, the Yung-cheng emperor set about overhauling the administration of customs income as well. Just as part of the intent of the *huo-hao* reforms was to protect the people from harsh official exactions, the reforms in the customs administration were designed to protect merchants from unjust surcharges. At the same time, distribution of the customs surplus was rationalized to guarantee the fullest possible remittance to the central government while satisfying local claims to supplemental customs income. Part of the requirements for such a plan were met by the *huo-hao kuei-kung* reforms themselves. By providing provincial officials with adequate sources of revenues, it was hoped that the demands for *lou-kuei* from the customs administration would be reduced. Serious efforts were made in many places to reduce or eliminate the customs surcharges levied on long-distance merchants that had previously entered the informal funding network.[140]

The efforts to regulate customs duties followed the same principles applied to taxes in the agricultural sector: uniformity, public announcement of rates, and improved bookkeeping techniques. In the sixth month of YC 4 (1726), Yung-cheng issued an edict calling on customs officials to collect and remit in full (*chin-shou chin-chieh*) all surplus merchant duties at each customs station in the empire.[141] In order to encourage officials to declare the actual revenue potential at their customs stations, a one-year deadline was allowed for such declarations and a moratorium was placed on repayment of previously undeclared surplus income.[142]

Two factors stood in the way of central-government control of customs revenues: a complete disregard for the legal rates of collection at individual duty stations and concealment of customs income through duplicate bookkeeping. In order to eliminate the first obstacle, a decree was issued requiring all customs stations to collect duties according to the rates issued by the Board of Revenue. To ensure adherence to these rates, they were to be engraved on blocks and printed so that they might be clearly posted at each collection point, much in the same way that officials had been ordered to post the land-tax rates at key points in each chou and hsien.[143]

The difficulty in enforcing compliance was apparent immediately. Although the official rates were expressed in terms of rates according to type of cargo, the volume of trade passing through certain customs points, coupled with a lack of staff, had forced some customs stations to collect duties on the basis of the capacity of the boat, without regard to the type of cargo. In the case of the Chiu-chiang customs in Kiangsi, this practice had been in effect as early as SC 2 (1645), when the customs station first opened. Initially there were no regulations governing collection, and the Board was satisfied so long as the quota of 99,000 taels was met. In SC 12 (1655), under the guidance of Customs Superintendent Fei-ta, each boat traveling the route that passed through the port at Chiu-chiang was given a registration number, and these numbers, along with the boat's specifications, were sent to the Board. However, as the boats stopping at the port proliferated, it became increasingly difficult for the station's staff to measure and investigate the contents of each boat. Although the quota itself had since doubled, customs inspectors could do no more than rely on visual estimates of each boat's capacity, levying duties at a uniform rate of approximately 0.02 tael per picul of cargo.[144]

The inefficiency of such a system had long been known to both provincial and court officials. In fact, all attempts at regulation had become futile. Boats varied in size, depth, and width. Some were old and some were newly built, and the capacity of these various types could not be judged at a cursory glance.[145] In Shantung, where duties were also levied on the capacity of the boat, shippers renovated their boats to make the cargo hold deeper and wider, thereby deceiving the official inspectors, who could make only a perfunctory estimate of capacity from onshore.[146] Moreover, although boats carried a variety of goods of vastly differing value, duties were applied uniformly. These anomalies had been reported to the court many times, but the fear that inadequate staff and confusion in levying customs duties would result in deficits in the regular quota prevented any change in the system of collections from being implemented.[147]

This resistance to change reflected an aversion to risk shared by both provincial and court officials. Officials preferred to maintain an inefficient method of collections that had at least produced a reliable minimum quota, rather than switch to a more complex system that could produce greater average income for the government but could also result in greater problems in particular years. Instead, the government turned to improvements in bureaucratic procedure to protect merchants from excessive demands by customs staff and to provide the central government with better information about the actual volume of trade passing through each port. This was accomplished by issuing registers (*hao-pu*) to each customs station on which were recorded the name of the duty station, the date, and the amount of silver collected as tax from each merchant. In order to avoid falsification of these records, the merchants were to fill out and sign these registers themselves. Moreover, in the manner of the three- and four-stub receipts used in the collection of the land and head tax, the customs inspector's portion of the "receipts in payment" (*wan-shui ch'üan-ken*), issued upon payment of the duties, was also sent along to the Board for comparison with the records in the *hao-pu*.[148]

The need for improved accounting is vividly illustrated by the state of customs collection in Fukien. The province had sixteen customs stations in the early Ch'ing. Yet despite regulations requiring the documentation of all customs transactions, at year's end the quota for the whole province would simply be divided among all the stations and false records would be compiled under the auspices of the stations at Nan-t'ai and Hsia-men.[149] Any surplus above the quota would then presumably be divided among the staff of all sixteen stations, with payments to civil officials in the province being made in the form of customary fees. As a result of the reforms, not only were accounting methods made more stringent, but variations in the rates of collection between and within customs stations in the province were made uniform, in order to simplify collection and ensure that the increase in prices as a result of taxation was shared more equitably by consumers throughout Fukien.

The combination of the *huo-hao kuei-kung* reforms and the order to eliminate corruption within the customs administration at the same time that efforts were being made to remit all surplus customs revenues in full to the imperial capital could not but cause some consternation and confusion at the local level. This was particularly true in those areas where the reforms were implemented early. As explained in chapter 2, apart from blatant falsification of customs revenues, many customs stations gained extra revenues by charging fees to cover the costs of customs administration and *lou-kuei* to superior officials. Because *lou-kuei* to superiors had been eliminated and officials had been provided with *yang-lien*, it was not considered unreasonable that customs duties now be collected according to the established Board rates. However, when the emperor issued his edict calling for the complete remittance of excess revenues (*ying-yü*), many customs officials feared that without collection of surcharges their *ying-yü* remittances would drop and they would be accused of stealing. Therefore, in some areas officials continued to sanction the collection of duties at rates above those promulgated by the Board.[150]

Yung-cheng's assurances that his edict on *ying-yü* was simply intended to guarantee complete remittance of legally collected duties seems to have assuaged some of the fears of officials in charge of customs revenues. However, as in the case of salt fees, it soon became apparent that some provision had to be made to allow a share of customs revenues to continue to flow into the provincial coffers. The emperor's order to eliminate surcharges and fees within the customs administration was not met with unanimous approval. Some officials felt that additional levies on merchants were justifiable because merchants could afford them and had paid them willingly for as long as could be remembered.[151] Although all agreed that hiding and pocketing customs revenues was not to be condoned, many provincial officials were concerned that the customs administration itself could not operate without some transfer of funds from the customs surplus to its own coffers. Ch'ang Pin, who had been a customs official himself, pointed out that runners at the Canton customs collected various inspection fees that were used to pay wages, transportation costs, and so on. In an impassioned plea he asked the emperor how the clerks and runners and other staff members of the customs administration could be expected to work on empty stomachs.[152]

Ch'ang Pin was not alone in his concern. Superintendent of Fukien Customs Chun-t'ai argued that the number of employees in the customs administration went far beyond the statutory quota and that expenses accrued in running this agency were great. Only by allowing the regulated collection of long-standing customary fees for their support could one guard against the more serious problem of embezzlement and deficits.[153] Kiangsi Governor Pu-lan-t'ai went into even greater detail in describing the expenses incurred by the customs administration in his province, expenses for which, he claimed, it was imperative to skim a certain amount off the revenues remitted to the central government. To cover Board fees and the transport of documents and taxes alone, several thousand taels were needed. These expenses were covered by a *hao-hsien* on the regular tax as well as a transport fee (*chieh-fei*) deducted from the *ying-yü* collected at each station. To pay the living expenses of yamen runners, a fee called "list silver" (*tan-yin*) was charged to each merchant submitting a list of the taxable goods he carried. Moreover, every month, 400 to 700 taels were accumulated because of both differences in weights between the official scales and the market scales and variations in the fineness of silver. This miscellaneous customs revenue (*lin-kuan ling-shui*) was turned over to the supervising official at each customs station to pay for his daily living expenses, ink, paper, private secretaries' and clerks' salaries, and other costs. Any surplus at the year's end was reported and submitted to the governor's yamen.[154]

In order to meet the needs of customs administration, an arrangement was finally worked out whereby all customs expenses were deducted from the *ying-yü* before the latter was remitted to the imperial capital.[155] These funds were used to pay the *yang-lien* of customs officials and the wages of their clerks, runners, and private secretaries, as well as administrative expenses and the costs of compiling accounts and remitting taxes. Only after all such deductions were made and reported to the emperor in a palace memorial were the remaining "excess revenues" sent to the Board to be turned over to the Imperial Household treasury. Because the *ying-yü* thus remitted represented not the total surplus of the customs administration, but only the saved portion after expenses, it was often called "saved surplus" (*chieh-sheng ying-yü*).

The *ying-yü* total continued to represent both collections of fees beyond the Board's schedule of duties and increased income due to the growth of the volume of trade. In accordance with the spirit of the reforms, however, the amount of customary fees, too, were published so that merchants would know precisely what was expected of them. Moreover, instead of allowing the customs-administration staff to pocket fees personally, yamen expenses were budgeted from the excess revenues and monthly allowances were issued to support customs employees and curb corruption.[156]

Despite the proscription against the acceptance of customary fees, customs fees (*shui-kuei*), like salt fees, continued to play a role in the finances of the provinces. Following the reforms, fees that were previously paid to high provincial officials were returned to the provincial coffers to help cover the public expenses of the whole province. In many instances the first response of provincial governors to the reforms was to insist that because customs revenues rightly belonged to the central government, all former customary fees should be combined with the *cheng-hsiang* customs revenues and sent to Peking. In every case where such a request was made, the emperor refused to accept these revenues and authorized their use in the province of origin to supplement public expenses.

Yung-cheng's special edict to Acting Kiangsu Governor Ho T'ien-p'ei explains his reasoning on this matter. Ho reported that in addition to the maritime customs quota and excess revenues collected in Kiangsu, there was a surplus of 5,732 taels that did not belong to anyone. Rather than cover up the existence of this surplus, Ho reported it to the emperor and proposed that it be sent to the capital. The emperor replied:[157]

> This kind of surplus *lou-kuei* has never been predictable. Although you have loyally and sincerely memorialized the facts, it is not appropriate for me to permit you to voluntarily send [this money to the capital]. You need only memorialize about funds like this and keep them temporarily on reserve in the provincial treasury in case there are local public expenses or the need for funds to reward [outstanding soldiers or officials]. These funds belong to you to memorialize about and use as you see fit.

Yung-cheng was consistent in his policy of allowing provincial officials to return customs *lou-kuei* to the provincial coffers. In Kiangsi, customs and salt fees were retained to provide minor officials with *yang-lien*.[158] Kwangsi's revenues from the land and head tax were so low that in YC 5 (1727) the emperor issued a special edict granting over 15,000 taels from the province's customs surplus to supplement the costs of providing officials with *yang-lien*. When it was discovered that an additional 31,400 taels in surplus could be derived from Kwangsi's customs administration, this too was turned over to the governor, with instructions to divide it among the ranked and unranked officials in the province on the basis of the difficulty of their posts.[159] Evidence also exists for the return of customs surplus to the provincial coffers in Shantung, Fukien, and Fengtien.[160] In each case the basis for allowing retention of customary fees or surplus levies seems to have been that they were paid willingly by the merchants and did not interfere with the fulfillment of the quota due the central government.[161]

Revenues from Miscellaneous Commercial Duties

Customs duties were not the only form of commercial taxes that was legitimized as a source of local revenue during the reforms. Although the evidence surrounding these sources of provincial income is less abundant, local commercial duties were also a focus of reform.

As already pointed out in the description of the implementation of *huo-hao kuei-kung*, taxes on the sale of property, unloading of goods, brokerage licenses and so on played an important part in the revenues of several provinces. Like the land and head tax and customs and salt duties, local commercial taxes were legally the property of the central government, to be collected in full and remitted in full to the Board of Revenue. However, as we noted in our discussion of informal funding prior to the reforms, these so-called miscellaneous taxes (*tsa-shui*) were the most difficult taxes for the central government to control. Because the volume of commercial transactions fluctuated from year to year, magistrates generally remitted only a customarily agreed-upon quota to the central government, retaining the surplus to cover quota shortages in future years and to pay for their own expenses and for contributions to the expenses of superior administrative units.[162]

Throughout the early Ch'ing, as the volume of trade and transactions in the sale of land and buildings rose, the central government's ability to regulate trade and the remittance of taxes was further circumscribed. One indication of the extraordinary rise in local commercial activity was the increased issuance of brokerage licenses during the early-eighteenth century. Brokers were licensed middlemen who were particularly important in arbitrating prices and bringing together buyers and sellers in local periodic markets.[163] In order to control the volume of local trade and ensure the payment of taxes and maintenance of a "fair" price structure, the central government set limits on the number of brokers who could be licensed in each province. In Hupei, the Board of Revenue set a quota in YC 4 (1726) establishing the number of licenses the financial commissioner could issue to each chou and hsien to certify brokers in their jurisdictions. Legally, new brokerage households (*ya-hu*) could be authorized only by rescinding the license of one broker and substituting another. Nevertheless, according to a report by Governor Wei T'ing-chen, by YC 9 (1731) the number of licenses actually issued by the individual chou and hsien had increased tenfold over the quota set five years earlier.[164] The revenue derived from the sale of licenses was small. Annual licensing fees ranged from 0.5 tael for a large firm (*shang-hang*) to only 0.3 tael for a medium-sized (*chung-hang*) one and 0.15 tael for a small firm (*hsia-hang*). By selling an extra 1,000 licenses, the province might hope to increase its revenues by at most around 300 taels, hence it is likely that the violation of the quota reflected a real need to increase the number of brokers engaged in handling a growing trade, and was not a ploy to gain additional revenues. This fact was acknowledged by the Board of Revenue when it granted Governor Wei's request not to hold subordinates to fixed quotas in issuing licenses and collecting commercial taxes.[165]

Provinces could indeed generate a substantial surplus from the collection of taxes on commercial transactions. Inasmuch as this excess revenue was the result of legitimate tax collection and not the product of surcharges or monetary manipulation, it was not subject to the same proscriptions applied to *lou-kuei*. Instead of demanding a greater share of this surplus for the central government coffers, Yung-cheng allowed the provincial governments to retain surplus commercial taxes for their own use.

Although evidence is scanty, it is probable that commercial-tax surplus contributed some income to every province. For example, in YC 8 (1730) the Board of Revenue permitted Kiangsi province to retain part of its unloading tax (*lo-ti shui*) and property-deed tax (*t'ien-fang ch'i-shui*).[166] It was in areas where revenues from *huo-hao* were lowest that income from commercial taxes had the greatest impact on the provincial *kung-hsiang*. As pointed out in chapter 4, both Kwangsi and Yunnan relied heavily on revenues from mining, salt, and surplus comercial duties.[167] In Kwangtung, surplus revenues of at least 35,000 taels were collected from the unloading tax and an additional 48,448 taels from the property-deed tax.[168] By YC 12 (1734), the annual surplus from these two duties alone had risen to more than 120,000 taels. Seventy thousand taels were earmarked for provincial *yang-lien* and to cover the costs of boat repairs, and the remaining 50,000 taels were stored in the provincial treasury for emergency expenses.[169] The most dramatic example of the reliance on commercial taxes for the success of the reforms was in Kweichow. There, only 18 percent of the revenues returned to the provincial coffers derived from the land and head tax. A full 59 percent of all provincial revenues emanated from salt and commercial taxes retained by the province for its own use.[170]

The reliance of these provinces on salt, customs, and miscellaneous duties both for emergency expenses and to supplement the income necessary to allocate *yang-lien* and *kung-fei* demonstrates that the role of "surplus" taxes and fees from the commercial sector was far more important than is indicated by statutory quotas. Although their total contribution to local treasury stores was still not as great as that derived from the land and head tax, only a small number of provinces could survive without an infusion of some nonagricultural income. In the land-tax-poor areas beyond central China and the north China plain, commercial revenues were vital to the success of the *huo-hao kuei-kung* reforms. Unlike *lou-kuei*, which burdened the people and destroyed official morale, income from salt, customs, and commercial taxes took advantage of China's growing population and commercial activity to provide an expanding and legitimate source of local funds that neither violated dynastic law nor harmed the livelihood of the masses of common people.

6

OBSTACLES TO REFORM: LOW-LEVEL CORRUPTION AND THE KIANGNAN TAX-CLEARANCE CASE

THE DECISION TO TREAT TREASURY SHORTAGES AS an institutional, rather than a normative, problem was an important step in the development of the modern Chinese state. The transformation of that which was private (*ssu*) into that which properly belongs to the public realm (*kung*) suggested a major reinterpretation of the relationship between government and the people. This notion applied not only to corruption, that insidious impulse toward personal aggrandizement at the expense of the dynasty. Essential to the reform movement was the concept of government responsibility for a wide range of public services which fiscal insolvency had previously made impossible. Moreover, the provision of adequate revenues at the lowest levels of the bureaucracy improved official morale by facilitating adherence to Confucian values and codes of administrative conduct.

The reaction of most provincial officials to the new fiscal order was one of considerable excitement and hope. Even the misgivings of magistrates seem to have waned over time. The initial success of *huo-hao kuei-kung*, however, could not conceal the harbingers of its demise. For the reforms to fulfill their promise as a mechanism for rational local-government finance, one crucial condition had to be met: taxes had to be paid. Despite the reliance of many provinces on nonagricultural income to fill their coffers, *huo-hao* was still the primary source of local revenue. As a surcharge on the land and head tax, *huo-hao*'s role in fiscal administration was inextricably linked to the collection of the dynasty's regular tax quota.

The *huo-hao kuei-kung* reforms attacked the cause of deficits at the level of the bureaucracy, but the Ch'ing state had little power to affect the forces that undermined its finances outside the official hierarchy. The same informal networks of funding that had allowed the bureaucracy to operate before the Yung-cheng reforms had also nurtured the growth of corruption within local society. If free rein had not been given to yamen runners, clerks, and members of the local elite to wring additional revenues from the taxpaying population, it would have been impossible for magistrates to fuel the informal funding system that *huo-hao kuei-kung* replaced. Once these local arrangements were established, it was far more difficult to wipe them out.

Tax arrears, evasion, and corruption below the level of the bureaucracy continued to be part of the fabric of rural life. Nowhere were they a more serious problem than in the three Kiangnan provinces of Kiangsu, Kiangsi, and Anhui.

Measures to Control Arrears

As early as SC 15 (1658), the Kiangnan region was the focus of an imperially sponsored investigation of arrears. This early inquiry into popular tax resistance was prompted by Governor-general Lang T'ing-tso's report that accumulated unpaid taxes during the period from 1651 to 1656 had reached over 4 million taels.[1] Soon after the death of the Shun-chih emperor, the Kiangnan region was again the focus of an imperial tax investigation, in the form of the famous *Tsou-hsiao an* of 1661.[2] Despite the harsh punishment meted out to the Kiangnan gentry as a warning against tax evasion, these three provinces continued to be plagued by arrears throughout the K'ang-hsi reign. Although the people of this region were the beneficiaries of numerous imperial tax remissions issued during this period, the emperor felt compelled to single out Kiangsu taxpayers for a special exemption from unpaid taxes in 1712.[3] This act of imperial grace was followed by two more remissions of arrears granted by the Yung-cheng emperor during his first year on the throne.[4] Nevertheless, by YC 3 (1725), the bureaucracy of

Kiangsu was still trying to work out a formula for the repayment of outstanding taxes totalling 8,810,000 taels, almost three times the province's annual tax obligations.[5]

Some effort was made to alleviate the cause of Kiangnan's arrears by lowering tax quotas in those areas subject to Ming *fu-liang*. During the first few years of the Yung-cheng period, however, the primary focus of official energies here, as elsewhere in the empire, was on the investigation and clearance of deficit cases. The analysis of people's arrears continued to be simplistic. The high level of *min-ch'ien* was largely attributed to the machinations of local magistrates, who were accused of falsifying their accounts in order to transfer newly paid taxes to cover old deficits. During late YC 4 and early YC 5, at least twenty-one chou and hsien magistrates in Kiangsi were removed from office on charges of embezzlement or accumulation of deficits, much of which was concealed in their accounts in the guise of people's arrears.[6]

In part, the failure of provincial officials to rectify this problem lay in the difficulty of detecting arrears malpractices. As Acting Kiangsi Governor Yü Chu pointed out at the time, any internal investigation was almost useless. As soon as word got out that a prefect was about to carry out a *p'an-ch'a* of his subordinates' accounts, the chou and hsien magistrates in his jurisdiction would alter the *liu-shui hung-pu* in which the taxes collected each day were recorded. They would then alter the payment receipts (*ch'uan-ken*) stored in the local fiscal secretary's office (*hu-fang*) to match these falsifications. Only taxes already sent by the chou and hsien to the financial commissioner would be recorded as paid. The rest the magistrate would enter as *min-ch'ien*. According to Yü, even a thorough investigation at the village level would bring to light no misconduct, because the clerks in charge of tax collection in the villages (*ching-ch'eng*) were in collusion with the yamen personnel.[7]

Given the appalling state of fiscal administration in the Kiangnan region, it is no wonder that the Yung-cheng emperor chose it as the focus of his own investigation of people's arrears. By YC 6 (1728), the *huo-hao kuei-kung* reforms were being implemented with considerable success almost everywhere in the empire but here. In fact, it was the chaos in Kiangnan's tax administration that initially led the emperor to prohibit these three provinces from participating in the reforms. In that same year, Yung-cheng issued an edict to all high provincial officials that called attention to the possibility that the Achilles heel of Chinese fiscal administration now lay not at the bureaucratic level, but below, where the *huo-hao kuei-kung* reforms did not penetrate. Without immediate attention, the repercussions of this low-level corruption could cause the destruction of all that the emperor and his reforming administration had striven to accomplish.

Yung-cheng identified clerical engrossment (*hsü-li chung-pao*) as the single most important factor in the spread of low-level corruption. Clerks had long been targets of official disdain and were frequently used as scapegoats for malfunctions in local administration. However, the emperor was not simply indulging in empty rhetoric. As he had always been during the implementation of his reforms, Yung-cheng was concerned to discover the manifestations and techniques of corruption. Only then, through structural changes in tax administration or improved administration of existing laws, could officials devise the means to root out the cause of this blight on the body politic.

The emperor outlined several methods that might be employed by clerks to embezzle the people's taxes. Among these were proxy remittance (*pao-lan*), altering tax receipts (*hsi-kai ch'uan-p'iao*), opening and stealing from the tax envelopes deposited in government tax chests, and charging fees to conceal the names of households owing back taxes. Yung-cheng felt that such practices persisted because the magistrates rarely took the time to inform the people of their individual tax liabilities and the amount of taxes outstanding under their names. Magistrates may not have intended to become conspirators in tax fraud. In order to guarantee the functioning of the old informal funding network, however, they had simply ignored government regulations designed to enable the individual to take full responsibility for his own tax payments. As a result, what the officials considered tax arrears the people might regard as taxes paid in full, while clerks persisted in their treachery, deceiving both.[8]

As a first step in remedying clerical fraud, Yung-cheng ordered the chou and hsien to have the *shu-shou*[9] in each *hsiang* and *li* submit a list of all taxes paid and in arrears within his jurisdiction. The magistrates were then to check these lists against their own records. They were instructed that if there were no discrepancies they were to apply their official seal to the lists and have them posted in the *li* or *hsiang* concerned so that every household in arrears would be informed of its exact liabilities. If the amounts posted did not agree with a taxpayer's own estimation of what he had paid, he could bring his receipts to the yamen and register an accusation of clerical engrossment.[10] In this way, the emperor hoped to prevent clerks from engaging in what he called wanton banditry in the guise of official business. It should be noted that once again the emperor placed emphasis on the direct relationship between the individual taxpayer and the government and on providing the taxpayer with full and public information to enable him to protect his interests against rapacious yamen personnel.[11]

The chou and hsien magistrates themselves were not without culpability in the persistence of arrears. Because the accumulated arrears in the provinces were so large that the people would have difficulty paying them off, Yung-cheng had granted his subjects the privilege of paying their debt in installments. The period allowed for repayment averaged about ten years, depending on the amount owed and the distance of one's home from the capital. To the emperor this was an expression of his love for the people and should have given the people ample time to pay their debts to the government with ease. However, Yung-cheng had heard that unscrupulous magistrates in some jurisdictions had set up unofficial registers to record the amount of arrears collected each year. If the people paid more than the exact quota set for a particular year's installment, the magistrate remitted the quota and embezzled the rest. Because the amount called for was sent to the financial commissioner, no further investigation of the magistrate's accounts was required. Meanwhile, people who in their public-spiritedness had paid more than was necessary that year would be pressed for payment of their arrears as if they had never been paid off. It was to the people's despair over this practice that the emperor traced the rise in tax resistance and delayed payments. Again, the solution he proposed centered on the public posting of installment quotas and the amounts already paid by each household.[12] Moreover, "good people" who paid more than the installment, rather than being penalized, were to be rewarded and their actions reported to the magistrate's superiors.

The emperor's edict on arrears set off a flurry of new tax investigations, the largest of which were carried out in Hukwang, Chekiang, and Kiangnan.[13] However, it was in Kiangnan that the investigation of arrears developed into a full-scale tax-clearance case (ch'ing-ch'a) that would last three years and involve not only all the officials of the provincial administration, but special agents of the central government as well.

The Origins of the Kiangnan Ch'ing-ch'a

Following the emperor's edict calling for the investigation of arrears, Governor Chang Tan-lin submitted his own evaluation of the situation in Kiangsu. Most striking was the volume of taxes the people of this province owed to the government. The size of the Kiangsu debt was not simply a function of its high tax quota; it also reflected the exceptionally slow progress of arrears repayment. For example, in YC 4 (1726) only slightly over 11 percent of the outstanding taxes due that year had been remitted to the magistrate's yamen.[14] In view of the liberal repayment policy established by the central government, such delinquency could only be the result of flaws in the operation of local tax administration.

According to Chang, the most important impediment to efficient tax collection in his province was the inadequacy of chou and hsien tax registers. The large size of their jurisdictions and the broad range of duties for which an individual magistrate was responsible made it difficult to verify the accuracy of the records on which tax collection was based. Omissions and falsifications in the registration of land could be found in every subordinate unit in the region. Sometimes several tens of households were merged under the name of one household. At other times the property of one wealthy household was registered under scores of different *hu* designations. In the former case the party really responsible for tax payment was impossible to detect. In the latter, arrears in large amounts were hidden by dispersing them among a myriad of fictional landowners. As a result, Kiangsu's taxes were rarely paid in full.

Although the inaccurate registration of land served the interests of Kiangsu's more prosperous inhabitants, the paucity of reliable tax data forced magistrates to relegate responsibility for fulfillment of government tax quotas to yamen and village clerks. Proxy remittance (*pao-lan*) was therefore a common practice in Kiangsu. The imposition of a third party between the taxpayer and the government contributed to both arrears and their persistent default. Clerks and runners invariably pocketed a portion of the taxes consigned to them, recording them in the yamen accounts as people's arrears. In order to conceal their own embezzlement, subbureaucratic personnel were often instrumental in encouraging popular resistance to arrears repayment and in inciting antitax demonstrations.[15]

Governor Chang's suspicions that the common people were not responsible for much of the tax indebtedness in his province was rekindled once the new drive to recover arrears was under way. Almost immediately, petitions began pouring in to the yamen of Kiangsu's magistrates, expressing concern over the effect that the investigation would have on the region's poor. According to reports transmitted to the governor's office, the petitioners claimed that most of the outstanding taxes in Kiangsu were owed on land that had long since been sold by needy proprietors. Utilization of the land had passed to new owners, but the liability for past arrears remained with the household that had originally incurred them. Worried that these people would not be able to pay the government what they owed, the petitioners requested that all arrears be divided equally among the present landholding population.

Similarities in the content of requests coming in from all over the province raised doubts as to the spontaneous nature of the petition campaign. Inquiries into the identity of these "public-spirited" subjects convinced the governor that it was in fact households who controlled the *pao-lan* networks that were behind the move to redistribute the debt. Inasmuch as these households themselves were responsible for a large part of the unpaid tax quota, a redistribution of accumulated arrears would serve to transfer their own liabilities onto the shoulders of others. However, Chang had a more important reason for rejecting the plan. Even if all the households in Kiangsu complied with the reapportionment of existing arrears, such a move would do nothing to root out the causes of *pao-lan* and tax evasion. Within a few years the problem of unpaid taxes would have to be confronted again. Only a thorough *ch'ing-ch'a* could rectify the system of tax collection and eliminate the source of abuses once and for all.

Chang Tan-lin was familiar with the methods used to carry out a *ch'ing-ch'a* because his cousin, Chang Tan-jang, had just assisted in such an investigation in nearby Chekiang. Armed with his cousin's advice, the governor memorialized the emperor to carry out a full-scale tax audit in Kiangsu as well. What distinguished Chang's proposed *ch'ing-ch'a* from a routine investigation of provincial fiscal administration was the role assigned to officials outside the provincial bureaucracy. Normally it was the duty of assistant and subassistant prefects to inspect the tax records of subordinate chou and hsien. Ostensibly to avoid overburdening these provincial officials, Chang requested that the Board of Civil Appointments and the top officials in the province be authorized to select officials not yet assigned to regular posts to take on this responsibility. Because Suchow, Sung-chiang, and Ch'ang-chou prefectures had the greatest deficits and arrears, the governor suggested that four officials be assigned to each. The number of special investigators sent to the other prefectures in the province could be fewer, depending on the size of their debt and the problems anticipated in their recovery. Altogether, Chang estimated that twenty-four "expectant" officials would be necessary to investigate the tax-collection records and procedures of all the prefectures in the province and assist in the compilation of new, accurate tax registers to avoid future malfeasance. In addition, the governor proposed that once the task was completed these men be kept on in the province to help carry out a much-needed land survey to guarantee that the government's information on landholdings was indeed up-to-date.[16] Chang Tan-lin was transferred to Kiangsi before he had a chance to test his plan in Kiangsu, but his proposal was quickly taken up by the new governor, a young Manchu bannerman named Yin-chi-shan.

The task facing Yin-chi-shan was even more difficult than his predecessor had anticipated. Not only was pressure being placed on the provincial government to shift the burden of arrears to innocent taxpayers, but the emperor's call for stricter prompting of payment of old debts soon gave rise to overt resistance to government tax collectors in the countryside. As early as the second month of YC 6 the magistrate of Chia-ting hsien had encountered resistance to the payment of old arrears. In this case, "evil people" had called the inhabitants of one village together by beating a gong and incited them to cut down the suspension bridge in order to deny the tax collector access to the village.[17] The reaction to the tightening of sanctions against tax defaulters in Wu-hsi hsien was even more hostile. In the sixth month of the same year, Wu-hsi magistrate Chiang Ch'ang-jung escalated his campaign to collect past taxes by making the heads of all households with arrears wear the cangue. Soon after this order was issued, a group of "evil people" rioted in the hsien yamen and released the prisoners being held in the hsien jail. As a final act of defiance, they even burned the government's boats to prevent the hsien police from pursuing them.[18]

Not all magistrates were as diligent as those of Chia-ting and Wu-hsi. Some feared that the provincial government's determination to retrieve old tax debts would reflect poorly on their own career evaluations. Thus, in spite of good fall harvests throughout the province, the government began to receive reports of crop devastation due to floods from a number of hsien, including An-tung, T'an-yuan, and Shu-yang. Subsequent investigations disclosed only minor damage from rains in a few isolated low-lying villages.[19] Although the governor did order the financial commissioner to provide flood relief for the few who were actually affected, it was clear that the magistrates in these hsien, unable to collect their full quota of arrears, had exaggerated reports of natural disaster in the hope of receiving an imperial tax exemption for their jurisdictions. The governor felt that they too were under the influence of locally powerful "evil people."

Who were these "evil people"? As is so often the case in official communications, the perpetrators of corruption and lawlessness were described in such vague terms as to include almost anyone, save perhaps "simple, ignorant peasants" and the local officials themselves. This ambiguity was in part deliberate, for the roots of corruption extended so deeply into the Kiangnan tax administration that without a thorough and honest investigation, the officials of the province could not know exactly who the "evil people" were or how they carried out their clever deceptions. However, even before the investigation had begun, an increasing number of officials had come to believe that the gentry, the mainstay of the imperial state, could not escape culpability in the sabotage of local fiscal management.

Chang Tan-lin had not been the only one to suspect that the chronic arrears in the region were not entirely an outgrowth of popular tax resistance. Wang Chin, an aging member of the gentry from Chiang-ning prefecture in Kiangsu, reported to the emperor that the fault lay not in the chou and hsien magistrates' lack of skill in collecting taxes, but in the abuses of gentry and members of large households (*shen-chin ta-hu*). During his term as a magistrate in both Hunan and Chekiang, Wang found that the "little people" who did not own much land tended to pay their taxes promptly. It was the gentry and large households, with vast holdings, who attempted to evade taxation by registering their land under fictitious names. However, without the connivance of clerks and runners, complete concealment would not have been possible.[20] Such "evil people" delayed remittance of their taxes in the expectation that an imperial tax remission would eventually relieve them of any obligation to repay arrears. From the ample evidence of such imperial acts of grace we can see that they were not wrong in assuming that the worse arrears became, the greater the likelihood that a remission would be granted.

Fa-hai, who was governor of Chekiang during the first half of the Yung-cheng reign, had already urged the emperor to investigate the illegal activities of Kiangnan's local degree-holders. He also attributed arrears to proxy remittance and tax resistance by gentry and local "ruffians," as well as embezzlement by yamen and village clerks.[21] Fa-hai felt that few officials understood the situation and praised Financial Commissioner Oertai and the Fan-t'u and Wu-hsi magistrates as the only members of the Kiangnan bureaucracy who wholeheartedly attacked the problem of arrears and neither pandered to the will of powerful local families nor acted with excessive leniency in order to win over the people's affections.

Some of the officials who were eventually charged with carrying out the Kiangnan *ch'ing-ch'a* were also sensitive to the fact that other kinds of malfeasance were often disguised as people's arrears. This was particularly true of those officials already in Kiangnan, engaged in the earlier investigation of government deficits. Among these men was the provincial censor, I-la-chi. In order to uncover the actual amount of deficits in areas like Suchow and Sung-chiang, I-la-chi and his fellow investigators had ordered each prefecture, chou, and hsien to compile an account of people's arrears. Among the items listed as *min-ch'ien*, I-la-chi had discovered many that could be traced to embezzlement by officials and their staff. However, he also contended that the vast majority of genuine arrears belonged not to the common people, but to the gentry. Moreover, of these gentry offenders, most were members of families that owned extensive fields. Tax delays by this group were clearly not due to financial distress, but were the result of deliberate tax resistance (*yu-i k'ang-ch'ien*).[22]

It is little wonder then that Governor Yin-chi-shan came to share his predecessor's suspicions of the so-called spokesmen of the people who clamored for the redistribution of arrears of taxes. Even after the latter's rejection of their proposal, pressure for such a move did not abate. A joint petition was sent to Yin-chi-shan by inhabitants of the chou and hsien of Sung-chiang prefecture, and requests from individual chou and hsien continued to pour in as well. Groups of literati and commoners even came to the governor's yamen to enjoin him to submit a memorial on the matter. The persistence of these groups only served to confirm in the governor's mind what earlier investigators had suggested, that very few of the arrears on record could really be blamed on poor people who did not have the means to pay. "The remainder," Yin-chi-shan insisted, "are the result of tax resistance by large households (*ta-hu chih k'ang-wan*), proxy remittance by village clerks (*t'u-shu chih pao-lan*), and embezzlement by yamen runners and clerks who tamper with the accounts, dividing embezzled taxes among many households and falsely registering land ownership (*hua-fen kuei-chi, i-ts'e kai-ming*)."[23] The claim that all these arrears were *wu-cho*, without anyone to whom responsibility could be assigned, would hold true only if they arose from the impoverishment of former landed households. If they were the result of personal aggrandizement by powerful members of the local community, then responsibility could be assigned and the funds recovered.

The outcome of Yin-chi-shan's own inquiry into the identity of the petitioners was similar to that of Chang Tan-lin. Many turned out to be taxpayers with large accumulated arrears, who stood to profit from the redistribution of unpaid debts.[24] Others, whom the governor labeled local ruffians, evil gentry, wicked runners, and traitorous clerks, hoped to halt any investigation that might interfere with their control of the tax-collection process. Although a large number of local officials were seduced by the simplicity of the petitioners' plan to eliminate arrears, particularly as some of the people's debts were decades old, the governor's mind was made up. A *ch'ing-ch'a* was essential.

The Ch'ing-ch'a Begins

The Kiangnan *ch'ing-ch'a*, as it finally developed under Yin-chi-shan's supervision, came to include at least seventy officials especially chosen on the basis of their integrity and experience in tax matters (*ching-yü ch'ien-liang*).[25] Particular emphasis was placed on separating the investigation from the normal functions of the bureaucracy in order to guarantee that those engaged in the review of local tax practices would be free of any ties that might prejudice their findings and would be able to devote all of their time to the task at hand. Three levels of officials from outside Kiangnan's official hierarchy were assigned to the investigation. At the top, the emperor appointed two imperial commissioners to superintend the *ch'ing-ch'a* of taxes (*ch'in-ming tsung-li ch'ing-ch'a ch'ien-liang*), Board of Works Vice-president Ma-erh-t'ai and Censor An Hsiu-te.[26] Below them were nine imperially appointed branch investigators (*fen-ch'a ta-ch'en*), amongst whom the various jurisdictions in Kiangnan were divided.[27] These *fen-ch'a* officials came mainly from the ranks of circuit intendants and were in charge of the everyday supervision of the investigation at the local level.[28] At the bottom of the *ch'ing-ch'a* hierarchy were the *hsieh-ch'a* officials. These men were chosen from the ranks of minor officials, expectant magistrates, and assistant prefects and subprefects.[29] Officers showing promise in this capacity could hope to receive promotion to more permanent positions in the regular bureaucracy.

Although the greatest volume of arrears originated in Kiangsu province, the *ch'ing-ch'a* was designed from the start to deal with Kiangsi and Anhui as well. Officials assigned to Chekiang were also consulted on occasion, because it was recognized that many of the problems affecting Kiangsu were prevalent throughout the region.[30] Thus, although most of the extant documentation refers specifically to Kiangsu, we can assume that the general procedures and many of the findings were typical of Kiangnan as a whole. Because the investigation covered so large an area, centralized supervision was tempered by a recognition of the need to grant inspectors flexibility in their actions at the local level.[31] Moreover, high-level provincial and *ch'ing-ch'a* officials divided up the territory in order to facilitate closer supervision of *fen-ch'a* officials and coordination of all investigative efforts. All those assigned to the *ch'ing-ch'a* were instructed by the emperor to meet often in order to share information and help each other with the development of efficient auditing techniques.

During the initial stages of the *ch'ing-ch'a*, the main concern was not to recover arrears, but to determine their cause and designate responsibility for future repayment. The emperor even issued a two-year injunction against the collection of back taxes, after which time all debts were to be cleared and the investigators were to certify the accuracy of all tax registers in the chou and hsien.[32] It soon became apparent that even this would require more than the allotted time and manpower. Therefore, the commissioners concentrated first on clearing up old arrears and investigating corrupt practices. Verification of tax registers was begun, but it was recognized that a complete cadastral survey would be necessary and could not be carried out with the existing complement of *ch'ing-ch'a* personnel.

The first task of officials sent to the chou and hsien was to determine what portion of arrears really belonged to the people and what portion could be categorized as officials' embezzlement (*kuan-ch'in*) or runner and clerk engrossment (*i-shih*).[33] In order to encourage cooperation with the investigators, the emperor issued an edict suspending punishment of any embezzler or tax farmer who confessed his crime and agreed to pay back the funds stolen from the government and the people (*chun pao-lan ch'in-shih chih-jen tzu-shou mien-tsui*).[34] Repayment in installments was permitted in order to avoid forcing the offenders to resort once again to extortion of the common people. In addition, Yung-cheng expanded his previous suspension of arrears collections to include all taxes in the region. In this way, the emperor hoped that the collection of regular taxes would not interfere with the investigations that were under way.[35] The curtailment of compulsory debt repayment did not mean that the government ceased its recovery of back taxes. In fact, tax chests were set up in each chou and hsien and the people were encouraged to deposit in them as much as they were able toward paying off their own arrears. At the same time, a bureau was established in each chou and hsien to investigate the sources of arrears and to compile a "clear account" of all unpaid taxes, classified by household. Once again, there was widespread publicity and the posting of the emperor's instructions in every village so as to let the people know what their obligations were.[36] The *ch'ing-ch'a* officials also encouraged households with arrears to go to the bureaux in person to verify the amounts under their names and to correct any mistakes in the records,[37] presumably by presenting receipts for taxes already paid. In the process of compiling "clear accounts," local officials were also enjoined to determine the correct name and residence of each taxpaying household to facilitate a house-by-house investigation of tax liabilities at a later date.[38] By midyear it was the opinion of most officials involved in the *ch'ing-ch'a* that to a large extent the arrears were really the product of clerical engrossment, the most difficult category of debts to uncover. For the moment, however, it was hoped that by verifying people's arrears and encouraging officials to confess to embezzlement, funds belonging to the third category would automatically become visible (*shui-lo shih-ch'u*).

Despite these elaborate preparations, the investigation of arrears did not go as smoothly as anticipated. In some cases the choice between testing the government's ability to carry out its investigation and avoiding punishment by the confession of one's crimes did result in offenders in all three categories coming forward. Wen Erh-sun, who was in charge of arrears investigations in T'ai-ts'ang chou, reported a fair response by the middle of YC 7 (1729). Arrears in Ch'ung-ming hsien were so small that the task of recovering them was left entirely in the hands of the magistrate. In the remaining chou and hsien, Wen reported the following results:[39]

Locale	Arrears (taels)	Confessed to (taels)	Amounts Paid (taels)
T'ai-ts'ang chou	166,894	121,779	5,130
Chen-yang hsien	181,066	115,482	1,645
Chia-ting hsien	711,954	22,567	0
Pao-shan hsien	768,909	83,215	0

However, these preliminary responses accounted for only a portion of all arrears and were not accompanied by large voluntary repayments. It remained to be seen whether those who confessed to responsibility for arrears would reimburse the government, and whether the majority of unaccounted-for arrears could be tracked down.

Trouble Within the Ranks

In this endeavor, the *ch'ing-ch'a* apparatus encountered immediate obstacles. One was at the highest level of the investigative hierarchy. The other penetrated to the lowest levels of the provincial subbureaucracy. For such a large-scale *ch'ing-ch'a* to succeed, it was necessary to have the complete cooperation of local officials, and for those in supervisory positions to consult and assist each other in providing information and establishing rules for the inspection and retrieval of funds. However, signs of rivalry and outright dishonesty appeared within the ranks of *tsung-li* and *fen-ch'a* officials as soon as the *ch'ing-ch'a* had begun.

Upon his arrival in Kiangnan, Ma-erh-t'ai found an air of hostility growing among *ch'ing-ch'a* officials already in the province.

Although all actions were to be decided on in concert, Ma-erh-t'ai reported that Financial Commissioner Chao Hsiang-kuei had taken all responsibility for directing the investigation upon himself, refusing to discuss proposals with the Board officials sent to supervise the *ch'ing-ch'a* or with the branch investigators. Resentment over this usurpation of power was so strong that the special investigators simply ignored Chao's orders and abandoned any effort at joint planning. This created serious problems for subordinates involved in the audit of taxes, who were constantly faced with conflicting instructions. According to Ma-erh-t'ai, petty infighting of this kind had set the investigation back at least six months.[40]

Ma-erh-t'ai's report to the emperor confirmed the rumblings that had already been emanating from the ranks of the *fen-ch'a* officials themselves. Soon after his assignment to the superintendency of the Kiangnan *ch'ing-ch'a*, Wang Chi was appointed acting governor at Suchow. When Censor I-la-chi was ordered to assist in the investigation of debts in Kiangsu as well as those in Anhui, Governor-general Fan Shih-i instructed him to coordinate his actions with Governors Yin-chi-shan and Wang Chi. They, in turn, would handle all communications with the Board of Revenue. However, because Yin-chi-shan was temporarily acting superintendent of river conservancy and engaged in a crucial construction project, the work of the *ch'ing-ch'a* was left entirely to Wang Chi. According to I-la-chi, Wang did all he could to subvert his position and authority. The acting Suchow governor failed to include I-la-chi in the drafting of notices regarding the audit of people's arrears and even drafted memorials to which I-la-chi's name was appended without consulting I-la-chi on their contents. Moreover, when I-la-chi's name was included on official papers, his post and rank were not mentioned.[41] It was only after Board of Civil Appointments Vice-president P'eng Wei-hsin showed him a particularly stern imperial rescript appended to one of these memorials that I-la-chi even learned of Wang's obstructionist activities.

I-la-chi felt that his role as an imperially appointed special investigator was being challenged by a conspiracy within the regular provincial bureaucracy. Although the task of identifying deficits and arrears belonged to I-la-chi and the other *ch'ing-ch'a* officials and their staffs, recovery of funds was the duty of regular local officials. Every day that recovery was delayed increased the risk that the property of a guilty party would be spent or hidden so that arrears would never be repaid. Although 600,000 taels had al-

ready been retrieved from over 170 cases, I-la-chi calculated that
there were still more than 600 cases in the financial commissioners' files pertaining to embezzlement by officials alone. Total revenues still unaccounted for came to more than 5,300,000 taels. Yet,
despite direct imperial orders to hasten the recovery of back taxes,
Financial Commissioner Chao Hsiang-kuei, with the support of
Governor Wang Chi, had given the matter only perfunctory attention (*pu-kuo i-fan chi-wan*).[42] Inasmuch as the governor and financial commissioner were unwilling to devote any energy to the
matter, it was only natural that officials in charge of recovering
these funds treated their assignments as a mere formality.

I-la-chi feared a total breakdown in communications between
local officials and imperially commissioned investigators, which
would destroy any hope of the *ch'ing-ch'a's* success. In a display of
frustration not uncommon in secret communications to the emperor, I-la-chi placed the blame on his own incompetence as an
official.[43]

> I am really useless in Kiangsu. My Chinese is inade-
> quate. Therefore, the memorials I write cannot be clear
> and detailed. I respectfully beg the emperor to extend
> his grace and send down an edict bringing me back to
> the capital so that I may kneel and memorialize the
> emperor on the situation I witnessed in the provinces
> and the various impediments [to my freedom of ac-
> tion]. Then send me to the Board for deliberation [of
> my case] and punishment as a warning to those who
> are ordered to carry out a mission and prove to have
> no ability. I will close my eyes and depart this world in
> peace.

Submission of such an appeal, whining and childish as it may
seem, was a technique employed fairly often by officials caught in a
bureaucratic bind. Although I-la-chi did risk being called back to
the capital, he probably would not have written such a memorial if
he had not believed that the emperor had confidence in him. If
such was the case, the memorial would have the effect of forcing
the emperor to take some action to confirm I-la-chi's position.

I-la-chi's boldness may have derived from his knowledge that he
was not alone in his suspicions of Chao Hsiang-kuei and Wang
Chi. At the same time that he submitted his memorial, an even
more scathing indictment of the two leaders of the provincial bureaucracy was delivered by the T'ai-ts'ang *fen-ch'a* official Wen

Erh-sun.[44] Wen was also under the impression that all *tsung-li* and *fen-ch'a* officials were supposed to meet and consult on the implementation of the *ch'ing-ch'a*. When he arrived in Kiangnan, however, he was told that an argument was going on between Governor Wang Chi and the *fen-ch'a* official in charge of Huai-an prefecture, Ch'ien Chao-yuan. As a result, no joint meetings of investigative personnel were held and the *fen-ch'a* officials simply went off to their assigned areas. When Wen visited the governor, he admonished him on this issue but did not receive any satisfaction. Later, Wen met with the *tsung-li* officials sent by the emperor and was told that without consulting them, Financial Commissioner Chao had issued a detailed set of orders to all prefects and chou and hsien magistrates. Wen was as concerned as I-la-chi that communication not break down between the *ch'ing-ch'a* officials and the local bureaucracy. The *tsung-li* officials having already ordered their subordinate *hsieh-ch'a* officials to compile registers of arrears (*ch'ien-ts'e*), Wen suggested that when these were completed and household-by-household investigations were begun, the magistrates be required to come to the capital to consult with the special investigators.

Although Wang Chi agreed to support Wen's efforts to foster cooperation between *hsieh-ch'a* officials and the local bureaucracy, his own cooperation with investigators on the provincial level was not forthcoming. Rather than aid Wen Erh-sun in familiarizing himself with the situation in Kiangsu, Wang left the chore to P'eng Wei-hsin and I-la-chi, who were only vaguely acquainted with local conditions. After reaching T'ai-ts'ang, Wang heard that there had been a Board communiqué ordering *ch'ing-ch'a* officials to ferret out deficits as well as arrears. Not only was a copy of this document never sent to Wen, but when he went to Suchow in person and pressed Wang Chi and Chao Hsiang-kuei on the matter, they kept him waiting ten days before refusing to show him the order in question. In the end Wen could get the information he needed only by transcribing a copy of the document in P'eng Wei-hsin's yamen and then going to I-la-chi's office to obtain the relevant figures for T'ai-ts'ang chou.

Wen suspected that the behavior of the governor and financial commissioner was motivated by a desire to protect their friends in the officialdom. For example, among the cases being handled by Wen was that of former Grand Secretary Wang Yen, who, along with his son, uncle, and nephew, owed the government 46,000 taels in back taxes. Because the records of the case had not yet arrived in T'ai-ts'ang, Wen was unable to take action to recover the funds. To make matters worse, Wen discovered that the *hsieh-ch'a* official, Sun Chien-lung, sent by Financial Commissioner Chao to assist Wen in inspecting T'ai-ts'ang's granaries and treasuries, was a disciple of Wang Yen. Wen strenuously pushed for Sun's transfer, but to no avail.[45] In the end, investigations by *ch'ing-ch'a* officials uncovered evidence of the private use of government funds by both Financial Commissioner Chao and Hsü Yung-yu, an official who had held posts as both a hsien magistrate and a prefect in the province. Wang Chi was also cited for misuse of his power as governor and for nepotism in appointing his cousin Ning Shu-yeh and his family disciple Sun Chien-lung to *ch'ing-ch'a* posts. These two officials were removed from office and an investigation was begun to determine which of the other officers recommended by Wang and Hsü deserved dismissal.[46]

The inquiry into Chao Hsiang-kuei's and Wang Chi's activities in office brought to light other crimes as well. Both were found guilty of embezzlement and collusion with yamen personnel to collect customary fees (*lou-kuei*) in the form of gate fees extracted from lower provincial officials. This type of *lou-kuei* was vigorously attacked after the implementation of *huo-hao kuei-kung* because it drained local resources and fostered a corrupt dependency relationship between officials at different levels of the bureaucracy. Both the Chen-yang magistrate, T'ao Shih-ch'i, and the acting Hsin-yang magistrate, Chu Kuei-yang, reported that every time they had business with Wang they were forced to pay ten to twelve taels before being allowed past the yamen entrance. A local jail warden stated that he had been forced to pay identical sums to members of Wang's staff on at least thirty different occasions.[47] When we consider that this amounted to over 300 taels, the impact on the jail warden's own ability to deal honestly with the local people is obvious.

Both Governor Wang and Financial Commissioner Chao were removed from office, eliminating an important stumbling block in the way of local official cooperation with the *ch'ing-ch'a*. However, this was not the only impediment to be overcome. The more covert and dispersed obstructionist activities of local clerks, runners, and gentry would prove far more difficult to counteract.

Subbureaucratic Subversion

The elaborate methods utilized by yamen functionaries and members of the local elite to subvert the collection of arrears had been established long before the *ch'ing-ch'a* apparatus descended on Kiangnan, and the question of whether even so intense an investigation could deal with them was not an idle one. Some clerical malfeasance took the form of overt embezzlement and was relatively easy to detect, once avenues of communication were opened up between the government and the taxpayers. For example, in one hsien in Sung-chiang prefecture an expectant subprefect named Chu had unpaid taxes totaling over 900 taels. As part of the *ch'ing-ch'a*, the hsien magistrate issued a summons for him to be investigated (*ch'u-p'iao t'i-chiu*). Fearing punishment, Chu immediately volunteered to pay his arrears in full, whereupon the magistrate sent a hsien clerk named Chin Yung-lin to compel him to do so speedily.

This took place in the sixth month, before the regular tax collection season. Chin Yung-lin took advantage of the fact that the locked tax chests had not yet been set up to swindle Chu out of his 900 taels. It was only after the magistrate reported to the prefect for the second time on Chu's intention to pay his debt that he discovered that the funds had already been pocketed by Chin Yung-lin. The magistrate, fearful that his own reputation would be tarnished if the money was not remitted to the central government, pressed Chu for payment of his arrears again (*ch'ung-wan*). In a rage, Chu went to Chin Yung-lin and tried to force him to return the money, but could not get him to turn over a single tael. Under normal circumstances, Chu might never have retrieved his stolen remittance, but because the province was in the midst of an investigation of just such malpractices, he was able to obtain immediate redress at a higher level. The *fen-ch'a* official Feng Ching-hsia had Chin Yung-lin arrested and obtained a confession not only to the theft of Chu's money, but to that of over 2,000 taels from other taxpayers as well. The *ch'ing-ch'a* superintendent, Ma-erh-t'ai, had Chin turned over to the new financial commissioner for further interrogation and also ordered the investigation of all local officials guilty of "failure to investigate" (*shih-ch'a*) the misconduct of their subordinates, with a view toward future impeachments.[48]

In fact, the *ch'ing-ch'a* officials appear to have been quite successful in uncovering cases of overt embezzlement by individual members of the local bureaucracy. During the second half of YC 7, I-la-chi reported on the progress of the investigation of such cases in the prefectures of Suchow, Sung-chiang, Ch'ang-chou, and T'ai-ts'ang-chou.[49] Under the classification of official embezzlement (*kuan-ch'in*), it was discovered that as the magistrate of Li-shui hsien, Chao Hsiang-kuei had stolen several thousand piculs of rice which he disguised as having been used for famine relief. In K'un-shan hsien, Wang Su-wei and others had embezzled more than 2,000 taels obtained from the sale of firewood on government land (*kuan-ti ch'ai-chia*). Former Hua-ting magistrate Lin K'uang pocketed 8,600 taels which he falsely reported as arrears, and another 4,200 taels were embezzled by the Wu-chin magistrate, Ch'en Shen, using the same method. All of these officials confessed to their crimes under the pressure of the *ch'ing-ch'a* investigation.

A number of cases of runner, clerk, and gentry embezzlement were also discovered through the investigative efforts of the *ch'ing-ch'a* officials. A few examples may be cited here. In Lou hsien, a tax-collection clerk was accused of "cheating the people out of their taxes" (*k'uang-p'ien liang-hu yin*).[50] A *chien-sheng* named Ch'in Pen-heng in Wu-hsi was found to have contracted to pay people's taxes, embezzling their remittances by issuing false tax notification receipts (*chia-ch'uan pao-ch'in ch'ien-liang*). Ch'in was deprived of his *chien-sheng* status and his case was turned over to the financial and judicial commissioners for investigation and sentencing.[51] A similar case was uncovered by a *hsieh-ch'a* officer in cooperation with the Shang-hai hsien magistrate. Here, a *chien-sheng* named Fan was in league with the local tithing chief (*chia-shou*) to engage in proxy remittance and the registration of landholdings under fictitious names (*hua-fen kuei-hu*).[52] In P'ei chou and Sui-ning hsien, *hsieh-ch'a* officers reported that the head yamen clerks had conspired with the local *li-shou* to steal government funds. Investigation into areas exempted from arrears payments because of flood damage to crops disclosed that in at least four villages no reduction in harvests had occurred. The collection of arrears had continued and the revenues were pocketed by the clerks themselves.[53]

These isolated successes began to pale in the face of revelations regarding the depth to which clerical malfeasance had penetrated local tax administration. The most shocking discovery occurred by accident. One of the most effective and hardworking of the *fen-ch'a* officials was a man named Feng Ching-hsia. It was under

Feng's supervision that many of the above crimes were discovered. In mid-YC 7, information reached Feng's office that a *ch'ü* clerk in Wu-hsi hsien named Li Ming-ju had embezzled a large amount of tax revenue. Feng ordered him to produce his accounts. Quite unexpectedly, a commoner named Yang Shih-yü, who had been hired by Li Ming-ju to do his paperwork, came forward with all the private records (*ssu-shou ti-pu*) compiled during Li's fifteen years in charge of tax collection in T'ien-shang *ch'ü*. In all they came to 200 volumes, which Feng had Yang Shih-yü deliver to Suchow. In contrast to the registers in the magistrate's yamen, the clerk's accounts contained a complete record of the taxpayers in the area, the land they owned, the taxes due on each holding, and how much was paid and in arrears. However, after two days of careful scrutiny, Feng and Yang discovered that Li Ming-ju was able to manipulate the tax-collection process by an inconspicuous system of secret marks placed beside each entry.[54] In effect, this code provided the clerk with a duplicate set of books so that information about his own activities could be concealed from the magistrate. Only by decoding these accounts could anyone begin to unravel the mystery of who really owed the government money and how the embezzlement of taxes had been accomplished.[55] When Feng asked Yang Shih-yü if the other *ch'ü* clerks also used such books, Yang replied that not only did they exist in the fifteen *ch'ü* in Wu-hsi, but there was not a prefecture, chou, or hsien in the region in which *ti-pu* were not compiled. Clerks would even sell these registers, presumably to incoming clerks, in order to enable them to continue the corrupt practices of their predecessors.[56] The names applied to these registers varied and the codes were not the same, but *ti-pu* were an indispensable tool for the clerk wishing to profit from his post.

Armed with this information from Feng Ching-hsia, I-la-chi met with Ma-erh-t'ai and decided to call a meeting of all nearby *ch'ing-ch'a* officials to be held in the governor's yamen. The urgency of confiscating all such books was impressed upon them, and written instructions to that effect were sent out to all other local and *ch'ing-ch'a* officials. Before long, *ti-pu* were confiscated in Suchow, Sung-chiang, and Ch'ang-chou prefectures, and the *hsieh-ch'a* set to work decoding the secret markings, volume by volume, so that embezzled items and manipulation of the tax rolls could be exposed.[57] By the tenth month of YC 7, Ma-erh-t'ai reported that 60 to 70 percent of the *ti-pu* in Suchow, Sung-chiang, Chen-chiang, and Chiang-ning prefectures had been seized.[58] As each case of embezzlement and arrears was disclosed, the information was turned over to the *fen-ch'a* officials, who carried out surprise inspections of the areas involved in order to verify the facts.[59]

The discovery of the duplicate accounts led to a new influx of petitions from gentry, clerks, and commoners who pledged to pay up their taxes, but begged to have their areas excused from compiling accounts and carrying out a thorough *ch'ing-ch'a*.[60] Some officials feared that the large number of confessions to embezzlement received from yamen runners might be part of a cover-up in which runners were being bribed to take the blame for arrears in the hope that once the government was reimbursed the investigations would cease.[61] If anyone had such hopes, he was soon disappointed, for from the start, the intention of the emperor was to disclose the origins of corruption and arrears at the local level and rectify the irregularities that made them possible. Actual reimbursement of arrears was a secondary issue at this time. Again and again the emperor reminded his emissaries in Kiangnan that the "important thing in this *ch'ing-ch'a* of accumulated arrears is to ferret out abuses. You must not devote yourselves exclusively to the collection of taxes."[62] Therefore, Ma-erh-t'ai refused these requests and reminded the Kiangnan public that the purpose of the *ch'ing-ch'a* was to remove the burdens on the people and thoroughly clean up Kiangnan's tax administration. This was to be accomplished by isolating those households that were falsely registered and discovering the real parties responsible for each *mou* of land so that accurate registers could be compiled.[63] Because most of those who were now volunteering to pay up probably had something to hide, Ma-erh-t'ai was adamant that their tax obligations receive special attention.

With the help of the duplicate registers, confessions by clerks, runners, officials, and gentry, and interviews with ordinary villagers, the *ch'ing-ch'a* officials were able to begin to assemble a profile of abuses in Kiangnan's tax administration. Following the guidelines established by the emperor, these were divided into three categories: official embezzlement, clerk and runner engrossment, and evasion of taxation by the taxpayers themselves.

The Anatomy of Tax Corruption

The fabrication of "people's arrears" by chou and hsien magistrates was the most easily detected of the malpractices examined by the *ch'ing-ch'a* investigators. Many of the methods used had already been discovered during the deficit inquiries that accompanied the *huo-hao kuei-kung* reforms. Chou and hsien officials with shortages in their own treasuries and granaries often falsified the *liu-shui ch'uan-ken* in their yamen in order to transfer taxes received from the people into their own coffers.[64] Although this was commonly done at the time that an official turned over his accounts to his successor, or in anticipation of a spot investigation by his superior, natural disasters also prompted officials to embezzle taxpayer remittances. In some instances, a magistrate who had obtained a tax deferment for his jurisdiction would conceal the emperor's benevolence from the local population. Because the government did not expect any remittances at this time, all taxes paid could be pocketed by the magistrate and recorded in his yamen accounts as "yet to be paid." At other times the magistrate chose not to risk punishment for failure to announce a tax remission, but pocketed all taxes received prior to the release of the announcement of the imperial grace period. In both instances the taxpayers would consider their taxes to have been paid, hence the embezzlement amounts would eventually show up in the yamen accounts as people's arrears due to tax resistance.[65]

Natural disaster provided an opportunity for malfeasance by clerks and taxpayers as well. Magistrates generally left to their clerks the determination of which households were entitled to tax relief. The clerks often exaggerated the extent of a disaster and the amount of taxes that required exemption. This enabled them to pocket the taxes paid by households that had not experienced financial hardship. It was also common for clerks to sell receipts verifying a household's inability to pay taxes because of damage to its crops in a flood or drought. Households untouched by disaster could avoid paying taxes by "purchasing barren status" (*mai-huang*), although it is likely that cultivators genuinely stricken by disaster were also forced to bribe the clerks in this fashion before obtaining their exemption. Clerks, runners, and officials also tried to get tax exemptions for their own land in the area under their jurisdiction. This practice was known as "falsely declaring barren status" (*mao-huang*).[66] These practices were so widespread and had been carried out for so many years that Yin-chi-shan felt it would be impossible to distinguish between households whose crops had really been destroyed and those that had procured exemption under false pretenses. In order to avoid burdening innocent people, investigation of arrears arising from these methods was halted.

A third technique used by officials to embezzle taxes involved their relationship with members of the region's economic and social elite. It will be recalled that taxpayers were supposed to deposit their own taxes in the yamen's locked tax chests. Before the tax-collection season began, magistrates often borrowed silver from gentry and wealthy households in their jurisdictions on the pretext of needing money to carry out public business. They would usually pledge to apply the borrowed funds to the concerned household's taxes that year. Once in the hands of the magistrate, such loans were rarely reimbursed to the public coffers. Naturally, the resultant arrears for that year would not be attributed to the powerful households from which the funds were originally borrowed, but would be apportioned in tiny amounts among the taxes due from numerous small commoner households.[67]

By far the greatest number of arrears resulting from corruption were attributed to clerks. By the end of YC 7, confessions had been obtained from these members of the yamen staff accounting for over 2,400,000 taels in embezzled taxes.[68] Because clerks were in charge of the tax registers and were the agents of the government actually sent to the countryside to supervise the collection of taxes,[69] they were in a unique position to manipulate the tax system to their own benefit. In many cases the head clerks (*ching-ch'eng*) in the yamen and the clerks in charge of the tax chests (*kuei-shu*) conspired with the officials themselves to alter register receipts and directly steal paid taxes.[70] Clerks, however, had a number of independent means of siphoning off the people's remittances, creating arrears which chou and hsien officials never suspected had been embezzled.

Clerks sometimes imitated the methods utilized by magistrates, particularly when the latter did not supervise the compilation of tax registers. In such instances it was relatively easy for clerks to pocket a portion of the taxes they collected, distributing the amount stolen into the arrears of all the households in the area.[71] A similar technique, known as *tsai-liang*, involved increasing the tax obligations of the weakest households by minute amounts, even before the tax-prompting process began.[72]

Because the land registers were in the hands of the yamen's fiscal clerks, it was also possible for them to make changes in the actual classification of land. By altering the ratings on property, designating medium-quality land as low-quality and vice versa, it was possible to collect taxes at the usual rate, keeping the difference between the amount paid and the amount due in the registers. The difference in taxes due for the whole hsien when ratings were lowered to that of less fertile land was made up in the registers by elevating the ratings on land in other parts of the hsien. Because the taxpayer, however, still paid his usual rate, in the latter case the difference in assessments would appear as arrears in the yamen accounts. This practice was known as *kai-tse*.[73]

Other forms of embezzlement by clerks involved the alteration of tax receipts. One simple method of pocketing paid taxes was simply not to issue a receipt. This being a common practice throughout the Kiangnan region, in many places the people never demanded proof of payment. As a result, the taxpayers had no recourse against corrupt clerks. A closely related practice was to pocket the remittances of small households and report that these taxpayers had fled the land to evade taxation.[74] Some magistrates did enforce the regulations requiring the use of three- and four-stub receipts, but these were also easily circumvented. For example, the practice known as *ta-hsiao p'iao* entailed issuing a receipt to the taxpayer bearing the actual amount remitted. However, on the stub sent to the hsien yamen, only 10 to 20 percent of the payment was recorded. The remainder was stolen by the clerks. Some clerks did not even bother to alter receipts and simply manufactured their own duplicates, complete with forged official seals.[75]

Probably the most difficult form of tax manipulation to deal with was that perpetrated by the families of gentry and retired officials (*shen-huan*), local powerful households, "wicked" lower-degree holders, and "local rowdies" (*ti-kun*). Without denying that there were gentry in Kiangsu who were possessed of integrity and a spirit of public service, the *ch'ing-ch'a* officials found that a large number were willing to evade taxation and pass their debt on to the ordinary village population. Some simply neglected to pay their taxes at all. By promptly remitting the *huo-hao* portion of their taxes to the magistrate, many were able for many years to forestall local-government pressure to pay the *cheng-hsiang* part of their taxes. Others discovered that by bribing the head clerk with 10 to 20 percent of the taxes due, they could avoid being harassed when each period for the prompting of outstanding taxes arrived. Similar bribes could also be made to subordinate clerks in return for alteration of the yamen accounts. For example, for a fee, a clerk might be willing to allow a taxpayer to pay 40, 50, or 60 taels, which he would then register as a payment of 100 taels. The subordinate clerks were not liable for discrepancies between the silver on hand and that recorded in the accounts, hence the magistrate would end up responsible for the difference.[76] Such methods, of course, were available only to landowners with considerable holdings.

Members of the rural elite had other, more devious methods of evading taxes and profiting from the tax-collection process. The most destructive of the entire tax structure was the practice known as *kuei-li hu-ming*, the registration of false households and fictitious names.[77] In the Kiangnan region, it was not uncommon for large landowners to divide their holdings into several tens or even several hundreds of different household registrations, each claiming a minute amount of land. The name of the household heads for each of these *hu* would be falsified, using the names of dead ancestors, people who had migrated from the area, temple names, and so on. Ownership of the land was rendered difficult to trace, and the small amount of arrears from each *hu* discouraged investigation. Even if they were found out, their familiarity with the malpractices of officials and clerks and their own influence in the community allowed the rural elite to blackmail the regular bureaucracy into granting them almost total immunity from taxation. It was this power that encouraged local gentry and "strongmen" to engage in proxy remittance. Often, if a member of the local gentry owned little or no land himself, he would invite friends or relatives to register their holdings under his name. The latter would comply in the hope of paying their taxes at a lower "gentry rate." As the actual owners of the land gave their taxes to him to pay, the local "strongman" or lower-degree-holder could pocket the money and resist payment to the local government. Similar opportunities arose when a member of the gentry sold land. By coercing the purchaser into keeping the registration of the land under his own name, the previous owner could force the new owner to consign all his taxes to him. Involvement in proxy remittance also extended to lands with which the local elite had no direct connections. They, like the clerks and runners in the hsien yamen, used the common people's fear of any involvement with the bureaucracy to relieve them of the task of depositing their taxes in the yamen tax chests. The petty taxpayer usually paid his taxes in full, along with a fee to the magnanimous middleman, but only a portion of these remittances ever reached the magistrate's treasury.

It should be obvious from the above discussion that the average small taxpayer did not have access to these methods of tax evasion and embezzlement. Their implementation depended entirely on wealth, status, and access to force. At first, the *ch'ing-ch'a* officials predicted that as much as 80 to 90 percent of the taxes that had been designated as people's arrears would ultimately be revealed to have been the result of abuses by yamen personnel and powerful members of the local community.[78] These taxes proved far more difficult to collect because their theft was hidden in a cloud of false registrations and local particularistic ties and was carried out before the taxes ever reached the local government.

The root of all these abuses was traced to the system of land and tax registration. Meticulous procedures for registering land by household and guaranteeing individual responsibility for tax remittance were delineated in the Ch'ing code. Nevertheless, without scrupulous attention to the maintenance of chou and hsien tax records, these regulations were no more than "empty words on paper." Although tax evasion and hidden land were problems in every province, in Kiangnan the system of land and tax registration had disintegrated to such a degree that in some places it was barely distinguishable from the old *li-chia* system under the Ming, without any of the protections that that system had once promised. Because the registration of land for tax purposes bore so little resemblance to actual land ownership, taxes in many areas of Kiangsu were collected by locality and not by household.[79] In some cases, the "real collection registers" (*shih-cheng e-ts'e*) on which tax collection was supposed to be based bore no more than the name of the *li-chang* for each area. No pretense was even made at recording the names of taxpaying households, false or otherwise.[80] Even in cases where lists of taxpayers were kept, the clerk or runner in charge of tax collection in a village was charged only with filling the quota. Magistrates, with little knowledge of the locale and too many duties to allow them to investigate each village in person, were not concerned with the liabilities of individual households. When it came time, therefore, for an inquiry into arrears, the records often contained not a single real taxpayer who could be pressed for payment.[81] The names applied to the village clerks and runners in charge of taxation varied from place to place, but almost all were indicative of their evolution from the tax-prompting headman of the previous dynasty.[82]

Perhaps the most important reason that clerks and runners could persist in the manipulation of land and tax registration was that in many areas tax-collection posts had, in effect, become hereditary. Whereas clerical posts in the central government had come under severe scrutiny earlier in the dynasty, so-called *shih-ch'üeh*, passed on from father to son and brother to brother, were still widespread at the local level.[83] Efforts to investigate abuses through the offices of the regular provincial bureaucracy were also obstructed by the fact that even the financial commissioner's yamen was controlled by hereditary clerks. According to Censor Kao Shan, who was sent to Kiangnan by the emperor to assist in the *ch'ing-ch'a* of arrears, the clerks in the fiscal section of the financial commissioner's yamen were organized so that one clerk had exclusive control over the affairs of each chou and hsien. Only these clerks knew how much tax revenue was to be retained or remitted in each area. Likewise, only these clerks knew the extent of embezzlement, misappropriation, and excessive spending in the local yamen. If the financial commissioner wanted to investigate the taxes of a certain chou or hsien he had to rely on the responsible clerk in his own office. If clerks employed by the chou and hsien were engaged in manipulation of tax registers, these provincial level clerks were so adept at tampering with the higher-level records that they could conceal such practices completely. Most of the financial commissioner's clerks were either in collusion with their local counterparts to steal taxes at the source, or conspired with those chou and hsien clerks who were in league with the gentry in order to profit indirectly from proxy remittance. The hereditary nature of these fiscal clerkships meant that the taxes of many areas in the province had virtually become the family property of those whose job it was to collect them.[84]

This being the case, it is not surprising that the *ch'ing-ch'a* officials found that Kiangnan's "fish-scale registers," the land records upon which all local-land and head-tax registers were based, were utterly useless. "Fish-scale registers" were supposed to be the product of imperial land surveys. At the time of such a survey, each parcel of land in an area was given a registration number and was classified as either high (*shang*), medium (*chung*), or low (*hsia*) in productivity, for the purpose of assessing rates of taxation. Two copies of these registers were compiled, one to be kept in the financial commissioner's yamen and one to be stored in the chou or hsien treasury. It was now revealed that most of the "fish-scale registers" in Kiangnan had been burned, hidden, or revised beyond recognition.[85] Without collusion between the financial commissioner's clerks and the staff of the chou and hsien yamen, the situation could never have deteriorated to this extent.

Two approaches were devised to alleviate these basic weaknesses in tax administration. One entailed stricter supervision of clerks and runners. The *huo-hao kuei-kung* reforms had already taken a step in the right direction by providing for clerical salaries from public-expense funds. It was now decided to extend punishment for missing funds to clerks and runners as well as to regular officials.[86] Efforts were made to prohibit magistrates from charging fees to clerks in return for the privilege of supervising tax collection, a practice that served only to encourage clerical corruption.[87] In order to prevent cover-ups at the clerical level, some officials also favored a system of rewards for information about corruption to supplement punishment for wrongdoing.[88]

Besides these attempts to tighten government control over clerical behavior, efforts were made to improve land and tax registration so that embezzlement would be more difficult. The obstacles to such an endeavor were numerous and there was no consensus on the best method to follow. One of the major impediments to reform of tax registration was the fact that whereas taxes were assessed on the land, they were collected from individual households. In the north, where a large portion of the land was tilled by those who owned it or rented from nearby landlords or fellow peasants, this did not pose a great problem for administrators. However, in the Kiangnan region, where absentee landlordism was high and the market in landed property was very active, tax registration by household led to serious defects in tax records.

Clearly, for the *ch'ing-ch'a* to have lasting results, it was necessary to conduct a complete cadastral survey of all cultivated land in the region so that new "fish-scale registers" could be compiled.[89] However, the question still remained as to how the data so derived were to be organized to best ensure full tax collection. As early as 1723, a new method of land registration had been attempted in several areas in an effort to eliminate the remnants of the *li-chia* system and make up for deficiencies in the *Fu-i ch'üan-shu*.[90] This method, known as *shun-chuang chih-fa* or *shun-chuang kun-ts'un*, had as its basis the division of the rural population into *pao-chia* units to facilitate local control. The residents of each town and village were divided into *chia* of ten households each. For each *chia* a list was drawn up similar to the door placards (*yen-hu men-tan*) used in the mutual-security-guarantee system. These lists were then passed from one household to the next, allowing the taxpayer to fill in the information required by the local government. Space was provided for the real name of the household head, the address and number of people in the *hu*, the amount of land owned, how much of the land was cultivated and how much was barren, the amount of tax in grain and silver due on each parcel, and the village, *t'u*, and *chia* in which each was registered.[91] The principle behind this system was that even if a person's land was scattered among a number of *t'u*, it should be registered together at the owner's place of residence. Tax payments could then be administered by one agent and prompted by the use of "rolling lists."[92] The accuracy of these declarations was checked by having the clerks in charge of the tax registers in each *t'u* draw up similar lists, which were then compared with the "real collection registers" in the magistrate's yamen and the data provided by the people themselves.[93]

The greatest weakness of this system was that not everyone's land was situated in the *t'u* in which he lived.[94] In some cases, landowners deliberately established residence away from their land in an effort to evade taxation. Under these circumstances they were unlikely to report this land when filling out their *shun-chuang* forms. The time and effort required of the clerks in charge of one *t'u* to track down land possessed by its residents in other *t'u* would be enormous, hence such absentee landowners often escaped taxation. This practice, known as *kuo-hu fei-liang*, was especially effective in evading taxes in places like Kiangnan, where the government's own land registers were almost useless.

Another problem arose from the high turnover of land ownership in the Kiangnan region. Utilization of a system of registration based on the household and not the land itself made it difficult for officials to keep track of the land as it changed hands. One common practice used by wealthy households to evade taxes involved their role as moneylenders to the poor. Rather than sell land outright, a poor household would often mortgage it to a wealthy household. The original owner would receive perhaps half the value of his land, but had the right to buy it back within a fixed time period. Use of the land generally passed into the hands of the holder of the mortgage, but title was not necessarily transferred to the wealthier party. Consequently, the property was lost to the original owner, but his tax liability remained (*ch'an-ch'ü liang-ts'un*). The party mortgaging his land did not have the ability to pay his taxes because he could no longer farm it, or was able to do so only by paying the mortgage holder rent. The person who had lent him the money for which his land was collateral was equally unwilling to pay the tax, because technically the land was not his own. As a result, the tax went unpaid and the government could not determine responsibility for the plot.[95] The lucrative nature of such arrangements encouraged many usurers to refuse title to such land even after the time limit for redemption was up. Even in the case of outright sale of land, however, failure to report the transaction to the government could result in exemption from taxation for many years.

Two measures were introduced to deal with the defects in this system of land registration. One was the method of tax registration by territorial division (*pan-t'u wan-liang chih-fa*), suggested in Kiangnan by the *fen-ch'a* official Wen Erh-sun. All the territory under a magistrate's jurisdiction was still divided along a grid, but registration for tax purposes was now based on the land, not on the household. If a plot of land was situated in a certain *t'u*, then taxes on it were to be registered in that *t'u* regardless of who owned the land or where the owner lived. If a plot of land extended over more than one *t'u*, a separate registration was established for that portion of the land in each. Once a complete land survey was carried out, no matter how often a plot of land changed hands or where the owner moved, the records would be clear because the land itself could not be moved or hidden. It was only a matter of keeping an account of who owned each plot.[96] It was felt that this would be easy, because the tenants on any piece of absentee-owned land would always know to whom they paid their rent.

To guarantee that the government should be informed of land and property transactions and that the magistrates, the clerks, or the taxpayers not conspire to hide landownership from the government, a new system of land and property contracts was also established. The original plan was proposed by Honan Governor T'ien Wen-ching in YC 5 (1727). Previously, when land or buildings changed hands, any sheet of blank paper could be used to draw up a contract between the two parties involved in the transaction. Such a contract became legally binding only when an official document called a *ch'i-wei* was attached to one corner. *Ch'i-wei* were issued by the financial commissioner of each province to the chou and hsien magistrates. The latter sold them to the people and affixed his seal across the *ch'i-wei* and the contract to avoid fraud. The number of *ch'i-wei* distributed by the magistrates was an indication to the financial commissioner of the amount of taxes due in the area. The submission of contracts for the application of *ch'i-wei* was one of the few ways the magistrate had to determine who was responsible for the taxes on each piece of land in his jurisdiction. For the new owner, the existence of the *ch'i-wei* on his contract or deed constituted legal proof of ownership in the event of a property dispute.

By YC 5, this system had broken down. Magistrates utilized the issuance of *ch'i-wei* as a source of revenue, often charging as much as five *ch'ien* for this service. People making large purchases might not mind the cost, but small-holders, who often dealt in transactions which themselves were worth no more than a few *ch'ien*, simply stopped buying the *ch'i-wei* or declaring responsibility for the tax. Moreover, since it was to the magistrate's advantage to hide the amount of taxable land in his jurisdiction, many local officials disregarded the requirement to affix *ch'i-wei*, using up that which was sent by the financial commissioner without asking for more when additional sales were brought to their attention. *Ch'i-wei* gradually ceased to function as necessary proof of purchase, and increasingly the people neglected to report transactions in land.[97]

In order to ensure that the people would report land sales, T'ien Wen-ching suggested the use of a system of contract paper (*ch'i-chih*). According to his plan, when people bought buildings or land, they would no longer be allowed to use any blank piece of paper to draw up a contract. Instead, special contract paper, similar to the perforated sheets used to issue *san-lien yin-p'iao*, would be printed by the financial commissioner. He would issue a certain number to every chou and hsien, according to the size of the jurisdiction and the number of acres of agricultural land within its borders. The contract paper would be bound in volumes of 100 sheets each and sent directly from the printer to the chou and hsien to avoid any corruption by the financial commissioner's own staff. Every sheet would have a serial number against which the financial commissioner could check the issue made to each magistrate. When the contract paper arrived, the magistrate would tear off the number stubs and send the contract paper to paper shops for direct sale to the people. To guard against overcharges for the paper, on each sheet would be printed the words, "Each sheet of contract paper is to be sold by the magistrate for five *wen* [approximately 0.005 tael], which will be sent to the financial commissioner to cover the costs of ink and paper. It is forbidden to burden the people by charging more." A register would be issued to each shop selling the paper, in which the shopkeeper would record the personal data of the individual to whom each sheet was sold. If a mistake was made or a deal did not go through, the purchaser was to bring the original sheet back to the shop so that the shopkeeper could send it to the magistrate to return to the financial commissioner as evidence that no transaction was being hidden.

After purchasing the contract paper, the seller of the property would record on his section how much land and buildings or other structures were included in the sale, who the seller and the purchaser were, how much the property sold for, a statement that the property was sold outright and not mortgaged or pawned, a bond that neither neighbors nor relatives disputed ownership of the land, and the date of the transaction. Once the deal was finalized, the new owner would then bring the contract to the magistrate. After the new owner paid the property-deed tax (*t'ien-fang ch'i-shui*), the magistrate would affix his seal to the contract and the middle stub, which he sent to the financial commissioner along with the tax. In addition, he would copy the information concerning the contract onto the stub kept in his office as a record for readjusting the land-tax registers.[98] No contract would be considered valid if it was not made on government contract paper and did not bear the magistrate's seal. The stores selling the paper kept a record of who purchased each piece, hence the magistrate could easily track down anyone who did not bring his contract in to pay the tax and register the transfer of property.

The purpose of contract paper was thus as much to provide the magistrate with accurate information regarding land transactions as to control the magistrate's remittances of the property-deed tax. It is difficult to know how well this system worked in helping to rectify the inaccuracies in local tax records. However, the necessity of using clerks to collect the tax and affix the seal seems to have led to new opportunities for corruption.[99] Nevertheless, in conjunction with the *pan-t'u wan-liang chih-fa* it was hoped that at least a start could be made in clearing up Kiangnan's land and tax records and with them, the region's extraordinary accumulation of arrears.

The Final Reckoning

The Kiangnan *ch'ing-ch'a* was brought to a close at the end of YC 8 (1730), when the "clear accounts" (*ch'ing-ts'e*) for each jurisdiction and for the province as a whole were submitted to the emperor.[100] The findings of investigators in Kiangsu broken down by prefectural-level administrative unit are delineated in table 6.1.[101] The enormous task undertaken by the men assigned to the Kiangnan *ch'ing-ch'a* can be inferred from these figures. In the end, it was determined that only 54 percent of the total arrears in Kiangsu province were attributable to popular tax delinquency. The remainder was the result of corruption on the part of officials, their staff, and members of the local elite. We do not know what proportion of those taxes classified as genuine "people's arrears" were the result of tax evasion by wealthy and powerful landowners in the province. However, the fact that only 0.5 percent of this tax debt was acknowledged by the taxpayers prior to the investigation is vivid testimony to the chaotic state of Kiangnan's tax rolls.

Determination of these figures and the reckoning of responsibility for every tael listed had by no means been an easy process. Once the private record books of the chou and hsien clerks were confiscated and decoded and confessions of embezzlement were obtained from local officials and their subordinates, the *hsieh-ch'a* officials still had to undertake house-to-house investigations in many areas in order to verify their findings.[102] Occasionally these investigators met with violence at the hands of the local people. When officials were sent to one area of Anhui accused of falsifying flood and drought damage to obtain exemption from taxes, "the local people" rioted in an effort to drive them away.[103] In some instances, resistance may have been justified. A report by an imperial emissary to Kiangnan held that Feng Ching-hsia had been overly zealous in his pursuit of arreared taxes in Ch'ang-chou prefecture, forcing confessions of clerical embezzlement and *pao-lan* even where they did not exist. According to Hai-pao, Feng even compelled people to confess to having arrears that exceeded their original tax liabilities, with the result that Ch'ang-chou reported about 60,000 taels more income than the original tax shortage. Whether or not Hai-pao's account of the situation was accurate, "the people of the prefecture" clearly were not happy with the investigation. When Yin-chi-shan, now governor of Kiangsu, visited the prefectural capital, a huge crowd surrounded him to voice their

Table 6.1 *Kiangsu Arrears, 1712–26 (in taels)*

	Original Arrears	Arrears originally acknowledged by taxpayers	Total arrears under investigation	Responsibility as determined by ch'ing-ch'a			Actual people's arrears	People's arrears as a percentage of missing taxes
				Officials	Staff	Tax farmers		
Suchow fu	2,579,594	125,536	2,454,058	3,740	978,287	3,967	1,593,600	61.8
Sung-chiang fu	2,309,457	65,470	2,243,987	17,679	877,873	263,997	1,149,980	49.8
Ch'ang-chou fu	1,967,198	15,086	1,952,112	7,226	745,426	55,849	1,158,697	58.9
T'ai-ts'ang chou	1,844,148	64,700	1,779,448	—	1,026,719	—	817,429	44.3
Chen-chiang fu	680,259	15,594	664,665	—	114,987	53,253	512,019	75.3
Wei-an fu	376,034	1,315	374,719	—	310,903	26,934	38,197	10.2
Kiangning fu	332,877	15,540	317,337	751	106,435	196	225,495	67.7
Yangchow fu	154,031	2,047	151,984	—	89,411	47	64,573	41.9
T'ung chou	44,599	2,969	41,630	—	18,489	1,762	24,348	54.6
Hsü chou	40,060	882	39,178	—	360	47	39,653	98.9
All wei-so	38,655	434	38,221	17	2,291	—	36,347	94.0
P'ei chou	36,061	506	35,555	1,071	12,457	—	22,533	62.5
Hai chou	26,978	3,510	23,468	—	5,928	—	21,050	78.0
Total	10,429,951	313,589	10,116,362	30,484	4,289,566	406,052	5,703,849	55.0

SOURCE: "Ch'a Kiangsu ku-shu KH 51–YC 4 chi-ch'ien ch'ien-liang nien-k'uan ch'in-ch'ien shu-mu wen-ts'e," YC 8,11,21, *Nei-ko ta-k'u hsien-ts'un Ch'ing-tai han-wen huang ts'e* no. 598.

grievances. It was only after the governor met with representatives of the disgruntled taxpayers in a nearby Buddhist temple that the people were placated and agreed to return home.[104]

Officials also had to cope with demonstrations by people who hoped to avoid repayment of taxes determined to be "people's arrears." Toward the end of the *ch'ing-ch'a*, a new magistrate was appointed to Shang-hai hsien. By inspecting yamen records he learned that the people in several *t'u* had paid up no more than 10 to 20 percent of their arrears, and many had not paid anything at all. The magistrate twice sent his deputy to press for payment and both times the local people rioted. Then the magistrate assigned the mutual-responsibility headman (*chia-shou*), Chao Wei-ch'en, to assist his deputy in arresting recalcitrant taxpayers. However, when Mr. Chao was found to be one of the taxpayers with long-standing arrears, he too was arrested. Mr. Chao's aging wife came upon this scene, and the sight of her husband being arrested while a mob attacked the magistrate's deputy drove her to suicide. Soon afterwards, the magistrate, accompanied by an entourage of yamen runners, went on a tour of inspection in this area and was met by a large crowd led by Mr. Chao's wife's brother's children. Together they stoned the members of the magistrate's retinue and drove the magistrate out of town, ending, at least temporarily, any efforts to collect arrears from members of the community.[105]

Similar riots also broke out in An-fu hsien in Kiangsi, after the magistrate personally directed the collection of old tax debts in Shang-hsi *hsiang*. When he returned to the hsien city he was met by a group of villagers who surrounded his yamen and began beating up the runners who had accompanied him on his tour. The leaders of the rioters complained that the magistrate had used three former bandits as volunteers to exact tax payments and that these thugs, as well as regular yamen runners, were riding rough-shod over the villagers. Investigators subsequently found that the accused men were former bandits and that the methods used to exact payment of arrears did result in undue harassment of the local population. Nevertheless, it was felt to have been necessary to punish the leaders of the rioting villagers for their failure to press their case peacefully by petitioning the magistrate's superiors.[106]

Instances of overt popular resistance such as these were exceptional. More subtle resistance to the *ch'ing-ch'a*, however, also hampered the work of investigators. Some residents still held out hope of avoiding a *ch'ing-ch'a* by paying off the arrears before guilt was determined. One such case occurred in She hsien in An-hui's Hui-chou prefecture.[107] Here, for reasons unknown, a group of salt merchants volunteered to pay the 26,549 taels of accumulated arrears still outstanding in the hsien. The leader of the merchants was a native of She hsien named Huang Kuang-te. Claiming that the arrears were all owed by households that had fled or had died out, or were old, young, women, or very ill members of the rural population, Huang and his followers begged the Salt Commissioner to transmit their desire to use this opportunity to show their gratitude for the emperor's benevolence. The higher officials of the province and the governor-general were extremely suspicious of this gesture and insisted that even if the salt merchants did pay up the debt of the people, a thorough *ch'ing-ch'a* would still be carried out to determine the source of arrears and prevent future malpractices and tax evasion. Moreover, although the merchants had proposed canceling the debt over a period of four years, the government demanded that they comply with the two-year time limit originally set for the repayment of arrears. After much pressure from the Anhui governor, the merchants agreed to submit the entire sum within one year. However, by the time this payment was due, only 1,980 taels had actually reached the government's coffers.

While the upper echelon of the provincial bureaucracy was debating whether or not to accept this contribution, it was discovered that the former magistrate of She hsien had already erected a stone tablet in his yamen courtyard engraved with the names of the salt merchants and the amount of taxes they had pledged to contribute. There was no one in the hsien who did not know of the merchants' act of charity. The officials were faced with a real dilemma. Even if the tax arrears were paid by a third party, it was still their duty to carry out a *ch'ing-ch'a* in She hsien. On the other hand, if they now sent a team of *hsieh-ch'a* officials to the area, it would cause a public disturbance. Although the taxes had not even been paid, to the people this was a closed case. How could they conceive of government agents who were interested only in information and not in extorting more of their hard-earned money? Rather than create a situation in which the salt merchants would be made to look like the saviors of the people and the government as a pack of vultures after the last ounce of the people's blood, the *ch'ing-ch'a* in She hsien was called off.

Whether the merchants were really motivated by a desire to help the poor of their native place or had hopes of hiding land holdings of their own will probably never be known. That the government was so hesitant to disturb the people by sending a *ch'ing-ch'a* team, and debated the issue for at least six months before deciding against it, indicates how sensitive they were to the possibility of violence resulting from their investigations. Perhaps the few instances for which we now have evidence were indicative of a widespread popular inability, by the eighteenth century, to distinguish between government efforts to help them and government efforts to oppress them.

As the "clear accounts" were drawn up, the *ch'ing-ch'a* officials also began to worry that their estimates of arrears and embezzlement might not be accurate. The original records of Kiangnan's land and head taxes were in such disarray that much of the investigators' work depended on oral declarations and written bonds obtained from the local people. One problem arose from the fact that commoners sometimes registered their land under the names of gentry households. The government hoped that once the campaign to collect arrears on such land began, the actual ownership would become known. However, Kiangsi Financial Commissioner Wang Hung even doubted the veracity of those bonds that had recently been solicited as testimony to the accurate registration of land. These falsifications may have resulted from gentry efforts to protect their *pao-lan* activities, or from commoners' own hopes of evading eventual repayment under the protection of powerful local households. In either case, the government could not begin to determine the truth if the people did not come forward and confess.[108]

Another obstacle to the accurate categorization of taxes in arrears resulted from the fact that the taxes in each chou and hsien were handled by clerks who were local people and had a vested interest in sabotaging the investigations. The backgrounds of these people varied. Some were gentry and some were commoners. Some had considerable land holdings of their own, but between 60 and 70 percent were landless. According to the guidelines established by the government, if a landless clerk admitted responsibility for arrears, then the arrears had to be classified as embezzlement and a list of the households in the particular *t'u* from which the taxes were stolen had to be compiled in order to exonerate the innocent taxpayers accused of owing back taxes. If a landowning clerk admitted to arrears, then his debts were listed as *min-ch'ien*, unless it could be proved that he had also stolen taxes from other households.[109]

Given the frequency of false registration, *pao-lan*, and *ch'an-ch'ü liang-ts'un*, such determinations were not easy to make. In cases where land had been mortgaged, it was decided that the original owner would still be responsible for the tax and the missing funds were listed as *min-ch'ien*. However, if a piece of land had been sold, but the new owner had prevented a change in tax registration in order to evade taxation or carry out proxy remittance, the missing taxes were listed as having been embezzled. This was not merely a problem of semantics. As we shall see, the speed with which these taxes had to be repaid depended entirely on their classification by the *ch'ing-ch'a* officials. Moreover, the investigators had to be extremely cautious in their reliance on members of the local community to rectify errors in tax registration. If the investigations fell under the control of the embezzlers themselves, there would be no way to determine who were the real owners of the land. On the other hand, if the zeal of *ch'ing-ch'a* officials was too great, they ran the risk of accepting popular accusations against innocent runners and clerks.[110]

Clerks also interfered with the determination of responsibility for arrears. It was discovered that some of these men were able to conceal their theft of tax remittances by recording the funds paid as arrears and falsifying the name or location of the responsible taxpayer. By use of these so-called "destroyed receipts" (*tang-p'iao*), the source of the arrears could not be traced and the clerk was made to appear without culpability.[111] During the course of the *ch'ing-ch'a*, some runners were found to have taken responsibility for people's arrears which they had not even embezzled, in the hope of pocketing the payments made by the real guilty parties after the *ch'ing-ch'a* officials left. Impoverished runners and their relatives were even known to take bribes in return for receiving the punishment that should have been meted out to a delinquent taxpayer. In the end the real culprits were never apprehended, and often the taxes were not repaid.[112]

In view of the problems faced by *ch'ing-ch'a* officials seeking to ascertain responsibility for over 10 million taels of oustanding taxes that had been piling up in Kiangsu for fifteen years, it is not surprising to discover that many of their findings were not the product of their investigative expertise. At least 67 percent of all the missing taxes attributed to embezzlement were so classified because someone came forward and confessed to responsibility. If independent verification of malfeasance was so difficult, how effective could the *ch'ing-ch'a* be in eradicating the abuses that Yung-cheng felt stood in the way of the implementation of the *huo-hao kuei-kung* reforms in Kiangnan?

The misgivings of Kiangnan's highest officials should not have encouraged the emperor to expect that the *ch'ing-ch'a* had greatly altered the extent of corruption in the region. As the investigations drew to a close, Yung-cheng ordered that 100,000 taels in regular taxes be stored in the treasuries of busy prefectures, chou, and hsien in order to facilitate disbursement in times of emergencies. Instead of accepting this boon, Governor-general Shih I-chih argued that Kiangnan could handle any exigency with internally generated revenue stores. If the emperor insisted on this largesse, Shih felt it would be best to store it all in the provincial treasuries. Kiangnan's extraordinary system of riverine transport would provide rapid deployment wherever the need arose. The governor-general's real concern was that if such funds were stored in local treasuries, they would be embezzled. Even with a rigorous *ch'ing-ch'a* in progress, Shih felt ill prepared to guard against corruption. If the funds were deposited locally, they would probably sit for years before an emergency arose requiring their use. In the meantime, magistrates would manipulate their accounts in order to steal the funds, and the circuit intendants sent to inspect the stores would conspire to conceal the missing funds by issuing false bonds of guarantee (*fu-t'ung nieh-chieh*).[113] When the money was really needed, there would be nothing left to spend.

The governor-general was not being overly cautious. The limited evidence describing the outcome of the audit of Kiangnan arrears indicates that the failure to effect any real changes in the structure of local power or tax administration ultimately doomed the *ch'ing-ch'a* to the status of a futile exercise. Of the original 4,726,102 taels attributed to embezzlement, only 86,583 taels, or approximately 2 percent, was repaid by 1730.[114] Following the close of the investigation, vigorous efforts to recover stolen taxes from guilty officials were consistently thwarted. Even the confiscation of an official's property did not guarantee the reimbursement of missing tax revenues. Favoritism by incumbent officials resulted in the placing of inflated valuations on confiscated goods. Poor storage and long delays in the sale of some items made them virtually worthless. In a few cases, clerks and runners were found to have stolen the property that was confiscated, for which they substituted inferior goods. Tenants were allowed to continue cultivating confiscated land until it was sold, in order to apply the rent they paid to the original owner's debt. Default by tenants was reported so frequently, however, that additional investigations were necessary to determine when tenants had actually refused to pay their rents and when the rent had been embezzled by the responsible members of the yamen staff.[115] By the time the emperor died, in 1735, these problems had still not been solved.

In YC 10 (1732), Yung-cheng issued an edict allowing all persons found responsible for arrears during the Kiangnan ch'ing-ch'a to pay their debt to the government in installments. Beginning in that year, all persons found guilty of embezzlement and pao-lan were given ten years to reimburse the amounts they owed. Shortages proven to have been the result of default by ordinary taxpayers, on the other hand, could be paid up over a period of twenty years. In order to encourage honesty and public-spiritedness, anyone paying the arrears due in a particular year's installment would be exempt from an equal amount of his following year's quota. The same principle was applied to those guilty of corruption.[116]

Given the extraordinary leniency of these terms, it was expected that taxpayers, officials, clerks, and runners alike would have no trouble complying with the government's demands. Yet, by YC 12 (1734), after the deadline for the first two installments had passed, less than 10 percent of the quota due in each period had been paid. This was due partly to a lack of attention on the part of hsien magistrates, who were more concerned with the collection of current taxes that would reflect upon their official evaluations. Many people, nevertheless, particularly yamen runners, took advantage of a Board decision that held that in cases where the guilty party had died and his property was exhausted, repayment could be exempted. As a result, the number of reports of death from disease among yamen runners soared to as many as 110 per county. Most of these were spurious, and a strict investigation was ordered, along with a stiffening of the punishments for magistrates who failed to press for collection of arrears.[117]

Another group guilty of resisting the payment of arrears was that of absentee landlords. The land of people residing in one hsien but located in another was called chi-chuang land.[118] Owners of such land were able to continue tax resistance because magistrates found it inconvenient to cross borders and arrest a household head with arrears who lived outside their jurisdiction. Moreover, the officials of the chou or hsien in which the recalcitrant taxpayer dwelt generally delayed pursuit of such people because capture did not affect their own chances for promotion.[119] This problem persisted long after the *ch'ing-ch'a* was but a memory, and may have been a further inducement to landowners contemplating residence in distant urban centers.[120]

Even the main purpose of the *ch'ing-ch'a*, the reorganization and rectification of Kiangnan's tax registers, does not seem to have had lasting results. Although the evidence after Yung-cheng's death is sparse, a report from one hsien in Kiangsu, dated CL 18 (1753), points to the continuation of problems attacked more than twenty-five years earlier. According to the magistrate of Chin-t'an hsien in Chen-chiang prefecture, his post was responsible for an annual tax quota of approximately 72,300 taels. Although classified as a medium post, this hsien had tremendous difficulties in getting the taxpayers to pay their taxes in full. Between CL 1 and CL 13, a total of 244,100 taels were in arrears. All except that which was exempted by special imperial edict still remained unpaid. Moreover, in spite of extremely energetic efforts by the magistrate, the governor, and the governor-general, an additional 15,800 taels were in arrears for the period since CL 14. One of the main reasons for this appalling situation was that the land and tax registers were inadequate.[121]

The problems that arose during the Kiangnan *ch'ing-ch'a* were not unique to these three provinces. Examples of false registration, clerical manipulation, official laxity and outright embezzlement could be found everywhere in China,[122] though nowhere were they as deeply embedded in the fabric of local life as in this region. At least for the remainder of the century, arrears do not appear to have had the devastating impact in other provinces that they had in Kiangsu, and to a lesser extent in Anhui and Kiangsi. But, however much the reforms of the early eighteenth century might have helped alleviate the strains on local finances and the fiscal pressures on individual officials, so long as tax collection remained the purview of clerks and runners, so long as local gentry and wealthy households held a monopoly of power and influence below the hsien level, so long as communications remained poor and the heavy burden of official duties made it impossible for any one man to "see everywhere" in his jurisdiction, the ability of the imperial government to institute rationalizing reforms would always be limited.

The problem of "evil gentry and local bully" usurpation of government authority and subversion of local government was thus not a problem peculiar to China in the nineteenth and twentieth centuries. It had deep roots in the very structure of imperial rule. The specific actors who took on these roles may have changed and the power they exercised may have grown, but their existence must be seen as one of the fundamental contradictions within the late-traditional Chinese state. The Kiangnan *ch'ing-ch'a* demonstrates that the dynasty was neither unaware of the problem nor unwilling to take vigorous action to combat it. But without a commitment to social reform, the only tools available to a reform-minded dynasty were bureaucratic. Bureaucratic methods were quite successful in eliminating the causes of corruption within the administrative hierarchy of the provinces until inflation and other factors began to erode the benefits gained from the implementation of *huo-hao kuei-kung*. Below the level of the hsien, however, they only meant a proliferation of paperwork. If three-stub receipts did not halt corruption in the collection of taxes, perhaps four-stub receipts would. If *ch'i-wei* did not ensure honest registration of land transactions, perhaps contract paper would. If magistrates could not control the embezzlement of their subordinates, perhaps keeping three different sets of records which could be checked against each other would help.

In provinces such as Honan and Chihli in the north, where land tenure was relatively simple, the turnover of land slow, and the power of the gentry over the population comparatively weak, the methods introduced during the eighteenth century to halt arrears and deficits worked surprisingly well. In the south, and in Kiangnan in particular, the complexity of land-tenure arrangements, the small size of individual plots, the extremely active land market, the growing number of absentee landlords, and the close links between clerks and gentry in the countryside made any bureaucratic solution impossible. Without a vastly expanded bureaucracy capable of supplanting the informal networks of local power, no dynasty could hope to use bureaucratic solutions to solve the problem of local competition for resources.

Whether in recognition of these problems or in a traditional attempt to establish his reputation as a benevolent ruler, one of the first acts of the Ch'ien-lung emperor upon taking the throne was to declare a tax amnesty for all taxes of over ten years standing and all *min-ch'ien* for YC 12 and earlier.[123] At the same time, Ch'ien-lung opened the way for a reexamination of the reforms his father had so painstakingly guided to fruition during his short but vigorous reign. Thus, politics as well as society came to threaten the very existence of the *huo-hao kuei-kung* reforms.

7

LOOKING AHEAD: THE BREAKDOWN OF THE *HUO-HAO KUEI-KUNG* REFORMS

EVEN UNDER AN ABSOLUTIST REGIME, NO ADMIN-istrative system remains precisely as those who established it intended. Opposition from within the elite and outside it will usually compel modification of the original ideal, as will the necessity to make radical change conform to the widely held norms of a society. In addition, changes may occur in the economic, political, social, and natural environments of a state, which were not anticipated by the originators of reform or which might even have been a by-product of the reforms themselves.[1] Even when they do not completely reverse earlier innovations, later rulers and administrators often do not hold the same vision of a system as that of their predecessors nor have the same commitment to its principles. Finally, within a sociopolitical system, there might be contradictions and defects that no piecemeal effort at reform could rectify, and that, with time, erode earlier achievements.

Following the Yung-cheng emperor's death, a renewed concern for Confucian principles of benevolent rule contributed to the introduction of measures that rendered *huo-hao kuei-kung* unworkable by the end of the eighteenth century. It was not simply traditional philosophy, however, that stood as a barrier to the development of a strong centralized state in China. Behind Confucian exhortations to decrease taxes and protect "the people" lay the more fundamental realities of the late Ch'ing economy and social structure.

Even during the reign of the Yung-cheng emperor, the requirements of widely differing economic and social patterns caused provincial variations in the implementation of *huo-hao kuei-kung*. Ancillary problems connected with arrears and deficits led to a wide range of bureaucratic reforms designed to improve the government's control of official malfeasance, but they left unresolved the issue of clerk and runner engrossment. Furthermore, absentee landlordism and the concentration of landholdings, particularly in the wealthy Kiangnan provinces, were beginning to pose a new threat to the government's ability to collect the taxes needed to make *huo-hao kuei-kung* a success.

The predominance of the agrarian sector in the Chinese economy of the eighteenth century made dependence on revenues from the land a necessity. With this dependence came a natural concern that the demands of government not exceed the ability of the people to pay. In part, the resurgence of traditional rhetoric was a reflection of the competition between the government and the local elite for the productive output of the countryside. But it was also a manifestation of an awareness that the demographic changes fostered by Ch'ing rule would diminish the per capita income of China's growing peasant population.

For the *huo-hao kuei-kung* reforms to continue to function as a deterrent to corruption and a stimulus to greater government participation in the development of the local economic infrastructure, two things were necessary. Local autonomy in the management of *huo-hao* revenues had to be protected in order to ensure flexibility in the collection and allocation of funds. Equally important, local government had to be able to increase levels of income to meet the rising costs of government services that would inevitably result from economic and demographic growth. Neither of those conditions existed during the years after the Yung-cheng reign. Low levels of communications technology and the difficulties encountered in collecting agricultural taxes provoked an increase in bureaucratic control over local *kung-fei* expenditures. At the same time, fear that rising taxes would lead to instability and even popular revolt led to the limitation of the revenues legally available to local government.

The modifications in *huo-hao kuei-kung* introduced during the Ch'ien-lung period were not calculated to destroy the reforms, but

this is precisely what they did. By the end of the reign, local officials were even more handicapped in the fulfillment of their duties
than they had been fifty years before, and corruption became a
threat to the very survival of the unified Chinese state.

The Debate over Huo-hao kuei-kung in the
Early Ch'ien-lung Period

Unlike the Wang An-shih reforms of the Sung dynasty, the reforms of the Yung-cheng period did not polarize the bureaucracy
in such a way as to invite a complete reversal of the programs upon
the death of the emperor in whose name they were carried out. In
part this was due to the decline of "cabinet politics" with the elimination of the post of prime minister. Although the Yung-cheng
emperor attempted to make the reforms effected during his reign
appear to be the result of "grass-roots" impulses, without a clear
forum for policy formation outside the person of the emperor, any
direct attack on the *huo-hao kuei-kung* reforms would appear
to be an attack on the emperor himself. This was even more the
case given the greatly circumscribed role of eunuchs, members of
the imperial family, and central-government ministers under the
Ch'ing. Moreover, the Yung-cheng emperor's untimely death, and
his institution of an indisputable method for naming an heir, precluded the factional struggles surrounding rival claimants to the
throne that had so plagued the K'ang-hsi emperor in the last years
of his reign. Yung-cheng's meticulous use of the palace-memorial
system and selective appointments to high official posts assured
that most of the officials in positions of power supported his programs and had been intimately involved in their implementation
for more than a decade. Many of these officials continued to hold
responsible posts in government for as much as twenty years after
the Ch'ien-lung emperor took the throne.

Yet opposition to *huo-hao kuei-kung* did exist.

It was not uncommon for high officials to send a new emperor
advice during the first few months of his reign. To accept such
counsel was a symbol of the new ruler's intention to open the "avenues of discussion" (*yen-lu*) and govern in a sage manner. A great
many of the memorials dispatched to the Ch'ien-lung emperor following his father's death were simply traditional diatribes on the
need to improve official discipline and morale, though some did

offer specific suggestions for the perfection of government.[2] A number of these addressed the issue of *huo-hao*.

Although no one seems to have been bold enough to suggest the immediate abolition of the Yung-cheng reforms, many of the memorialists were openly critical of certain aspects of their implementation. The old fear that legalization would lead to the collection of new illegal surtaxes in excess of the *huo-hao* quota was voiced with particular vigor.[3] Even though grudging acknowledgement was made of the fact that *huo-hao* was necessary as a source of *kung-fei* and *yang-lien*, critics of the reforms insisted that it be viewed as no more than a temporary expedient. Even the Yung-cheng emperor, they claimed, had pledged that when deficits were cleared up and the treasuries were full, *huo-hao* could gradually be reduced and ultimately banned. Until that time, the new emperor was urged to decrease *huo-hao* to the bare minimum necessary for *yang-lien* and *kung-fei*, so that even those who wished to embezzle would have nothing to embezzle from, and all would know that *huo-hao* was something that could be lowered but could never be raised.

The authors of these memorials shared several basic views on the nature of government. First, their arguments all reflected a belief in a static economy. Hsü Wang-yu began his memorial with one of the traditional formulae for good kingship. The way to ensure the sufficiency of the state's wealth is first to ensure the sufficiency of the people's resources. The way to ensure the sufficiency of the people's resources lies in light taxation. According to Hsü, "there is a fixed amount of wealth on heaven and on earth. If it does not belong to the officials then it belongs to the people."[4] Hsü therefore felt that every penny not taken by the government as taxes was a penny that could benefit the common folk.

Such beliefs were closely linked to a nonactivist conception of the role of local administration. As metropolitan officials, these men had little knowledge of the real costs of public services, nor, it seems, did they recognize their possible benefits to the people. One metropolitan censor later even suggested that *huo-hao* be reduced to a sum equivalent to *yang-lien* alone, on the theory that any expenditures that needed to be made at the local level could be covered by regular *ts'un-liu* taxes.[5]

Finally, though they acknowledged the efficacy of the reforms in counteracting many of the causes of official corruption, the critics of *huo-hao kuei-kung* continued to harbor a deep distrust of local officials. In their judgement, magistrates would always find new ways to milk the people. Furthermore, they felt that by legitimizing one form of surcharge, the effect of *huo-hao kuei-kung* would be to legitimate all surcharges in the eyes of greedy bureaucrats.

It should be noted that most of these memorials displayed a certain ignorance of the reforms, and particularly, how they had come about. Some contained trivial mistakes, such as the belief that T'ien Wen-ching was already governor of Honan when the reforms were proposed.[6] Other mistakes were more important, such as the statement that Yung-cheng had immediately ordered all magistrates to remit *huo-hao* directly to their financial commissioners,[7] or that court approval of the reforms had been swift and implementation uniform and speedy in all places.[8] Few seem to have been cognizant of the lengthy process of deliberation and accommodation that had brought the reforms to their present state. These and other misconceptions no doubt made it easier to propose changes in the system that could substantially alter their original intent.

Because most of these memorials arrived while the Ch'ien-lung emperor was still officially in mourning, they were handled mainly by the Grand Secretariat. In most instances the well-meaning advice of officials was disposed of with a simple "No need to deliberate this memorial," written in black to indicate that the decision had not been made by the emperor. However, in the case of at least two of the memorials calling for a decrease in *huo-hao*, the court felt that a more detailed comment was necessary. They agreed that the people would benefit from a reduction in *huo-hao*, but were also concerned that the elimination of that levy would leave the chou and hsien without a source of *yang-lien*. Although they did not comply with the request that *huo-hao* be lowered, the Grand Secretaries did recommend that the emperor issue a forceful edict condemning exactions in excess of the legal quota and confirming the memorialists' claim that *huo-hao* could be lowered but could not be raised.[9]

The Ch'ien-lung emperor's own approach to *huo-hao* was an ambivalent one. Initially, he tried to present himself to his subjects as a benevolent and lenient ruler in the tradition of his grandfather, K'ang-hsi. Many viewed his exemption of accumulated arrears as a repudiation of the vigorous *ch'ing-ch'a* undertaken during the last half of the Yung-cheng reign.[10] Ch'ien-lung also canceled a *ch'ing-ch'a* of *huo-hao* revenues scheduled by the late emperor shortly before his death.[11] At the same time he took the advice of the Grand Secretariat and issued an edict banning future increases in *huo-hao*.[12] In several provinces, *huo-hao* rates were actually lowered in keeping with the spirit of the new policy.[13] *Huo-hao* in Szechuan, which, at 25 percent, had been the highest in the empire, was lowered to 15 percent, as were the rates in Kweichow and Kansu.[14] Yet, just two years later the emperor granted all provinces an increment to their public-expense funds in the form of *p'ing-yü*, a small surcharge which had originally been remitted to the Boards.[15] This action was taken in recognition of the fact that local governments were experiencing shortages in their *kung-fei* budgets.

Throughout these early years, Ch'ien-lung never questioned the importance of his father's reforms in the fight against corruption in the provinces, and gave no succor to those who hoped for their demise. Nevertheless, the few pronouncements he did make on the subject reflected his sympathy with the primary concern of the critics of *huo-hao kuei-kung*, that is, provincial misconduct in the handling of the newly instituted system of local funding.

If *huo-hao kuei-kung* could not be eliminated altogether, its detractors could at least lobby for stricter supervision of local fiscal management. It will be recalled that under the Yung-cheng emperor, the disbursal and expenditure of *huo-hao* revenues was left entirely to the discretion of the provincial governments. Except for an edict in 1730 that required Board of Revenue approval for any changes in *yang-lien* quotas, the provinces were not required to report to the central government on any matters concerning *huo-hao*. The storage and accounting of such funds, as well as the method of remittance and allocation, was left entirely up to the governors, governors-general, and financial commissioners, although at the emperor's urging, most provinces had adopted direct remittance of *huo-hao* to the financial commissioner. The purpose of allowing provincial governments such unprecedented freedom in handling their own resources was to permit enough flexibility in local finance to conform to local needs and changing fiscal conditions.

The fear that local officials could not be trusted to administer their own finances honestly had been raised even before the late emperor's death. In 1735, the discovery of an 87,000-tael discrepancy in his predecessor's accounts prompted Fukien Financial Commissioner Chang T'ing-mei to propose that there be an audit of all *kung-fei* and *yang-lien* deposited in financial commissioners' treasuries.[16] In response, Yung-cheng agreed to instigate a *ch'ing-ch'a* of all *huo-hao* revenues, an order later canceled by Ch'ien-lung. However, he could not accede to Chang's second request—that each province be required to compile an annual account of its *kung-fei* and *yang-lien* to be sent to the Board of Revenue for examination and approval along with the annual *tsou-hsiao* of regular taxes. This would have constituted too great a breach of the provincial fiscal autonomy the reforms were intended to provide.

Almost immediately after the death of the Yung-cheng emperor, efforts to impose greater control over local fiscal administration were renewed. The first step in this direction was a campaign to create uniformity (*hua-i*) in the rates at which *huo-hao* was levied. During the Yung-cheng period, officials had been successful in fixing rates of collection and lowering existing levels of customary exactions, but the percentage of regular tax quotas levied as *huo-hao* still varied among the provinces and within some provinces as well. In Chihli, for example, several chou and hsien collected no *huo-hao* at all, whereas others collected anywhere from 5 to 16 percent, depending on the level of regular taxation and on the people's ability to pay.[17] The Board of Revenue recognized that differing local conditions made uniformity among the provinces impossible. However, following a memorial by the censor, Yang Ssu-ching, it recommended that rates within each province be made the same in order to facilitate central-government supervision of local finances and make more difficult manipulation of the rates at taxpayers' expense.[18]

The provinces were quick to resist this interference in their fiscal affairs. In those where *huo-hao* rates were already uniform, the move was resented as a dangerous violation of the principle of provincial fiscal discretion. Officials in the few provinces where the rates did vary argued that local conditions made uniformity impossible.[19] In the end the drive failed,[20] but the notion that some form of standardization would be essential to prevent corruption among the empire's nearly two thousand local administrators continued to gain adherents.

After four years of virtual silence on the subject, the new emperor opened the fifth year of his reign with what was to be his major policy statement on the *huo-hao kuei-kung* reforms.[21] It began with a lament over the paucity of virtue within the bureaucracy not unlike hundreds of imperial remonstrances issued during the centuries of dynastic rule in China. What was unusual about this edict was the fact that the emperor, in the very first line, lumped *huo-hao* together with other forms of taxation that both legally and by common practice were the exclusive property of the central government. During the Yung-cheng reign, references to corruption in tax collection involving *huo-hao* had always included a disclaimer to the effect that *huo-hao was not the same* as regular and miscellaneous taxes. Thus, the Ch'ien-lung emperor had taken the first step in fulfilling the prophecy that *huo-hao* would some day come to be regarded as the same as *cheng-hsiang*.

This was not unintentional, for the emperor's purpose was to reform the reforms, and to do so he would need to authorize far more centralized control over their implementation than had ever been allowed during his father's time. Although he recognized the success of *huo-hao kuei-kung* in freeing officials from financial difficulties and in ridding the people of the burden of extortion, Ch'ien-lung was deeply troubled by the evidence that many officials had continued to indulge in excessive and unnecessary expenditures. In order to control the mismanagement and abuse of local revenues, he ordered the Board of Revenue to undertake a total reassessment of the operations of local-government finance.

In order to accomplish this task, the governor and governor-general of each province were directed to evaluate every item for which public monies were spent within their jurisdiction and to draw up a schedule of proposed allowable expenditures (*li-ting chang-ch'eng*). Once approved by the Board, these categories of expenditure would function as a kind of budget against which local income and expenditure each year would be compared. The *yang-lien* of each official would be treated in a similar fashion, though the amount allocated would vary in relation to his time in office and whether the post was held in an acting capacity.[22] Armed with these figures, the governor and governor-general were to determine which officials had delayed remittance of funds or had disbursed *huo-hao* in excess of the authorized amounts. At the end of the year, the province would then submit a register of all local revenues saved, paid, and in arrears, to be audited by the Board of Revenue.[23]

In this way, the emperor gave the Board of Revenue full authority to approve or reject the *huo-hao* expenditures of individual provinces, in the same manner that it approved or rejected their expenditures of *cheng-hsiang*. At the same time, by requiring that expenditures be categorized and that reasonable quotas be set for each category of public spending, this edict greatly limited the ability of local-government officials to shift provincial funds to meet their changing fiscal needs. Distrustful of local officials, and concerned that acceptance of *huo-hao* would lead to the introduction of new surcharges, critics of *huo-hao kuei-kung* had favored increased central-government supervision of provincial income and expenditure. The emperor came to share their fears. What neither had considered was that the very act of imposing stricter controls over the use of provincial revenues might produce just the results they were intended to avert. For, as we shall see, the introduction of Board scrutiny over the entire management of *huo-hao* created conditions that greatly handicapped the smooth functioning of local finance and did indeed make *huo-hao* appear to be the same as *cheng-hsiang*.

Changes in the method of administering *huo-hao* revenues did not silence the staunchest detractors of the Yung-cheng emperor's reforms. One crucial question remained unanswered. Did the legalized collection of *huo-hao* and its remittance to the public coffers conform with traditionally accepted tenets of good government? Or was it a terrible source of hardship for both honest officials and the common people? Always concerned with his image as a sage ruler, this question seems to have haunted the new emperor. Finally, in early 1742, Ch'ien-lung decided to open the issue to public discussion by posing the question of continued implementation of *huo-hao kuei-kung* as part of the palace examination for aspirants to the *chin-shih* degree.

In what appears to be his address to the students, the emperor frankly revealed his uncertainties regarding his father's efforts at reform.[24] A chief cause of concern was that *huo-hao kuei-kung* might not conform to the way of the ancients. Echoing the classics, Ch'ien-lung acknowledged the importance of light corvée and low taxes as an expression of a ruler's love of his people. Inasmuch as the Ch'ing did not levy taxes in the form of labor service, there was no question of their transgressing the first requirement. But, Ch'ien-lung wondered, did the legalization of *huo-hao* in addition to the regular land tax constitute a violation of the latter? If it did not exist in ancient times, how could it now be condoned? On the other hand, if it only recently came under official supervision, how could we know it did not exist in the days of the sages? Having wormed his way out of this initial dilemma, the emperor turned to the real problem posed by the classical test of benevolent rule. What effect did current fiscal policy have on the government and on the people?

Ch'ien-lung quickly dismissed the claim by opponents of the reforms that the Yung-cheng emperor's use of administrative techniques to control corruption was a result of his personal failure as an emperor to inspire virtue in his officials.[25] Less easily dispelled was the accusation that the collection of *huo-hao* constituted an increase in taxes (*chia-fu*). This would be not only a violation of the ancient proscription against heavy taxation, but also a direct violation of K'ang-hsi's promise of 1710 never to raise taxes again (*yung-pu chia-fu*). To contravene one's predecessor's supreme act of benevolence would truly be a sign that the empire was beyond purification. Nevertheless, there was always the possibility that the reforms were precisely what the dynasty required to improve the life of the people and that the criticism now being voiced was really the work of men who hoped to profit by the restoration of *huo-hao* to the status of a private levy.

It was this confusion that prompted the emperor to put the question of *huo-hao kuei-kung*'s fate to the students assembled for the palace examination. As men of character, recently arrived from the countryside, they would be able to judge whether the reforms were beneficial or harmful to the people. They could help him make up his mind whether or not to change the law.

Ch'ien-lung seems to have been sincere in his desire to solicit opinions on *huo-hao*. In his opening remarks in the examination hall he urged the students to speak frankly, without fear of punishment for expressing unpopular opinions. In another edict issued the same day, he instructed the Grand Secretaries Oertai and Chang T'ing-yü to order the officials reading the examination papers to devote special attention to the sections concerning the meltage fee. The authors of any suggestions worthy of implementation were to be selected for the honor of an imperial audience.[26] In addition, a separate order was sent out to all ministers of the central government, members of the Hanlin Academy, censors, and provincial governors and governors-general, calling for their analysis of the Yung-cheng emperor's reforms.[27]

Nevertheless, the emperor's hesitation on the issue of *huo-hao kuei-kung* may have been due less to questions of its benefits than to fear of being branded, along with Yung-cheng, as a tyrannical and unjust ruler. Did he really seek an open debate on its merits and demerits, or did he hope for a mandate for its continuation, perhaps with minor adjustments? Unlike his father, Ch'ien-lung was not willing to boldly challenge "public opinion." Yung-cheng would never have posed problems of public policy in terms of ancient precedent or the purity of the empire. Perhaps Ch'ien-lung was considering the abrogation of the reforms, but if this were so, how can we explain his outrage when he received the opinions he had so keenly sought? According to the emperor's edict of the sixteenth day of the fourth month of the seventh year of his reign, none of the answers composed by the students displayed careful consideration of the matter at hand. Some dragged in issues totally unrelated to *huo-hao*. Even those who did mention the reforms did not seem to fully understand them, or made suggestions which, in Ch'ien-lung's opinion, it would be impossible to carry out. On the whole, the emperor labeled their responses stupid and unfounded.

It is not likely that all the responses were simply inane or off the subject, as Ch'ien-lung would have us believe. Most of his edict was addressed to the need for greater official obedience to the law. In particular, he cautioned those officials who would question the very system of government (*cheng-t'i*) with their "numerous and wild" memorials. By rights, he said, these officials should be disciplined, but because they were responding to an edict calling for opinions, he would grant them special leniency. However, such actions would be punished in the future as a warning to "those who spout lies" (*wang-yen che*).[28] Such venom could not have been directed against officials simply for bringing up extraneous issues. Ch'ien-lung did mention one official who used the opportunity to request the opening up of contributions to purchase degrees and another who offered suggestions on coinage. However, although the original memorials no longer exist, the emperor's attack on "those who spout lies," and especially his warning against those who would speculate on the basic system of government, indicates that a fair number of the responses from officials must have contained not suggestions for improving *huo-hao kuei-kung*, but outright appeals for its abolition.

This is confirmed by a memorial written by T'an Hsing-i only two months after the emperor called upon officials and students to assist him in deciding the fate of the reforms. T'an noted that opponents of the return of the meltage fee to the public coffers (*kuei-kung*) were now numerous, and divided them into two groups:

those who favored its total elimination as a public levy—the "return to the people" (*kuei-min*) faction—and those who favored its retention by the chou and hsien magistrates without remittance to the provincial treasury—the "return to the officials" (*kuei-kuan*) faction.[29]

Several years later, the censor Chao Ching-li submitted a refutation of these two groups that sheds some light on the arguments offered by each of the factions in the debate.[30] Returning *huo-hao* to the people meant, in effect, that *huo-hao* would no longer be collected, either as a public or as a private levy. This might be called the purist view, because all would agree that *huo-hao* had originated as an illegal surcharge that should not have been levied in the first place. Chao admitted that in terms of morality this position was correct, and that, if implemented, its benefits would be extensive. However, in terms of "the times and the circumstances" it was impractical. Now, through the use of *huo-hao*, there was a constant source of income for state expenses and for each official's *yang-lien*. He hoped that the emperor would not forget this fact and would opt for the long-term welfare of state and society, rather than try to satisfy present public opinion.

Those who favored return of *huo-hao* to the officials did not seek the total abolition of the meltage fee, but wanted it to revert to the kind of private levy, collected by and used by the chou and hsien officials themselves, that had existed prior to the reforms. In this way, it was argued, officials would collect only what was needed and could adjust (*t'ung-jung*) *huo-hao* rates to their requirements. The *kuei-kuan* faction was clearly the same group that was spreading the idea that *kuei-kung* constituted an increase in taxes. Chao was at a loss, however, to explain how this system would any less result in an increase in popular remittances, inasmuch as it entailed no regulation by outside authorities.

Chao Ching-li attacked the *kuei-kuan* faction on four counts. First, if the *huo-hao* quota was eliminated and magistrates were left to collect it at their own discretion, there would be no guarantee that future magistrates would not renew the unrestrained exploitation of the common people. Secondly, if *huo-hao* were returned to the hands of the magistrates, it would again become their private property. When local official business arose, they would have to levy further taxes on the people to make up for the funds they had already applied to their personal expenses. High and low officials in need of funds would return to the practice of covering up for each other and investigations of local finances would become impossible. Thirdly, if one advocated the return of *huo-hao* to the magistrates, one had also to advocate a return to sending gifts to superiors and the favoritism and bribery that accompanied such *lou-kuei*. Finally, Chao pointed out that *huo-hao kuei-kung* served a redistributive purpose. If magistrates kept their *huo-hao*, in areas with high tax quotas there would be a surplus, whereas in areas where the quotas were low, there would be great hardship in carrying out the duties of government.

Apart from expressing his outrage at the stupidity of those who responded immediately to his call for opinions, Ch'ien-lung took no action regarding *huo-hao* for months. Perhaps he was awaiting further discussion after making known his disappointment with the early respondents. Several memorials preserved in the *Huang-ch'ao ching-shih wen-pien* that defend the reforms may have been part of this second wave of replies, for by the end of the year the Grand Secretariat reported that "popular opinion" had swung overwhelmingly to the side of preserving the reforms as they were.[31] In general, they sought to show (1) that *huo-hao* was not an invention or a product of the Yung-cheng reign; (2) that *huo-hao kuei-kung* had resulted not in an increase but in a decrease in the tax burden imposed on the people; (3) that *huo-hao* was indispensable as a source of local-government revenues; and (4) that there was no danger that legalization of *huo-hao* would result in its being regarded as *cheng-hsiang*, thereby encouraging the collection of additional surcharges.[32]

These arguments were not new, but the way in which they were presented tended to highlight the differences between the more progressive advocates of the reforms and their conservative opponents. Given the link between the spread of *huo-hao* and the growing monetization and diversification of the economy in the late imperial period, it is no surprise that those who sought to ban its collection were often the same people whose writings were filled with nostalgia for China's ancient agrarian past. In the days when the land was divided into well-fields[33] and everyone was contentedly engaged in farming, there was no need to debate the merits and demerits of an evil like *huo-hao*, nor was the people's livelihood threatened by the unequal distribution of land. At least one champion of the reforms saw fit to point out that this undifferentiated agrarian paradise had never existed. Neither its passing nor the imposition of *huo-hao* levies could be blamed for the plight of the Chinese masses. What was now needed were efforts to improve agricultural productivity and a realization that it was diligence and hard work that brought about economic prosperity, whatever one's occupation or relation to the land. In fact, the continuation of *huo-hao kuei-kung* would contribute to the improvement of the general welfare. Uncollected, *huo-hao* was just a few more unproductive coppers in the pockets of millions of individual taxpayers, but combined in the public coffers, it was an invaluable pool of revenue for public works and other projects for the common good.[34]

In the eleventh month of CL 7 (1742) the Grand Secretariat delivered its verdict on the matter of *huo-hao*.[35] Responses to the emperor's call for opinions had continued to pour in from all over the empire and the consensus was that *huo-hao kuei-kung* should be retained unchanged. According to the Grand Secretaries, the one or two dissenting views they received had shown no grasp of the situation and had failed to understand the need to "measure income against expenditure." What ultimately saved *huo-hao kuei-kung* was the recognition that no other policy could solve the pressing need for regular funding at the local and provincial level. Those who opposed it held to outmoded ideals of righteous government that could not serve the needs of the present day.

The Grand Secretariat did not attempt a detailed analysis of *huo-hao kuei-kung* at this time. However, it did address one issue raised by supporters of the reforms. Several memorialists were concerned that the imposition of Board scrutiny over *huo-hao* revenues ran counter to the Yung-cheng emperor's original intentions. One in particular, Sun Chia-kan, pointed out that the increasingly restrictive regulations now governing the allocation of *huo-hao* threatened to destroy any usefulness the reforms may have had in controlling corruption at the local level.[36] Expenditures not approved by the Board of Revenue would still have to be defrayed, whether by exacting gifts from one's subordinates or, in the case of low-level officials, by levying surtaxes on the people. It was not without reason that the late emperor had firmly resisted any moves to eliminate local discretion in the management of *huo-hao* funds. The Grand Secretaries acknowledged the Board's inability to appreciate fully the details of local finance and the likelihood that in exercising its authority it would greatly impede the freedom of action of provincial officials. However, their overriding concern remained the unreliability of local official morality. An annual Board of Revenue audit of provincial *huo-hao* accounts was the only method they could envisage to control embezzlement and excessive expenditure of *yang-lien* and public-expense funds.

Following the Grand Secretariat's recommendations, the emperor issued his own pronouncement on the future of *huo-hao kuei-kung*. He also concluded that the reforms were absolutely essential for the regulation of the country and its people. After reviewing their history and their importance to local finance, Ch'ien-lung made one more attempt to answer the charges of the critics of his father's most controversial policy. His tone was almost that of a hurt parent addressing his ungrateful children.

The emperor first assured his subjects that *huo-hao kuei-kung* had been a product of love for the people and of a desire to preserve order in government. It had not, as some people held, been contrived to increase the revenues of the central government. The state derived no profit when it allowed the government of a locale to supply its own needs by tapping the resources of its own people. In fact, Ch'ien-lung maintained that in the entire empire there were no more than two or three provinces in which the *huo-hao* collected was sufficient to meet all provincial and local expenses. In the remaining places, regular tax funds (*cheng-hsiang*) were allocated by the central government to make up the shortfall. This, the emperor lamented, was something of which the officials and the people were not completely aware.

Ch'ien-lung reminded officialdom of his own hesitation and painstaking consideration of the issue. In particular, he expressed his suspicion that those who favored returning *huo-hao* to local officials (*kuei-kuan*) really desired to satisfy their personal greed. Ending with an exhortation to all officials to be virtuous, the emperor once more affirmed his belief in *huo-hao kuei-kung*. To change the regulations now would not only lead the people to avarice, but even worse, would constitute a reversal of the late Yung-cheng emperor's legacy of benevolence toward the people and guidance of his officials. For *huo-hao kuei-kung* the future seemed assured. But was it? To understand well the fate of the Yung-cheng emperor's legacy, we must examine the actual operation of *huo-hao kuei-kung* during the next hundred years and how government policy and external circumstances acted upon it.

The Operation of Huo-hao kuei-kung in the Ch'ien-lung Period

On the surface, the fiscal record of the first half of the Ch'ien-lung reign was an impressive one. After the initial debates on their implementation, the *huo-hao kuei-kung* reforms had become part of the routine management of local finances. The surplus *huo-hao* available in some provinces seems to have diminished in the latter part of the century, but even in this there was no clear pattern. Random samples of fiscal accounts for those years show that the total deposits after expenditures fluctuated greatly depending on harvests, imperial tax remissions, and the number of emergency outlays in the particular province. Nevertheless, in those provinces for which data are available, reports of continuing *huo-hao* reserves present a picture of general prosperity (see table 7.1), although central-government reserves may not have been as abundant as they had been during the early years of the reforms.[37]

Yang-lien quotas remained largely the same as they were under the Yung-cheng emperor. *Yang-lien* was provided for newly created posts.[38] There is also limited evidence that some officials were granted increases in *yang-lien* commensurate with the augmentation of their official responsibilities. In CL 6, submagisterial officials in Honan were given additional *yang-lien* if they were called upon to supervise water-conservancy projects in addition to their regular duties.[39] The *yang-lien* of military officials in Chekiang were also raised when certain jurisdictions were consolidated.[40] Moreover, the *yang-lien* of a number of officials in Hunan were adjusted to correspond better to the simplicity or complexity of their posts.[41]

One major innovation in the handling of *yang-lien* was introduced during the Ch'ien-lung period. A frequently cited cause of official corruption was the high cost of traveling from the capital in Peking to posts in the provinces. Many officials simply did not have the funds and were forced to borrow from usurers in the capital. These loans, known as *ching-tai*, were generally granted at rates of interest ranging from 20 to 40 percent, deducted from the principal in advance.[42] Pressure to repay them was a powerful incentive to steal public funds once an official reached his post.[43]

The recognition of officials' need for adequate funds that grew out of the *huo-hao kuei-kung* reforms also focused attention on this problem. During the Yung-cheng period, several proposals were offered to alleviate this source of corruption, but no action was taken to relieve the burdens on newly appointed officials until the reign of Ch'ien-lung. In CL 14 (1749), a metropolitan censor named Ko Chün memorialized requesting harsh punishment of officials who took out private loans and equally severe treatment

Table 7.1 *Sample Provincial* Huo-hao *Reserves in the Ch'ien-lung Period (in taels)*

	CL 20	CL 38, 41, or 42
Chihli	175,158	55,363
Shansi	357,118	347,340
Shensi	180,486	168,876[c]
Honan	379,098	506,918
Shantung	263,966	179,798
Hupei	322,311	76,876
Hunan	25[a]	
Kiangsu	362,396	160,372
Kiangsi		260,060
Kwangtung	148,924	273,590
Kwangsi	9,308	45,279
Kweichow	582,725	525,185
Yunnan	408,572	235,135
Szechuan	154,548[b]	

SOURCES: KCT CL 9425, Honan Governor Chiang Ping, CL 20,5,24; KCT CL 9317, Kwangsi Governor Wei Che-chih, CL 20,5,13; KCT CL 9598, Chihli Governor-general Fan Kuan-ch'eng, CL 20,5,29; KCT CL 9504, Kweichow Governor Ting Ch'ang, CL 20,5,29; KCT CL 9475, Kwangtung Governor Hao Nien, CL 20,5,28; KCT CL 9457, Yunnan Governor Ai-pi-ta, CL 20,5,26; KCT CL 9981, Kiangsi Governor Chuang Yu-kung, CL 20,7,13; KCT CL 6824, Hunan Governor Hu Pao-ch'üan, CL 19,5,29; KCT CL 10075, Acting Shensi Governor T'ai-chu, CL 20,7,25; KCT CL 12200, Szechuan Governor-general K'ai-t'ai, CL 216,22; KCT CL 9482, Shensi Governor Heng Wen, CL 20,5,29; KCT CL 9761, Shantung Governor Kuo I-yü, CL 20,6,22; KCT CL 38423, Shensi Governor Fu Kang, CL 44,5,1; KCT CL 35091, Kiangsi Governor Hao-shih, CL 43,5,29; KCT CL 35121, Hupei Governor Ch'en Hui-tsu, CL 43,6,3; KCT CL 28934, Yunnan Governor Li Hu, CL 39,5,27; KCT 28999, Honan Governor-general Ho Wei, CL 39,6,8; KCT CL 28951, Kwangsi Governor Hsiung Hsüeh-p'eng, CL 39,6,2; KCT CL 31408, Shantung Governor Kuo-t'ai, CL 42,5,9; KCT CL 31598, Shansi Governor Chueh-lo Pa-yen, CL 42,5,26; KCT CL 31630, Chihli Governor Chou Yuan-li, CL 42,5,30; KCT CL 31629, Kiangsu Governor Yang K'uei, CL 42,5,29; KCT CL 31588, Kwangtung Governor Li Chih-ying, CL 42,5,26.
[a] Only available data are for CL 19.
[b] Only available data are for CL 21.
[c] Only available data are for CL 43.

of those who profited by making such advances to officials. The emperor sympathized with the officials, however, feeling that they would turn to usurers only if they were in dire economic difficulty. Rather than deprive them of access to loans altogether, the emperor proposed that loans from the government be made available. Only officials chosen in the monthly selections in the capital would be eligible for such assistance. The financial and judicial commissioners, who were chosen by a special process, and minor officials, who did not come to the capital for selection, would not be included. All others could receive an advance from their *yang-lien*, calculated on the basis of their rank and the distance of their posts from the capital.[44] (See table 7.2.) Once an official arrived at his new post, the *yang-lien* advanced would be paid back in four quarterly installments, or in six installments if an official's salary was smaller than or just equivalent to the loan.[45]

As always seemed to be the case when changes in administration designed to curb corruption were made, new abuses arose after a few years. The original regulations held that if an official failed to repay his debt to the Board, the responsibility would fall on the officials of the whole province.[46] So many officials took advantage of these loans without paying them back that in CL 27 (1762) the emperor had them discontinued. They were soon reinstituted, however, with stricter regulations for repayment and stipulations designed to prevent those who had purchased office and those who had failed to repay previous *yang-lien* advances from receiving these funds.[47]

Another innovation that grew out of a practice first introduced under the Yung-cheng emperor was the investment of public funds at interest. During the Yung-cheng period the emperor made grants of regular tax revenues to military garrisons in several provinces. These funds, called *sheng-hsi yin*, were to be invested with merchants, generally salt merchants or pawnbrokers. The accrued interest was then used to provide money for soldiers' aid, weddings, funerals, and so on. The principal itself was not spent, and it provided a perpetual endowment for the welfare of the empire's military men.[48] In YC 13, officials in Kiangsi extended this method of funding to the civilian realm when the emperor gave them a grant of 1,000 taels to open an academy. Traditionally such grants would be invested in land and the rents derived from the land would be used to support the school and its students. This was done, but the income from rents was insufficient to provide for all the school's operating costs. Rather than make up the shortage on a year-to-year basis from current *kung-fei* revenues, the provincial officials decided to allocate one large loan from the provincial treasury and invest it at interest with salt merchants and pawnbrokers. The interest was then used to finance the academy and gradually repay the principal borrowed from the province.[49]

Other provinces also made use of this modern technique of

Table 7.2 *Rates of Yang-lien Advanced for Travel to Official Posts*

	Yunnan	Kweichow	Hunan Kansu Fukien Kwangsi Kwangtung Szechuan	Shensi Kiangsu Anhui Hupei Chekiang Kiangsi	Shantung Shansi Fengtien Honan	Chihli
Circuit intendants, prefects	1,000	900	800	700	500	300
Chou and hsien magistrates	600	500	500	300	200	150
Subprefects, assistant subprefects	400	350	300	250	150	100
Assistant chou magistrates, subassistant chou magistrates	200	150	120	100	80	60
Miscellaneous officials chosen by the Board	60	50	40	40	40	30

SOURCE: Saeki Tomi, *Ch'ing-tai Yung-cheng ch'ao ti yang-lien yin yen-chiu*, p. 157.

financing local expenditures. When the central government cut off the supply of customs *lou-kuei* that had previously supplemented the income of the Kiangsu governor's yamen, enterprising officials decided to invest the *lou-kuei* remaining in the provincial treasury so that the interest could be used to pay the expenses that would arise in future years.[50] Similar steps were taken in Hunan, producing an extra 9,000 taels per year to meet the pressing needs of local public expenditure.[51] Even the Imperial Household invested surplus revenues from the salt administration with salt merchants to provide funds for imperial rewards and other expenditures.[52] It is thus clear that commercial forms of generating wealth were quite acceptable in eighteenth-century Chinese official circles. The general economic prosperity of this period and the stability of the fiscal system meant that whereas various agencies of government in Europe and Japan were borrowing heavily from private commercial sources during their early modern period, in China the government itself was still the largest source of liquid capital in the land.[53]

This account of a flourishing fiscal system, however, must not be exaggerated. By the end of the eighteenth century, signs of decay had already begun to appear. Part of the problem may be traced directly to the evolution that took place in the *huo-hao* system itself. One of the first principles of the Yung-cheng reforms violated under the Ch'ien-lung emperor was that of provincial jurisdiction over *huo-hao* income. Unlike *cheng-hsiang*, *huo-hao* was to be the exclusive property of the province in which it originated. As we have seen, Yung-cheng opposed any suggestion that *huo-hao* be used for state or military purposes outside a province or to aid other provinces. Early in his term as emperor, however, Ch'ien-lung set a precedent that opened the way for the central government to shift *huo-hao* revenues from province to province and eventually to its own coffers.

During the first few years of the Ch'ien-lung reign, a large portion of the regular taxes of Chihli, Anhui, and Kiangsu were exempted from payment by imperial decree. Because these tax remissions were granted to relieve the burden on taxpayers affected by natural disaster, the *huo-hao* due on these taxes were also exempted. As a result, the three provinces faced shortages in funds for official *yang-lien* and *kung-fei*. In an effort to solve his province's financial difficulties, the Chihli financial commissioner memorialized, requesting that 100,000 taels of Honan's 400,000-tael *huo-hao* surplus be appropriated to aid Chihli. Ch'ien-lung not only approved this request, but ordered the Board to determine how much of Honan's excess reserves should be granted to help Kiangsu and Anhui as well. Ch'ien-lung knew he was violating an important precept, but felt he could justify doing so as a temporary expedient. After all, this still constituted the use of the wealth of the people of the empire to help the people of the empire.[54]

It was not long before this "temporary expedient" became a common practice. In CL 16 (1751) Shantung, Shansi, and Honan were ordered to send part of their surplus *huo-hao* to Chihli to assist in the repair of city walls in that province.[55] The next year it was discovered that Hupei and Anhui had large reserves of *huo-hao* and miscellaneous duties in their treasuries. The governors of those two provinces were ordered to calculate how much they could spare to assist other provinces.[56] We do not know how much Anhui contributed, but for the next few years Hupei deducted 150,000 taels from its *huo-hao* revenues for distribution outside its borders.[57] In CL 23 (1758), this process was formalized. After analyzing the *huo-hao* schedules submitted by the provinces, the Board of Revenue determined that thirteen provinces had just enough *huo-hao* for their own needs, but Kweichow, Hunan, and Kansu were found deficient in *huo-hao* income. To supplement their insufficient treasury stores, Honan, Shantung, and Shansi, each of which had surplus *huo-hao*, were instructed to contribute 6,000 taels annually to their poorer neighbors.[58] Other, temporary transfers for which we no longer have a record probably continued throughout the dynasty, as in the case of a transfer of 150,000 taels from Honan and Kiangsu in CC 17 (1812), when a tax remission following a natural disaster depleted Anhui's *huo-hao* reserves.[59]

Thus, instead of trying to broaden the fiscal base in provinces with chronic shortages, the central government chose to manipulate the levels of funding already available. The surpluses recorded by individual provinces no longer represented a cushion to cover changing local needs. Even more important was the fact that the provinces could no longer expend these surpluses as they saw fit. Large reserves piled up in some treasuries at the same time that shortages began to plague officials in the field.

The cause of this paradox was the imposition of Board scrutiny over provincial income and expenditure. Board scrutiny did not simply give the Board of Revenue the authority to audit and reject provincial *huo-hao* expenditures. It also involved the establishment of schedules for expenditure in which all income and expenses were divided into rigid categories and the amount of funds to be allocated for each item was predetermined. Some flexibility was allowed by dividing all expenses into those with and without fixed categories (*yu-ting-hsiang wu-ting-hsiang*).[60] *Huo-hao* funds for which there were no fixed categories were known as *sui-shih tung-yung chih hsiang* and served as a discretionary fund from which unpredictable expenditures could be made.[61] In addition, some provinces also had an item called *hsien-k'uan*, which, though small, also served as a discretionary fund for emergency use.[62] These funds did not actually originate as *huo-hao*, but as profits from the sale of stabilization rice and confiscated goods.[63] Items for which there was a fixed category in the provincial *huo-hao* schedule were also divided into those for which a fixed amount of funds was allocated annually, and those for which the amount of allowable expenditure was not fixed (*wu-ting-shu*). The latter included items such as clothing, food, and money for prisoners, which could vary from year to year. Allocations were set aside and averaged over a five-year period for items of this kind.[64]

Difficulties should have been anticipated from the beginning. So great was the discrepancy between the provinces' concepts of their fiscal needs and the Board's own analysis of these needs that it took almost ten years for the Board to approve all the schedules of *huo-hao* expenses ordered compiled in CL 5 (1740).[65] Once these schedules were established, if an expenditure was not already certified, a memorial had to be sent to the Board requesting permission to disburse funds. Failure to receive Board authorization before making unscheduled allocations could result in impeachment.[66] Because many expenditures of this type were emergencies, officials occasionally did not have time to go through the tedious procedures outlined above. In such cases, even if the expenditure was legitimate, the official concerned could be held personally responsible for repayment of the money involved.[67]

Approved expenditures outside the established schedules were called "items beyond the normal regulations that should be disbursed" (*ch'ang-li wai ying-hsing tung-yung chih hsiang*). The rigidity of the *huo-hao* schedules is demonstrated by some of the items included as "beyond the normal regulations." In Honan, *yang-lien* allocated for two newly created posts was considered to be *ch'ang-li chih-wai*.[68] In a number of provinces, additional funds used to make up the difference between the Board price and the market price of goods sent to the capital were also designated as *ch'ang-li chih-wai* and had to be memorialized year after year.[69] The variety and small size of expenditures that could require Board approval are vividly illustrated by a memorial requesting approval of disbursements beyond the normal regulations in Chihli. These included 48 taels for the wages of guards posted on bridges over two rivers in Mi-yün hsien, 105 taels for sailors' wages, and 12 taels to supplement government allowances granted to two chaste widows.[70] One of the reasons for the proliferation of such requests was that once these schedules were drawn up they were not revised to take into consideration new expenses or changing fiscal needs arising from inflation or other external causes.

Petition to the Board of Revenue did not guarantee approval, even of legitimate expenditures. The dilemma facing Kwangtung Governor Hao Nien was probably not exceptional. Kwangtung province was responsible for purchases of white wax for the capital. However, the Board price of 0.3 tael was 0.653 tael less than the market price. In addition, the price did not include the costs of shipping and *fan-shih* for the Board staff. During the Yung-cheng reign, the difference was made up from the province's *huo-hao*. When the governor reported this to the Board and requested additional allocations from the *huo-hao* for which there was no fixed category of expenditures, the Board refused approval on the ground that the additional sum, more than twice the Board price, could not have been an honest calculation. Instead, they ordered the governor to lower his estimates. Repeated attempts to explain the reasons for so large a discrepancy proved futile, and the Board continued to return Hao's memorials with orders to recheck his figures.[71]

Consequently, not only was the paperwork involved in handling *huo-hao* increased by the imposition of Board scrutiny, but the risk of punishment or impeachment for "mishandling" *huo-hao* revenues was greatly enhanced. In view of this, and the fact that management of *huo-hao* became a criterion in an official's evaluation for promotion,[72] there is little wonder that many officials were disinclined to be creative or innovative in the management of local resources.

Although none of the original schedules established in CL 15 have been preserved, we are fortunate that there is a surviving *hao-hsien* register, compiled by the Board of Revenue during the Kuang-hsü reign (1875–1907).[73] This document illustrates the rigidity of the system of accounting imposed on local finances after Yung-cheng's death. It appears to be an exact duplicate of the schedules established during the early Ch'ien-lung period, with annotations of minor changes made during subsequent reigns.[74] It is evident that until the end of the Ch'ing no major effort was made to overhaul the allocation of *huo-hao* to meet the growing costs of government or to allow for new types of expenditures at the local level.

Variations in the budget for a particular year did exist. These were handled by the inclusion of classifications of expenditure such as "items with fixed categories and fixed allocations where expenditure is more (or less) than the scheduled amount" and "unpredictable expenses." An examination of the former demonstrates that, in all the provinces listed, reductions in fixed allocations far exceeded additions. In Honan, for example, more than 9,000 taels were deducted from the original quotas for fixed allocations, whereas only about 2,300 taels were added to existing levels of funding. Even more striking is the case of Hunan, where 26,143.2 taels were cut from the Ch'ien-lung quotas, largely because of a massive reduction in *yang-lien*, whereas only 205 taels were added to fixed expenditures, almost all of which went toward Board fees and travel expenses for deputies on official business.

It is under "unpredictable expenses" that we would expect to find those items for which *huo-hao* made its most vital contribution to local revenues—relief, construction, water conservancy, and so on. In fact, this was only occasionally the case. For the most part, *sui-shih tung-yung chih k'uan* encompassed routine expenditures which for one reason or another tended to fluctuate. These included clothing and food for prisoners, travel and transport expenses, partial allocations of *yang-lien*, and in rare instances, supplemental local expenses for such tasks as conducting sacrifices and apprehending criminals. Moreover, of the four provinces listed in this register, only Honan and Chekiang recorded a specific category of *kung-fei* for subordinate administrative units in general. We can only assume that local governments elsewhere were once again forced either to rely on irregular modes of funding or to limit greatly their role in local affairs.

A final category of funds not mentioned in the statutes appears at the end of several of these provincial accounts. Supplemental expenditures (*pu-kei chih k'uan*) were funds that should have been disbursed in previous years but were not. Among these were numerous items of *yang-lien*. That they were not received must have been a hardship for the officials involved. The reason for such a category is not given, but it may have been the high levels of *huo-hao* arrears evident in the register. Budgeted expenditures often exceeded annual income, and collections in any one year always included a certain amount of taxes that should have been paid in the past. Inability to collect the full quota of land and head taxes was a problem that increased seriously during the second half of the dynasty and severely impeded the effectiveness of the *huo-hao kuei-kung* reforms.[75]

Both in shifting *huo-hao* from one province to another and in setting up rigid schedules for expenditure, the central government demonstrated its view that provincial fiscal needs were basically immutable. In the former instance, instead of promoting the expansion of government services and its contribution to local society, as the Yung-cheng emperor had done, the Ch'ien-lung court held that after *yang-lien* and certain *kung-fei* had been paid, any surplus revenues were excessive (*to-yü*). In the latter instance, the court locked local finance into schedules that might have corresponded to minimum needs in CL 15 but failed to respond to changes in the economy, population, and administrative requirements. These schedules were not constantly revised budgets or guidelines, but were regulations. To cope with rigidity, some officials were content simply to follow the regulations in a perfunctory manner so as to avoid disciplinary sanctions. Others, as we shall see, saw no option other than to bend or circumvent the rules and hope that they were not caught.

Several additional factors adversely affected the functioning of *huo-hao kuei-kung*. Whenever natural disaster prompted the emperor to issue an exemption of regular tax payments, the *huo-hao* levied as a percentage of those taxes was also exempted. Provinces that did not rely exclusively on revenues from land taxes still had a "cushion" with which to sustain local government in lean years. In contrast, provinces that derived most of their income from *huo-hao* were often left without funds to pay for *yang-lien* and *kung-fei*. This is precisely why, during the Yung-cheng period, Honan Governor T'ien Wen-ching had argued for maintenance of large *huo-hao* reserves in individual provincial treasuries. If no *huo-hao* was collected in a given year, a province could still cover that year's expenses by disbursing surplus *huo-hao* accumulated in the past. This is exactly what happened in Chihli and Shensi in CL 16

(1751).[76] If the resources of a province were meager, however, or natural disasters brought famine for more than one year at a time, a province could be left with no resources to cover local and provincial expenses and salaries. The government dealt with this problem by transferring *huo-hao* funds from one province to another, as explained above. Unfortunately, this served to deplete the reserves of the donor province and could potentially leave it vulnerable to the same problems faced by its poorer neighbors.

So great were such problems that even so solvent a province as Honan faced extreme difficulties by the end of the Ch'ien-lung reign.[77] Successive years of bad harvests made it impossible to collect the *cheng-hsiang* tax. As a result, the funds from the provincial treasury had to be transferred to pay for labor and materials used in river works that normally would have been paid for from regular taxes. Surcharges of sixty-nine *wen* per tael were also levied in chou and hsien along the river to help defray the costs of construction. However, after CL 43 (1778), flooding along the Yellow River necessitated so many emergency repairs that this small fee was raised to as much as three *ch'ien* per tael. Claims of large provincial reserves must therefore be seen as deceptive. They could quickly be depleted in times of flood or drought. Moreover, they sometimes represented funds that could not be used because of the strict rules against shifting *huo-hao* earmarked for one item of expenditure to another purpose. Consequently, by the late eighteenth century the imposition of special surcharges for public expenses was once again a common occurrence.

Another problem facing local officials during the Ch'ien-lung reign was that of levies to cover the expense of imperial tours. During the K'ang-hsi period, the main burden for such tours was naturally borne by the provinces, by means of "contributions" exacted from the people. The question of how to pay for such tours under the new system of funding did not arise during the Yung-cheng reign, because that emperor rarely traveled far from Peking. Ch'ien-lung, in contrast, was notorious for his southern excursions, undertaken ostensibly to entertain his mother. The costs of such trips fell only on those provinces visited by the emperor and empress dowager, and were particularly great in Kiangnan. In preparation for one southern tour, Kiangsu Governor Chiang Yu-kung was ordered to repair all the bridges and roads along the imperial route. Provincial *kung-fei* revenues were to be used for this purpose, although merchant contributions were solicited to provide for the arrangement of visits to scenic places and of entertainments for the imperial party. In all, 568,351 taels were approved for the occasion, 149,796 taels of which were allocated from *cheng-hsiang* revenues stored in the provincial treasury. The remainder came from merchant contributions (150,000 taels) and *hsien-k'uan* and fines (268,555 taels) that otherwise would have been available for the expenses of the province itself.[78]

Despite the severity of the central government's controls over *huo-hao* expenditure, one crucial aspect of *huo-hao kuei-kung* was changed so many times that it probably completely lost its effectiveness. By the end of the Yung-cheng period, most provinces had implemented remittance of *huo-hao* directly to the financial commissioner for redistribution as *yang-lien* and *kung-fei*. But in CL 3 (1738), a communiqué was issued by the Board of Revenue ordering provinces to allow the chou and hsien to deduct the *yang-lien* of all officials of the rank of magistrate and below to avoid their having to go to the capital to receive their salaries from the financial commissioner.[79] In CL 48 (1783), this ruling was reversed at the behest of the Shantung financial commissioner, Lu Shao.[80] Lu reported that under these new regulations, the chou and hsien magistrates sent only the regular tax to the provincial treasury. Their own *huo-hao* and funds for the purchase of grain were stored in their own yamen. As a result, magistrates had begun to siphon off these funds as they pleased and local-government deficits were once again increasing. This was the very problem that remittance to the financial commissioner (*kuei-kung*) was designed to prevent. Nevertheless, vacillation between remittance and nonremittance seems to have continued, for in the *Su-chou fu-chih* there is a report that prior to Tao-kuang 5 (1825) the *yang-lien* of all officials of the rank of magistrate and below was deducted at the hsien level. After that date, magistrates were required to receive their share of local *huo-hao* directly from the financial commissioner, but payment to miscellaneous officials was still made at the source.[81]

Ironically, it was probably in the poorest provinces that the reforms were retained in their most pristine form, for it was there that supplementary commercial revenues and *huo-hao kuei-kung*'s redistributive mechanisms played their most important role. The governors and governors-general of Kwangsi and Kweichow fought vigorously against deduction of *huo-hao* by the magistrate on the grounds that few hsien in their provinces collected enough *huo-*

hao to cover all administrative costs. The Board of Revenue had hoped to solve this problem by instructing poorer chou and hsien to procure their additional allowances directly from the magistrates of their richer neighbors, a system that could only have increased the opportunities for corruption and fiscal manipulation. Nevertheless, in the mountainous areas of the southwest, poor transportation often made it easier to go to the provincial capital than to travel the shorter distances to a nearby county seat.[82] Even more important was the fact that in both Kwangsi and Kweichow it was only by the addition of customs revenues that sufficient funds were made available for local expenses. In Kwangsi, direct deduction of *huo-hao* would have provided, on the average, only 20 percent of a magistrate's *yang-lien*, much less any surplus for the other costs of local administration.[83] Hence, once again, the quest for uniformity fell afoul of China's diverse local conditions.

One area in which uniformity did prevail was in the provinces' continued struggle to find new sources of revenues to meet rising administrative expenses. Some provinces suffered from the central government's persistent drive to lower *huo-hao* rates.[84] Kiangsu not only experienced a reduction in *huo-hao* rates but also lost over 100,000 taels in *huo-hao* revenues because of benevolent actions such as the elimination of *fu-liang* and reductions in *pai-liang* quotas.[85] Supplementary sources of income were also occasionally lost, as when the central government eliminated the surcharge collected in Kwangtung on military-colony rice[86] or declared provincial *p'ing-yü* to be an illegal surcharge.[87] These revenues were sometimes made up in other ways, but few provinces could finance the added expenses incurred when the central government created new administrative jurisdictions without providing new sources for their funding.

Hardest hit by this practice was the southwest, where, during the eighteenth century, numerous new prefectures and counties were carved out of former wastelands and aborigine territories. Already suffering from the lowering of its *huo-hao* rate to 15 percent and the elimination of its *huo-hao* on commercial taxes (*shui-hao*), Kweichow was faced, in the early Ch'ien-lung period, with a shortage of 23,418 taels. Most of this arose from additional *yang-lien* and *kung-fei* which had to be paid to new officials installed on the frontier.[88] In Hunan, the creation of Yung-shun prefecture cost the province 4,000 taels a year in *yang-lien* for its four subordinate hsien. For a few years this was paid from customs surplus, but in

1734 this supplement was converted to *cheng-hsiang* and remitted to the central government. The following year the addition of another prefecture and a post and salt intendancy required yet another infusion of *yang-lien*. By 1744, over 40,000 taels had been "advanced" (*no-i*) to cover the increasing shortages that resulted from this bureaucratic reorganization.[89] Even provinces in the long-settled economic heartland, like Kiangsu, saw their fiscal burden increased by the creation of new prefectures and the division of hsien.[90]

The most difficult problems, however, with which local officials had to cope were only indirectly the outgrowth of government policies. Nothing seems to have so impeded the efforts of the provincial bureaucracy to deal with fixed salaries and a rigid system of local funding as the apparent rise in prices and population in the second half of the eighteenth century.

One clear indicator of rising provincial expenses was the funds necessary for the purchase of local specialty products sent to the capital. The Board of Revenue set rates by which regular tax funds were allocated for the purchase of these goods in the provinces. During the early part of the dynasty, as we have seen, local officials often made a profit by buying tribute goods at the market price, which was generally cheaper than the Board price. By the early Ch'ien-lung period, however, numerous provinces were discovering that rather than yielding a surplus, the Board price for tribute goods was insufficient. On the contrary, it now became necessary to allocate additional funds from provincial *huo-hao* to make up the difference between the Board price and the cost of goods in the marketplace.[91]

As early as CL 10 (1745), a censor named Ch'ai Hu-sheng memorialized concerning the narrow margin within which government finances operated.[92] Ch'ai acknowledged that fiscal difficulties had always plagued Chinese governments, but claimed that in the past the solution had been to economize. This could be done by cutting down on supernumerary soldiers and officials and by eliminating government waste. Now, Ch'ai felt, there were neither superfluous officials nor extravagance at court. Moreover, every possible method was being used to wring the surplus from the population. Until the late Ming, officials had been expected to collect only 80 to 90 percent of the tax quota, but under Chang Chu-cheng, 100-percent collection had become the standard for official evaluations. Now, not only were few taxes retained by the provinces, but they themselves were drawing in all possible revenues in the form of *huo-hao* on the land and head tax, *ying-yü* on the customs tax, and excess quota (*i-e*) on the salt tax. Yet, the sum available to administer the empire was barely sufficient. In the future, he feared, expenses would certainly outstrip income. It was therefore imperative to increase income and reduce expenditures (*k'ai-yuan chieh-liu*) now.

Ch'ai proposed several solutions to the problem. The first was to open new colony land (*t'un-t'ien*) in Manchuria to provide for those who had left their native places for lack of work. Secondly, the government should issue several years' wages and disband the Han army. Finally, he suggested that the regulations for purchase of degrees (*chüan-chien*) be liberalized and the revenues generated made available to supplement local public expenses (*kung-fei*). Ch'ai also felt that the stringent Board regulations governing the use of provincial *huo-hao* would impede local finance and initiative by causing officials to fear any action that could involve them in rejected accounts or poor official evaluations. As evidence of the effect this could have on the economy, he noted that large areas of land in Kwangtung had not been reclaimed, waterworks in Shensi had deteriorated to a state unknown since ancient times, and, although Hukwang rice production was vital to the supply of staples in the southeast, the dikes along the lakes in that region were suffering from neglect. All of these projects should have been undertaken by local officials using *kung-fei*, but because of a combination of fear and revenue shortages, they were not. Moreover, Ch'ai claimed that the *yang-lien* allocated to officials was also inadequate, providing only enough to pay private secretaries and servants' wages, entertainment costs, and the costs of carts and horses, firewood, and fuel. With nothing left over, it was difficult for officials to initiate any programs of benefit to agriculture, sericulture, and the education of the people.

Although Ch'ai may have exaggerated the financial stringency that officials were experiencing during the early Ch'ien-lung reign, the recollections of officials and gentry show that one clear indicator of inflation, rice prices, was increasing. In a memorial arguing against large government purchases of rice that took the staple off the open market and drove prices up, Kweichow Censor Sun Hao presented a vivid picture of hardships facing the people in the southeast. Sun recalled that in his home province of Chekiang several decades earlier, the price of one picul of rice had been only 8 *ch'ien* (0.8 tael).[93] Now it had doubled, costing between 1.5 and 1.8 taels per picul. One factor was population growth which was not matched by a comparable increase in arable land. Another was the severe shortage of copper coins that plagued China during the early eighteenth century.[94]

Later writers confirm the continuation of a serious inflationary trend during the eighteenth century. Writing in CL 57 (1792), Wang Hui-tsu stated that the price of one peck (*tou*) of rice fluctuated between 180 *wen* and 310 *wen*. Yet Wang could recall that when he was a little over ten years old (around CL 10), the price of rice was only 90 to 100 *wen*. When, occasionally, it rose to 120 *wen*, everyone was astonished by its high cost. After CL 13 (1748), the price rose as high as 160 *wen* and hunger was not uncommon. But in the last ten years or so, even a price of 200 copper cash for a peck of rice was considered low.[95]

Ch'ien Ping offered similar testimony concerning rice prices in Kiangnan. According to Ch'ien, in the Yung-cheng and early Ch'ien-lung periods the price of a pint (*sheng*) of rice, the equivalent of one-tenth of a peck, was around 10 *wen*. However, in CL 20 (1755) there was a plague of insects, and the price of rice in Suchow, Sung-chiang, Ch'ang-chou, and Cheng-chiang rose to as much as 35 or 36 *wen*. Countless people died of starvation as a result. Even after the harvests had returned to normal several years later, the price stabilized at 14 or 15 *wen*. In CL 50 (1785), there was a great drought and the price of a pint of rice rose to the incredible sum of 56 or 57 *wen*. Thereafter, regardless of the state of the harvest, the price never fell below 27 *wen* and could rise to as much as 34 or 35 *wen*, more than three times the price prevalent in the Yung-cheng period.[96]

Ch'ien also remarked on changes in the price of land.[97] By his calculations, in the early Shun-chih reign a *mou* of land had not cost more than 2 or 3 taels. These rates rose in the K'ang-hsi period to 4 or 5 taels per *mou*. During the Yung-cheng period, land prices fell to the levels common during the early years of the dynasty, perhaps because of the numerous land-reclamation projects promoted during those years. In the early Ch'ien-lung period, the price rose again to 7 or 8 taels and occasionally even 10 taels per *mou*. By the late Ch'ien-lung and early Chia-ch'ing reigns, land prices per *mou* had risen to an average of 50 taels.

One of the most interesting contemporary efforts to explain the inflation under way in China during the eighteenth century was presented in CL 13 (1748) by Hupei Governor Yang Hsi-fu.[98] Yang felt that the prevailing high prices for rice and other grains were not primarily due to natural disaster or to hoarding, the usual explanation given for rising prices, but were caused by the large number of people buying food. The reason they bought food was that they were poor. This was not a sudden occurrence, but the result of what Yang call four "gradual circumstances." These were (1) population growth, (2) increasingly extravagant habits, (3) the concentration of land in the hands of wealthy households, and (4) government purchases of granary stores.

Regarding the first issue, Yang pointed out that most of the land that could be reclaimed had already been opened to cultivation. Now the population was growing in excess of available tillage. The inevitable result was a rise in grain prices as demand exceeded supply. Yang recalled that he himself had grown up in the countryside, where his family had tilled the soil for generations. In the K'ang-hsi period, paddy rice had sold for no more than 2 or 3 *ch'ien* a picul. By the Yung-cheng period the price had risen to 4 or 5 *ch'ien*, and never fell to the prices seen under K'ang-hsi. Now the price was even higher, 5 or 6 *ch'ien* per picul, and the prices known during the Yung-cheng period were no more than a memory.

Extravagant life-styles also drove up the price of grain. When the dynasty first entered China, there was disorder and life was hard. People's habits were of necessity frugal. Once peace was restored and people could obtain employment, they began to yearn for elaborate clothing and food and stylish appearances in marriages and funerals. This trend began in the large towns and cities and spread even to out-of-the-way mountain villages. Yang offered more than a traditional diatribe against luxurious living and wasteful habits. For he recognized that one consequence of selling crops to buy luxuries was the increased involvement of the peasantry in the market economy. Although he did not express it in these terms, Yang was lamenting the effects of the increasing commercialization of agriculture. More people sold their crops after the harvest and were forced to buy rice later in the year. As the number of people purchasing rice in market towns increased, so did the price of that crucial commodity.

The concentration of land in the hands of wealthy households also contributed to the rising price of grain and was closely related to the above two factors. Governor Yang's description of these effects conveys a keen understanding of what would later be called monopoly capitalism.

> When the dynasty began there was more land than people. Thus the price of land was cheap. After peace [was restored] there was enough land to nourish the people, so land prices were stable. After a long period of peace there were more people than land, so land became expensive. In the past every *mou* was one or two taels. One sold after becoming poor and once having sold [one's land] one did not have the means to buy it back. One bought after becoming wealthy and having bought [land] one did not have to resell.

> Recently about 50 or 60 percent of the land has become the property of wealthy households. People who in the past were landowners are now all tenant farmers. Their annual income is barely enough to feed their families. They must buy rice to tide themselves over. But after the wealthy farmers have brought in their harvest, if they cannot get a high price [for their grain] they are not willing to sell cheaply. In the case of any commodity, if one person buys it, the price cannot increase. If ten people buy it, then the price will suddenly grow. If ten people sell, they cannot ask a high price. If one person sells exclusively, then he can demand as high [a price] as he wants. Under such circumstances, how can grain not be expensive?[99]

Finally, the government policy of buying grain for storage in case of emergencies exacerbated the already serious general grain shortage. According to Yang, almost half the grain produced by the people was removed from the market through government purchase, and rigid guidelines allowed the return of only 30 percent of these grain stores during the slack season between harvests.

Try as it might, the government could do little to reverse any of these trends. It was, in fact, the benevolent policies of the government and the peace brought about by Ch'ing rule that had led to the enormous increase in population during the century. Although several folk methods of birth control were practiced during that period, they were not sufficiently effective to control China's eighteenth-century demographic growth. Moreover, both the government and the people tended to view high birth rates as a positive good to be encouraged, not banned. Concentration of landownership also presented an insuperable dilemma for the government. Only a policy of land equalization could end the monopoly power of large landed interests and help achieve the ancient ideal of a large, independent peasantry. But those who owned the land were still the major bulwark of dynastic power, a fact that tempered even the mildest efforts to alleviate poverty and land hunger. Yang's assertion that such a policy would be "difficult to carry out" was a gross understatement. As a last resort, the dynasty could fall back on the old strategy of encouraging frugality, but even this, Yang felt, would not produce immediate results, human nature being what it is.

Nevertheless, Yang was not entirely pessimistic. The problems brought about by overstocking government granaries could be eased by reductions in stores and flexibility in the application of rules governing the sale of stabilization rice. More important, the governor recommended increased government activity aimed at improving production. Although much of the available land had been reclaimed, agricultural output could still be improved by means of greater government encouragement of, and participation in, irrigation projects. However, the combination of factors underlined by Yang was largely beyond the control of any Chinese government in the eighteenth and nineteenth centuries. Granary stores were unlikely to be reduced, because they were the government's one defense against famine. This, together with the fact that officials were even less likely to initiate new projects now that their *huo-hao* accounts were part of their official evaluations, meant that hopes for alleviation of this inflationary trend were slim indeed.

By the middle of the Ch'ien-lung reign, an important new factor began to contribute to China's inflationary spiral. The growth of Chinese trade with the West, and especially Great Britain, led to a great influx of silver into the economy. By increasing the money in circulation, this trade contributed to the rise in prices of even the most basic commodities.[100] If the figures cited by officials at the time are accurate, we can assume that the rise in prices between the time *huo-hao kuei-kung* was first implemented and the early Ch'ien-lung period was substantial. The difference between prices in the Yung-cheng period and those of the late Ch'ien-lung and early Chia-ch'ing reign was enormous. Based on scattered reports by officials throughout the eighteenth century, Wang Yeh-chien has estimated that prices underwent an almost threefold increase during this period. Moreover, he has postulated that this inflationary trend was a steady one, providing few periods of relief for a beleaguered bureaucracy.[101]

The effects of inflation on the *huo-hao kuei-kung* reforms cannot be underestimated. Not only would increases in the cost of living for officials place tremendous strains on unchanging *yang-lien* quotas, but the costs of construction materials, wage labor, and salaries for private secretaries and clerks must also have risen considerably. Moreover, as Wang Yeh-chien has pointed out, as population grew, a growing number of clerks were needed to handle local administration and more and more funds were required for expenses such as poor relief.[102] It is little wonder that reports of official and clerical corruption continued to appear intermittently throughout the Ch'ien-lung period. However, it was not until the reign of the Chia-ch'ing emperor that *huo-hao kuei-kung* began to appear to be damaged beyond repair.

Huo-hao kuei-kung in the Chia-ch'ing Period

Had the officials engaged in the debates over *huo-hao* in the early Ch'ien-lung period lived to the Chia-ch'ing reign, they would have seen all their worst predictions borne out. Inflation, rising population, and increased government regulation of local finance had taken their toll. Although not yet totally defunct, the great panacea of local fiscal reform barely resembled the vigorous program first instituted almost a century before.

Deficits were not the only indicators of local fiscal difficulties.[103] Finances were so tight in Chihli that when taxes were exempted, loans had to be made to the province by the central government. However, the province found itself handicapped in repaying these funds because of the cancellation of past arrears in provincial land taxes and *huo-hao*.[104] So small were the reserves of regular taxes in Kiangsu that the governor was forced to advance provincial *huo-hao* to cover expenses that had normally been disbursed from *cheng-hsiang*.[105]

In some places, deficits became so serious that deductions were made from the *yang-lien* of each official in the province to repay shortages accumulated by previous officials. This practice may have arisen out of the Chia-ch'ing emperor's own zeal in preventing official mishandling of local funds. By the mid-Chia-ch'ing period, Anhui province had deficits totaling over 2 million taels.

Although schedules had been established for repayment, only a quarter of these debts had actually been cleared by CC 14 (1809). The governor felt that deficits were unavoidable, because the burden of government business in busy chou and hsien far exceeded their fiscal resources. The emperor, however, saw these deficits as the result of excessive expenditure and laxity in arranging repayment. Insisting that budgeted funds existed for every item of acceptable public expenditure, Chia-ch'ing ordered the governor to encourage his subordinates to exercise greater economy. Officials with new deficits that could be shown not to be the result of embezzlement were allowed to repay their shortages within four years. But in the case of old arrears and deficits, the emperor instructed the governor to deduct 50 percent of the *yang-lien* of each commissioner, circuit intendant, prefect, and magistrate until the missing funds were cleared.[106]

During the Yung-cheng period, the *wu-cho* deficits of a province could be made up by using the *huo-hao* of the whole province. However, this was never allowed to interfere with the payment of *yang-lien* to individual officials. By the end of the Chia-ch'ing period, deductions of *yang-lien* to repay deficits seem to have become institutionalized. In CC 23 (1818), Kweichow Censor Wu Chieh complained bitterly about the demands placed on officials' *yang-lien*, one item of which was called "apportioned reimbursements" (*t'an-p'ei*).[107] By this method the *wu-cho* deficits of previous officials were apportioned among all the officials in a province in yearly installments. A vicious cycle was thus set in motion. If shortages in local revenues had contributed to deficits, this system of deficit repayment could only increase local fiscal difficulties by depriving officials of a large portion of the funds on which they depended to live and to operate their yamen.

Deductions from *yang-lien* were not limited to deficit reimbursements. The central government itself faced shortages by the Chia-ch'ing period, and turned to local officials for assistance in the form of "contributions to demonstrate gratitude" (*chüan-shu pao-hsiao*). Although these were technically voluntary, the provincial governors and governors-general clearly felt that their careers depended on their performance in providing the central government with additional funds, particularly to supplement imperial military expenditures. The source of these high officials' "gifts" to the court was once again forced deductions (*t'an-k'ou*) from the *yang-lien* of each official in the province.[108] In both this and the above case, not only was the strict prohibition against deductions from officials' *yang-lien* violated, but the inalienability of provincial *huo-hao* was dealt a blow even more severe than that when Ch'ien-lung issued his edict allowing *huo-hao* surplus to be transferred from one province to another.

Even without these drains on provincial *huo-hao*, officials in the field were beginning to notice serious insufficiencies in the *huo-hao* revenues available for provincial administration and public services. As we have seen, Anhui Governor Tung Chiao-tseng felt that deficits in his province were the result of inadequate funds in busier chou and hsien.[109] In Kiangsu, high officials pointed out that since the *huo-hao* expenditure schedules (*chang-ch'eng*) had been established for their province in CL 12 (1747), no increases in allocations had been made. Nevertheless, during that time the cost of such items as paper and food had increased several fold.[110] To make matters worse, in CC 6 (1801), the Board of Revenue had ordered each province to make substantial reductions in its *kung-fei* expenditures. In Shantung this included 20-percent cuts in the *kung-fei* allowed for stationery expenses and clerical wages in county-level units.[111] In Kiangsu, the Board called upon officials to reduce allocations for the governor's, governor-general's, and two financial commissioners' clerks' paper and wages, wages for the governor's and governor-general's regimental soldiers, and travel expenses for missions carried out by members of the governor's staff.[112] These reductions were not the first that officials had been asked to make, and they seem to have been resisted, though to what effect we do not know.

What is known is that the central government's view of *huo-hao* had changed dramatically since the debates of the early Ch'ien-lung period. For the first time, rather than defending the distinction between *huo-hao* and *cheng-hsiang*, the emperor declared that they were really one and the same: "Each province's *hao-hsien yin* is collected along with the *cheng-hsiang*. Thus, it is no different from regular taxes and should not be disbursed as one pleases."[113] Not only were the provinces required to request an edict in order to disburse *huo-hao* funds, but expenditure of *huo-hao* was now considered a last resort, and not the regular source of provincial funding that it was originally intended to be. According to Chia-ch'ing, when a province had public expenses, it should first use up the *hsien-k'uan* in its treasury. "Only if this is insufficient may *hao-hsien* be borrowed and disbursed."[114]

The pressures placed on provincial finances had predictable results. As superior officials found themselves with diminished real income, they too began to shift the burden of expenses onto their subordinates. As in the days before *huo-hao kuei-kung*, officials on missions in the provinces began to demand from the officials through whose territory they passed the costs of food, firewood, servants, carts and horses, entertainment, and gifts. Deductions were taken from officials' *yang-lien* to pay not only for *wu-cho* deficits but also for public expenses incurred by officials higher up in the provincial hierarchy.[115] The demands made on the *yang-lien* of lower officials were so great that in CC 25 (1820) the emperor could issue an edict stating that "the contribution they must make toward official missions increases daily. Some have their [*yang-lien*] deducted in full, leaving nothing."[116]

Deprived in large measure of their own legitimate sources of income, it is not surprising that local officials began to resort to illegal surcharges, forced contributions, customary fees (*lou-kuei*), manipulation of silver-copper ratios, and other devices for raising funds.[117] Even the Chia-ch'ing emperor was forced to admit that local officials had no choice but to rely on *lou-kuei*. Rather than allow them to extort from the people as they pleased, the emperor made the extraordinary recommendation that *lou-kuei* be legalized and schedules set up for its collection.[118]

Thus, in one hundred years, history had come full circle. *Huo-hao* had indeed become the same as *cheng-hsiang* and equally inadequate to meet the needs of provincial and local government. The "lesson" of *huo-hao kuei-kung* seems to have ruled out the implementation of Chia-ch'ing's plan, but thenceforth, the acceptance of *lou-kuei* became the mark of even a virtuous official. From that point on, any effort by the government to improve official discipline was doomed to failure. Rational fiscal administration was dead, and informal networks of funding once again became the hallmark of the Chinese bureaucracy.

CONCLUSION

The bankruptcy of China's villages in recent years is recognized by the whole nation. Although there are many causes, the most direct is the heavy oppression imposed by surtaxes on the land. If we want to save the village economy from decline, we must first reduce the burden on the peasants. If we want to reduce the burden on the peasants, then we must carefully devise means to eliminate surtaxes on the land. This is one of our urgent tasks for the future.

    K'o Han-fen, "Ch'ing-tai t'ien-fu chih hao-hsien," *Nung-hsüeh*,
May 1939

IT WAS WITH THIS IMPASSIONED PLEA THAT K'O Han-fen ended one of the earliest scholarly articles on the *huo-hao kuei-kung* reforms. K'o blamed the excessive collection of surtaxes in the 1930s on the legalization of *huo-hao* during the Yung-cheng period of the last imperial dynasty. In doing so, he echoed the fears of those early opponents of the reform who warned that the institutionalization of surcharges would lead only to more surcharges beyond the legally established limits. History proved them correct, but not simply because of the venality of local officials. The unrestrained collection of surtaxes that K'o Han-fen decried in the 1930s was indeed a blight on the Chinese polity and economy. It served no purpose other than the enrichment of those whose good fortune it was to hold a position of power in a pitifully fragmented political system. By K'o's time, a centralized bureaucracy played only a minor role in the taxation of the hundreds of millions of Chinese who eked their living from the soil. The imposition of surtaxes continued, but now they merely lined the pockets and fueled the military machines of powerful warlords, local strongmen, and semi-independent provincial officials. But this was a far cry from the situation that prevailed in the 1720s.

The Yung-cheng emperor's reforms were first and foremost an attempt to strengthen the institutions of bureaucratic rule. This was accomplished not by giving free rein to the forces of corruption, but by bringing them under the control of the legitimate agencies of government. The underlying theme of *huo-hao kuei-kung* was that the surplus productive capacity of China be used for the public good. Revenues derived from the legalization of *huo-hao* were to be applied to the improvement of administration as well as to the expansion of government-funded projects to enhance China's transportation, public-welfare, and water-conservancy facilities. This marked an important step in the development of a modern state in which the concept of government responsibility goes beyond the collection of taxes and the maintenance of public order. Moreover, by assuring adequate income for all levels of government, *huo-hao kuei-kung* helped to reconcile the tensions between central and local administration that had always threatened the stability of the Chinese state and laid the groundwork for a rational system of rule in which corruption would no longer play an essential role.

If the roots of China's twentieth-century fiscal anarchy are to be sought in the Yung-cheng emperor's reforms, then they must be sought in their failure, not in their design. The return to informal funding that occurred in the late eighteenth century and was exacerbated by Ho-shen's reign of terror was undoubtedly a key factor in the decline of the nineteenth-century Ch'ing state. By the end of the Chia-ch'ing reign, *huo-hao kuei-kung* had ceased to be an effective system of local fiscal administration. The central government's appropriation of large portions of local officials' *yang-lien* in order to finance the suppression of the Taiping rebels was but the final act in this drama of unfulfilled possibilities. Officials in the nineteenth century occasionally looked back on the period of fiscal reform in the 1720s as a golden age of Ch'ing administration. The distribution of fiscal resources and administrative power, however, was so altered by the rebellions of the Hsien-feng reign that no solution of the kind attempted in the early eighteenth century could ever be successful again.

The failure of the *huo-hao kuei-kung* reforms was largely a result of China's agrarian economic structure. Prior to the industrial revolution, every state had to confront the limitations of revenue derived from the product of the land. Low per-capita yields and difficulties in the assessment and collection of levies from a large rural population cultivating small and scattered plots were not problems unique to China's dynasties. Some countries, such as France, relied on professional tax farmers to assure the collection of the state's quota and left the management of local society to hereditary and clerical elites. The obstacles that such a system presented for the development of integrated governmental institutions are obvious. In principle, at least, China rejected such a compromise, but the realities of agrarian-based taxation made some such accommodation a necessity, even if it caused the erosion of state power.

In England, the growth of the centralized monarchy was facilitated by the decision to rely primarily on indirect taxation. England's power in the eighteenth century was in many ways the product of its income from commercial tariffs, particularly those derived from its growing overseas trade. The Ch'ing also recognized the potential of commercial taxation, imposing levies on both internal and external marketing activities. Moreover, unlike the land tax, which was collected according to fixed quotas that barely rose during the 268 years of Ch'ing rule, commercial taxes were collected to the full extent that the market would bear. The fact that the English monarchy filled its coffers primarily from the profits of maritime customs is significant, for only tax barriers at the borders of the state could guarantee that the revenue from such duties would go directly to the central treasury. China's trade in the late-imperial period was primarily domestic. In a sense, China attempted to imitate the conditions found in a multistate system by establishing internal customs barriers through which it took its share of commercial profits. As such, commercial taxes were much more likely to be absorbed locally in China than they were in the West.

In one respect, *huo-hao kuei-kung* was an acknowledgement of this tendency. By recognizing the claim of local administration to commercial revenues, the central government hoped to safeguard its own share of land-tax and customs quotas. Both customary fees from the merchant class and surplus revenues from maritime and domestic trade made an important contribution to the postreform budgets of both the provinces and their subordinate chou and hsien. However, the fact that the combined total of maritime customs, salt gabelle, and miscellaneous duties did not exceed that of the land tax until almost the end of the dynasty indicates that the abandonment of the agrarian tax base would have been impossible during the Ch'ing.

As we have seen, the difficulties encountered in collecting the land tax, upon which the *huo-hao* revenues of local government depended, was a major obstacle to mid-Ch'ing fiscal reform. It has often been suggested that the small size of China's late-imperial bureaucracy was responsible for its poor performance in such areas as tax collection. As G. William Skinner has pointed out, China in the 1720s had fewer county-level administrative units than it had had in the Han dynasty, when both its population and its territory were far smaller. Although the question of expanding the number of hsien was occasionally raised, a quick glance at the economics of such a proposal makes it clear why it was never pursued. During the Yung-cheng period, China had 1,360 hsien. To match the ratio of population to administrative unit that prevailed during the early years of imperial rule would have necessitated increasing that number to around 8,500.[1] If we assume the provision of *yang-lien* for the magistrate and a bare minimum of income for basic administrative tasks, each hsien required at least 3,000 taels. At the county-population level of the 1720s this meant that approximately 4,080,000 taels were expended on local administration, an attainable figure given the economy of the time. To provide China with enough hsien to ensure efficient control of the local population, the Ch'ing would have had to allocate more than 25,500,000 taels to county-level government alone, not to mention the addition of higher-level administrative units to supervise the activities of magistrates and their subordinate personnel. At this rate, almost the entire land- and head-tax income of the dynasty during the early eighteenth century would have been expended in measures to improve its collection.

The penetration of the bureaucracy to lower levels of society was not an option in late imperial times. Even in the People's Republic of China the institutions of territorial administration have not been extended much below those that existed in the Ch'ing. The reformers of the 1720s tried to deal with the limitations of the existing system of territorial control in the most efficient way they could: (1) by improving funding of local government so that magistrates would no longer have to rely on the illegal activities of their subordinates to carry out local administration, (2) by paying those lower yamen personnel upon whom a dispersed administration depended, (3) by making yamen runners and clerks subject to the same administrative sanctions as officials, and (4) by attempting to reorganize tax collection to eliminate the middlemen who stood between the government and the individual taxpayer.

Huo-hao kuei-kung was a powerful tool to achieve these goals, but by itself it was insufficient. The informal networks of local power and influence, which had facilitated corruption below the level of the bureaucracy before the reforms, survived. Given the communications technology of the eighteenth century, the small size of the bureaucracy, and the continued reliance on agricultural taxation, the government could do little to increase its share of the rural surplus. Rationalization of local-government finance did much to prevent the dissipation of revenues collected from the taxpayers, but could do little to prevent the tax evasion and tax farming that decreased the level of remittances in the first place. Gentry resistance and low government income combined to prevent the implementation of the thorough cadastral surveys that might have enabled the government to tap more fully the potential of the agrarian economy. But even had this been accomplished, the fluid land market in the areas of greatest tax evasion would have made such surveys useless within a short time.

The predominance of the agrarian sector of China's economy contributed to the demise of the mid-Ch'ing reforms in other ways as well. One of the main reasons that *huo-hao kuei-kung* ceased to function by the end of the Ch'ien-lung reign was the central government's refusal to authorize the periodic increase in *huo-hao* levies that would have enabled local officials to cope with increased costs brought about by inflation and population growth. If Confucianism was an obstacle to the evolution of a strong modern state, its effects were felt here. Confucian concepts of benevolent rule precluded the expansion of taxation to the point that it risked the destruction of the peasantry. The increase in rural population in the eighteenth century was so great that the government was correct in fearing the consequences of any further drain on percapita income.[2] However, the reaffirmation of the concept of a nonexpanding fiscal base could not but lead to renewed competition between local and central government for limited resources. Local autonomy in fiscal matters ensured the flexibility necessary for successful implementation of the *huo-hao kuei-kung* reforms, but afforded no institutional means to control malfeasance among provincial officials. Given the low level of communications technology available prior to the twentieth century, the only way a government could control the fiscal activities of its constituent parts was through a system of quotas on income and expenditure. However, strict controls by the central government would inevitably reduce the effectiveness of the reforms by eliminating provincial- and county-level fiscal discretion. Neither alternative was wholly acceptable. Nevertheless, the central government, with its overriding concern for the protection of state finances and the people's livelihood, chose the latter course, with the deleterious effects we have described.

It was not a lack of vision or a lack of will that determined the collapse of the centralized Chinese state. It was a lack of means. The demise of rational fiscal administration heralded a new era of corrupt local administration, low official morale, and ineffective control of the Chinese countryside. The poverty of China's rural population contributed to the failure of *huo-hao kuei-kung*. In turn, the instability of late Ch'ing finance impaired the dynasty's ability to maintain previous levels of water-conservancy projects and other services vital to the well-being of China's agrarian economy. As students of modern China, we must not take the nineteenth century as our model of the possibilities for change in the "late-imperial state." The nineteenth century, with its increasing regionalism, domestic rebellion, and weakened state control over society and the bureaucracy, represents the culmination of an administrative cycle that began in the late Ming. The *huo-hao kuei-kung* reforms present us with an example of creative and rational reform in the late-imperial period, the effects of which we are only now beginning to explore. The factors contributing to the demise of this fiscal institution and the outcome of the reversion to uncontrolled fiscal competition in the nineteenth century must be taken into account if we are to really understand the fall of the Ch'ing state and the disintegration of the Chinese polity in the modern age.

NOTE ON SOURCES

A large portion of the materials used in this study was gathered in the imperial archives housed in the National Palace Museum in Taipei, Taiwan. The collection known as the *Kung-chung tang* contains over 400,000 individual memorials addressed to the Ch'ing emperors as part of the secret palace-memorial system of communications. Citation of these documents is as follows: Catalogue number in the museum archive (i.e., KCT 19901), the name of the memorialist(s), and the date of the memorial. In the case of reign periods other than Yung-cheng, the abbreviation of the reign period follows the letters KCT (i.e., KCT CL 489). In some instances where the memorial in question was first found in the mid-eighteenth-century collection known as the *Yung-cheng chu-p'i yü-chih*, that source is cited following the same format. A small number of secret palace memorials pertaining to *huo-hao* were overlooked when I was working in the archives in Taiwan because they were not filed under categories that would have indicated their relevance to this study. In such cases, the photo-offset version of these memorials, the *Kung-chung tang Yung-cheng ch'ao tsou-che*, produced after my return from Taiwan, made it possible to assure examination of all Yung-cheng-period sources in Taiwan.

The secret palace memorials of the Yung-cheng period, and to a lesser extent, those of the Ch'ien-lung and Chia-ch'ing periods, constitute the most complete data available on the implementation of *huo-hao kuei-kung*. They do not, however, provide adequate information on the routine operation of government. In order to explore the effects of the reforms and of corruption on early fiscal administration, it was necessary to examine a number of archival sources not available in Taiwan. Many of these are housed in the Number One Historical Archives in Peking. There I found additional secret palace memorials that were crucial in understanding the early Ch'ien-lung period reactions to the reforms. These are catalogued under the title *Chu-p'i tsou-che*. In addition, I was able to examine routine memorials in the Board of Revenue section of the Grand Secretariat Archives (*hu-k'o t'i-pen*). The most valuable of these pertained to bureaucratic corruption (*t'an-wu*). Unlike secret palace memorials, these are catalogued by the number of the document and the box in which it is stored. The third new source in the archives in Peking was the collection of *huang-ts'e*. These are registers, often thousands of pages in length, in which data on population, fiscal, and other matters were reported to the emperor. Two separate catalogues exist for these documents, listing each by title and catalogue number.

Abbreviations

CC	Chia-ch'ing reign
CCWHTK	Ch'ing-chao wen-hsien t'ung-k'ao
CL	Ch'ien-lung reign
CLSL	Ta-ch'ing shih-tsu chang huang-ti shih-lu
CPTC	Chu-p'i tsou-che
CPYC	Yung-cheng chu-p'i yü-chih
HCCSWP	Huang-ch'ao ching-shih wen-pien
HCSHC	Huang-ch'ao shih-huo chih
HPTL	Ch'in-ting hu-pu tsu-li
KCT	Kung-chung tang
KCTYCCTC	Kung-chung tang Yung-cheng ch'ao tsou-che
SC	Shun-chih reign
TCHT	Ta-ch'ing hui-tien
TCHTSL	Ta-ch'ing hui-tien shih-li
TP	Yung-cheng hu-k'o t'i-pen
YC	Yung-cheng reign
YCSL	Ta-ch'ing shih-tsung hsien huang-ti shih-lu

NOTES

Preface

1. Ray Huang, *1587, A Year of No Significance: The Ming Dynasty in Decline*, pp. 20, 86. One of the implications of Huang's superb characterization of the Wan-li reign is that the importance of ideology in Ming administration almost guaranteed that the emperor would be little more than a figurehead.

2. See Silas Wu, *Communication and Imperial Control in China: Evolution of the Palace Memorial System, 1693–1735*, pp. 107–23. According to Wu, K'ang-hsi valued harmony, a fact that led him to avoid drastic changes, treat officials with leniency, and rely on moral suasion rather than punitive sanctions in dealing with bureaucratic malfeasance. Yung-cheng's stricter approach toward officials and his advocacy of radical reform are seen as the result of his adherence to efficiency as the principal value in his administration. One striking characteristic of the Yung-cheng emperor was his dedication to his position as ruler and his attention to the details of government. His rescripts to palace memorials were often pages long, in contrast to the one or two words that often served as the imperial comment of his predecessor. On several occasions the Yung-cheng emperor depicted himself hunched over these provincial reports, composing his replies by candlelight in a hand made shaky by weariness. Although we now know that he himself did not write all of his rescripts, it is clear that the image of the indefatigable monarch was not mere pretense.

3. Jonathan Spence describes several instances in which K'ang-hsi's aversion to conflict within the bureaucracy led to his refusal to take stern measures to combat corruption. Jonathan Spence, *Ts'ao Yin and the K'ang-hsi Emperor, Bondservant and Master*, pp. 186, 189, 212.

4. Harold Kahn provides an excellent analysis of the way in which Confucian ideals of kingship molded the Ch'ien-lung emperor's behavior.

Two poignant examples are his excessive displays of filial sentiment toward his mother and his almost compulsive attempts to appear as a patron of the arts and letters. See Harold Kahn, *Monarchy in the Emperor's Eyes, Image and Reality in the Ch'ien-lung Reign.*

Chapter 1

1. Tan Shou, *Ch'ing-ch'ao ch'üan-shih*, p. 124. The tael is a Chinese ounce of silver. Except where payment was in kind or conversion to copper coins was allowed by local officials, all taxes in China were paid in weights of unminted silver. The Chinese terms for decimal fractions of an ounce were *ch'ien* (0.1), *fen* (0.01), *li* (0.001), and *hao* (0.0001).

2. Hsiao I-shan has estimated that the total income from salt, customs, and miscellaneous taxes in the late K'ang-hsi period was about 6,370,000 taels. Added to the approximately 23 million taels in land and head taxes designated for remittance to the central government, total central-government income in the late K'ang-hsi reign was about 29,370,000 taels. Hsiao I-shan, *Ch'ing-tai t'ung-shih*, vol. 2, p. 354; *Ta-ch'ing hui-tien, chüan* 32, *hu-pu* 10, *fu-i* 2, *ch'i-yün* (hereafter cited as TCHT).

3. The most famous was the Kiangnan tax-arrears case of 1661 in which over 13,000 members of the Kiangnan gentry were implicated. For a discussion of the case, see Robert Oxnam, *Ruling from Horseback, Manchu Politics in the Oboi Regency, 1661–1669*, pp. 102–108.

4. Wang Yeh-chien, *Land Taxation in Imperial China, 1750–1911*, p. 91.

5. Hsiao I-shan, vol. 2, p. 353.

6. Ibid. This sum includes revenues from the salt gabelle, which were difficult to collect during the first few years of the dynasty.

7. Ibid.

8. During this period there were smaller and much less costly expeditions to subdue Mongolian tribes and other non-Chinese peoples living along China's northwestern frontier.

9. The Ch'ing dynasty also protected the state from the exertion of undue imperial pressure on its finances by establishing an Imperial Household treasury separate from that of the state Board of Revenue and drawing upon its own sources of funds. See Chang Te-ch'ang, "The Economic Role of the Imperial Household in the Ch'ing Dynasty."

10. *Ta-ch'ing shih-tsung hsien huang-ti shih-lu, chüan* 3, YC 1,1,14 (hereafter cited as YCSL). Deficits at the central-government level may have resulted in part from the acceptance of bribes to ignore shortages in provincial remittances.

11. *Kung-chung tang* 4623, Prince I, no date (hereafter cited as KCT). This memorial is clearly from YC 1, because Huang Ping is named as governor of Shantung.

12. *Yung-cheng chu-p'i yü-chih*, Shansi Financial Commissioner Kao Ch'eng-ling, YC 3,10,4 (hereafter cited as CPYC).

13. KCT 14122, Kiangsi Governor P'ei Shuai-tu, YC 3,9,26; KCT

15129, Kiangsi Governor P'ei Shuai-tu, YC 2,12,18; *Kung-chung tang Yung-cheng tsou-che*, Chekiang Financial Commissioner Wang Ch'ao-en, YC 2,1,25 (hereafter cited as KCTYCCTC). The list of provinces with deficits is a long one. Fukien reported a deficit of 109,000 taels resulting from the shifting of regular tax funds to unauthorized purposes, and Kansu, with a total tax quota of only 250,000 taels, still owed the central government 290,000 taels in 1725. Although the evidence is not complete, few provinces seem to have escaped incurring some deficits. KCTYCCTC, Fukien Financial Commissioner Huang Shu-wan, YC 1,12,26; KCT 15827, Kansu Governor Shih Wen-cho, YC 3,11,16.

14. See, for example, CPYC, T'ien Wen-ching, YC 3,2,12; CPYC, T'ien Wen-ching, YC 6,7,11; *Yung-cheng hu-k'o t'i-pen, t'an-wu*, box 556, no. 0007 (hereafter cited as TP); TP, *t'an-wu*, box 568, no. 0107.

15. Ray Huang, "Fiscal Administration During the Ming Dynasty," p. 83.

16. The gazetteer of Anyang hsien in northern Honan lists more than thirty items of local produce that were purchased with local taxes and sent to the capital to fill the imperial storehouses. *An-yang hsien-chih, t'ien-fu chih*, pp. 7–8.

17. Huang, "Fiscal Administration," p. 83.

18. Several excellent studies of these institutions are available in English. See Liang Fang-chung, "Local Tax Collectors in the Ming Dynasty"; John Watt, *The District Magistrate in Late Imperial China*; Hsiao Kung-chuan, *Rural China, Imperial Control in the Nineteenth Century*.

19. That the occasional *liang-chang* was rewarded for his service with entry into the regular bureaucracy does not change the basic extramural nature of the position.

20. See Liang, "Local Tax Collectors."

21. See Hsiao Kung-chuan, pp. 113–24.

22. *Huang-ch'ao shih-huo chih, chüan 2, fu-i 1*, SC 1 (hereafter cited as HCSHC).

23. Huang, "Fiscal Administration," pp. 87–89.

24. *An-yang hsien-chih, t'ien-fu chih*, p. 9; Kitamura Hironao, *Shindai shakai keizai shih kenkyū*, pp. 50–87. During the early Ch'ing, local officials were urged to carry out a policy known as *ting-sui-ti*, in which the head tax was abolished and the revenues previously derived therefrom were apportioned into the tax on land.

25. Ray Huang, *Taxation and Government Finance in Sixteenth Century Ming China*, pp. 184–85.

26. The origins of this principle can probably be traced to Mencius. His principles of moral rule were the foundation of the neo-Confucian orthodoxy of the late-imperial period. The classical text bearing his name contains numerous references to low taxation as a criterion of benevolent rule. See, for example, bk. I, pt. A, sec. 5; bk. II, pt. A, sec. 5. Mencius appears to have had a very limited view of the purposes to which tax revenues were applied, seeing them mainly as a source of funds to support warfare or the luxurious life style of the political elite.

27. These should be distinguished from general tax amnesties in which

the emperor excused all or part of the population from tax payments in celebration of an imperial birthday, ascent to the throne, or other auspicious event. Both types of exemptions served as a kind of safety valve, periodically relieving the pressure of taxes on a rural economy poised on the margin of subsistence.

28. Several works discuss the role of tax farmers in traditional China. See for example Ch'u T'ung-tsu, *Local Government in China under the Ch'ing*, and Hsiao Kung-chuan, *Rural China*. The best study of *pao-lan* to date is Nishimura Genshō, "Shinchō no horan."

29. Following a memorial by the censor Hsü Hsü-ling, suggesting reasons why previous efforts to open new land had failed, the K'ang-hsi emperor issued two orders designed to encourage reclamation through increased material incentives. He extended the period of tax exemption for newly opened lands from three to four, six, and ultimately ten years. In addition, the sponsorship of reclamation was made a road to official rank. Anyone opening twenty *ch'ing* and able to pass a literary examination would automatically receive the rank of assistant magistrate. If he could not pass the test he would receive the rank of *pa-tsung*, a low-level military position. A person ambitious enough to open 100 *ch'ing* would receive the rank of hsien magistrate after his literary competence was established and that of *shou-pei*, a second captain in the army, if it was not. Shang Hung-kuei, "Lueh-lun ch'ing-ch'u ching-chi hui-fu ho kung-ku ti tui-ch'eng chi ch'i ch'eng-chiu," p. 116.

30. Hsiao Kung-chuan, pp. 89–90.

31. HCSHC 2, *fu-i*, 6 KH 51; HCSHC 2, *fu-i* 5, KH 37. Only taxes earmarked for the Imperial Household treasury were exempt from such supervision. These funds included revenues derived from imperial domains, surplus customs duties, and certain fines and property confiscated from officials. They were not considered part of the regular tax revenues (*cheng-hsiang*), but even some of these were remitted first to the Board of Revenue before being sent to the Imperial Household.

32. HCSHC 2, *fu-i* 1, SC 1.

33, HCSHC 2, *fu-i* 4, KH 24.

34. For example, the Ming tax on artisan households (*chang-pan*), a vestige of earlier Ming occupational registration of the population, was eliminated. HCSHC 2, *fu-i* 5, KH 36, KH 39, and KH 41.

35. Saeki Tomi, *Chukokushi kenkyū*, p. 427. See *Ta-ch'ing shih-tsu chang huang-ti shih-lu*, *chüan* 25, SC 3,4,*jen-yin*.

36. Saeki, *Chukokushi*, p. 428. See *Ta-ch'ing shih-tsu chang huang-ti shih-lu*, *chüan* 57, SC 8,6,*hsin-hsi*.

37. *Ta-ch'ing hui-tien shih-li*, *chüan* 177, *hu-pu*, *t'ien-fu*, *tsou-hsiao*, SC 9 (hereafter cited as TCHTSL).

38. HCSHC 2, *fu-i* 4, KH 11.

39. This was a problem especially in areas undergoing extensive land reclamation. However, the practice of altering land- and head-tax receipts and account books to make paid taxes appear to be in arrears was also widespread.

40. HCSHC 2, *fu-i* 4, KH 28; HCSHC 2, *fu-i* 5, KH 39, *hu-pu i-chun*.

41. For examples of *fen-p'ei* in practice, see KCT 20245, Tung Wang-hsiang, no date; KCT 4623, Prince I, no date.

42. See Wang Yeh-chien, *Land Taxation*, p. 10.

43. TCHTSL, *chüan* 177, *hu-pu, t'ien-fu, tsou-hsiao*, KH 7 *t'i-chun*.

44. As we shall see, it was far more difficult for the central government to control receipts of these tax items because there was no rigid quota, a measure taken in recognition of the frequent fluctuations that could occur in the volume of trade and market transactions. See chap. 2 for the role of some of these items in the process of informal local-revenue accumulation. Some of them were later included in *tsou-hsiao* reports, but underreporting continued. HCSHC 2, *fu-i* 4.

45. TCHTSL, *chüan* 177, *hu-pu, t'ien-fu, tsou-hsiao*, KH 7 *t'i-chun*. The deadline for submission of the *tsou-hsiao ts'e* was changed by the Yung-cheng emperor to the fourth month of the following year for Chihli, Shantung, Honan, Shensi, and Shansi, the fifth month of the following year for Chekiang, Anhui, Kiangsi, Kiangsu, and Hukwang, and the sixth month of the following year for Fukien, Szechuan, Kwangtung, Kwangsi, Yunnan, and Kweichow. This change was made to give high provincial officials enough time to check local accounts, which could not be submitted before the end of the year when tax collection was completed. It also allowed for distances between the province and the imperial capital, to which the *ch'i-yün* portion of the tax was delivered. The scattering of *tsou-hsiao* deadlines aided the Board in completing its audits by spreading out the receipt of taxes and accounts over a three-month period. TCHTSL, *chüan* 177, *hu-pu, t'ien-fu, tsou-hsiao*, YC 7 *i-chun*.

46. For a while, local officials were even required to await Board approval of the latter before disbursing any funds. However, by the late K'ang-hsi period this seems to have given way to a system in which officials could disburse funds for routine expenditures and simultaneously report the amount spent to the Board. HCSHC 2, *fu-i* 6, KH 51; HCSHC 2, *fu-i* 5, KH 37.

47. *Ch'ing-ch'ao wen-hsien t'ung-k'ao*, *chüan* 41, *k'uai-chi*, KH 17, *hu-pu i-tsou* (hereafter cited as CCWHTK).

48. TCHTSL, *chüan* 177, KH 15 *fu-chun*.

49. TCHTSL, *chüan* 177, KH 22 *t'i-chun*.

50. See table 2.7 for a list of *feng-yin* granted to local- and provincial-level officials.

51. Wang Yeh-chien, "Ch'ing Yung-cheng nien ti ts'ai-cheng kai-ko," pp. 50–53.

52. See chap. 2 for a discussion of *chüan-feng* as an example of the informal accumulation of provincial revenue.

53. HCSHC 2, *fu-i* 1, SC 1, memorials by Governor Fang Ta-yu and Censor Ning Ch'eng-hsün.

54. HCSHC 2, *fu-i* 4, KH 26 edict. The use of *yu-tan* was continued only in Kiangsu, where a small printing tax was already being levied as part of the land and head tax.

55. HCSHC 2, *fu-i* 5, KH 30.

56. HCSHC 2, *fu-i* 5, KH 39, *hu-pu i-chun*.

57. Ibid.

58. Ibid. Further evidence of the emphasis on wrapping one's own taxes and depositing them personally in the tax chest (*tzu-feng t'ou-kuei*) is provided in K'ang-hsi's attack on the division of taxpayers in some provinces into *ta-hu* and *hsiao-hu*. For example, under the *li-chia* system as practiced in Hunan, the *ta-hu* contracted to collect and pay the taxes of the *hsiao-hu*. Powerful local strongmen or members of wealthy households, persons registered as *ta-hu*, sometimes treated the *hsiao-hu* as their virtual slaves. K'ang-hsi issued a strongly worded prohibition of the practice and ordered that the two groups be separated on the tax rolls. In addition, the emperor warned that if practices such as tax farming, tax resistance, extortion, and levying illegal surcharges persisted, the governors and governors-general of the provinces concerned would be impeached and punished. CCWHTK, *chüan* 2, *fu-i* 2, KH 35.

59. See, for example, TP, *t'an-wu*, box 570, no. 0131. In one hsien in Shantung, clerks admitted that in a portion of the taxes they collected, only one-tenth of every tael collected was recorded in the tax-collection registers. In this way they were able to steal almost 10,000 taels of the taxes submitted by the people of their hsien between KH 61 and YC 6. TP, *t'an-wu*, box 569, no. 123.

60. HCSHC, *fu-i* 4, KH 28; HCSHC, *fu-i* 5, KH 43.

61. See chap. 6.

62. HCSHC 2, *fu-i* 6, KH 49.

63. Wang Yeh-chien, "Ts'ai-cheng kai-ko," pp. 50−53.

64. CPYC, T'ien Wen-ching, YC 2, *jun* 4,6.

65. HCSHC, *fu-i* 6, KH 51.

66. Early Ch'ing tax quotas were based on the quotas found in the Ming dynasty Wan-li period (1573−1619) revisions of the *Fu-i ch'üan-shu*.

67. *Yin-lou* referred to taxes that were collected but not reported to the central government, whereas hidden lands were technically lands that had been opened to cultivation but not registered for taxation.

Chapter 2

1. Among these were levies in beans and horse fodder which probably originated as levies of supplies for local yamen during the Ming dynasty.

2. Ch'u, p. 140. The provinces that sent tribute grain to the court were Shantung, Honan, Hupei, Kiangsi, Kiangsu, Anhui, and Chekiang.

3. Ibid., p. 144.

4. Wang Yeh-chien, "The Fiscal Importance of the Land Tax during the Ch'ing Period," p. 832.

5. TCHT, *chüan* 32, *hu-pu* 10, *fu-i* 2, *ch'i-yün*. See, for example, the lists of KH 24 retained and remitted taxes as compared with those for YC 2.

6. *Ch'in-ting hu-pu tsu-li*, *chüan* 11, *k'u-ts'ang*, *ch'un-ch'iu e-po* (hereafter cited as HPTL).

7. Ibid. Shensi's and Kansu's near neighbors (*lin-chin sheng*) were designated as Honan and Shansi, and their next-nearest neighbors (*tz'u-chin sheng*) were Shantung and Chihli. For Szechuan, Kweichow, and Yunnan the near neighbors were Kiangsi and Hukwang and the next-nearest neighbor was Chekiang. Thus, we can see which provinces were viewed as chronically short of funds and which were viewed as having a surplus. It is interesting to note that Kiangsu was not a primary or secondary source of assistance for any province. Despite its very large tax quota, Kiangsu suffered from constant arrears and deficits. (See chap. 6.)

8. TCHTSL, *chüan* 169, *hu-pu, t'ien-fu, ch'i-yün*; HPTL, *chüan* 9, *t'ien-fu* 3, *hu-chieh ch'ien-liang*; HPTL, *chüan* 10, *k'u-ts'ang k'u-ts'un k'uan-mu*. Although it is not necessarily indicative of expenses in the early part of the dynasty, it may be noted that in CC 2 (1797) the Chihli governor-general complained that post-station expenses alone in that province exceeded 610,000 taels annually. KCT CC 3194, Liang K'en-t'ang, CC 2,9,24.

9. The importance of military expenditures to the central government is self-evident. Funds for supplies, salaries, and rations for the Manchu and Chinese garrisons in the province were allocated almost exclusively from retained regular taxes. The maintenance of post stations, feeding of horses, and payment of porters', laborers', and grooms' wages were likewise of vital interest to the central government. It was by means of such stations that the government received and transmitted all urgent communications between itself and its representatives in the provinces. Taxes were conveyed along the post-station routes and officials on tours of inspection or going to administer the provincial examinations were also provided with transportation by the stations.

10. HPTL, *chüan* 9, *hu-chieh ch'ien-liang*; "Tsou hsiao ti-ting ch'ien-liang shih wen-ts'e," *Nei-ko ta-k'u hsien-ts'un ch'ing-tai han-wen huang-ts'e*, no. 501.

11. This is not made clear in such compilations as the *Ta-ch'ing hui-tien*, but can be seen when we examine actual *tsou-hsiao ts'e*. In the Shansi case, if one adds together all the *ts'un-liu* deducted by the chou and hsien it comes to precisely the amount listed earlier in the accounts as the total *ts'un-liu* for the whole province. This is given added credence in a memorial by the Honan financial commissioner, in which he states that the wages for runners in the yamen of the governor, financial commissioner, judicial commissioner, and each of the circuit intendants and prefects was deducted from the *ts'un-liu* allotted to each chou and hsien. *Chu-p'i tsou-che, ts'ai-cheng, ching-fei*, Honan Financial Commissioner Hsü Shih-lin, CL 1,8,9 (hereafter cited as CPTC). Unfortunately, it is impossible to check this for other *tsou-hsiao ts'e* of the early Ch'ing because most are damaged and portions are missing.

12. See, for example, *An-yang hsien-chih, t'ien-fu chih*, p. 15.

13. See, for example, CPYC, T'ien Wen-ching, YC 2,11,2. An imperial edict was sent to the Board of Revenue ordering Honan to use funds in the financial commissioner's treasury to buy grain for delivery to Suchow for sale to stabilize rice prices there.

14. TCHT, *chüan* 32, *hu-pu* 10, *fu-i* 2, *ch'i-yün*, KH 2 *t'i-chun*. Transportation expenses called *shui-chiao* were allowed for shipments of dyes to the capital in KH 28 (1689), based on the amount being shipped and the distance traversed. The rates allowed for both of these forms of transport expenses were raised for most provinces in 1725. TCHT, *chüan* 32, *hu-pu* 10, *fu-i* 2, *ch'i-yün*, KH 28 *fu-chun*, YC 3 *i-chun*.

15. KCT 12533, Yunnan Governor-general Kao Ch'i-cho, Yunnan Governor Yang Ming-shih, YC 1,12,20; CPYC, T'ien Wen-ching, YC 6,3,4. In 1726, T'ien received an edict from the Board of Revenue ordering local officials to report cases of old and collapsing granaries to their superiors. Their superiors were to send officers to examine the granaries and make estimates of repair costs. These estimates were submitted to the Board, which allocated *cheng-hsiang* revenues to undertake emergency repairs. Where granaries were few and grain was being stored in the open air or in the courtyards of temples, the magistrate was to report to the governor, requesting that he investigate and memorialize the Board on how many new granaries should be built.

16. Miyazaki Ichisada, *Aijiashi ronkō*, pp. 389–90.

17. This perhaps accounts for the Yung-cheng emperor's willingness to postpone implementation of his local fiscal reforms in this area until more urgent problems relating to local tax collection had been rectified. See chap. 4.

18. *An-yang hsien-chih, t'ien-fu chih*; Miyazaki, *Aijiashi*, p. 389.

19. CPYC, Liang-kuang Governor-general Kao Ch'i-cho, YC 9,11,9, rescript.

20. CPYC, Kansu Governor Hsü Jung, YC 7,3,12.

21. *An-yang hsien-chih, t'ien-fu chih*; TP, *t'an-wu*, box 558, no. 0026.

22. Miyazaki, *Aijiashi*, p. 324. It is here that we begin to see the real differences in administrative costs that could exist among hsien throughout the empire. A higher tax quota alone would require employing more clerks and runners, for which *ts'un-liu* quotas made no provision.

23. See, for example, CPYC, Oertai, YC 5,10,8; CPYC, Hsü Jung, YC 7,3,12; CPYC, Shensi Governor Chang Pao, YC 5,8,16. In addition, clerks had to be given a regular wage or be allowed to collect fees for the services they performed.

24. Miyazaki, *Aijiashi*, pp. 330–31. Miyazaki relies on Wang Hui-tsu's *Tso-chih le-yen* for his estimates. For a detailed discussion of private secretaries in the Ch'ing, see Miao Ch'üan-chi, *Ch'ing-tai mu-fu jen-shih chih-tu*.

25. See chapter 7 for a discussion of loans made to officials to pay for the expense of moving to a new post after the implementation of the *huo-hao kuei-kung* reforms.

26. Officials were legally required to pay their own expenses on tour, though prior to the Yung-cheng emperor's reforms, most officials passed these costs onto their subordinates or the population of the areas they visited. See, for example, CPYC, Fukien Governor-general Liu Shih-ming, YC 7,11,7; Kwangsi Governor Chin Kung, YC 10,1,12.

27. CPYC, Hsü Jung, YC 7,3,12.

28. See, for example, CPYC, T'ien Wen-ching, YC 5,8,4 and YC 3,6,10.

29. CPYC, Shantung Governor Huang Ping, YC 1,12,13. CPYC, T'ien Wen-ching, YC 5,8,4.

30. TP, *t'an-wu*, box 569, no. 0110. The Number One Historical Archives in Peking contain a useful collection of routine Board of Revenue memorials concerning cases of impeachment for corruption. Although many are damaged, a number exist that detail the complete proceedings of the case, including transcripts of interrogations of officials, staff, and local inhabitants. These not only shed considerable light on the actual operations of local government, but also are valuable sources for understanding local social structure.

31. The end portion of this memorial is missing, but Ho also appears to have been responsible for 300 taels spent to transport the grain purchased in other areas to stabilize rice prices in Yin hsien. Fifteen boats were hired for the purpose, four taels being paid for the wages of the boatmen on each. In addition, 3,000 sacks had to be made to carry the rice, at a cost of 0.08 tael each for labor and materials.

32. TP, *t'an-wu*, box 558, no. 0026.

33. Ibid.

34. Ibid. Irregular methods were also utilized to hire yamen runners in Chü-ning hsien. Through a system of *pao-chia* contributions, 110 taels per year were raised for the employment of two messengers, four sedan-chair bearers, one parasol carrier, and one cook. According to the village elders of the hsien, this was a long-standing practice for which the magistrate was not responsible.

35. According to Board of Revenue statutes promulgated in 1714 and 1720, an official whose deficits could be shown to be the result of advancing funds for unauthorized public expenses (*no*), as opposed to embezzlement (*ch'in*), would be excused from banishment. If the missing funds were repaid within one year, he would be restored to official status (*k'ai-fu*). See, for example, the case of Li Fan, magistrate of Ch'i-yuan hsien, Shantung, who was found guilty of taking 2,932 taels in regular tax revenues and spending it for relief, the purchase of pack animals, and the payment of salaries to minor officials. TP, *t'an-wu*, box 570, no. 0134.

36. Ch'en Teng-yuan, *Chung-kuo t'ien-fu shih*, p. 222; Wang Yeh-chien, "Ts'ai-cheng kai-ko," pp. 50–53. Ch'en cites the *K'ang-hsi tung-hua lu*, *chüan* 84. See also KCT 4520, Shantung Governor Huang Ping, YC 1,12,13. Huang states that during the K'ang-hsi reign a request was made to pay back Shantung deficits by means of *feng-kung* contributions, but this was never carried out because *feng-kung* was discontinued entirely.

37. This law was promulgated in 1662. TCHTSL, *chüan* 170, *hu-pu*, KH 1.

38. Ibid. CL 1 edict. This practice, known as *k'ou-huang*, became the subject of controversy during the Ch'ien-lung period, although it dated back at least to the time of K'ang-hsi. Ch'ien-lung did not object to the practice itself, but to the habit of making up the missing funds through confiscation of the salaries and wages of officials and functionaries at the

prefectural level and below. Instead, he ordered that deductions be made from the salaries of all officials in the provinces except those of the exceedingly low-paid ranks of miscellaneous functionaries and education officials.

39. KCT 2966, Chihli Pa-ch'ang tao Kao Shun, YC 6,12,7.

40. Ibid. See also *An-yang hsien-chih, t'ien-fu chih.*

41. See, for example, CPYC, T'ien Wen-ching, YC 2,11,20 and YC 3,3,3.

42. HPTL, *chüan* 11, *k'u-ts'ang, fan-k'u ch'u-na.*

43. YCSL, YC 1,1,14, edict to the Grand Secretariat. Similar fees were sent to the Boards of Works and Punishments by the local officials who dealt with them.

44. Miyazaki Ichisada has made a detailed study of the contribution of salaries and wages. See his "Yo-sei te ni yoru kōkōkin kōen no teishi ni tsuite."

45. CPYC, T'ien Wen-ching, YC 5,8,4. Total expenses for the project were over 200,000 taels, most of which was raised from levies on the local population and contributions from wealthy local inhabitants.

46. CPYC, Shantung Governor Huang Ping, YC 1,12,13.

47. HCSHC, *fu-i* 5, KH 43.

48. CPYC, Oertai, YC 1,11,26.

49. CPYC, Li Wei, YC 2,9,6.

50. CPYC, T'ien Wen-ching, YC 5,8,4.

51. CPYC, Oertai, YC 5,10,8 and YC 6,6,12.

52. KCT 4748, Fukien Censor Chou Kuang-t'ao, no date (YC period); Hsiao I-shan, vol. 2, p. 355.

53. Ch'u, p. 28.

54. KCT 4748, Fukien Censor Chou Kuang-t'ao, no date (YC period).

55. KCT 5544, Kiangnan Censor Chiang Ping, YC 13,10,10.

56. Ibid. In Kiangnan, the fee was usually about 0.06 tael per tael of silver weighed.

57. KCT 5008, Director of the Court of Judicature and Revision Yü Kuang, no date (YC period); KCT 5544, Kiangnan Censor Chiang Ping, YC 13,10,10; KCT 20940, Honan Censor Yang Shih-chien, no date (YC period).

58. KCT 20940, Honan Censor Yang Shih-chien, no date (YC period); KCT 20970, Yen Tsu-hsi, no date (YC period); KCT 8889, Shantung Educational Commissioner Wang Shih-ch'en, no date (YC period).

59. KCT 8889, Shantung Educational Commissioner Wang Shih-ch'en, no date (YC period).

60. Ibid. TP, *t'an-wu*, box 570, no. 0131 and box 569, no. 0123.

61. KCT 21301, Hanlin Bachelor Tung Chün-wei, no date (YC period).

62. KCT 20970, Yen Tsu-hsi, no date (YC period).

63. Regarding *tsa-shui*, see under "Retained and Remitted Taxes," above.

64. For example, in Honan a duty was charged when people offered incense at Mount T'ai. This was a regular tax and should have been remitted in full by the chou magistrate. Instead, less was reported than was

collected and a portion was shared with each of the magistrate's superiors in the form of annual gifts called *hsiang-kuei*. KCT 6727, T'ien Wen-ching, YC 6,9,8.

65. CPYC, Yun-kuei Governor-general Kao Ch'i-cho, YC 2,5,8. See also KCT 13726, Acting Kwangtung Governor Shih-li-ha, YC 5,11,22; CPYC, Szechuan Governor Fa-min, YC 4,6,4.

66. For a discussion of hidden land, see chap. 1. Also, KCT 15957, Chekiang Governor-general Ch'eng Yuan-chang, no date (YC period); KCT 11847, Prince I, YC 3,8,16; KCT 17855, Wang Shih-chün, YC 7,9,15.

67. KCT 11847, Prince I, YC 3,8,16; KCT 11918, T'ien Wen-ching, YC 3,10,13.

68. KCT 5514, Grand Secretary, Acting Censor So Chu, YC 13,10,27.

69. KCT 5624, Chekiang Censor Weng Tsao, no date (YC period).

70. KCT 5010, Office of the Provincial Commander-in-Chief, no name, no date (YC period); KCT 3239, Junior Metropolitan Censor, Kuei Hsüan-kuang, YC 9,7,7.

71. Ch'u, p. 29.

72. The use of a similar technique by the financial commissioner is described under "Funds Skimmed Off in the Process of Purchase and Allocation," below.

73. KCTYCCTC, Hanlin Reader Wu Lung-yuan, YC 1,11,26.

74. KCT 5589, Board of Rites Vice-president Li Tsung-wan, no date (YC period).

75. KCT 20112, Shansi Censor Yen Ssu-sheng, no date (YC period).

76. See chap. 6.

77. KCT 16657, Acting Kiangsi Governor Chang Tan-lin, YC 7,5,6; KCT 13467, Chihli Governor-general Li Fu, YC 4,3,27.

78. KCT 15105, Kwangtung Governor-general Yang Lin, no date (YC period). This figure appears somewhat high and may have included other forms of customary fees from the customs and salt administrations.

79. KCT KH 1473, Kwangsi Governor Kao Ch'i-cho, KH 60,5,2. It is clear that these *chieh-li* were fixed assessments on subordinates. Remittances were allocated as follows (in taels):

Financial Commissioner	1,600
Judicial Commissioner	600
Ts'ang-wu Circuit	600
Yu-chiang Circuit	200
Tso-chiang Circuit	200
Kuei-lin, Wu-chou, Nan-ning prefects	2,000
Liu-chou, T'ai-p'ing, Ch'ing-yuan, Ssu-en prefects	800
All chou and hsien	6,400

Some officials, such as the financial commissioner, sent *chieh-li* for each of the four seasonal festivals, whereas others, including the judicial commissioner, sent a lump sum annually. The chou and hsien varied, sending gifts at one, two, three, or all four seasons, and some sent no *chieh-li* at all.

80. KCT 14029, Shantung Governor Sai-leng-e, YC 5,5,22.

81. KCT 6727, T'ien Wen-ching, YC 6,9,8.

82. KCT 11816, Kansu Governor Hsü Jung, YC 7, *jun* 7, 9; KCT 14159, Assistant Director of Water Conservancy Ch'i Tseng-chün, YC 6,8,28; KCT 6727, T'ien Wen-ching, YC 6,9,8.

83. KCT 17027, Acting Kwangtung Financial Commissioner Kan Ju-lai, YC 10,9,3. Given an annual tax quota of about 1 million taels, the amount of *hsiao-fei yin* remitted each year came to around 3,000 taels.

84. KCT 16354, Chihli Governor-general Li Wei, YC 11,4,26.

85. KCT 22159, Reader of the Grand Secretariat Hsi Chu, YC 7,11,29. Chao Hung-en also memorialized reporting that the *fan-shih* of the financial commissioner's yamen clerks required from 4,000 to 5,000 taels per year and were derived from *lou-kuei*. KCT 19845, Prince I, Board disposition slip, no date (YC period).

86. KCT 13976, Yang Wen-ch'ien, YC 6,3,2, transmitting a report by Kwangtung Judicial Commissioner Yin Chi-shan. See also KCT 2085, Censor (no name), YC 11,4,27. Lower yamen which had direct dealings with the Board also sent *fan-shih yin*. For example, the Superintendent of Water Conservancy sent it when reporting the annual accounts of his yamen. KCT 12691, Kiangnan Superintendent of Water Conservancy, Ch'i Tseng-chün, YC 12,10,28.

87. KCT 22264, Szechuan Financial Commissioner Kao Wei-hsin, no date (probably YC 7 or 8).

88. KCT 5164, Ho-tung Governor-general Wang Shih-chün, YC 13,7,24.

89. Ibid.

90. KCT 13600, Liang-kuang Governor-general K'ung Yü-hsün, YC 5,8,19.

91. KCT 20817, Yin Chi-shan, no date (YC period); KCT 3078, Wang Mu, no date (YC period). Inasmuch as the people holding such posts received little or no salary, fees of this type were clearly paid in anticipation of lucrative opportunities for graft once they came to their posts.

92. KCT 18933, Acting Kwangtung Governor Fu T'ai, YC 7,9,19.

93. KCT 20817, Yin Chi-shan, no date (YC period). It is important to note that Kuan was faulted not so much for accepting bribes as for extorting more than the customary amount.

94. KCT 555, Yueh Chung-ch'i, YC 6,9,16; KCT 15726, Hunan Governor Wang Ch'ao-en, YC 3,4,3; KCT 20820, Yin Chi-shan, YC 6,12,11.

95. KCT 12326, Shantung Financial Commissioner Yueh Chün, YC 6,5,24.

96. KCT 1301, Acting Fuchow Manchu General-in-chief Chun-t'ai, YC 13,4,24.

97. KCT 4085, Kwangchow Manchu Brigade General and Superintendent of Customs Mao-k'o-ming, no date (YC period).

98. KCT 14045, Shantung Governor Sai-leng-e, YC 5,9,3.

99. KCT 557, Yueh Chung-ch'i, YC 6,9,16.

100. KCT 555, Yueh Chung-ch'i, YC 6,9,16. Similar discrepancies existed for other goods as well.

101. KCT 4088, Mao-k'o-ming, YC 11,11,27.

102. KCT 1299, Superintendent of Fukien Maritime Customs Chunt'ai, YC 8,5,26.

103. Ibid.; KCT 15449, Kwangtung Governor-general K'ung Yü-hsün, YC 6,10,8; KCT 1464, Kiangsu Governor Chang Ch'ia, YC 3,6,18.

104. KCT 22307, Fengtien Metropolitan Prefect Yang Ch'ao-tseng, no date (YC period).

105. KCT 14641, Kiangsu Governor Chang Ch'ia, YC 3,6,18.

106. Ibid.

107. Ibid.

108. Although it was not until the Ch'ien-lung period that foreign trade was restricted to Canton, most trade by western merchants had already gravitated to Canton by the seventeenth century. See Frederic Wakeman, *The Fall of Imperial China*, p. 120.

109. KCT 15450, Liang-kuang Governor-general K'ung Yü-hsün, YC 6,11,7. The rate for *shang-huo fen-t'ou* was 3.9 percent when levied on the value of merchandise, at which time it was called *tan-t'ou yin*. When levied on the value of cargo, the rates varied. For example, 0.018 tael was collected on every *chin* by weight of most cargo and 0.01 tael on every bolt of silk cloth.

110. KCT 4110, Kwangchow Superintendent of Maritime Customs Mao-k'o-ming, YC 10,12,28.

111. Ibid. At this time a Mexican silver dollar was valued at 0.72 tael. It should be noted that the emperor felt a tax with so inelegant a name could only harm the reputations of those involved and ordered that prohibitions on *jen-shui* be strictly enforced.

112. KCT 2037, Kiangsi Governor Chang An, YC 12,11,20; KCT 16516, Kiangsi Governor Pu-lan-t'ai, YC 5,11,1.

113. KCT 16516, Kiangsi Governor Pu-lan-t'ai, YC 5,11,1.

114. At the Chiu-chiang and Kan-chou customs this was called *p'ingyü ling-yin* and came to 7,000 to 8,000 taels annually. KCT 16657, Acting Kiangsi Governor Chang Tan-lin, YC 7,5,6.

115. KCT 13767, Kao Pin, YC 11,12,2.

116. KCT 1298, Controller of Fukien Customs Chun-t'ai, YC 9,6,13.

117. KCT 15629, Kwangsi Governor Chin Kung, no date (YC period).

118. KCT 21603, Yueh Chung-ch'i, YC 6,9,9.

119. For more information on the operation of the salt administration see Thomas Metzger, "The Organizational Capabilities of the Ch'ing State in the Field of Commerce: The Liang-huai Salt Monopoly"; Ho P'ing-ti, "The Salt Merchants of Yang-chou: A Study of Commercial Capitalism in Eighteenth Century China."

120. E-tu Zen Sun, *Ch'ing Administrative Terms*, p. 163.

121. In the Yung-cheng period much of this surplus was used to supplement military supply and for waterworks repairs. KCT 4332, Shensi Judicial Commissioner Shih-se, no date (YC period); KCT 3379, Sun Chia-kan, no date (YC period).

122. KCT 16499, Hunan Governor Pu-lan-t'ai, YC 4,6,22.

123. KCT 5747, Board of Punishments Metropolitan Censor Chao Tien-tsui, no date (YC period).

124. KCT CL 3548, Pan-ti, CL 18,4,11.

125. See, for example, KCT 17147, Kiangsi Financial Commissioner I-la-chi, no date (YC period).

126. KCT 17145, Kiangsi Financial Commissioner I-la-chi, no date (YC period).

127. KCT 19177, Shantung Salt Controller Ch'i Shao-wen, no date (YC period).

128. KCT 16657, Acting Kiangsi Governor Chang Tan-lin, YC 7,5,6. See also KCT 13654, Chihli Governor-general I Chao-hsiung, YC 5,9,15; KCT 4288, T'ien Wen-ching, YC 7,3,11; and KCT 3730, Fa-hai, no date (probably YC 3) regarding *yen-kuei* sent to lower officials in Chihli, Honan, and Chekiang respectively.

129. KCT 14093, Fu-min, Pu-lan-t'ai, and Chu Kang, YC 5,7,9.

130. KCT 3730, Fa-hai, no date (YC period).

131. KCT 5747, Board of Punishments Metropolitan Censor Chao Tien-tsui, no date (YC period).

132. KCT 4336, Shensi Judicial Commissioner Shih-se, YC 6,9,21.

133. KCT 17328, K'o-erh-t'ai, YC 5,1,4.

134. CPYC, Acting Suchow Governor Ch'iao Shih-ch'ien, YC 9,12,7. See also KCT 15972, Chekiang Governor-general Ch'eng Yuan-chang, no date (YC period), on merchant offers to contribute funds to make up an official's 216,500-tael deficit; KCT 18660, Suchow Governor Ch'en Shih-hsia, YC 6,4,18, on merchant offers to contribute 7,000 taels for boat construction; KCT 13755, Kao Pin, no date (YC period), on merchant subscriptions to the construction of a state-sponsored temple in Kiangnan.

135. The government could have provided local revenues from the salt monopoly by increasing the tax on salt. In some cases a meltage fee on the salt gabelle was allowed, but the income from this source was small. (See, for example, "Hao-hsien yin-liang ts'e," *Nei-ko ta-k'u hsien-ts'un ch'ing-tai han-wen huang ts'e*, no. 942). Any large-scale move in this direction would have necessitated extending regular revenue sharing to the salt gabelle. The salt administration being a separate agency and one of the central government's most reliable sources of income, it was understandably unwilling to do so. Moreover, because in theory salt prices were tied to the gabelle, it was perhaps only by means of customary fees that the government saw itself able to appropriate the excess profits of salt merchants without having the increase in taxation passed on to the consumer.

136. KCT 17027, Acting Kwangtung Financial Commissioner Kan Ju-lai, YC 10,9,3.

137. KCT 17673, Shantung Financial Commissioner Chang Pao, YC 4,7,13.

138. KCT 12337, Acting Shantung Governor, Financial Commissioner Yueh Chün, no date (YC period).

139. KCT 11352, Suchow Financial Commissioner Chang Tan-lin, YC 5,11,1.

140. *Ping-feng* refers to the process of opening the wrapped tax envelopes deposited by individual taxpayers and recombining them for trans-

port to the provincial capital. According to Yueh Chün, when the chou and hsien remitted taxes much of the silver received was in small pieces weighing less than a tael, reflecting the low liabilities of most taxpayers. However, in remitting and disbursing funds, higher levels of government used the hundredth of a tael as the lowest denomination. All smaller fractions of an ounce were rounded off to the nearest *li* and the remaining silver was kept by the financial commissioner. KCT 12337, Acting Shantung Governor, Financial Commissioner Yueh Chün, YC 6,8,12. See also KCT 17027, Kan Ju-lai, YC 10,9,3.

141. KCT 22134, Acting Kwangtung Financial Commissioner Wang Mu, no date (YC period). Board of Works President Li Hsien-fu reported that in KH 38 (1699) the issuing of rations to the Green Standard Army was placed under the supervision of provincial officials, the financial commissioner, and the grain intendant at the provincial level and the prefects and magistrates at the local level. The civil officials were originally assigned this duty to prevent military officers from overreporting expenses (*hsü-mao*) and taking deductions from their subordinate troops' rations (*k'ou-k'o*). However, civil officials throughout the empire were later found to be demanding *lou-kuei* before they would issue the bond of guarantee (*chieh-kuei*) necessary for the release of the rations. KCTYCCTC, Board of Works President Li Hsien-fu, YC 2,1.

142. KCT 22134, Acting Kwangtung Financial Commissioner Wang Mu, no date (YC period).

143. KCT 6727, T'ien Wen-ching, YC 6,9,8. See also KCT 16895, Chekiang Grain Intendant Ts'ai Shih-shan, YC 2,11,25.

144. KCT 17673, Shantung Financial Commissioner Chang Pao, YC 4,7,13.

145. KCT 17027, Acting Kwangtung Financial Commissioner Kan Ju-lai, YC 10,9,3.

146. KCT 12510, Kiangning Financial Commissioner Chueh-lo Shih-lin, YC 5,8,6.

147. KCT 15958, Anhui Governor Ch'eng Yuan-cheng, no date (YC period).

148. KCT 10969, Acting Kiangning Financial Commissioner Liu Nan, YC 9,6,1.

149. KCT 17058, Kiangning Financial Commissioner (no name), YC 11,8; KCT 22358, Kiangning Post and Salt Intendant Ch'ien Hung-mou, YC 10,5,11.

150. KCT 12511, Kiangning Financial Commissioner Chueh-lo Shih-lin, YC 5,8,6.

151. KCT 17058, Kiangning Financial Commissioner (no name), YC 11,8.

152. KCT 12511, Chueh-lo Shih-lin, YC 5,8,6.

153. KCT 14161, Kiangnan Superintendent of Water Conservancy Ch'i Tseng-chün, YC 8,12,6; KCT 16895, Chekiang Grain Intendant Ts'ai Shih-shan, YC 2,11,25.

154. Two less common sources of profit from purchases and allocations should be mentioned. Officials with purchasing responsibilities oc-

casionally falsified the expenditure of regular tax revenues (*mao-hsiao*) or commandeered taxes without authority (*mao-ling*). This probably yielded a sizable sum but should not be considered part of the informal funding network, because it was illegal and sanctions against it were usually enforced strictly even in the early Ch'ing. If detected, the official concerned would be impeached and his family property confiscated. See, for example, KCT CL 2406, Fukien Financial Commissioner Te Shu, CL 17,9,3. The financial commissioner also might take a cut from funds allocated from his treasury to subordinates. This was the case in Shantung, where the financial commissioner would routinely deduct 0.06 tael from every tael of funds he issued to circuit intendants, prefects, and magistrates engaged in the repair of waterworks. However, there is no evidence that this practice was common in other provinces. KCT 12351, Shantung Financial Commissioner Yueh Chün, YC 6,1,28.

Chapter 3

1. CCWHTK, *chüan* 1, *t'ien-fu* 1, Shun-chih 1; CCWHTK, *chüan* 2, *fu-i* 2, K'ang-hsi edicts to the Board of Revenue, KH 4 and KH 7; Hsiao I-shan, vol. 2, p. 355.
2. Hsiao I-shan, vol. 2, p. 355.
3. Wang Ch'ing-yün, *Shih-ch'ü yü-chi*, pp. 300–1.
4. Following the implementation of *huo-hao kuei-kung*, magistrates in several provinces resisted the remittance of their *huo-hao* to the financial commissioner, despite evidence that the reforms would ultimately lessen their fiscal burden. See, for example, the section of this chapter headed "Backlash in Honan."
5. For an excellent discussion of the way in which degree holders in one county were able to shield a large portion of the cultivated land in their area from the government's tax collectors, see Jerry Dennerline, *The Chia-ting Loyalists*, pp. 327–29.
6. Dennerline, chap. 4, nn. 5,6, and 7.
7. Two instances of this use of the tax amnesty are cited in chap. 1 under the heading, "Imperial Benevolence and Fiscal Administration."
8. An instance of such tolerance is noted in chap. 1 under the heading, "Imperial Benevolence and Fiscal Administration."
9. See, for example, KCT 4520, Shantung Governor Huang Ping, YC 1,12,13; KCT KH 2038, Chekiang Governor Wang Tu-chao, KH 51,11.
10. KCTYCCTC, Kiangsu Financial Commissioner Oertai, YC 2,1,11.
11. See, for example, KCTYCCTC, Honan Governor Shih Wen-cho, YC 2,1,22; KCT 4916, Shih I-chih, YC 1,8,8; KCT 16514, Shantung Governor Pu-lan-t'ai, YC 3,4,7; KCT 21080, Commissioner of the Transmission Office Chang Mao-ch'eng, no date (YC period).
12. See, for example, KCTYCCTC, Board of Punishments President Fu-ko, YC 1,11,4; KCT 4502, Board of Punishments Vice-president Huang Ping, YC 5,11,20; KCT 5742, Hanlin Compiler Chuang K'ai, YC 1,7; KCT 20916, Censor Wang Chih-lin, no date (YC period).

13. Board fees are described in chap. 2 under the heading, "Customary Fees." In an edict to all provincial governors, Yung-cheng stated that "in the past all matters reported [to the Board] in a routine memorial were accompanied by Board fees (*pu-fei*)." YCSL, *chüan* 25, YC 2,10,23.

14. YCSL, *chüan* 3, YC 1,1,14.

15. HCSHC, *fu-i* 6, KH 61.

16. YCSL, *chüan* 3, YC 1,1,14, *chüan* 4, YC 1,2,25, *chüan* 25, YC 2,10,23. I wish to thank Beatrice Bartlett for bringing these references to my attention.

17. HCSHC, *fu-i* 6, KH 61. Shensi was temporarily excluded because it was the headquarters for military operations against non-Chinese tribes to the northwest.

18. YCSL, *chüan* 3, YC 1,1,1.

19. KCT 4696, Board of Punishments Vice President Huang Ping, YC 2,8,1; KCTYCCTC, Honan Governor Shih Wen-cho, YC 2,1,22.

20. See, for example, KCT 13603, Liang-kuang Governor-general K'ung Yü-hsün, YC 3,11,10; KCTYCCTC, Honan Governor Shih Wen-cho, YC 2,4,22.

21. Officials in Chekiang and Kiangnan were particularly burdened by the policy of property confiscation because so many officials came from these provinces. See, for example, KCT 8031, Director of the Court of Judicature and Revision Hsing-kuei, YC 6,12,5.

22. In Shantung alone it was found that more than 900,000 piculs of grain were missing from local granaries. KCT 4623, Prince I, no date (YC period).

23. See, for example, KCTYCCTC, Shantung Governor Huang Ping, YC 2,4,3.

24. KCT 14098, Acting Hupei Governor-general Fu-min, YC 5,4,21. See also the case of magistrate Ho, pp. 42–43.

25. Most of these took the form of suggestions to increase the number and type of inspectors to which local treasuries were subjected and to make accounting fraud more difficult by introducing officially issued and numbered tax registers and receipts. See, for example, KCT 21080, Commissioner of the Transmission Office Chang Mao-ch'eng, no date (YC period); KCT 4769, P'u-chao, YC 2,7,25.

26. KCT 20916, Censor Wang Chih-lin, no date (YC period); KCT 21301, Hanlin Bachelor Tung Chün-wei, no date (YC period); KCT 4717, Hukwang Censor Ch'eng Jen-ch'i, YC 3,1,12.

27. Not all central-government officials attributed deficits to mere greed on the part of their colleagues. For example, Li Fu and Ch'ien I-k'ai suggested that the sale of government positions (*chüan-na*) was the main cause of peculation in office. Officials accrued large debts in order to buy their posts, leaving them with no choice but to steal from their yamen treasuries to pay them off. KCT 20981, Board of War Vice-president Li Fu, no date (Li held this post only during YC 1); KCT 5806, Commissioner of the Transmission Office Ch'ien I-k'ai, YC 1,8,10. This explanation cannot account for all the deficits uncovered in the early YC reign, the sale of office having been relatively infrequent during that period.

28. KCT 20907, Grand Secretary and Board of Rites Vice-president Hu Hsü, no date (YC period).

29. KCTYCCTC, Kwangsi Financial Commissioner Liu T'ing-tsung, YC 2,4.

30. See, for example, KCT 12522, Prince I, no date (YC period). In Shansi, at least 175,162 taels of the deficit for the period 1716–23 turned out to have originated as arrears.

31. See, for example, KCTYCCTC, Chekiang Financial Commissioner Wang Ch'ao-en, YC 2,1,25; KCT KH 1872, Acting Chihli Governor Chao Chih-yuan, KH 61,12,22; KCTYCCTC, Fukien Financial Commissioner Huang Shu-wan, YC 1,12,26; KCT 4696, Board of Punishments Vice-president Huang Ping, YC 2,8,1.

32. KCT 5730, Censorate Vice-president Ch'en Yün-kung, YC 1,10,24.

33. The complete transcript of the Board inquiry may be found in KCTYCCTC, Board of Punishments President Po-ko, YC 1,11,4. No follow-up memorials appear to have survived among the records of the Grand Secretariat in the Number One Historical Archives in Peking.

34. KCT 18677, Honan Governor Shih Wen-cho, YC 1,8,27; KCT 5706, Subdirector of the Court of Judicature and Revision T'ang Chih-yü, no date (YC period).

35. KCT 18677, Honan Governor Shih Wen-cho, YC 1,8,27; KCT 4520, Shantung Governor Huang Ping, YC 1,12,12; KCT 5742, Hanlin Compiler Chuang K'ai, YC 1,7 (on deficits in Shansi); KCT 14048, Acting Shantung Governor Sai-leng-e, YC 5,2,10.

36. KCT 4623, Prince I, no date (YC period).

37. KCTYCCTC, Wu Lung-yuan, YC 2, *jun* 4,9.

38. Numerous complaints were made during this period that officials with deficits transferred their family property to another household in order to evade confiscation. This was possible because of the delays inherent in initiating confiscation proceedings in another province and because officials who were still in office were usually given time to repay their deficits from the assets possessed at their posts. See, for example, KCT 5806, Commissioner of the Transmission Office Ch'ien I-k'ai, YC 1,8,10.

39. CCWHTK, *chüan* 3, *t'ien-fu* 3, YC 2, edict to the Board of Revenue.

40. KCTYCCTC, Fukien Financial Commissioner Huang Shu-wan, YC 1,12,26; KCT 15827, Kansu Governor Shih Wen-cho, YC 3,11,16; KCT 4520, Shantung Governor Huang Ping, YC 1,12,13; KCTYCCTC, Chekiang Financial Commissioner Wang Ch'ao-en, YC 2,1,25.

41. KCT 15129, Kiangsi Governor P'ei Shuai-tu, YC 2,12,18; KCT 18677, Honan Governor Shih Wen-cho, YC 1,8,27; KCTYCCTC, Board of Punishments President Fu-ko, YC 1,11,4; KCT 20642, Szechuan-Shensi Governor-general Nien Keng-yao, YC 2,10,17; KCTYCCTC, Wu Lung-yuan, YC 2, *jun* 4,9; KCT 20240, no date, name removed.

42. KCTYCCTC, Kiangsi Governor P'ei Shuai-tu, YC 1,12,12.

43. According to Ch'ien Ta-hsin, the Monograph on Law (*Hsing-fa chih*) in the Yuan History states that local officials in mining areas were

able to manipulate their scales in order to collect more than the legal quota of the annual duty on extracted metals. The term *huo-hao* was coined by a censor during that dynasty to describe this practice. K'o Han-fen traces *huo-hao* to the Sung period, and argues that from the start it was a surcharge on taxes paid in silver. The added revenue derived in this fashion was used by officials to bribe the emperor into granting them promotions. This use of *huo-hao*, according to K'o, was outlawed by Sung T'ai-tsu. See Ch'ien Ta-hsin, *Shih chia-chai yang-hsin lu*, *chüan* 19, p. 8; K'o Han-fen, "Ch'ing-tai t'ien-fu chung chih hao-hsien," pp. 45–46.

44. In SC 6 (1646), Lo Yang-hsing requested that the customary practice of adding a 3-percent *huo-hao* to land and head taxes be legalized. By KH 34 (1695), Censor Ch'ien Chuen could memorialize that Shansi's *huo-hao* had already reached 30 or 40 percent. Similarly high rates were reported for Shensi the following year. Ch'en Teng-yuan, p. 213.

45. See, for example, HCSHC 2, *fu-i* 2, SC 13. In fact, during the Ch'ing dynasty the term *p'ing-yü* was generally used to designate legitimate surcharges established to offset the loss of silver in the process of tax collection and remittance.

46. CCWHTK, *chüan* 2, *fu-i* 2, KH 7. K'ang-hsi's efforts to improve methods of informing the taxpayer of his liabilities stemmed in part from his feeling that magistrates could levy *huo-hao* only because the taxpayer was ignorant of his individual tax responsibilities.

47. Wang Ching-yün, *chüan* 3, p. 300.

48. Ibid. K'ang-hsi 48,9 edict.

49. For a discussion of the origins of the secret palace-memorial system see Jonathan Spence, *Ts'ao Yin and the K'ang-hsi Emperor* and Silas Wu, *Communication and Control in Imperial China*. More recent work on this institution has been published in Taiwan. See, for example, Beatrice Bartlett, "Ch'ing Palace Memorials in the Archives of the National Palace Museum," and Chuang Chi-fa, "Ch'ing shih-tsung yü tsou-che chih-tu ti fa-chan."

50. The constraints on the emperor's freedom of expression under the traditional memorial system are illustrated in Ray Huang's *1587, A Year of No Significance, the Ming Dynasty in Decline*; see, for example, p. 20.

51. KCTYCCTC, Kiangsi Governor P'ei Shuai-tu, YC 1,12,12; KCT 15129, P'ei Shuai-tu, YC 2,12,18.

52. KCTYCCTC, Liang-kuang Governor-general K'ung Yü-hsün, YC 2,6,7. The emperor's comments implied rejection of K'ung's proposal.

53. CPYC, Chekiang Governor Huang Shu-lin, no date (YC period). Officials in other provinces also attempted to continue the use of *feng-kung* contributions. See, for example, KCTYCCTC, Chihli Governor Li Wei-chün, YC 2,2,13. Other provinces continued to make up deficits using salt and customs fees, fees on mining, customary fees, and so on. See KCTYCCTC, Wu Lung-yuan, YC 2, *jun* 4,9; CPYC, Mao Wen-ch'üan, YC 2,5,29.

54. CPYC, Hukwang Governor-general Yang Tsung-jen, YC 1,5,15.

55. KCT 20208, Shansi Financial Commissioner Kao Ch'eng-ling, YC

3,2,8. That No-min did implement such a plan is further confirmed by one of his successors as governor. See KCT 12520, Shansi Governor Chueh-lo Shih-lin, YC 6,3,22.

56. CPYC, Chihli Governor Li Wei-chün, YC 2,3,23. Looking back five years later, Shun-te Prefect Te-hsi recalled that Chihli had begun to use *huo-hao* to make up deficits as early as YC 1 (1723). KCT 3971, Shun-te Prefect Te-hsi, YC 6,9,25.

57. KCTYCCTC, Shantung Governor Huang Ping, YC 1,12,1.

58. KCTYCCTC, Shantung Governor Huang Ping, YC 2, *jun* 4, 16.

59. KCTYCCTC, Wu Lung-yuan, YC 2, *jun* 4, 9.

60. CPYC, Honan Governor Shih Wen-cho, YC 1,8,27.

61. KCTYCCTC, Honan Governor Shih Wen-cho, YC 2,1,22.

62. Ibid. Yung-cheng's rescript.

63. KCT 4916, Shih I-chih, YC 1,8,8. Although other sources make no mention of Shih as instrumental in the institution of *yang-lien yin*, it is likely that Shih's memorial received the emperor's careful attention. Shih was a protegé of Nien Keng-yao, who was himself one of the Yung-cheng emperor's closest confidants during the first year of his reign. Moreover, after an exceedingly uneventful career prior to Yung-cheng's ascent to the throne, Shih suddenly rose to high office within the bureaucracy.

64. KCT 20916, Censor Wang Chih-lin, no date (YC period).

65. KCTYCCTC, Subdirector of the Banqueting Court Lo Ch'i-ch'ang, YC 2,4,7.

66. KCT 20240, no name, no date. The name on this memorial was cut off, indicating that it was circulated for official comment. This was done to conform to the guarantee of confidentiality that was a vital part of the secret palace-memorial system. From the content of his remarks, this official appears to have been either an imperial commissioner or a censor assigned to Hunan province.

67. Arthur Hummel, *Eminent Chinese of the Ch'ing Period*, pp. 639–40.

68. KCT 21350, Shen Chin-ssu, no date (YC period).

69. KCTYCCTC, Board of Punishments Vice-president Chuang Ch'ing-tu, no date (YC period).

70. KCT 20208, Shansi Financial Commissioner Kao Ch'eng-ling, YC 3,2,8.

71. No-min, Shih Wen-cho, Yang Tsung-jen, and T'ien Wen-ching were all bannermen who entered the bureaucracy by purchasing *chien-sheng* degrees. See their respective biographies in *Kuo-ch'ao ch'i-hsien le-cheng*, *chüan* 170 and *chüan* 65; *Ts'ung-cheng kuan-fa lu*, 9.14.226; *Manchou ming-ch'en chüan*, 9.18.66.

72. The same was probably true of the others as well. As Chang Chung-li points out, prior to the Taiping Rebellion, the purchase of a *chien-sheng* degree normally gave one access only to the lowest levels of official appointments. See Chang Chung-li, *The Chinese Gentry*, p. 5. In T'ien's case the evidence of imperial patronage is more direct. In an edict transmitted to T'ien in early 1725, Yung-cheng stated, "Indeed, T'ien

Wen-ching was not recommended by anyone, but was specially promoted by me." CPYC, T'ien Wen-ching, YC 2,11,20.

73. Although in public pronouncements Yung-cheng denied knowing T'ien Wen-ching personally, their correspondence in secret palace memorials reveals an intimacy that went far beyond that usually expected between minister and king. In 1728, when T'ien requested an audience with the emperor to consult on his new duties as governor-general of Honan-Shantung, Yung-cheng denied T'ien permission to leave his post, with these words: "If you did not know me and I did not know you, then it would be appropriate for me to give you instructions face to face. You say we have been apart for five years. The way I see it, though the months and years are many, we have been separated by only an inch." CPYC, T'ien Wen-ching, YC 6,6,21.

74. The other two were Li Wei and Oertai.

75. For an excellent example of T'ien's intense distrust of members of the local gentry, see his *Chou-hsien shih-i*. The emperor was even more outspoken in his condemnation of degree-holding officials. In a 1727 edict calling for increased sales of degrees, Yung-cheng said, "Recently I see that among those who rise through the examination system, not only are many careless and perfunctory, but many are also corrupt and lawbreaking. The practice of teacher student and classmate relationships associated with favoritism and appeals to feelings is seen everywhere and unbreakable. If the official career should be left completely to those who rise through examinations, they would join together and work for their private interest against the public interest. This is a great harm to the public welfare and to the livelihood of the people." Chang Chung-li, *The Chinese Gentry*, p. 115.

76. T'ien first proposed the use of *shih-yung kuan* in a long secret palace memorial in 1727. The idea was initially rejected, but was later implemented by the Yung-cheng emperor. See CPYC, T'ien Wen-ching, YC 5,2,18.

77. More of T'ien's memorials than of any other official's were selected by the Yung-cheng emperor for publication in the *Yung-cheng chu-p'i yü-chih* during this reign. *Chou-hsien shih-i*, a collection of essays on local government, and *Fu-yü hsüan-hua lu*, a selection of T'ien's memorials as governor of Honan, were also compiled at the suggestion of the emperor.

78. Although the Yung-cheng emperor always spoke of No-min as the originator of the policy of *huo-hao kuei-kung*, in later discussions, particularly by the Ch'ien-lung emperor, equal credit was given to T'ien Wen-ching. See, for example, *Chang-te fu-chih*, vol. 1, pp. 53–55.

79. T'ien often bemoaned the fact that by carrying out the emperor's wishes he earned the hatred of those who served under him. See, for example, CPYC, T'ien Wen-ching, YC 2,8,8.

80. CPYC, T'ien Wen-ching, YC 2,5,12. This statement is quoted in the imperial edict cited by T'ien.

81. KCTYCCTC, Honan Governor Shih Wen-cho, YC 2,5,18.

82. CPYC, T'ien Wen-ching, YC 2,5,12.

83. KCTYCCTC, T'ien Wen-ching, YC 2,6,22.

84. CPYC, T'ien Wen-ching, YC 2,5,12.

85. Ibid.

86. CPYC, T'ien Wen-ching, YC 2,6,22. For a fuller discussion of the examination boycott and its connection with the new policy of merging the land and head taxes (*ting-sui-ti*), see my "T'ien Wen-ching and Radical Fiscal Reform during the Yung-cheng Period" (unpublished paper, Berkeley, 1975). See also Araki Toshikazu, "Yosei ninen no hikō jiken to Den Bunkyō."

87. CPYC, T'ien Wen-ching, YC 2,6,22. The educational commissioner was a man named Chang T'ing-lü. Chang was the brother of Chang T'ing-yü, scion of a powerful Anhui gentry family and himself a Grand Secretary with enormous influence in government during the Yung-cheng and early Ch'ien-lung reigns.

88. CPYC, T'ien Wen-ching, YC 2,6,22.

89. CPYC, T'ien Wen-ching, YC 2,8,8.

90. CPYC, T'ien Wen-ching, YC 2,6,22.

91. CPYC, T'ien Wen-ching, YC 2,9,3.

92. KCT 3595, edict, YC 2.

93. The original memorial no longer exists. Inasmuch as it was submitted to the Grand Secretariat for comment under No-min's own name, it was probably sent in the form of a *t'i-pen*. The fact that officials used *t'i-pen* only to memorialize on routine matters suggests that the emperor himself instructed No-min to present his plan at this time. Yung-cheng often did so when creative new ideas were presented to him in secret palace memorials. Thus, it is fair to assume that the appearance of No-min's proposal in early YC 2 indicated the emperor's desire to publicize *huo-hao kuei-kung* and encourage its widespread implementation.

94. *Tung-hua lu*, Yung-cheng *chüan* 4, YC 2,6, *i-yu*.

95. *Shen Tuan-k'o kung i-shu, nien-p'u*, pp. 248–49.

96. Ch'a Ssu-t'ing was a *chin-shih* from Chekiang whose career began in the Hanlin Academy. After serving as vice-president of the Board of Rites, he was purged and eventually died in prison, a victim of one of Yung-cheng's few literary inquisitions. Hummel, p. 22.

97. KCT 4898, Ch'a Ssu-t'ing, no date (YC period).

98. KCT 20204, Shansi Financial Commissioner Kao Ch'eng-ling, YC 2,6,8.

99. Ibid. The emperor's warning was toned down considerably in the version that appears in the *Shih-lu*.

100. *Tung-hua lu*, Yung-cheng *chüan* 5, YC 2,7, *ting-wei*.

101. Abe Takeo, *Shindaishi no kenkyū*, pp. 682–90.

102. In 1657 the Ch'ing eliminated the exemption of degree holders from labor service assessed on land holdings. In addition, exemption from all other forms of personal service was limited to the degree holder or official himself. Hsiao Kung-chuan, p. 125. For a discussion of the implications of this law for gentry landowners, see Hillary Beattie, *Land*

and Lineage in China: a study of T'ung-cheng county, Anhui in the Ming and Ch'ing dynasties, pp. 70–71.

103. See Frederic Wakeman, "The Shun Interregnum," p. 73.

Chapter 4

1. Ch'u, p. 22.

2. See table 2.7 for a list of official emoluments under the regular system of revenue sharing.

3. KCTYCCTC, Hunan Examiner, Board of Punishments Vice-president Chuang Ch'ing-tu, no date (YC period)

4. Ibid.

5. I have chosen to discuss the implementation of the reforms in Honan rather than in Shansi in part because the documentation for Honan is greater and in part because examples of other provinces that were guided by the Honan experience are more numerous. The "Shansi Method" is sometimes mentioned by memorialists to connote the full remittance of *huo-hao* to the provincial treasury. Since T'ien Wen-ching was embroiled in a dispute with members of the local gentry at the time Yung-cheng opened the matter of reform to court debate, it is possible that he used Shansi as a test case to avoid extraneous issues that might influence the court's decision.

6. KCTYCCTC, Honan Governor Shih Wen-cho, YC 2,1,22.

7. KCTYCCTC, Honan Governor Shih Wen-cho, YC 2,3,3.

8. Ibid.

9. Ibid.

10. See pp. 116–17.

11. See, for example, CPYC, T'ien Wen-ching, YC 7,5,4; CPYC, Anhui Governor Wei T'ing-chen, YC 7,10,25.

12. KCTYCCTC, Honan Governor Shih Wen-cho, YC 2,3,3.

13. KCTYCCTC, Honan Governor Shih Wen-cho, YC 2,1,22.

14. Abe Takeo, "Kōsen teikai no kenkyū," p. 228.

15. For example, Shensi's quota was similar to that of Fukien. However, as we shall see, expenditures for military purposes not funded by the central government placed extraordinary burdens on local-government finances in the provinces.

16. For an excellent account of the gentry's ability to intervene in the tax-collection process to prevent accurate assessment of landownership and tax liabilities, see Beattie, pp. 69–83.

17. Members of the local elite tried to elicit commoner support for their grievances by rallying them to boycott the construction project. Although they appear to have disrupted work for a short time, they were unable to generate much popular enthusiasm for their cause, and the laborers soon returned to work. CPYC, T'ien Wen-ching, YC 2,6,22.

18. CPYC, T'ien Wen-ching, YC 3,2,12.

19. CPYC, T'ien Wen-ching, YC 6,3,4. In all, 826 new granaries were built and plans were made to build additional ones as the need arose.

20. CPYC, T'ien Wen-ching, YC 5,6,20 (see emperor's rescript); CPYC, T'ien Wen-ching, YC 6,2,3. Following T'ien's recommendations, independent chou magistrates received an extra 300 taels and chou and hsien magistrates received an additional 400 taels apiece.

21. CPYC, T'ien Wen-ching, YC 3,3,17.

22. As we shall see, the emperor was not disappointed. *Yang-lien* for minor officials was implemented in almost every province by the end of his reign.

23. CPYC, T'ien Wen-ching, YC 6,2,3.

24. *Ta-ch'ing kao-tsung ch'un huang-ti shih-lu, chüan* 93, CL 4,5, *i-chou* (hereafter cited as CLSL). For a discussion of the transfer of *huo-hao* from one province to another during the Ch'ien-lung period see chap. 7.

25. In Shansi the surplus reached a high of 770,000 taels in 1734. The surpluses in Chihli and Shensi were much smaller. KCT 12636, Shansi Governor Chueh-lo Shih-lin, YC 12,7,15; KCT 0686, Yueh Chung-ch'i and Hsi Lin, YC 6,5,7; KCT 16348, Chihli Governor Li Wei, YC 12,4,28.

26. KCT 20208, Shansi Financial Commissioner Kao Ch'eng-ling, YC 3,2,8.

27. CPYC, Shansi Board of Revenue Metropolitan Censor Sung Yün, YC 6,9,13. Sung's findings confirm the theory of some historians that surcharge rates were arrived at through informal negotiations between local leaders and the magistrate. Variations in *huo-hao* rates were common even after the reforms, but the ceiling established in each province was not usually exceeded.

28. CPYC, Shansi Board of Revenue Metropolitan Censor Sung Yün, YC 6,9,13.

29. Ibid.

30. Several instances of magisterial resistance are described in chap. 3 under the heading, "Backlash in Honan."

31. KCT 12518, Shansi Governor Chueh-lo Shih-lin, YC 5,12,18.

32. CPYC, Acting Chihli Governor Yang K'un, no date. The date of this action can be established from KCT 19894, a disposition slip issued by Prince I regarding Yang's request to utilize YC 7 *huo-hao* surplus for public expenses.

33. KCT 21738, Acting Shensi Governor-general Yueh Chung-ch'i, YC 3,5,18; CPYC, Shensi Governor Wu Ko, YC 7,9,3. Under Nien, for every 2 taels of *huo-hao*, 0.02 tael was sent to the prefecture for the *yang-lien* of the judicial commissioner, post intendant, prefect, and sub-prefect. The remaining 0.18 tael was sent to the financial commissioner who distributed 0.04 tael among the province's high officials and returned 0.14 tael to the magistrates as *yang-lien* and to make up deficits.

34. Yueh had good reason to try to portray Nien's administration in the worst possible light. Nien, formerly one of Yung-cheng's most trusted supporters, had just been removed from office amidst a cloud of accusations, including bribery and the protection of traitors.

35. CPYC, Shensi Governor Wu Ko, YC 7,9,3.

36. KCT 0686, Yueh Chung-ch'i and Hsi Lin, YC 6,5,7.

37. CPYC, Acting Chihli Governor Yang K'un, no date. In YC 7 alone, Chihli sent 25,592 taels to the Board in the form of "food money" when submitting its annual accounts and an additional 14,698 taels when the actual tax silver was sent to the Board.

38. KCT 15162, Acting Chihli Governor-general T'ang Chih-yü, YC 9,3,17. The clerks and officers were allowed to keep 7,000 taels of the initial fee for their own salaries.

39. KCT 16348, Chihli Governor Li Wei, YC 12,4,28. In Chihli, the public-expense allowances allocated to individual officials was called *pan-kung yin-liang*.

40. The Board's remission of these fees was itself a product of the heightened awareness of the demands placed on the provinces, which were a by-product of the reforms.

41. After two years of experimenting with a system whereby magistrates retained their own *yang-lien* and distributed a contribution to each of their superiors, Kwangtung finally instituted partial remittance in 1726. By this method magistrates were authorized to collect 16.9 percent, 0.9 tael having been appended to cover the costs of reporting the annual accounts to the Board of Revenue and the costs of reporting criminal cases to the Board of Punishments. Of the remaining 0.16 tael, 0.07 was sent to the provincial treasury to cover the *yang-lien* of high officials and the rest was retained by the chou and hsien for their own *yang-lien* and expenses. CPYC, Kwangtung Governor Yang Wen-ch'ien, YC 4,4,14; CPYC, Kwangtung Governor-general Hao Yü-lin, YC 7,12,27; KCT 19833, Prince I, no date (YC period); KCT 5215, Kwangtung Financial Commissioner Wang Shih-chün, YC 8,4,11. The *yang-lien* of the governor, governor-general, and financial commissioner were supplemented by surplus revenues from the unloading tax, deed tax, and commercial duties. In YC 8, revenues from these sources were also applied to the provision of *yang-lien* for minor officials. See KCT 12203, Kwangtung Governor Fu T'ai and Governor-general Hao Yü-lin, YC 8,3,11; KCT 14244, Kwangtung Governor Fu T'ai and Governor-general Hao Yü-lin, YC 7,11,24.

42. KCT 0448, Shensi Governor-general Yueh Chung-ch'i and Szechuan Governor Hsien Te, YC 5,9,4.

43. Ibid.; KCT 13085, Szechuan Governor Hsien Te, YC 8,5,22. The formula for collecting *pang-t'ieh* was originally linked to supplementary wages for yamen runners. The wage was set at 12 taels per runner, and hsien were divided into three grades depending on the level of business within their jurisdiction. On this basis they were allowed to collect an extra 40, 35 or 30 taels, used for a variety of chou and hsien expenses.

44. KCT 13085, Szechuan Governor Hsien Te, YC 8,5,22.

45. CPYC, Kweichow Governor Chang Kuang-ssu, YC 7,8,6.

46. KCT 13085, Szechuan Governor Hsien Te, YC 8,5,22.

47. Ibid.

48. Ibid. Edict dated YC 8,5,11.

49. KCT 13086, Szechuan Governor Hsien Te, YC 8,11,9. Szechuan was also permitted to keep surplus "retained extra-day funds" (*chieh-*

k'uang yin) to supplement its income from *huo-hao.* "Retained extra-day funds" usually referred to commercial duties collected during the last few days of a long month and were used to pay wages and administrative expenses.

50. CPYC, Lanchow Governor Hsü Jung, YC 7,3,12; KCT 11817, Kansu Governor Hsü Jung, no date (YC period).

51. TCHT, *chüan* 32, *hu-pu* 10, *fu-i* 2, *ch'i-yün.*

52. KCT 14381, Kansu Governor Mang Ku-li, YC 6,3,23.

53. CPYC, Lanchow Governor Hsü Jung, YC 7,3,12.

54. The fact that Kansu was a border province and, along with Shensi, was the main staging point for the control of northwestern Mongolian tribes probably influenced the emperor's decision to allow this compromise of the principles of the reforms.

55. CPYC, Acting Fengtien Metropolitan Prefect Wang Ch'ao-en, YC 7,6,4. Fengtien's *yang-lien* schedule was as follows:

Metropolitan prefect	700 taels
Vice-governor	300 taels
Submetropolitan prefect	165 taels
Assistant prefect	165 taels
Chin-chou prefect	400 taels

56. CPYC, Acting Fengtien Metropolitan Prefect Wang Ch'ao-en, YC 7,6,4; KCT 3877, Fengtien Metropolitan Prefect Li Cheng-yuan, YC 8,11,9.

57. KCT 2493, Fengtien Metropolitan Prefect Yang Ch'ao-tseng, YC 10,8,3.

58. TCHT, *chüan* 32, *hu-pu* 10, *fu-i* 2, *ch'i-yün*; KCT 8357, Kwangsi Governor Kuo-t'ai, no date (YC period). Li Fu's reduction of Kwangsi's *huo-hao* was viewed by Yung-cheng as a manifestation of his generally treacherous behavior as an official. See the emperor's rescript to KCT 8357.

59. KCT 6151, Yunnan Governor-general Oertai, YC 8,3,26; KCT 13467, Chihli Governor Li Fu, YC 4,3,27.

60. TCHT, *chüan* 32, *hu-pu* 10, *fu-i* 2, *ch'i-yün.*

61. During the period between KH 60 and early YC 1, approximately 19,250 taels in taxes on copper were paid to the Board of Revenue. KCT 12533, Yun-kuei Governor-general Kao Ch'i-cho and Yunnan Governor Yang Ming-shih, YC 1,12,20.

62. For a discussion of the trend toward private mining in the eighteenth century see Wei Ch'ing-yuan, *Ch'ing-tai ch'ien-ch'i ti shang-pan kuang-yeh ho tzu-pen chu-i meng-ya.*

63. KCT 12533, Yun-kuei Governor-general Kao Ch'i-cho and Yunnan Governor Yang Ming-shih, YC 1,12,20.

64. At times the government was so desperate to unload its surplus copper that it hired men to stand watch at major transportation junctions to lure passing merchants to make purchases at the nearby warehouses where copper was stored. Ibid.

65. Ibid.

66. KCTYCCTC, Yunnan Governor Yang Ming-shih and Governor-general Kao Ch'i-cho, YC 1,12,19.

67. KCTYCCTC, Yunnan Governor-general Kao Ch'i-cho, YC 2,2,18.

68. KCTYCCTC, Governor-general Kao Ch'i-cho, YC 2,5,28; CPYC, Governor-general Kao Ch'i-cho, YC 3,1,26; KCT 17607, Acting Kwei-chow Governor Shih-li-ha, YC 2,6,3. According to Governor-general Kao Ch'i-cho, the total annual quota of commercial duties remitted by Yunnan to the Board of Revenue in the early Yung-cheng reign was only 14,700 taels. However, an average prefecture could take in anywhere from 100 to 5,000 taels in excess of the amount reported to the central government. Likewise, a magistrate might find himself with a surplus of between forty and several hundred taels. This was aside from the customary fees on commercial duties (*shui-kuei*) that these jurisdictions traditionally sent to the governor, governor-general, and financial commissioner.

69. CPYC, Governor-general Kao Ch'i-cho, YC 3,1,26; KCT 17607, Acting Kweichow Governor Shih-li-ha, YC 2,6,3.

70. KCT 9549, Kweichow Governor Chang Kuang-ssu, YC 8,3,27.

71. Ibid.; KCT 14806, Kweichow Governor Ho Shih-ch'i, YC 4,11,15.

72. KCT 9549, Kweichow Governor Kao Ch'i-cho, YC 8,3,27.

73. For example, whereas in Kiangsu the gentry and wealthy households (*shen-chin fu-hu*) paid *huo-hao* at a rate of between 6 and 8 percent, the combined burden of surcharges levied on the common people brought the rate to well over 10 percent. KCT 18637, Suchow Governor Ch'en Shih-hsia, YC 5,11,6.

74. KCT 17111, Shantung Financial Commissioner Chang Pao, YC 4,4,5.

75. Ibid.

76. CPYC, T'ien Wen-ching, YC 6,9,8.

77. KCT 14044, Acting Shantung Governor Sai-leng-e, YC 5,1,24.

78. CPYC, T'ien Wen-ching, YC 6,9,8. These shortages were not entirely due to corruption. A small portion was the result of imperial tax deferments granted in YC 2,3, and 4 in response to unusually heavy rains that caused severe crop damage in low-lying areas of the province. However, when these taxes were not paid within the period of grace allowed by the emperor, the officials in the affected hsien had to reimburse the central government. KCT 17124, Shantung Financial Commissioner Chang Pao, YC 5,5,29.

79. Among the items coopted into the new *kung-fei* stores were fees from customs stations, surplus from duties levied on boats carrying commercial goods, fees from the incense tax in T'ai-an chou, customary fees from post stations, customary fees from officials handling the tribute grain, surplus "food money" sent to the judicial commissioner by lower officials for the handling of criminal cases, and fees fraudulently exacted from the chou and hsien on the pretext of supplementing Board fees. Between YC 2 and YC 5 the total revenue from all these sources exceeded 155,800 taels. KCT 16468, Shantung Financial Commissioner Fei Chin-wu, YC 7,6,8.

80. CPYC, T'ien Wen-ching, YC 6,10,27.

81. Ibid.; CPYC, T'ien Wen-ching, YC 6,9,8.

82. CPYC, T'ien Wen-ching, YC 7,3,6.

83. CPYC, T'ien Wen-ching, YC 7,8,3.

84. CPYC, Shantung Financial Commissioner Sun Kuo-erh, YC 8,4,11.

85. KCT 14316, Governor-general Fan Shih-i, YC 4,7,20. This figure was derived from the governor-general's statement that at a repayment rate of 189,000 taels annually, it would take ten years to clear all of the province's deficits.

86. KCT 14662, Kiangsu Governor Chang K'ai, YC 3,12,11.

87. Ibid.

88. See, for example, CPYC, Kiangsu Governor Chang K'ai, YC 4,1,1.

89. The new financial commissioner, Chang T'an-lin, favored a policy of partial remittance directly modeled on that implemented in Hukwang. KCT 18637, Suchow Governor Ch'en Shih-hsia, YC 5,11,6; KCT 11350, Kiangsu Financial Commissioner Chang T'an-lin, YC 5,11,1.

90. KCT 14845, Suchow Governor Ch'en Shih-hsia, YC 6,7,25.

91. KCT 19634, Acting Suchow Governor Wang Chi, no date (YC period).

92. KCT 20845, Yin Chi-shan, YC 9,4,9.

93. KCT 1765-1, Kiangsi Financial Commissioner Ch'ang Te-shan, YC 3,4,3.

94. KCT 16664, Acting Kiangsi Governor Chang T'an-lin, YC 7,4,26.

95. For example, the fifteen hsien collecting a tax quota of between 10,000 and 20,000 taels were originally allowed to retain 39 percent of their *huo-hao* as *yang-lien*. This was now modified to allow deduction of 50 percent of their *huo-hao*, producing fifteen different quotas ranging from 995 taels in Wu-ning hsien to 513 taels in Hsin-feng hsien. Although hsien with higher tax quotas were now allowed to retain smaller percentages of their *huo-hao*, in each case the amount of *yang-lien* rose along with total tax obligations. KCT 10982, Kiangsi Financial Commissioner Li Lan, YC 7,2.

96. An additional 8,000 taels was later budgeted from the provincial public-expense fund to provide salaries for minor officials.

97. KCT 20458, Yunnan Censor T'ien Chia-ku, no date (YC period); KCT 3730, Fa-hai, no date (early YC 3).

98. CPYC, Chekiang Financial Commissioner T'ung Chi-t'u, YC 2,8,28.

99. CPYC, Chekiang Governor Shih Wen-cho, YC 2,10,15; CPYC, Acting Chekiang Governor Fu-min, YC 3,11,27.

100. KCT 3730, Fa Hai, no date (early YC 3).

101. CPYC, Chekiang Governor Shih Wen-cho, YC 2,10,15.

102. Four prefectures were taxed at excessively high rates during the Ming and early Ch'ing: Suchow and Sung-chiang in Kiangsu and Chia-hsing and Hu-chou in Chekiang. The founder of the Ming punished the gentry in those areas for supporting his rival, Chang Shih-ch'eng, in the struggle for control of China after the defeat of the Mongol Yuan. The lands of wealthy inhabitants were registered as imperial lands (*kuan-*

t'ien) and taxed at the same high rates as rents on private holdings. The Ch'ing continued these high imposts until YC 3, when the *fu-liang* in Suchow and Sung-chiang was rescinded. According to Yung-cheng, similar action was delayed in Chekiang until the people there proved willing to abandon their "evil customs."

103. YCSL, YC 5,10, *i-hsi*, edict to the Board of Revenue.

104. CPYC, Li Wei, YC 5,12,3. Chekiang also supplemented *huo-hao* income with a small amount of fees and surplus revenues from the salt administration. For example, in YC 12, 14,000 taels, amassed from the loose bits of silver left over after the salt gabelle was remitted to the capital, were sent to the provincial treasury by the Salt and Post Intendant. KCT 3114, Chekiang Financial Commissioner Chang Jo-chen, YC 12,9,21.

105. KCT 15062, Acting Kiangsi Governor Hsieh Min, YC 10,8,6; KCT 6639, Acting Kiangsi Governor Hsieh Min, YC 11,7,28.

106. KCT 3480, Kiangsi Financial Commissioner Tiao Ch'eng-tsu, YC 12,9,22; KCT 6639, Acting Kiangsi Governor Hsieh Min, YC 11,7,28. This item was known as shipping silver (*shui-chiao yin*). In YC 3 (1725) the allowance was reduced from 0.01 tael to 0.008 tael per tael of taxes delivered. The province required only 0.003 tael per tael for actual transportation expenses, the remainder being set aside for public expenses. By YC 11 (1733), more than 15,000 taels had been accumulated from this one source.

107. KCT 15069, Acting Kiangsi Governor Hsieh Min, YC 8,1,20.

108. KCT 15052, Acting Kiangsi Governor Hsieh Min, YC 9,6,24.

109. KCT 6639, Acting Kiangsi Governor Hsieh Min, YC 11,7,28.

110. CPYC, Fukien Governor Liu Shih-ming, YC 7,6,16.

111. KCT 15371, Acting Fukien Governor Mao Wen-ch'üan, YC 5,6,4; KCT 11196, Fukien Governor Chu Kang, YC 6,8,8; CPYC, Fukien Governor Liu Shih-ming, YC 7,1,25.

112. KCT 19111, Prince I, no date (YC period); CPYC, Fukien Governor Liu Shih-min, YC 7,10,13.

113. KCT 19111, Prince I, no date (YC period).

114. KCT 12202, Fukien Governor-general Hao Yü-lin and Governor Chao Kuo-lin, no date (YC period).

115. KCT 12230, Fukien Governor-general Hao Yü-lin and Governor Chao Kuo-lin, YC 11,5,1.

116. YCSL, YC 8,10, *jen-tzu*.

117. KCT 14494, Acting Liang-chiang Governor-general Shih I-chih, YC 8,12,2.

Chapter 5

1. See, for example, the emperor's edict to the court defending Kao Ch'eng-ling's plan for *huo-hao kuei-kung* in Shansi, pp. 126–27.

2. For an exhaustive study of the terminology used to describe public expenses, see Iwami Hiroshi, "Yosei jidai ni okeru kōhi no kosatsu."

3. KCT 19812, Prince I, no date (YC period).

4. See, for example, Yung-cheng's rescript to Kansu Governor Shih Wen-cho's memorial, KCT 15831, Kansu Governor Shih Wen-cho, YC 3,11,16.

5. KCT 19111, Prince I, no date (YC period).

6. KCT 5558, Board of Works President Lai-pao, YC 13,13,10. The list of projects for which contributions were previously made is as follows:

1. In KH 29, Shantung Governor Fo-lun memorialized requesting a levy of 53,400 taels on the people for dredging of the Grand Canal in the Ch'i-ning and Lin-ch'ing area.

2. In YC 6, Kiangnan Governor-general Fan Shih-i requested a levy of 5 *wen* per *mou* for annual repairs on the Sung-chiang ocean wall.

3. In YC 7, Governor-general Fan Shih-i requested that eight prefectures and chou in Kiangnan be levied 6,000 taels for dredging of the Grand Canal, to be apportioned according to their quota of tribute grain.

4. In YC 8, Governor Hsien Te requested that several chou and hsien provide funds for their annual wall repairs by assessing the people between 0.002 and 0.001 tael per *mou* for a total of 1,300 taels per year.

5. In YC 11, Superintendent of River Conservancy Wang Ch'ao-en requested that eleven chou and hsien in Chihli contribute *pang-t'ieh yin* of 0.001 tael per *mou* for a total of 5,500 taels annually to dredge the Grand Canal.

6. In YC 13, Governor-general Chao Hung-en memorialized that landed villagers in four hsien had volunteered to provide food for tenant farmers who would work on major dike and flood-gate repairs in six prefectures. Contributions of one to five *wen* per *mou* were offered by thirty-three other chou and hsien. A total of 100,200 strings of cash were provided in this manner.

7. Ibid. The decision did not apply to contributions from wealthy merchants. As we shall see, such contributions were often regularized and integrated into the new system of local funding.

8. Wang Ching-yün, *chüan* 4, *chi-k'u*.

9. Ibid. Distribution of these funds was as follows:

Kiangsu, Anhui, Kiangsi, Chekiang, Hunan, Kansu,
    Szechuan, Kwangsi, Kweichow: 300,000 taels each
Fukien: slightly over 300,000 taels
Shansi, Honan, Hupei, Shensi, Kwangtung, Yunnan:
    200,000 taels each
Shantung: 100,000 taels

Because of its proximity to the imperial capital and the ease in disbursing emergency funds directly from the Board of Revenue treasury, initially no special funds were stored in Chihli. In CL 36, the amount of money stored in Kiangsu was increased so that each of its two financial commissioners' treasuries, in Suchow and Kiangning, would be the repository of 300,000 taels. The increases promulgated in CL 41 resulted in the following distribution of emergency funds (in taels):

Szechuan	1,050,000	Honan	350,000
Yunnan	480,000	Hunan	320,000
Kiangning	480,000	Shensi	310,000
Suchow	480,000	Shansi	310,000
Kweichow	450,000	Chekiang	300,000
Anhui	400,000	Kansu	280,000
Fukien	400,000	Shantung	250,000
Hupei	400,000	Kwangtung	200,000
Kwangsi	380,000	Chihli	30,000
Kiangsi	370,000		

10. KCT 14494, Acting Liang-chiang Governor-general Shih I-chih, YC 8,12,2.

11. Ibid. The breakdown of funds distributed to the prefectures, chou, and hsien in each province was as follows (in taels):

Shensi, Kansu, Szechuan	300,000
Fukien, Yunnan, Kweichow	200,000
Chihli, Shantung, Shansi, Honan, Kwangsi	150,000
Kiangsi, Anhui, Kiangsu, Hunan, Hupei, Chekiang, Kwangtung	100,000

12. Ibid. The method of distribution was changed slightly in CL 5 at the same time that quotas were raised.

13. KCT 2954, Hunan Educational Commissioner Hsi Sui, YC 7,3,13; KCT 0449, Shensi Governor-general Yueh Chung-ch'i, YC 5,5,13; KCT 13093, Szechuan Governor Hsien Te, YC 5,8,18.

14. KCT 17345, Kwangtung Governor-general Shih Yü-lin, YC 9,2, 21. It is interesting to note the governor-general's concern for efficiency, in addition to his humanitarian motives. One very important benefit of such a policy for allocating funds to purchase supplies and hire laborers was that it lessened waste and improved the workmanship on government projects.

15. Ibid.

16. See chap. 4.

17. KCT 17111, Shantung Financial Commissioner Chang Pao, YC 4,4,15.

18. Ibid.

19. KCT 11817, Kansu Governor Hsü Jung, no date (YC period).

20. KCT 17130, Acting Shensi Governor Chang Pao, YC 5,9,25.

21. See table 4.4.

22. KCT 17130, Acting Shensi Governor Chang Pao, YC 5,9,25.

23. It should be noted that part of the justification for the collection of *pang-t'ieh* in Szechuan was that the chou and hsien in Shensi were granted both *yang-lien* and *kung-fei* whereas officials in Szechuan had barely enough funds for *yang-lien*. KCT 0448, Shensi Governor-general Yueh Chung-ch'i and Szechuan Governor Hsien Te, YC 5,9,4.

24. KCT 20269, Imperial Diarist, Tutor of the Imperial Academy Ts'ui Chi, no date (YC period).

25. Ibid.

26. KCT 16357, Li Wei, no date (YC period).

27. KCT 16348, Chihli Governor-general Li Wei, YC 12,4,28. The distribution of *pan-kung yin-liang* was approved by the emperor as follows (in taels):

16 chou and hsien	200 each
18 chou and hsien	160 each
25 chou and hsien	120 each
Ch'ing-yüan hsien	400
Tientsin	300

28. KCT 20208, Shansi Financial Commissioner Kao Ch'eng-ling, YC 3,2,8.

29. *An-yang hsien-chih, t'ien-fu chih*.

30. See table 4.13.

31. KCT 8630, Anhui Governor Wei T'ing-chen, YC 7,1,10.

32. KCT 19634, Acting Suchow Governor Wang Chi, no date (YC period).

33. KCT 10982, Kiangsi Governor Li Lan, YC 7,2.

34. KCT 13741, Acting Kweichow Governor Shih-li-ha, YC 3,8,3; KCT 13738, Acting Kweichow Governor Shih-li-ha, YC 3,8,3.

35. There is also evidence that *kung-fei* allowances were provided for the wages of the clerks of high officials in Kansu and Shantung. See KCT 11817, Kansu Governor Hsü Jung, no date (YC period); KCT 17117, Shantung Financial Commissioner Chang Pao, YC 5,1,12; KCT 17126, Shantung Financial Commissioner Chang Pao, YC 5,5,29.

36. Of particular interest is the evidence that *huo-hao* funds were used to provide wages for yamen clerks and extra-quota runners. As we shall see in chap. 6, these two types of yamen personnel were instrumental in perpetuating fiscal malfeasance at every level of government. This was a result of their familiarity with the territory in which they worked, their control over the daily management of fiscal records, and the failure of the regular funding system to provide them with wages. There is not enough evidence to determine whether magistrates made similar efforts to raise the pay levels of local yamen personnel. The failure to do so may have been a key factor in the failure of some provinces to maintain sufficient control of local revenue sources to make the *huo-hao* reforms work.

37. Among the fixed allocations referred to here were the *kung-fei* specifically disbursed to high and low officials and expenditures related to

central-government remittances and tax accounting. The latter will be discussed in the following section.

38. CPYC, T'ien Wen-ching, YC 3,4,2; YC 3,2,29; YC 3,2,12.

39. CPYC, T'ien Wen-ching, YC 5,6,3.

40. CPYC, T'ien Wen-ching, YC 5,8,28.

41. CPYC, T'ien Wen-ching, YC 7,3,20.

42. CPYC, T'ien Wen-ching, YC 7, *jun* 7,10.

43. CPYC, T'ien Wen-ching, YC 8,2,25.

44. CPYC, T'ien Wen-ching, YC 9,5,24.

45. See table 4.4.

46. CPYC, T'ien Wen-ching, YC 2,10,26.

47. CPYC, T'ien Wen-ching, YC 8,7,8.

48. Ibid.; CPYC, T'ien Wen-ching, YC 7,12,8; YC 8,1,2.

49. CPYC, T'ien Wen-ching, YC 3,3,3; YC 2,12,15.

50. CPYC, T'ien Wen-ching, YC 8,2,1; YC 8,2,25; YC 2,11,20.

51. CPYC, T'ien Wen-ching, YC 3,5,16; KCT 16268, Chihli Governor-general Li Wei, YC 13,4,29; KCT 6639, Kiangsi Governor Hsieh Min, YC 11,7,28.

52. KCT 8630, Anhui Governor Wei T'ing-chen, YC 7,1,10.

53. KCT 19634, Acting Suchow Governor Wang Chi, no date (YC period).

54. KCT 15061, Kiangsi Governor Hsieh Min, YC 7,11,9.

55. CPYC, Acting Chihli Governor-general Yang K'un, no date.

56. KCT 11817, Kansu Governor Hsü Jung, no date (YC period).

57. See table 4.8.

58. In YC 5, Chekiang General-in-chief Shih Yün-cho sent a memorial to the emperor expressing his concern over the disposition of certain military rations allocated to the Green Standard Army. These so-called "empty rations" (*k'ung-liang*) were allowances to soldiers who were no longer in the army. The funds so derived were usually returned to the *kung-fei* account of the military unit. Afraid that he would be impeached for concealing these funds, Shih had considered reporting their existence in a routine memorial to the Board of War. However, he was worried that this would violate the proscription against reporting *kung-fei* matters through routine channels. The emperor informed him that the same procedures should be used in reporting these funds as were used in dealing with income from *huo-hao*. The only appropriate channel was a secret memorial sent directly to the emperor. KCT 6486, Chekiang General-in-chief Shih Yün-cho, YC 5,4,21. For a similar case involving T'ien Wen-ching see Sun Chia-kan, "Pan-li hao-hsien shu." In this case the emperor noted that a main reason for prohibiting officials from reporting *huo-hao* matters to the Board was to prevent *huo-hao* from being viewed as part of the regular tax (*cheng-hsiang*).

59. For examples of such reports see KCT 12640, Shansi Governor Chueh-lo Shih-lin, YC 9,9,12; KCT 11854, Honan Governor T'ien Wen-ching, YC 3,2,24; KCT 16465, Shantung Financial Commissioner Fei Chin-wu, YC 7,6,8.

60. For examples of more detailed reports, see KCT 15181, Chihli Governor-general T'ang Chih-yü, no date (YC period): KCT 0686, Yueh Chung-ch'i, YC 6,5,7; KCT 17126, Shantung Financial Commissioner Chang Pao, YC 5,5,29.

61. KCT 12203, Kwangtung Governor-general Hao Yü-lin and Acting Kwangtung Governor Fu T'ai, YC 8,3,11.

62. KCT 13848, Wei T'ing-chen, YC 4,6,8.

63. KCT 18076, Hukwang Governor-general Yü Chu and Hunan Governor Wang Kuo-tung, no date (YC period).

64. KCT 15053, Kiangsi Governor Hsieh Min, YC 9,6,24.

65. High provincial officials could also instigate reductions in *yang-lien*. For example, when T'ien Wen-ching was appointed governor-general of Honan-Shantung he discovered that circuit intendants in Shantung were receiving 6,000 taels apiece. Comparable posts in Honan were allocated only 3,000 taels. Therefore, he cut the *yang-lien* of the former in half. CPYC, T'ien Wen-ching, YC 6,9,8.

66. For examples of officials thanking the emperor for their *yang-lien*, see KCT 16173, Acting Shensi Governor Liu Yü-i, YC 10,9,13; KCT 2954, Hunan Educational Commissioner Hsi Sui, YC 7,3,13; KCT 9053, Shansi T'ai-yuan brigade-general (no name), YC 2, *jun* 4,24.

67. KCT 17769, Hupei Governor Wang Shih-chün, YC 10,3,8.

68. See, for example, KCT 19901, no date, concerning Oertai's request to raise the Kwangsi *yang-lien* quota and KCT 19802, 19891, 19894, 19895, Prince I, no date (YC period) commenting on *huo-hao* "yellow registers" submitted to the emperor by Chihli Governor-general Yang K'un.

69. KCT 13846, Wei T'ing-chen, YC 9,7,13; KCT 12640, Shansi Governor Chueh-lo Shih-lin, YC 9,9,12; KCT 12641, Shansi Governor Chueh-lo Shih-lin, YC 10,7,1.

70. See table 4.15.

71. KCT 12230, Fukien Governor-general Hao Yü-lin and Fukien Governor Chao Kuo-lin, YC 11,5,1.

72. CPYC, T'ien Wen-ching, YC 6,3,2.

73. KCT 22360, Chekiang Educational Commissioner Wang Lan-sheng, YC 5,7,8.

74. KCT 15053, Kiangsi Governor Hsieh Min, YC 9,6,24.

75. Ibid.

76. KCT 20843, Yin Chi-shan, YC 7, *jun* 7,9.

77. KCT 9135, Hupei Financial Commissioner Hsü Ting, YC 6,9,25.

78. KCT 17457, Szechuan Governor-general Huang T'ing-kuei, YC 10,1,16.

79. Ibid. For other examples of individual *yang-lien* increases see KCT 5215, Kwangtung Financial Commissioner Wang Shih-chun, YC 8,4,11; KCT 19833, Prince I, no date (YC period); KCT 6151, Yunnan Governor-general Oertai, YC 8,3,26.

80. KCT 16490, Kiangsi Governor Pu-lan-t'ai, YC 6,7,27.

81. KCT 11162, Hunan Financial Commissioner Chu Kang, YC 5,1,22.

82. KCT 12635, Shansi Governor Chueh-lo Shih-lin, YC 11,9,13.

83. CPYC, T'ien Wen-ching, YC 7,5,4.

84. See, for example, KCT 13973, Kwangtung Governor Yang Wen-ch'ien, YC 5,2,10.

85. KCT 21927-1, Shensi Governor Yueh Chung-ch'i, YC 5,5,13.

86. KCT 17339, Hupei Educational Commissioner Yü Chen, YC 6,4,16.

87. KCT 13973, Kwangtung Governor Yang Wen-ch'ien, YC 5,2,10.

88. KCT 13093, Szechuan Governor Hsien Te, YC 5,8,18.

89. KCT 0044, Shensi Governor Yueh Chung-ch'i, YC 5,3,25.

90. Ibid.

91. KCT 13093, Szechuan Governor Hsien Te, YC 5,8,18; KCT 0044, Shensi Governor-general Yueh Chung-ch'i, YC 5,3,25.

92. CPYC, T'ien Wen-ching, YC 3,3,17.

93. Ibid.

94. CPYC, T'ien Wen-ching, YC 6,2,3.

95. KCT 18076, Hukwang Governor-general Yü Chu and Hunan Governor Wang Kuo-tung, no date (YC period). The edict in question was received on YC 6,8,25.

96. Ibid.

97. Ibid. The new allocations of *yang-lien* were as follows (in taels):

Financial Commissioner's Law Secretary and Judicial Commissioner's Correspondence Secretary	50 each
Financial Commissioner's Treasury Keeper, Judicial Commissioner's Jail Warden, Post and Grain Intendant's Treasury Keepers, 7 Prefectural Jail Wardens, 3 Assistant Chou Magistrates, 5 Subassistant Chou Magistrates, 12 Assistant Hsien Magistrates	40 each
56 Hsien Jail Wardens, 8 Chou Jail Wardens, 48 Subdistrict Magistrates	30 each

The remainder of the 8,000 taels was used to pay *yang-lien* to officials in areas that were in the process of being converted from administration by native chiefs to administration by civil officials.

98. KCT 19892, Prince I, no date (YC period).

99. KCT 15155, Acting Chihli Governor-general T'ang Chih-yü, YC 7,9,26.

100. Ibid. The *yang-lien* rates agreed upon for minor officials in Chihli were as follows (in taels):

Assistant chou magistrates	60 each
Subassistant chou magistrates	45 each

Prefectural commissioners of records,
  assistant hsien magistrates   40 each
Registrars   33.114 each
Judicial commissioner's jailor,
  prefectural jailors, granary keepers,
  chou and hsien jail wardens,
  and other minor officials   31.52 each

The allocation of *yang-lien* for these officials required an additional expenditure of 8,641.486 taels.

101. KCT 14244, Kwangtung Governor-general Hao Yü-lin and Acting Governor Fu T'ai, YC 7,11,24.

102. KCT 12203, Kwangtung Governor-general Hao Yü-lin and Governor Fu T'ai, YC 8,3,11.

103. Ibid.

104. Ibid.

105. KCT 9685, Kiangnan Governor-general Kao Ch'i-cho and Anhui Governor Hsü Pen, no date (YC period).

106. Ibid.

107. Hsiao Kung-chuan, pp. 89–90.

108. See, for example, CPYC, T'ien Wen-ching, YC 3,8,3; YC 3,9,11. These memorials deal with the addition of newly reclaimed and hidden lands to the tax rolls.

109. KCT 18076, Hukwang Governor-general Yü Chu and Hunan Governor Wang Kuo-tung, no date (YC period).

110. KCT 12962, Fukien Governor-general Hao Yü-lin and Governor Chao Kuo-lin, no date (YC period).

111. KCT 16468, Shantung Financial Commissioner Fei Chin-wu, YC 7,6,8.

112. Ibid.

113. See, for example, KCT 3730, Fa Hai, no date (early YC 3).

114. See, for example, KCT 13436, Hupei Governor Ma Hui-po, YC 5,9,22; KCT 13436, Hupei Financial Commissioner Hsü Ting, YC 7,10,3; KCT 0448, Shensi Governor-general Yueh Chung-ch'i and Szechuan Governor Hsien Te, YC 5,9,4; KCT 16664, Kiangsi Governor Chiang Tan-lin, YC 7,4,26; KCT 3730, Fa Hai, no date (early YC 3) on Chekiang; CPYC, T'ien Wen-ching, YC 7,2,1.

115. KCTYCCTC, Yunnan Governor Yang Ming-shih and Governor-general Kao Ch'i-cho, YC 1,12,19; KCT 3114, Chekiang Financial Commissioner Chang Jo-chen, YC 12,9,21.

116. KCTYCCTC, Shantung Governor Huang Ping, YC 1,11,22.

117. KCT 14367-1, Ch'ang-lu Salt Censor Mang Ku-li, YC 3,1,20; KCT 16500, Kiangsi Governor Pu-lan-t'ai, YC 6,7,3.

118. KCT 4336, Shensi Judicial Commissioner and Ho-tung Salt Superintendent Shih-se, YC 6,9,21.

119. Ibid.

120. Ibid. See the Board deliberation enclosed with this memorial.

121. KCT 3379, Acting Ho-tung Salt Commissioner Sun Chia-k'an, no date (YC period).

122. KCT 14093, Fu-min, Pu-lan-t'ai, Chu Kang, YC 5,7,9.

123. KCT 19215, Chihli Brigade General Hsü Pen, YC 1,7; KCT 14367-1, Ch'ang-lu Salt Censor Mang Ku-li, YC 3,1,20; KCT 19177, Shantung Salt Controller Ch'i Shao-wen, YC 3,8,18; KCTYCCTC, Ch'ang-lu Salt Censor Mang Ku-li, YC 2,4,15.

124. KCT 3730, Fa Hai, no date (early YC 3); KCT 13654, Acting Chihli Governor-general I Chao-hsiung, YC 5,9,15; KCT 4288, Ho-tung Governor-general T'ien Wen-ching, YC 7,3,11; KCT 19552, Kiangsi Governor Pu-lan-t'ai, YC 5,10,18; KCT 6583, Acting Kiangsi Governor Hsieh Min, YC 7,11,9; KCT CL 3548, Pan-ti, CL 18,4,11.

125. KCT 17147, Acting Liang-huai Salt Controller, Kiangsi Financial Commissioner I-la-chi, YC 9,10,10.

126. Ibid.

127. KCT 3379, Acting Ho-tung Salt Controller Sun Chia-k'an, no date (YC period); KCT 17145, Acting Liang-huai Salt Controller I-la-chi, YC 8,11,27.

128. KCT 17145, Acting Liang-huai Salt Controller I-la-chi, YC 8,11,27.

129. See, for example, KCT 6583, Acting Kiangsi Governor Hsieh Min, YC 7,11,9; KCT 14093, Fu-min, Pu-lan-t'ai, Chu Kang, YC 5,7,9 (on Hukwang); KCT 20845, Yin-chi-shan, no date (YC period) on Kiangsu.

130. KCT 12322, Acting Shantung Financial Commissioner Yueh Chün, YC 6,10,28.

131. Ibid.

132. KCT 12282, Shantung Governor Yueh Chün, YC 12,4,6.

133. Ibid.

134. See, for example, KCT 2929, Szechuan K'uei Customs Superintendent Fo-pao, YC 12,8,10.

135. KCT 22250, Huai-an Customs Superintendent Nien Hsi-yao, YC 6,9,24. It is interesting to note Yung-cheng's response to Nien's report: "If, as you state in your memorial, the customs quota cannot be met because the Kiangnan harvest was abundant, then I wish that [the quota] would not be met every year for this reason. The whole empire is aware that the [revenues collected at] the Huai customs are difficult to predict."

136. KCT 4210, K'uei Customs Superintendent Mu-ko-te-pu, YC 10,11,28.

137. KCT KH 1719, Chekiang Governor Chu Shih, KH 58,5,8.

138. KCT 4211, K'uei Superintendent of Customs Mu-ko-te-pu, YC 10,11,28.

139. For examples of the accumulation and remittance of "excess revenues," see KCT 1972, Superintendent of Customs Hai Pao, YC 10,7,27; KCT 13229, Kwangtung Governor O-erh-ta, YC 9,8,24; KCT 15081, Kiangsi Governor Hsieh Min, YC 10,1,2 (on the Ch'iu-chiang and Ta-ku-t'ang customs); KCT 15080, Kiangsi Governor Hsieh Min, YC 9,10,24 (on the Kan customs); KCT 1305, Superintendent of Fukien Customs Chün T'ai, YC 9,6,13; KCT 14643, Kiangsu Governor Chang K'ai, YC 3,10,2 (on maritime and Lung-chiang customs).

140. Evidence exists for the elimination of customary fees paid on carts and livestock passing through the Fengtien border customs (KCT

22307, Fengtien Metropolitan Prefect Yang Ch'ao-tseng, no date); for the elimination of excessive fees collected at the Kan pass in Kiangsi (KCT 16516, Kiangsi Governor Pu-lan-t'ai, YC 5,11,1); for the elimination of "extortion on the pretext of cargo registration" at the Canton and T'ai-p'ing customs in Kwangtung (KCT 13940, Yang Wen-ch'ien, YC 4,2,12); for the elimination of gifts and fees exacted from merchants passing through customs station in Fukien (KCT 1299, Deputy Director of Fukien Customs, no name, YC 8,5,26); and for the elimination of some forms of extortion practiced by clerks and runners at customs stations in Kiangsi (KCT 15124, Kiangsi Governor P'ei Shuai-tu, YC 2,12,18).

141. KCT 21603, Szechuan-Shensi Governor-general Yueh Chung-ch'i, YC 6,9,9.

142. Ibid.

143. KCT 15125, Kiangsi Governor P'ei Shuai-tu, YC 3,2,26; KCT 1297, Superintendent of Fukien Customs Chun T'ai, YC 7,5,12.

144. KCT 15125, Kiangsi Governor P'ei Shuai-tu, YC 3,2,26.

145. Ibid.

146. KCT 12322, Acting Shantung Governor, Financial Commissioner Yueh Chün, YC 6,10,28.

147. KCT 15125, Kiangsi Governor P'ei Shuai-tu, YC 3,2,26.

148. KCT 1297, Fukien Superintendent of Customs Chün T'ai, YC 7,5,12.

149. Ibid.

150. KCT 0555, Yueh Chung-ch'i and Hsi Lin, YC 6,9,16.

151. KCT 1299, Fengtien Metropolitan Prefect Yang Ch'ao-tseng, no date (YC period); KCT 22312, Fengtien Metropolitan Prefect Yang Ch'ao-tseng, no date (YC period).

152. KCT 15289, Yunnan Governor Ch'ang Pin, YC 6,6,4.

153. KCT 1299, Fukien Superintendent of Customs Chun T'ai, YC 8,5,26.

154. KCT 16516, Kiangsi Governor Pu-lan-t'ai, YC 5,11,1.

155. For examples of *ying-yü* being deducted for customs-administration expenses, see KCT 1300, Superintendent of Fukien Customs Chün T'ai, YC 13,4,24; KCT 1980, Superintendent of Customs Hai Pao, YC 10,7,27; KCT 14573, Kwangtung Governor Yang Yung-pin, YC 11,7,9; KCT 11559, Hukwang Governor-general Yü Chu, YC 6,8,18; KCT 4076, Kwangtung Superintendent of Maritime Customs Mao K'o-ming, YC 11,11,27; KCT 21603, Szechuan-Shensi Governor-general Yueh Chung-ch'i, YC 6,9,9.

156. See, for example, KCT 4085, Superintendent of Canton Customs Mao K'o-ming, YC 11,3,28; KCT 4080, Superintendent of Canton Customs Mao K'o-ming, YC 12,6,10.

157. KCT 18847, Acting Kiangsu Governor Ho T'ien-p'ei, YC 1,9,9.

158. KCT 6583, Acting Kiangsi Governor Hsieh Min, YC 7,11,9.

159. KCT 15629, Kwangsi Governor Chin Kung, YC 7,2,4.

160. KCT 12431, Shantung Governor Yueh Chün, YC 8,5,22; KCT 13355, Fukien Governor-general K'ao Ch'i-cho, YC 6,11,6; KCT 22312, Fengtien Metropolitan Prefect Yang Ch'ao-tseng, no date (YC period).

161. In many discussions of which *lou-kuei* would be retained and which would be eliminated, the term *wu-ai* was used to indicate that a particular fee presented no obstacle to the collection of the official tax quota and would not unduly harm the financial well-being of the group from which it was exacted. See, for example, KCT 22312, Fengtien Metropolitan Prefect Yang Ch'ao-tseng, no date (YC period).

162. KCT 17849, Kwangtung Financial Commissioner Wang Shih-chün, YC 7,7,24. The data for Kweichow are particularly striking. See table 4.7 for a comparison of the actual level of *tsa-shui* collected in the province and the quotas sent to the central government. For a discussion of the role of *tsa-shui* in the informal funding system, see chap. 2.

163. According to Susan Mann, "In the Chinese marketing system, brokers performed three basic functions: (1) they introduced buyer and seller; (2) they guaranteed the satisfactory completion of a sale; and (3) they reconciled and standardized the conflicting weights, measures, units of account, and currency exchange rates buyers and sellers brought to their transaction." Although most often thought of as middlemen in the marketplace, they also acted as wholesalers and shippers of goods. Susan Mann, "Brokers as Entrepreneurs in Presocialist China" (Paper prepared for the Conference on Chinese Entrepreneurship at Home and Abroad, 1900–82, Cornell University, 1–2 Oct. 1982).

164. KCT 14999, Hupei Financial Commissioner Chung Pao, YC 11,9,13.

165. Ibid.

166. KCT 15069, Acting Kiangsi Governor Hsieh Min, YC 8,1,20. A yellow register compiled in the Kuang-hsü period (1875–1907) indicates that fees from salt merchants and surplus commercial duties continued to be important sources of local revenue in Hunan, Chekiang, and Anhui as well. See "Hao-hsien yin-liang ts'e," *Nei-ko ta-k'u hsien-ts'un ch'ing-tai han-wen huang-ts'e*, no. 942.

167. For examples of the use of commercial surplus to supplement *huo-hao* in these two provinces, see KCT 6151, Yunnan Governor-general Oertai, YC 8,3,26; KCTYCCTC, Governor-general Kao Ch'i-cho, YC 2,5,28.

168. KCT 17849, Kwangtung Financial Commissioner Wang Shih-chün, YC 7,7,24.

169. KCT 17028, Kwangtung Financial Commissioner Kan Ju-lai, YC 12,3,7.

170. See table 4.6.

Chapter 6

1. HCSHC 2, *fu-i* 2, SC 15.

2. See Oxnam, pp. 102–8.

3. *Su-chou fu-chih, chüan* 18, *t'ien-fu* 7.

4. Ibid.

5. KCT 14662, Kiangsu Governor Chang K'ai, YC 3,12,11.

6. KCT 10456, Acting Kiangsi Governor Yü Chu, YC 5,1,24.

7. Ibid.

8. Ibid.

9. *Shu-shou* was a term originally used to designate clerks in hsien yamen. During the Ming dynasty they came to play a broader role in the accounting of taxes in the *li-chia* system. The *shu-shou* referred to here were probably clerks stationed outside the yamen, in charge of local tax records and the compilation of the tax liabilities of people living within a small portion of a hsien's territory.

10. CCWHTK, *ch'üan* 3, *t'ien-fu* 3, YC 6 edict.

11. Similar methods were used to control corruption in the collection of customs revenues. Not only were rates publicly posted, but merchants were authorized to fill out their tax forms themselves as a check on clerical malfeasance. Although there is no evidence of the effectiveness of such a policy in preventing extortion of merchants, it clearly was of limited value in protecting peasants from the excessive demands of tax collectors.

12. CCWHTK, *chüan* 3, *t'ien-fu* 3, YC 6 edict.

13. For descriptions of the investigation of tax-collection procedures in Hukwang and Chekiang, see KCT 8027, Director of the Court of Judicature and Revision Hsing Kuei, YC 6,9,28; KCT 16897, Chekiang Kuan-feng cheng-su Censor Ts'ai Shih-shan, YC 6,11,19; KCT 14405, Acting Chekiang Governor-general Hsiang Kuei, YC 7,4,20; KCT 10512, Hukwang Governor-general Yü Chu, YC 6,9,8.

14. KCT 11368, Acting Suchow Governor Chang Tan-lin, YC 6,8,15.

15. Ibid.

16. Ibid.

17. KCT 10248, Yin-chi-shan, YC 6,11,9.

18. Ibid.

19. Ibid.

20. KCT 20997, Expectant Magistrate Wang Chin, no date (YC period). This memorial was among a group of undated memorials from officials holding ranks generally considered too low to communicate directly with the emperor by memorial. It is likely that these were transcriptions of reports made to the emperor when the officials to whom they are attributed received an audience in the capital before being transferred to a new post.

21. KCT 3731, Fa-hai, no date (YC period).

22. KCT 17135, Censor I-la-chi, YC 7,2,11.

23. KCT 10254, Yin-chi-shan, YC 6,12,11.

24. Typical of this group were men like Chang Ch'ang, a lower-degree holder from Sung-chiang prefecture, and Wang I-ch'ing, a large landowner from T'ai-ts'ang chou, two of the areas with the largest recorded arrears. Both were signatories of petitions of the kind described, and both were found to have evaded taxes for a number of years. See KCT 17135, Censor I-la-chi, YC 7,2,11.

25. KCT 10248, Yin-chi-shan, YC 6,11,9. A number of those assigned to investigate Kiangnan tax arrears were Manchu bannermen. It is clear that in the case of several supervisory officials, especially Governor Yin-

chi-shan, it was hoped that appointment of a Manchu would guarantee against lenient treatment of recalcitrant members of the local elite. Although this investigation had none of the specifically racial overtones of the 1661 arrears case, the parallels in terms of personnel and the debasement of gentry privilege could not have been lost on the local population.

26. KCT 22108, Board of Works Vice-president Ma-erh-t'ai, YC 7,7.

27. KCT 19630, Board of Revenue Vice-president Wang Chi and Board of Civil Appointments Vice-president P'eng Wei-hsin, YC 7,4,13.

28. KCT 22105, Board of Works Vice-president Ma-erh-t'ai, YC 7,4,3. Among the *fen-ch'a ta-ch'en* assigned to investigate the Kiangnan region were Circuit Intendants Feng Chin-hsia, Wen Erh-sun, and Wang Su-wei and Censors Tai Yin-pao and Hsing Kuei.

29. KCT 19672, Board of Revenue Vice-president Wang Chi, et al., YC 7,3,28; KCT 17701, Censor I-la-chi, YC 7,2,11.

30. KCT 19672, Board of Revenue Vice-president Wang Chi, et al., YC 7,3,28; KCT 17701, Censor I-la-chi, YC 7,2,11; KCT 17706, Censor I-la-chi, YC 7, *jun* 7,4; KCT 16669, Acting Kiangsi Governor Chang Tan-lin, YC 7,4,26.

31. KCT 17701, Censor I-la-chi, YC 7,2,11.

32. KCT 20839, Yin-chi-shan, YC 7,1,25; KCT 22108, Board of Works Vice-president Ma-erh-t'ai, YC 7,7.

33. KCT 20839, Yin-chi-shan, YC 7,1,25.

34. KCT 19630, Board of Revenue Vice-president Wang Chi and Board of Civil Appointments Vice-president P'eng Wei-hsin, YC 7,4,13.

35. Ibid.

36. Ibid.; KCT 20839, Yin-chi-shan, YC 7,1,25.

37. KCT 22283, Fen-ch'a T'ai-ts'ang chou taxes Wen Erh-sun, YC 7,7.

38. KCT 22105, Board of Works Vice-president Ma-erh-t'ai, YC 7,4,3; KCT 22277, Fen-ch'a T'ai-ts'ang chou taxes Wen Erh-sun, YC 7,6.

39. KCT 22283, Fen-ch'a T'ai-ts'ang chou taxes Wen Erh-sun, YC 7,7; KCT 22277, Fen-ch'a T'ai-ts'ang chou taxes Wen Erh-sun, YC 7,6.

40. KCT 22105, Board of Works Vice-president Ma-erh-t'ai, YC 7,4,3.

41. KCT 17139, Censor I-la-chi, YC 7,6,11.

42. Ibid.

43. Ibid.

44. KCT 22281, Fen-ch'a T'ai-ts'ang chou taxes Wen Erh-sun, YC 7,6.

45. Ibid.

46. KCT 22108, Board of Works Vice-president Ma-erh-t'ai, YC 7,7.

47. Ibid. It should be kept in mind that this investigation was initiated before the emperor permitted the implementation of *huo-hao kuei-kung*.

48. KCT 22106, Board of Works Vice-president Ma-erh-t'ai, YC 7,4.

49. KCT 11709, Censor I-la-chi, YC 7,9,15.

50. Ibid.

51. Ibid.; KCT 22110, Board of Works Vice-president Ma-erh-t'ai, YC 7,9,6.

52. KCT 22110, Board of Works Vice-president Ma-erh-t'ai, YC 7,9,6.

53. Ibid.

54. KCT 17709, Censor I-la-chi, YC 7,9,15.

55. KCT 22109, Board of Works Vice-president Ma-erh-t'ai, YC 7,8,29.

56. Ibid.

57. KCT 17709, Censor I-la-chi, YC 7,9,15.

58. KCT 22112, Board of Works Vice-president Ma-erh-t'ai, YC 7,10,3. The number of duplicate record books confiscated was probably exaggerated to impress the emperor.

59. KCT 1662, Ma-erh-t'ai, YC 7,10,3.

60. Ibid.

61. KCT 17709, Censor I-la-chi, YC 7,9,15.

62. Ibid.; see also KCT 22112, Board of Works Vice-president Ma-erh-t'ai, YC 7,10,3.

63. KCT 1662, Ma-erh-t'ai, YC 7,10,3.

64. KCT 8284, P'eng Wei-hsin and Ma-erh-t'ai, YC 7,12,4.

65. Ibid.

66. KCT 20840, Yin-chi-shan, YC 7,12,4.

67. KCT 7565, Assistant Supervisor of the *ch'ing-ch'a* of Kiangnan taxes An Hsiu-te, YC 7,11,24.

68. KCT 8284, P'eng Wei-hsin and Ma-erh-t'ai, YC 7,12,4. The imperial act of grace which allowed the people to repay their debts in installments also applied to these clerical debts. However, some magistrates pressed clerks so hard for reimbursement of embezzled funds that the clerks began to devise new methods to accumulate the necessary funds immediately. For example, an ingenious group of clerks and runners in Chiang-tu hsien printed up subscriptions calling for popular contributions to a public-works project. The money they collected in response to this appeal was used to pay back the funds they were originally accused of having embezzled from the government. KCT 20840, Yin-chi-shan, YC 7,12,4.

69. KCT 8284, P'eng Wei-hsin and Ma-erh-t'ai, YC 7,12,4. In Kiangnan, the clerks chosen from the yamen clerical pool to handle the collection of the land and tribute taxes were called *liang-tsung* and *ts'ao-tsung* respectively.

70. Ibid.

71. Ibid.; KCT 20833, Censor Kao Shan, no date (YC period).

72. KCT 20833, Censor Kao Shan, no date (YC period).

73. Ibid.

74. KCT 8284, P'eng Wei-hsin and Ma-erh-t'ai, YC 7,12,4.

75. Ibid.

76. Ibid.

77. Ibid.; KCT 20833, Censor Kao Shan, no date (YC period). This practice was also known as *hua-fen tsu-hu*. (See KCT 8285, Board of Civil Appointments Vice-president P'eng Wei-hsin, YC 9,6,26). The existence of these practices is confirmed in reports by members of the gentry as well. See, for example, the reports submitted by expectant magistrate Wang Chin, from Chü-jung hsien, Kiangnan fu, Kiangsu, KCT 20997, no date (YC period); Kiangnan *chu-jen* Wang Tien-hsien, KCT 20395,

no date (YC period); expectant magistrate Shang Yuan-po, KCT 20395, no date (YC period); and KCT 20450, name cut off, no date (YC period).

78. KCT 8284, P'eng Wei-hsin and Ma-erh-t'ai, YC 7,12,4. Part of the reason that the rural elite could get away with nonpayment of taxes was the special treatment they received from the local bureaucracy. It was common throughout China for officials to divide taxpaying households into *ta-hu* and *hsiao-hu* or other comparable appellations to distinguish those households that were to be treated with deference. Classification as a gentry household often also was accompanied by special tax rates. This explains why people were willing to register their land under the names of powerful or degree-holding members of the local community.

79. KCT 8284, P'eng Wei-hsin and Ma-erh-t'ai, YC 7,12,4.

80. KCT 7565, Censor An Hsiu-te, YC 7,11,24.

81. KCT 8284, P'eng Wei-hsin and Ma-erh-t'ai, YC 7,12,4.

82. Ibid. In Shang-yuan hsien and Chang-ning hsien they were known as *li-hsieh ts'ui-i*. The title *ts'ui-t'ou* was used in Chu-jung hsien, *yün-shou* in Li-yang hsien, and *tan-t'ou li-chang* in Li-shui and Liu-ho hsien. In Hsiang-hu hsien and Ju-kao hsien these tax collectors were called *tsung-tsui* and in Chia-ting hsien, Pao-han hsien and Hsin-yang hsien they were known as *p'ai-nien*, a name reminiscent of the rotating tithing chiefs of the Ming dynasty. Other names applied to clerks and runners in charge of tax collection were the *hu-shou* of Ching-chiang hsien, the *she-tsung* of P'ei chou, and the *pao-ch'ang kung-cheng* of Shu-yang hsien and Sui-ning hsien.

83. KCT 5802, Acting Chekiang Circuit Censor, Shansi Metropolitan Censor Wang Chi-ching, YC 1,7,12; KCT 9135, Hupei Financial Commissioner Hsü Ting, YC 6,9,25; KCT 8284, P'eng Wei-hsin and Ma-erh-t'ai, YC 7,12,4.

84. KCT 20834, Censor Kao Shan, no date (YC period).

85. KCT 20833, Kao Shan, no date (YC period).

86. KCT 7565, Censor An Hsiu-te, YC 7,11,24; KCT 20834, Censor Kao Shan, no date (YC period).

87. KCT 7565, Censor An Hsiu-te, YC 7,11,24.

88. KCT 20824, Censor Kao Shan, no date (YC period).

89. KCT 20833, Kao Shan, no date (YC period).

90. KCT 5573, Director of the Court of the Imperial Stud, Director of the Court of Sacrificial Worship Chiang Lien, YC 13,12,9; KCT 13649, Hupei Financial Commissioner Hsü Ting, YC 7,3,8.

91. KCT 13649, Hupei Financial Commissioner Hsü Ting, YC 7,3,8.

92. KCT 5573, Chiang Lien, YC 13,12,9.

93. KCT 13649, Hupei Financial Commissioner Hsü Ting, YC 7,3,8.

94. KCT 22270, Fen-ch'a T'ai-ts'ang chou taxes Wen Erh-sun, YC 7,6; KCT 11543, Hukwang Governor-general Yü Chu, YC 7,4,21. Wen's frequent references to the existence of a system of registration based on the location of a household in a particular *chia* suggests that the *shun-chuang* method of assessing taxes was in effect in Kiangnan before the initiation of the *ch'ing-ch'a*. Wen also mentions the fact that under this

system rich households were able to join together to form arbitrary *chia* registrations which they used to force the common people to turn their taxes over to them for proxy remittance.

95. KCT 5573, Chiang Lien, YC 13,12,9.

96. KCT 22279, Fen-ch'a T'ai-ts'ang chou taxes Wen Erh-sun, YC 7,6. In the end a combination of the *shun-chuang* and the *pan-t'u* methods seems to have been attempted in Kiangnan. Both forms of registering land were carried out. The *pan-t'u* method was found to be most effective in investigating abuses and tax arrears, whereas the *shun-chuang* method was most convenient as a basis for the actual collection of taxes by rolling lists. KCT 8285, Board of Civil Appointments Vice-president P'eng Wei-hsin, YC 9,6,25.

97. CPYC, T'ien Wen-ching, YC 5,9,25.

98. Ibid. Yung-cheng was enthusiastic about this method, but asked T'ien to wait a while before submitting his plan to the court in a routine memorial. According to Acting Kiangsi Judicial Commissioner Ling T'ao, this system was being used throughout much of the empire by early YC 6. KCT 3451, Acting Kiangsi Judicial Commissioner Ling T'ao, YC 12,8,3.

99. KCT 1981, Hai-pao, YC 11,7,3; KCT 3451, Acting Kiangsi Judicial Commissioner Ling T'ao, YC 12,8,3. These malpractices involved overcharges by clerks for the purchase of the contract paper and efforts by magistrates to hide *t'ien-fang ch'i-shui* revenues from the provincial government. For the most part, abuses seem to have resulted from laxity in carrying out the plan rather than from weaknesses in the plan itself, indicating that where it was carried out with diligence the system of contract paper probably did contribute to the government's ability to obtain information regarding landownership. It should be noted that, here again, reform designed to prevent clerical corruption was administrative, not structural. In the end the success of this and other types of procedural reforms depended on efficient implementation by the very people whose interests they would undermine.

100. CCWHTK, *chüan* 3, *t'ien-fu* 3, YC 10; KCT 15538, P'eng Wei-hsin and An Hsiu-te, YC 9,9,26.

101. The original yellow register broke down the data both by year and by the chou and hsien within each prefectural level administrative unit. "Staff" refers to any type of corruption by yamen runners and clerks. The category of tax farmers accounts only for those people engaged in *pao-lan* who were not members of the yamen staff. Thus, it should not be interpreted as an indication that *pao-lan* played a relatively small role in the tax problems of the province. Moreover, it is likely that the high proportion of embezzled taxes attributed to clerks and yamen runners in part marked instances in which they conspired with officials and members of the local elite to steal people's remittances but were bribed to take full responsibility upon themselves.

102. KCT 8521, Fen-ch'a Sung-chiang taxes Wang Su-wei, YC 8,4,12.

103. KCT 9684, Anhui Governor Hsü Pen, no date (YC period).

104. KCT 1976, Hai-pao, YC 9,6,6.

105. KCT 15489, Acting Suchow Governor Ch'iao Shih-ch'en, YC 10,1,28.

106. KCT 15068, Acting Kiangsi Governor Hsieh Min, YC 8,7,8.

107. KCT 17142, Censor I-la-chi, YC 8,3,26; KCT 14484, Acting Liang-chiang Governor Shih I-chih, YC 8,9,7.

108. KCT 2824, Kiangsi Financial Commissioner Wang Hung, YC 10,6,6. The *ch'ing-ch'a* seems to have ended later in Kiangsi than in Kiangsu and Anhui, perhaps because it began later in that province.

109. KCT 8287, P'eng Wei-hsin and An Hsiu-te, YC 9,6,26. These concerns were prompted by an edict from the emperor warning investigators to make certain that no embezzled funds were being falsely designated as *min-ch'ien*.

110. Ibid.

111. Ibid.

112. KCT 13320, Governor-general, Acting Suchow Governor Kao Ch'i-cho, YC 12,3,6.

113. KCT 14494, Censor, Acting Liang-chiang Governor-general Shih I-chih, YC 8,12,2.

114. "Ch'a Chiang-su ke-shu KH 51-YC 4 chi-ch'ien ch'ien-liang nien-k'uan ch'in-ch'ien shu-mu wen-ts'e," YC 8,11,21, *Nei-ko ta-k'u hsien-ts'un ch'ing-tai han-wen huang-ts'e*, no. 598.

115. KCT 20821, Yin-chi-shan, YC 8,3,22; KCT 20822, Yin-chi-shan, YC 9,6,6; KCT 13324, Suchow Governor Kao Ch'i-cho, YC 13,3,3.

116. CCWHTK, *chüan* 3, *t'ien-fu* 3, YC 10 edict.

117. KCT 13321, Suchow Governor Kao Ch'i-cho, YC 13,3,3.

118. The term *chi-hu ch'ien-liang* was sometimes used to refer to taxes assessed on such lands.

119. KCT 4794, Kiangnan Circuit Censor Chu Shih-chi, YC 12,8,25.

120. See, for example, HCSHC, *fu-i* 15, CL 48, which cites a memorial on tax arrears by absentee landlords submitted by Shantung Financial Commissioner Lu Yao.

121. KCT CL 3797, Kiangsi Governor Chuang Yu-kung, CL 18,5,11. By the Chia-ch'ing period, Kiangsu was still considered the province most responsible for deficits and arrears. See, for example, HCSHC, *fu-i* 20, CC 18 edict.

122. See, for example, KCT 20564, Expectant hsien magistrate Wang I-yao, no date (YC period), on clerical corruption; KCT 5082, Acting Chekiang Censor, Shansi Censor Wang Chi-ching, YC 1,7,12 and KCT 9135, Hupei Financial Commissioner Hsü Ting, YC 6,9,25 on the hereditary transmission of yamen runners' and clerks' posts; KCTYCCTC, Yunnan Governor Yang Ming-shih, YC 2,2,4; KCT 4987, Chekiang, Ningpo fu, Tzu-ch'i hsien magistrate Chang Shu-mei, no date (YC period) on Chekiang corruption; KCT 4977, Board of Rites Vice-president Ching Jih-chen, no date (YC period) on the need to compile up-to-date tax registers in Kwangtung; KCT 5548, Shensi Censor Po Ch'i-t'u, YC 13,10,16 on gentry *pao-lan* in Chihli; KCT 16495, Hunan Governor Pu-

lan-t'ai, YC 5,8,9 on *pao-lan* in Hunan; KCT 12613, Shansi Governor Chueh-lo Shih-lin and Financial Commissioner Chiang Tung, YC 8,11,9 on corruption in Shansi.

123. KCT 5573, Director of the Court of the Imperial Stud Chiang Lien, YC 13,12,9.

Chapter 7

1. As we have seen, just such a process took place after the implementation of the Single Whip reforms. Changes in the economy and fiscal administration, brought about by increased monetization of taxation, probably led to greater corruption than had existed under the less rational system the reforms were designed to replace.

2. Among these were proposals regarding the elimination of corruption in drawing up fiscal accounts, appeals to allow officials to remain longer in their posts in order to gain fuller knowledge of the areas in which they served, and suggestions that landowners who had been granted tax exemptions be required to pass the benefits on to their tenants in the form of lower rents. See, for example, KCT 5550, Censor Fu-min, YC 13,10,26; KCT 5543, Censor Chiang Ping, YC 13,10,10; KCT 5555, Board of Works Metropolitan Censor Yang An, YC 13,10,24.

3. See, for example, KCT 5627, Censor Hsieh Wen, YC 13,11,19; KCT 5634, Censor Lu Yü-tsu, YC 13,11,13; KCT 5008, Vice-president of the Court of Judicature and Revision Yü Kuang, no date (YC period); KCT 5599, Supervisor of Imperial Instruction Hsü Wang-yu, YC 13,11,20.

4. KCT 5599, Supervisor of Imperial Instruction Hsü Wang-yu, YC 13,11,20.

5. CPTC, *ts'ai-cheng, ching-fei*, Shu Ho-te, CL 2,12,21. As we have seen, the inadequacy of retained *ti-ting* taxes to meet the costs of local administration was one of the main reasons for the implementation of *huo-hao kuei-kung* in the first place. Had Shu's suggestion been carried out, it would have resulted in the immediate reversion to informal networks of funding.

6. KCT 5599, Supervisor of Imperial Instruction Hsü Wang-yu, YC 13,11,20.

7. KCT 5634, Censor Lu Yü-tsu, YC 13,11,13.

8. KCT 5599, Supervisor of Imperial Instruction Hsü Wang-yu, YC 13,11,20.

9. KCT 20419, Nei-ko deliberation, no date (YC period). This memorial was written in response to the suggestions offered by Hsü Wang-yu and Hsieh Wen.

10. CLSL, *ch'üan* 17, CL 1,4, *keng-ch'en*.

11. CLSL, *ch'üan* 109, CL 5,1, *i-ch'ou*.

12. Portions of the emperor's edict on *huo-hao* may be found in Wang Ch'ing-yün, *chüan* 3, pp. 302–3, and the CLSL, *chüan* 7, YC 13,11,

kuei-hai. The most complete version I have found appears in the *Chang-te fu-chih, chüan* 1, pp. 53–55.

13. In Kiangnan this decision was based on the fact that *huo-hao* rates had actually been raised with the implementation of the reforms. Inasmuch as tax rates in this area were already the highest in the empire, this was felt to be an unfair burden on the taxpayers. KCT 20419, Nei-ko deliberation, no date (YC period).

14. CPTC, *ts'ai-cheng, ti-ting,* Acting Szechuan Governor Wang Shih-chün, CL 1,11,6; CPTC, *ts'ai-cheng, ti-ting,* Szechuan-Shensi Governor-general Liu Yü-i, CL 1,6,24; CPTC, *ts'ai-cheng, ching-fei,* Kweichow Governor-general Chang Kuang-ssu, CL 4,3,15.

15. CLSL, *chüan* 109, CL 5,1, *i-ch'ou;* CPTC, *ts'ai-cheng, ti-ting,* An-ch'ing Governor Ch'en Ta-shou, CL 5,3,11. The *p'ing-yü yin* referred to here was probably a fee added on to tax revenues remitted to the Board to make up for deficiencies in the quality of silver.

16. KCT 3406, Fukien Financial Commissioner Chang T'ing-mei, YC 13, *jun* 4,27.

17. CPTC, *ts'ai-cheng, ching-fei,* Chihli Governor-general Li Wei, CL 1,12,3.

18. CPTC, *ts'ai-cheng, ti-ting,* Shansi Governor Chueh-lo Shih-lin, CL 1,8,4.

19. See for example CPTC, *ts'ai-cheng, ching-fei,* Chihli Governor-general Li Wei, CL 1,12,3; CPTC, *ts'ai-cheng, ti-ting,* Shansi Governor Chueh-lo Shih-lin, CL 1,8,4; CPTC, *ts'ai-cheng, ching-fei,* Kweichow Governor-general Chang Kuang, CL 2,2,10; CPTC, *ts'ai-cheng, ti-ting,* Liang-kuang Governor-general O-erh-ta, CL 1,12,28; CPTC, *ts'ai-cheng, ti-ting,* Acting Hukwang Governor-general Shih I-chih, CL 1,11,6.

20. Ten years later, officials could still be found memorializing on the necessity for uniformity of *huo-hao* quotas. See, for example, CPTC, *ts'ai-cheng, ti-ting,* Honan Judicial Commissioner Wang P'i-lieh, CL 10,10,1.

21. CLSL, *chüan* 109, CL 5,1, *i-ch'ou.*

22. During the Yung-cheng period it was ruled that an acting official holding more than one post would be paid only half the *yang-lien* of the acting post. The assumption behind this decision was that although the official would need additional funds to operate a second yamen and maintain additional staff, he would not need that portion devoted to living expenses already covered by the *yang-lien* of the original post. The remaining *yang-lien* was returned to the provincial treasury to use in supplying all officials with *kung-fei.* See, for example, KCT 17130, Board of Punishments Vice-President, Acting Shensi Governor Chang Pao, YC 5,9,25; KCT 16467, Shantung Financial Commissioner Fei Chin-wu, YC 7,6,8; KCT 13095, Szechuan Governor Hsien Te, YC 8,3,20; KCT 0686, Yueh Chung-ch'i and Hsi Lin, YC 6,5,7.

23. CLSL, *chüan* 109, CL 5,1, *i-ch'ou.*

24. CLSL, *chüan* 164, CL 7,4,1.

25. This criticism was based, of course, on the Confucian adage that

good government depended on good men and not on contriving laws or methods.

26. *Chi-hsin tang*, CL 7,4,1.

27. CLSL, *chüan* 165, CL 7,4,16.

28. Ibid.

29. CPTC, *ts'ai-cheng, ti-ting*, T'an Hsing-i, CL 7,6,22.

30. Chao Ching-li, "Hao-hsien ch'ing jeng kuei-kung," in *Huang-ch'ao ching-shih wen-pien, chüan* 27, *hu-cheng* 2 (hereafter cited as HCCSWP).

31. CLSL, *chüan* 178, CL 7,11, *i-ch'ou*.

32. Ch'ien Ch'en-chün, "T'iao-ch'en hao-hsien shu," in HCCSWP, *chüan* 27, *hu-cheng* 2; Sun Chia-kan, "Pan-li hao-hsien shu," in HCCSWP, *chüan* 27, *hu-cheng* 2; P'eng Tuan-shu, "Hao-hsien ssu-i," HCCSWP, *chüan* 27, *hu-cheng* 2.

33. The well-field system was a method of state-regulated land distribution in which land was divided into nine parcels, resembling the grid used in a game of tic-tac-toe. People cultivated the lands on the periphery as private plots and tilled the center plot communally for the benefit of their overlord. This system is said to have originated during the Chou dynasty and was often recalled by reformers in later dynasties seeking to provide all the people with land—the key, in classical political economy, to a contented and prosperous population.

34. P'eng, *chüan* 27, p. 1.

35. CLSL, *chüan* 178, CL 7,11, *i-ch'ou*.

36. Sun Chia-kan, *chüan* 27, pp. 7–8.

37. On the occasion of a tax remission honoring the Ch'ien-lung emperor's mother's ninetieth birthday it was announced that the Board of Revenue treasury contained reserves of over 7 million taels. HCSHC, CL 42.

38. See, for example, KCT CL 5814, Honan Governor Chiang Ping, CL 19,2,9; KCT CL 2549, Acting Honan Governor Fan Shih-shou, CL 17,9,24; CLSL, *chüan* 71, CL 3,6, *ping-wei*.

39. CLSL, *chüan* 148, CL 6,8, *i-ssu*.

40. KCT CL 2927, Chekiang Governor Chueh-lo Ya-erh-ha-shan, CL 17,11,21.

41. KCT CL 2549, Acting Honan Governor Fan Shih-shou, CL 17,9,24.

42. Saeki Tomi, *Ch'ing-tai Yung-cheng-ch'ao ti yang-lien yin yen-chiu*, p. 155. Saeki cites Ku Yen-wu's *Jih-chih lü* on these loans.

43. KCT 21201, Hanlin Reader Ch'en Pang-yen, no date (YC period).

44. Saeki, *Yang-lien yin*, p. 156.

45. Ibid., pp. 157–58.

46. TCHTSL, *chüan* 263, *kuan-yuan yü-chieh yang-lien lu-fei*, CL 14.

47. Saeki, *Yang-lien yin*, pp. 159–61.

48. KCT 4114, Kuang-chou Deputy Lieutenant-general Mao K'o-ming, YC 11,8,28; KCT 19678, Fuchow Manchu General-in-chief A-erh-sai, YC 9,11,20; KCT 5513, Hukwang Brigade General Yueh Ch'ao-lung, YC 10,4,28; KCT 2452, Kwangsi Brigade General Chang Ying-tsung,

YC 9,11,1; KCT 4621, Sian Financial Commissioner Yang-pieh, YC 12,6,8; KCT 4234, Kiangsi Brigade General Li Lien, YC 11,11,9.

49. KCT 3475, Kiangsi Financial Commissioner Tiao Ch'eng-tsu, YC 13,6,6.

50. CPTC, *ts'ai-cheng*, *ching-fei*, Kiangsu Governor Chang Ch'ü, CL 4,6,24.

51. CPTC, *ts'ai-cheng*, *ching-fei*, Hunan Governor Chiang P'u, CL 9,2,28.

52. *I-tsou tang*, CL 15,11,25. I wish to thank Beatrice Bartlett for bringing this document to my attention.

53. The effect this may have had on the development of capitalism in China would provide an interesting focus for comparative economic history. However, resort to investment at interest in some instances was also a sign of the weakening of traditional funding arrangements. This was clearly the case in Kiangsu.

54. CLSL, *chüan* 93, CL 4,5, *i-ch'ou*; CPTC, *ts'ai-cheng t'ien-fu*, Anhui Governor Sun Kuo-hsi, CL 4,5,15.

55. KCT CL 515, Chihli Governor-general Fang Kuan-ch'eng, CL 16,9,9. Honan sent 150,000 taels and Shantung and Shansi each contributed 100,000 taels.

56. KCT CL 1552, Hupei Governor Heng Wen, CL 17,4,24.

57. KCT CL 1927, Hupei Governor Heng Wen, CL 17,5,29; KCT CL 9501, Hupei Governor Chang Jo-chen, CL 20,5,29.

58. TCHTSL, *chüan* 170, *hao-hsien tung-chih*, CL 23.

59. TCHTSL, *chüan* 170, *hao-hsien tung-chih*, CL 17.

60. See, for example, KCT CL 9475, Kwangtung Governor Hao Nien, CL 20,5,28; KCT CL 31629, Kiangsu Governor Yang K'uei, CL 42,5,29; TCHTSL, *chüan* 170, *hao-hsien tung-chih*, CL 23.

61. TCHTSL, *chüan* 170, *hao-hsien tung-chih*, CL 33.

62. See, for example, KCT CL 2567, Honan Governor Chiang Ping, CL 17,9,26.

63. TCHTSL, *chüan* 170, *hao-hsien tung-chih*, CC 5.

64. TCHTSL, *chüan* 170, *hao-hsien tung-chih*, CL 33.

65. TCHTSL, *chüan* 170, *hao-hsien tung-chih*, CL 23. The Board rejected the provincial *hao-hsien chang-ch'eng* and returned them for revision so many times that it was not until CL 15 (1750) that the final schedules were all approved.

66. TCHTSL, *chüan* 170, *hao-hsien tung-chih*, CL 33.

67. Such was the case when Shih-se was governor of Honan. In early CL 13 (1748) he discovered that there were not enough funds in the Board allocation for tribute goods (*kung-wu*). He therefore borrowed 1,000 taels from the provincial *hsien-k'uan*. Later in that year there was urgent business for which there was not enough time to get a Board allocation. Shih-se borrowed another 10,000 taels from the *hsien-k'uan*. The governor, though transferred to the post of Yun-kuei governor-general, was still attempting to repay these funds in CL 17 (1752). KCT CL 2567, Honan Governor Chiang Ping, CL 17,9,26.

68. KCT CL 5814, Honan Governor Chiang Ping, CL 19,2,9.

69. See for example KCT CL 163, Anhui Governor Chang Shih-tsai, CL 16,7,21; KCT CL 2063, Chihli Governor Fang Kuan-ch'eng, CL 17,7,14. The same process was applied to allocations of clothing, coal, and so on for prisoners in Shansi. KCT CL 232, Shansi Governor A-ssu-ha, CL 16,7,28.

70. KCT CL 2063, Chihli Governor Fang Kuan-ch'eng, CL 17,7,14.

71. KCT CL 6612, Kwangtung Governor Hao Nien, CL 19,5,3. The reason for the high price, according to the governor, was that Kwang-tung was not a white-wax-producing area. Purchases had to be made in Kiangsi, and prices there were on the rise. Bonds of guarantee were ob-tained from local officials in the area of purchase and from the Kiangsi governor certifying that the price had not been overstated, but the Board still delayed approval. As a last resort, Hao Nien appealed to the emperor, but it is not known whether the Board's recalcitrance was overcome.

72. HPTL, chüan 9, t'ien-fu 3, ch'ien-liang k'ao-ch'eng.

73. "Kuang-hsü 27 teng nien hao-hsien yin-liang ts'e," Nei-ko ta-k'o hsien-ts'un ch'ing-tai han-wen huang-ts'e, no. 942. This particular regis-ter appears to be the only one that has survived. It covers only Honan, Chekiang, Hunan, and Anhui provinces.

74. This is evident when one examines the entries listed under the cate-gory "kung-fei" in the register.

75. In some provinces, yang-lien was routinely given only in propor-tion to the amount of the tax quota a magistrate was able to collect. See, for example, CPTC, ts'ai-cheng, ching-fei, Ch'a-lang-a and Liu Yü-i, CL 1,9,6 reporting on the situation in Kansu and CPTC, ts'ai-cheng, ching-fei, Fukien Governor Lu Cho, CL 1,1,18.

76. KCT CL 956, Chihli Governor-general Fan Kuan-ch'eng, CL 16,12,12; KCT CL 3273, Shensi Governor Chung Yin, CL 16,2,18.

77. HCSHC, fu-i 15, CL 51.

78. KCT CL 4230, Kiangsu Governor Chuang Yu-kung, CL 18,7,13.

79. CLSL, chüan 65, CL 3,3, hsin-ssu. Kweichow did not choose to comply, because income from huo-hao accounted for only a small por-tion of each official's yang-lien and kung-fei.

80. HCSHC, fu-i 15, CL 48.

81. Su-chou fu-chih, chüan 15, t'ien-fu 4.

82. Of course, in areas where huo-hao income exceeded local yang-lien and kung-fei quotas, the difficulty of traveling in mountainous areas was precisely the reason given for allowing magistrates to deduct their own yang-lien. See, for example, CPTC, ts'ai-cheng, ching-fei, Acting Szechuan Governor Wang Shih-chün, CL 1,7,4.

83. CPTC, ts'ai-cheng, ching-fei, Kweichow Governor Yang Ch'ao-tseng, CL 3,9,6; CPTC, ts'ai-cheng, ching-fei, Kweichow Governor-general Chang Kuang-ssu, CL 3,3,15.

84. CPTC, ts'ai-cheng, ti-ting, Acting Kansu Governor Liu Yü-i, CL 1,6,24; CPTC, ts'ai-cheng, ti-ting, Acting Szechuan Governor Wang Shih-chün, CL 1,11,6; CPTC, ts'ai-cheng, ching-fei, Kweichow Governor-

general Chang Kuang-ssu, CL 4,3,15. For a complete breakdown of *huo-hao* rates in the nineteenth century see HPTL, *hao-hsien ting-e*.

85. CPTC, *ts'ai-cheng*, *ching-fei*, Liang-chiang Governor-general Na-ssu-t'u and Kiangsu Governor Yang Yung-pin, CL 3,5,24.

86. CPTC, ts'ai-cheng, ching-fei, Liang-kuang Governor-general O-erh-ta and Kwangtung Governor Wang Mu, CL 3,9,12.

87. In some provinces, a small portion of regular taxes, usually about 3 percent, was accumulated from bits and pieces of silver left over after the chou and hsien had opened their tax envelopes. This *yü-ping* was ostensibly used to pay clerk and runner wages. See, for example, CPTC, *ts'ai-cheng*, *ching-fei*, Anhui Governor Chao Kuo-lin, no date. In Szechuan a more sizable sum, 6 percent, which had been used for similar purposes, was declared illegal during the Ch'ien-lung period. CPTC, *ts'ai-cheng*, *ching-fei*, Szechuan Governor Yen Se, CL 3,1,28.

88. CPTC, *ts'ai-cheng*, *ching-fei*, Kweichow Governor-general Chang Kuang-ssu, CL 4,3,15.

89. CPTC, *ts'ai-cheng*, *ching-fei*, Hunan Governor Chiang P'u, CL 9,2,28.

90. CPTC, *ts'ai-cheng*, *ching-fei*, Liang-chiang Governor-general Na-ssu-t'u and Kiangsu Governor Yang Yung-pin, CL 3,5,24.

91. Numerous examples of officials requesting permission to use *huo-hao* to make up the difference between the Board price and the market price of tribute goods may be found throughout the Ch'ien-lung period. These are but a few samples. KCT CL 163, Anhui Governor Chang Shih-tsai, CL 16,7,21; KCT CL 118, Kiangsu Governor Wang Shih, CL 16,7,13; KCT CL 882, Liang-chiang Governor-general Yin-chi-shan, CL 16,2,3. Allocations of such supplementary funds often amounted to thousands of taels.

92. *Huang-ch'ing tsou-i*, Acting Chekiang Circuit, Shansi Circuit Censor Ch'ai Hu-sheng, CL 10.

93. *Huang-ch'ing tsou-i*, Acting Shantung Circuit, Kweichow Circuit Censor Sun Hao, CL 4.

94. Ch'en Chao-nan, *Yung-cheng Ch'ien-lung nien-chien ti yin-ch'ien pi-chia pien-tung*. See also KCT CL 6207, Kiangsi Governor Fan Shih-shou, CL 19,4,11; CLSL, *chüan* 151, CL 6,9, *ssu-mao* for discussions of the high price of copper coins.

95. Wang Hui-tsu, *Ping-ta meng-lang lü*, CL 57, cited in Ch'en Chao-nan, p. 58.

96. Ch'ien Ping, *Li-yuan ts'ung-hua*, *chüan* 1, *mi-chia*, cited in Ch'en Chao-nan, p. 58.

97. Ibid., cited in Wang Ch'ing-yün, p. 82.

98. *Huang-ch'ao tsou-i*, Hupei Governor Yang Hsi-fu, CL 13.

99. Ibid.

100. Ch'üan Han-shen, "Mei-chou pai-yin yü shih-pa shih-chi chung-kuo wu-chia ke-ming ti kuan-hsi." Mexican silver dollars were circulating in Canton even during the Yung-cheng period. See chap. 2, "Contributions from the Customs and Salt Administrations."

101. Wang Yeh-chien, "The Secular Trend in Prices during the Ch'ing Period (1644–1911)," p. 362.

102. Wang Yeh-chien, *Land Taxation*, pp. 58–60. As early as the 1730s, Chihli and Kwangtung had begun to plead for the allocation of legitimate funds to pay "extra-quota" clerks, a plea that was continuously rejected by the Board of Revenue. See CPTC, *ts'ai-cheng, ching-fei*, Liang-kuang Governor-general O-erh-ta and Kwangtung Governor Wang Mu, CL 3,9,12; CPTC, *ts'ai-cheng, ching-fei*, Chihli Governor Kao Pin, CL 9,3,17.

103. For examples of provincial deficits, see HCSHC, *fu-i* 17, CC 6 edict; HCSHC, *fu-i* 20, CC 14 edict in response to a memorial by the governor of Anhui; HCSHC, *fu-i* 20, CC 20 edict in response to a memorial by the governor of Shantung; *Huang-ch'ing tsou-i*, Liang-chiang Governor-general Sun Yü-ting, CC 25.

104. KCT CC 3194, Chihli Governor-general Liang K'en-t'ang, CC 2,9,24.

105. KCT CC 10467-1, Kiangsu Governor Wang Jih-chang, CC 13,4,12.

106. HCSHC, *fu-i* 20, CC 14 edict in response to Anhui Governor Tung Chiao-tseng's memorial requesting alterations in the schedule for repayment of Anhui's deficits.

107. *Huang-ch'ing tsou-i*, Kweichow Censor Wu Chieh, CC 23.

108. Ibid.

109. HCSHC, *fu-i* 20, Anhui Governor Tung Chiao-tseng, CC 14.

110. KCT CC 8586, Fei Shan and Yueh Ch'i, CC 7,7,26.

111. KCT CC 6468, Shantung Governor Hui-ling, CC 6,10,25.

112. KCT CC 8586, Fei Shun and Yueh Ch'i, CC 7,7,26.

113. HCSHC, *fu-i* 17, CC 6 edict.

114. Ibid.

115. *Huang-ch'ing tsou-i*, Kweichow Censor Wu Chieh, CC 23.

116. *Huang-ch'ing tsou-i*, Liang-chiang Governor-general Sun Yü-t'ing, CC 25, citing an edict issued by the emperor that year.

117. See, for example, HCSHC, *fu-i* 17, Censor P'eng Hsi-lo, CC 4; HCSHC, *fu-i* 18, CC 12 edict; *Huang-ch'ing tsou-i*, Kweichow Censor Wu Chieh, CC 23; *Huang-ch'ing tsou-i*, Liang-chiang Governor-general Sun Yü-t'ing, CC 25.

118. *Huang-ch'ing tsou-i*, Liang-chiang Governor-general Sun Yü-t'ing, CC 25, citing the emperor's edict of earlier that year.

Conclusion

1. G. William Skinner, "Introduction: Urban Development in Imperial China," p. 20.

2. The level of exploitation endured by the peasantry during the 1920s and 1930s might suggest that far higher levels of taxation were possible during the imperial period. However, the most horrifying stories of peasants being forced to pay taxes decades in advance and of villages being

taxed at rates that exceeded half their normal harvest probably depict isolated incidents. Such extreme oppression could not have been sustained in one place, much less the whole country, for long. Even more important, we must recognize the differences between the recipients of tax revenues in these two periods. The tax collector of the Ch'ing period, however despicable he may appear by present standards, did not have the coercive power of his early-twentieth-century counterpart. He was a member of a large bureaucratic machine, and even when engaging in embezzlement, he had to abide by, or at least manipulate, certain legal procedures. The tax collector of the twentieth century was bound by no such constraints. The power to tax emanated from the barrel of a gun and not a shared sense of political legitimacy. Knowledge of tax liabilities, land-ownership, crop yields, and so on were irrelevant when taxes were collected at will, whenever and from whomever one pleased. There is no doubt that some peasants were driven to starvation by the demands of the tax collector. Yet it is not at all clear that the brutal methods of the early twentieth century yielded China's rulers and petty satraps any greater per capita revenues from the land than were derived through the relatively civilized methods of the late imperial regime.

GLOSSARY

cha-pa	閘壩
ch'an-ch'ü liang-ts'un	產去糧存
chang-ch'eng	章程
ch'ang-li wai ying-hsing tung-yung chih hsiang	常例外應行動用之項
cheng-e	正額
cheng-hsiang	正項
cheng-t'i	政體
cheng-to pao-shao	徵多報少
ch'eng-yüan	城垣
ch'i-chih	契紙
chi-chuang	寄莊
Chi-hsin tang	寄信檔
chi-hu ch'ien-liang	寄戶錢糧
ch'i-ssu	祭祀
ch'i-wei	契尾
ch'i-yün	起運
chia	甲
chia-ch'uan pao-ch'in ch'ien-liang	假串包侵錢糧
chia-fu	加賦
chia-p'ai	加派
chia-shou	甲首
chiao-chia	脚價
chiao-lien	矯廉

365

chiao-tai	交代
chieh-fei	解費
chieh-kei	借給
chieh-kuei	結規
chieh-k'uang yin	截曠銀
chieh-li	節禮
chieh-sheng yin	節省銀
chieh-sheng ying-yü	節省贏餘
ch'ien	錢
chien-sheng	監生
ch'ien-ts'e	欠冊
chih-i	贄儀
chih-pi ch'ien	紙筆錢
chih-pi fan-shih	紙筆飯食
chin	斤
ch'in	侵
ch'in-ming tsung-li ch'ing-ch'a ch'ien-liang	欽命總理清查錢糧
chin-shih	進士
chin-shou chin-chieh	盡收盡解
ch'ing	頃
ch'ing-ch'a	清查
ching-ch'eng	經承
ching-fei tsa-chih	經費雜支
ching-shih	經世
ch'ing-ts'e	清冊
ching-yü ch'ien-liang	精於錢糧
chiu-kou	九扣
ch'ü	區
ch'u-chieh	出結
chü-jen	舉人
ch'u-p'iao t'i-chiu	出票提究
chüan-chien	捐監
chüan-feng	捐俸
ch'uan-ken	串根
chüan-na	捐納
chüan-shu pao-hsiao	捐輸報效
ch'üan-wu cho-lo	全無著落
chun	准
chun pao-lan ch'in-shih chih jen tzu-shou mien-tsui	准包攬侵蝕之人自首免罪

chung-hang	中行
ch'ung-kung	充公
ch'ung-wan	重完
fa	法
fan-ch'ien	飯錢
fan-shih yin	飯食銀
fan-yin	飯銀
fei-sa	飛洒
fen	分
fen-cha ta-ch'en	分查大臣
fen-chu chih-k'uan	分貯之款
fen-kuei	分規
fen-p'ai	分派
fen-p'ei	分賠
feng-yin	俸銀
Fu-i ch'üan-shu	賦役全書
fu-liang	浮糧
hao	毫
hao-hsien	耗羨
hao-hsien fan-shih chieh-sheng yin	耗羨飯食節省銀
hao-lieh chien-kun	豪劣姦棍
hao-mi	耗米
hao-pu	號簿
ho-fang	河防
hsi-kai ch'uan-p'iao	洗改串票
hsia-hang	下行
hsiang-shui	香稅
hsiao-fan yin	小飯銀
hsiao-hu	小戶
hsiao kou-tzu	小口子
hsieh-ch'a	協查
hsien-k'uan	閒款
hsien-yü	羨餘
hsien-yü lou-kuei	羨餘陋規
hsin-hung	心紅
Hsing-fa chih	刑法志
hsü-li chung-pao	胥吏中飽
hsü-mao	虛冒
hu	戶
hu-chieh ch'ien-liang	護解錢糧
hu-fang	戶房

hu-shou	戶首
hua-fen kuei-chi	花分詭寄
hua-fen kuei-hu	花分詭戶
hua-i	畫一
huang-ts'e	黃冊
huo-hao	火耗
huo-hao kuei-kung	火耗歸公
i-chih yu-tan	易知由單
i-e	溢額
i-hsin yen-chiu	以新掩舊
i-hsüeh	義學
i-kung wan-kung	以公完公
i-kung wei-kung	以公爲公
i-shih	役蝕
i-ts'e kai-ming	易冊改名
I-tsou tang	議奏檔
jen-ch'ing	人情
jen-shui	人稅
juan-t'ai	輭擡
k'ai-fu	開復
k'ai-hsiao	開銷
kai-tse	改則
k'ai-yuan chieh-liu	開源節流
k'ang-liang	抗糧
k'ao-p'eng kung-ying	考棚供應
k'o-p'ai	科派
k'ou-k'o	扣尅
k'u-p'in	孤貧
k'u-p'ing	庫平
k'u-t'ang	庫帑
k'u-ts'ang	庫藏
k'u-ts'un k'uan-mu	庫存款目
kua-hao	掛號
kuan-chiang	官匠
kuan-ch'in	官侵
kuan-feng i-shih	官俸役食
kuan-ti ch'ai-chia	官地柴價
kuan-t'ien	官田
k'uang-p'ien liang-hu yin	誆騙糧戶銀
kuei-kuan	歸官
kuei-kung	歸公

k'uei-k'ung	虧空
kuei-li	規禮
kuei-li hu-ming	詭立戶名
kuei-min	歸民
kuei-shu	櫃書
kun-tan	滾單
kung	公
kung-chien	公件
kung-chüan	公捐
Kung-chung tang	宮中檔
kung-fei yin	公費銀
kung-hsiang	公項
k'ung-liang	空糧
kung-shih	工食
kung-shih	公事
kung-wu	貢物
kung-yung yin	公用銀
kuo-chi min-sheng	國計民生
kuo-hu fei-liang	過戶飛糧
lan	覽
le-chüan	樂捐
li	厘
li-chang	里長
li-chia	里甲
li-hsieh	里歇
li-shu	里書
li-ting chang-ch'eng	立定章程
liang-chang	糧長
liang-ju wei-ch'u	量入爲出
liang-kuei	糧規
liang-tsung	糧總
lin-chin sheng	鄰近省
lin-kuan ling-shui	臨關零稅
ling-shan	廩膳
ling-t'ang	領帑
liu-shui ch'uan-ken	流水串根
liu-shui hung-pu	流水紅簿
liu-ti	流抵
lo-ti shui	落地稅
lou-kuei	陋規
lu-k'o	蘆科

mai-huang	買荒
mao-hsiao	冒銷
mao-huang	冒荒
mao-ling	冒領
mi-chia	米價
min-ch'ien	民欠
mou	畝
mu-yu	募友
no	挪
no-i	挪移
pa-tsung	把總
p'ai-nien	排年
p'an-ch'a	盤查
pan-kung yin-liang	辦公銀兩
pan-t'u wan-liang chih-fa	版圖完糧之法
pang-fei	幫費
pang-t'ieh yin	幫貼銀
pang-t'ieh kung-shih	幫貼工食
pao	保
pao-chang kung-cheng	保長公征
pao-chia	保甲
pao-lan	包攬
p'ei-chih	賠支
pei-kung yin	備公銀
piao-li	表禮
p'ing-fei	平費
ping-feng yin	併封銀
p'ing-kuei yin	平規銀
ping-mi	兵米
p'ing-t'ou yin	平頭銀
p'ing-yü	平餘
p'ing-yü ling-yin	平餘零銀
po	駁
pu-chia	部價
pu-fei	部費
pu-kei chih-k'uan	補給之款
pu-kuo i-shen chi-wan	不過一審即完
san-lien yin-p'iao	三聯印票
shan-tung	擅動
shang-hang	上行
shang-huo fen-t'ou	商貨分頭

she-tsung	社總
shen-chin fu-hu	紳衿富戶
shen-chin ta-hu	紳衿大戶
shen-huan	紳宦
sheng	升
sheng-ch'en kuei-li	生辰規禮
sheng-hsi yin	生息銀
sheng-k'o	陞科
sheng-yuan	生員
shih-ch'a	失察
shih-cheng e-ts'e	實徵額冊
shih-chia	市價
shih-ch'üeh	世缺
shih-p'ing	市平
shih-yung kuan	試用官
shou-liang	首糧
shou-pei	守備
shu-shou	書手
shuang-lien shui-tan	雙聯稅單
shui-ch'i hsien-yü yin	稅契羨餘銀
shui-chiao yin	水脚銀
shui-hao	稅耗
shui-hsien	稅羨
shui-lo shih-ch'u	水落石出
shun-chuang chih-fa	順庄之法
shun-chuang kun-ts'ui	順庄滾催
ssu	私
ssu-p'ai	私派
ssu-shou ti-pu	私收底簿
sui-cheng sui-chieh	隨徵隨解
sui-chieh fan-shih yin	隨解飯食銀
sui-feng yin	隨封銀
sui-p'ing yin	隨平銀
sui-shih tung-yung chih-hsiang	隨時動用之項
ta-hu	大戶
ta-hu chih k'ang-wan	大戶之抗完
ta-p'ing yin	搭平銀
tai-cheng	帶徵
t'an-k'ou	攤扣
tan-ku	瞻顧
t'an-p'ei	攤賠

371

tan-t'ou yin	單頭銀
tan-t'ou li-chang	單頭里長
t'an-wu	貪污
tan-yin tsa-hsiang	單銀雜項
tang-p'iao	宕票
tao	道
tao-jen ho-li	到任賀禮
t'i-an	隄岸
T'i-ch'ao	邸抄
ti-kun	地棍
t'i-pen chih-tu	題本制度
ti-pu	底簿
ti-ting ch'ien-liang	地丁錢糧
t'ien-fang ch'i-shui	田房契稅
t'ien-li	天理
ting-sui-ti	丁隨地
to-yü	多餘
tou	斗
tsa-shui	雜稅
ts'ai-cheng	財政
tsai-liang	裁糧
ts'ao-liang	漕糧
ts'ao-tsung	漕總
tso-p'ing yin	坐平銀
tso-tsa	佐雜
tsou-che chih-tu	奏摺制度
tsou-hsiao	奏銷
Tsou-hsiao an	奏銷案
tsou-hsiao ts'e	奏銷冊
ts'ui-i	催役
ts'ui-k'o	催科
ts'ui-t'ou	催頭
ts'un-liu	存留
t'u	圖
t'u-i	土宜
t'u-shu chih pao-lan	圖書之包攬
tuan-p'ing	短平
tui-fei	兌費
t'un-t'ien	屯田
t'ung-chih	同知

t'ung-jung	通融
t'ung-p'an	通判
tz'u-chin sheng	次近省
tzu-feng t'ou-kuei	自封投櫃
wan-shui ch'uan-ken	完稅串根
wang-tao	王道
wang-yen che	妄言者
wei-kuan	委官
wei-wan	未完
wen	文
wo-ch'ien	倭鉛
wu-ai	無碍
wu-cho chih-k'uan	無著之款
wu-liang	無艮
wu-mi chih-ch'ui	無米之炊
wu-ting hsiang	無定項
wu-ting shu	無定數
ya-hu	牙戶
yang-lien yin	養廉銀
yen-ch'a kuei	烟茶規
yen-hu men-tan	烟戶門單
yen-k'o	鹽課
yen-kuei	鹽規
yen-lu	言路
yen-pi yin	驗批銀
yen-p'iao ch'ien	驗票錢
yen-shang kuei-li	鹽商規禮
yen-yin	鹽引
yin-hsün	因循
yin-kung no-i	因公挪移
yin-kung p'ei-tien	因公賠墊
yin-lou	隱漏
yin-p'iao	印票
yin-ti	隱地
ying-pi	應比
ying-t'ai	硬擡
ying-yü	贏餘
yu chih-jen, wu chih-fa	有治人無治法
yu-i k'ang-ch'ien	有意抗欠
yü-p'ing	餘平

373

yu-ting hsiang	有定項
yü-yin	餘引
yüeh	約
yün-fei	運費
yung-pu chia-fu	永不加賦

BIBLIOGRAPHY

Abe Takeo, *Shindaishi no kenkyū* [Researches in the history of the Ch'ing period], Tokyo, 1971.
———, "Kōsen teikai no kenkyu" [A study of the return of the meltage fee to the public coffers], *Tōyōshi kenkyū*, 16.4, March 1958.
An-yang hsien-chih [Gazetteer of Anyang county], Chia-ch'ing edition.
Araki Toshikazu, "Yosei ninen no hikō jiken to Den Bunkyō" [T'ien Wen-ching and the examination boycott of Yung-cheng 2], Tōyōshi kenkyū, 15.4, March 1957.
Bartlett, Beatrice, "Ch'ing Palace Memorials in the Archive of the National Palace Museum," *National Palace Museum Bulletin*, 13.6, January–February 1979.
Beattie, Hilary, *Land and Lineage in China: A study of T'ung-cheng county, Anhui in the Ming and Ch'ing dynasties*, Cambridge: Cambridge University Press, 1979.
Chang Chung-li, *The Chinese Gentry: Studies in their role in nineteenth century society*, Seattle: University of Washington Press, 1955.
Chang Te-ch'ang, "The Economic Role of the Imperial Household in the Ch'ing Dynasty," *Journal of Asian Studies*, February 1972.
Chang-te fu-chih [Gazetteer of Chang-te prefecture], Hsüeh-sheng shu-chu edition.
Chao Ching-li, "Hao-hsien ch'ing jeng kuei-kung" [A request for the continued return of the meltage fee to the public coffers], HCCSWP, *chüan* 27, *hu-cheng* 2.
Ch'en Chao-nan, *Yung-cheng Ch'ien-lung nien-chien ti yin-ch'ien pi-chia pien-tung* [Fluctuations in the silver: copper ratio during the Yung-cheng and Ch'ien periods], Taipei, 1966.
Ch'en Teng-yuan, *Chung-kuo t'ien-fu shih* [The history of Chinese land taxation], Taipei: Shang-wu yin-shu kuan, 1966.
Chi-hsin tang, National Palace Museum Archives, Taiwan.

Ch'ien Ch'en-chün, "T'iao-ch'en hao-hsien shu" [A point-by-point discussion of hao-hsien], HCCSWP, *chüan* 27, *hu-cheng* 2.

Ch'ien Ta-hsin, *Shih chia-chai yang-hsin lu*, Chung-hua shu-chu.

Ch'in-ting hu-pu tsu-li (HPTL).

Ch'ing-ch'ao wen-hsien t'ung-k'ao (CCWHTK), Taipei, 1958.

Ch'u T'ung-tsu, *Local Government in China under the Ch'ing*, Stanford: Stanford University Press, 1962.

Chu-p'i tsou-che (CPTC), Number One Historical Archives, Peking.

Ch'üan Han-sheng, "Mei-chou pai-yin yü shih-pa shih-chi Chung-kuo wu-chia ke-ming ti kuan-hsi" [The relationship between American silver and the eighteenth-century Chinese price revolution], *Bulletin of the Institute of History and Philology*, Academia Sinica, vol. 28, 1957.

Chuang Chi-fa, "Ch'ing shih-tsung yü tsou-che chih-tu ti fa-chan" [The Ch'ing emperor Shih-tsung (Yung-cheng) and the development of the secret palace-memorial system], *Kuo-li Taiwan shih-fan ta-hsüeh li-shih hsüeh-pao*, vol. 4, April 1976.

Dennerline, Jerry, *The Chia-ting Loyalists: Confucian Leadership and Social Change in Seventeenth Century China*, New Haven and London: Yale University Press, 1981.

Ho Ping-ti, "The Salt Merchants of Yang-chou: A Study of Commercial Capitalism in Eighteenth Century China," *Harvard Journal of Asiatic Studies*, June 1954.

Hsiao I-shan, *Ch'ing-tai t'ung-shih* [Comprehensive history of the Ch'ing period], Taipei: Shang-wu yin-shu kuan, 1972.

Hsiao Kung-chuan, *Rural China, Imperial Control in the Nineteenth Century*, Seattle: University of Washington Press, 1960.

Huang Pei, *Autocracy at Work, a Study of the Yung-cheng Period, 1723–1735*, Bloomington: Indiana University Press, 1975.

Huang, Ray, *1587, A Year of No Significance: The Ming Dynasty in Decline*, New Haven and London: Yale University Press, 1981.

———. *Taxation and Government Finance in Sixteenth Century Ming China*, Cambridge: Cambridge University Press, 1974.

———. "Fiscal Administration during the Ming Dynasty," in Charles O. Hucker, ed., *Chinese Government in Ming Times: Seven Studies*, New York: Columbia University Press, 1969.

Huang-ch'ao ching-shih wen-pien (HCCSWP), Taipei: Kuo-feng ch'u-pan she, 1963.

Huang-ch'ao shih-huo chih (HCSHC), Imperial edition, National Palace Museum Archives, Taiwan.

Huang-ch'ing tsou-i, National Palace Museum Archives, Taiwan.

Hummel, Arthur, ed., *Eminent Chinese of the Ch'ing Period* (reprint), Taipei: Ch'eng-wen Publishing Co., 1972.

I-tsou tang, National Palace Museum Archives, Taiwan.

Iwami Hiroshi, "Yosei jidai ni okeru kōhi no kosatsu" [Public expense funds during the Yung-cheng reign], *Tōyōshi kenkyū*, 15.4, March 1957.

Kahn, Harold, *Monarchy in the Emperor's Eyes: Image and Reality in the Ch'ien-lung Reign*, Cambridge: Harvard University Press, 1971.

Kitamura Hironao, *Shinda shakai keizai shi kenkyū* [Researches in Ch'ing period social and economic history], Osaka: Osaka City University, Institute of Economics, 1972.

Ko Han-feng, "Ch'ing-tai t'ien-fu ching chih hao-hsien" [The meltage fee added to the land tax during the Ch'ing period], Nung-hsüeh, 1.5, May 1939.

Kung-chung tang (KCT), National Palace Museum Archives, Taiwan.

Kung-chung tang Yung-cheng ch'ao tsou-che (KCTYCCTC), Shih-lin: National Palace Museum, 1977–.

Kuo-ch'ao ch'i-hsien lei-cheng, Kuang-hsü edition.

Liang Fang-chung, "Local Tax Collectors in the Ming Dynasty," in E-tu Zen Sun, ed., *Chinese Social History*, New York: Octagon Books, 1966.

Man-chou ming-ch'en chüan, n.d.

Metzger, Thomas, "The Organizational Capabilities of the Ch'ing State in the Field of Commerce: The Liang-huai Salt Monopoly," in Willmott, ed., *Economic Organization in Chinese Society*, Stanford: Stanford University Press, 1972.

Miao Ch'üan-chi, *Ch'ing-tai mu-fu jen-shih chih-tu* [The system of private secretaries during the Ch'ing period], Chung-kuo jen-shih hsing-cheng yueh-k'an she, 1971.

Miyazaki Ichisada, *Aijiashi renkō* [Essays in Asian history], Tokyo.

———. "Yosei te ni yoru kōkōkin kōen no teishi ni tsuite" [On the suspension of salary contributions under the Yung-cheng emperor], Tōyōshi kenkyū, 22.3, December 1963.

Nei-ko ta-k'u hsien-ts'un ch'ing-tai han-wen huang-ts'e, Number One Historical Archives, Peking.

Nishimura Genshō, "Shinchō no horan" [Proxy remittance in the Ch'ing dynasty], Tōyōshi kenkyū, 35.3, December 1976.

Oxnam, Robert, *Ruling from Horseback, Manchu Politics in the Oboi Regency, 1661–1669*, Chicago: University of Chicago Press, 1975.

P'eng Tuan-shu, "Hao-hsien ssu-i" [A personal view on *hao-hsien*], HCCSWP, chüan 27, hu-cheng 2.

Saeki Tomi, *Chukokushi kenkyū* [Studies in Chinese history], Tōyōshi Kenkyū Monographs, no. 21, 1969.

———. *Ch'ing-tai Yung-cheng ch'ao ti yang-lien yin yen-chiu* [A study of the nourishing virtue silver of the Yung-cheng period of the Ch'ing dynasty], Taipei: Shang-wu yin-shu kuan, 1977.

Shang Hung-kuei, "Lüeh-lun ch'ing-ch'u ching-chi hui-fu ho kung-ku ti tui-ch'eng chi ch'i ch'eng-chiu" [A brief discussion of the process of economic recovery and consolidation in the early Ch'ing and its achievements], Pei-ching ta-hsüeh hsüeh-pao, vol. 2, 1957.

Shen Tuan-k'o kung i-shu, Taipei: Wen-hai ch'u-pan she, 1969.

Skinner, G. William, "Introduction: Urban Development in Imperial China," in Skinner, ed., *The City in Late Imperial China*, Stanford: Stanford University Press, 1977.

Spence, Jonathan, *Ts'ao Yin and the K'ang-hsi Emperor, Bondservant and Master*, New Haven and London: Yale University Press, 1966.

Su-chou fu-chih [Gazetteer of Suchow prefecture], T'ung-chih edition.

Sun Chia-kan, "Pan-li hao-hsien shu" [On the management of hao-hsien], HCCSWP, *chüan* 27, *hu-cheng* 2.

Sun, E-tu Zen, *Ch'ing Administrative Terms*, Cambridge: Cambridge University Press, 1961.

Ta-ch'ing hui-tien (TCHT), Yung-cheng edition.

Ta-ch'ing hui-tien shih-li (TCHTSL), Kuang-hsü edition.

Ta-ch'ing kao-tsung ch'un huang-ti shih-lu (CLSL), Taiwan re-print, 1964.

Ta-ch'ing shih-tsu chang huang-ti shih-lu, Taiwan reprint, 1964.

Ta-ch'ing shih-tsung hsien huang-ti shih-lu (YCSL), Taiwan reprint, 1964.

Tan Shou, *Ch'ing-ch'ao ch'üan-shih* [A comprehensive history of the Ch'ing dynasty], Taipei: Chung-hua Publishing Co., 1970.

T'ien Wen-ching, *Fu-yü hsüan-hua lu*, 1727 edition.

T'ien Wen-ching, *Ch'in-pan chou-hsien shih-i*, T'ung-chih 7 reprint.

Ts'ung-cheng kuan-fa lu, Tao-kuang 10 edition.

Wakeman, Frederic, *The Fall of Imperial China*, New York: The Free Press, 1975.

———. "The Shun Interregnum," in Spence and Wills, ed., *From Ming to Ch'ing: Conquest, Region, and Continuity in Seventeenth Century China*, New Haven and London: Yale University Press, 1979.

Wang Ch'ing-yün, *Shih-ch'ü yü-chi*, Chin-tai chung-kuo shih-liao tsung-k'an series 8, no. 75, Taipei: Wen-hai ch'u-pan she, 1974.

Wang Hsien-chien, *Tung-hua lu*, Kuang-hsü 10 edition.

Wang Hui-tsu, *Tso-chih le-yen*, Shanghai: Shang-wu yin-shu kuan, 1937.

Wang Yeh-chien, *Land Taxation in Imperial China, 1750−1911*, Cam-bridge: Harvard University Press, 1973.

———. "Ch'ing Yung-cheng nien ti ts'ai-cheng kai-ko" [The fiscal re-forms of the Yung-cheng period], *Bulletin of the Department of History and Philology, Academia Sinica*, 32:47−75, 1961.

———. "The Fiscal Importance of the Land Tax during the Ch'ing Pe-riod," *Journal of Asian Studies*, 30.4, August 1971.

———. "The Secular Trend in Prices during the Ch'ing Period (1644−1911)," *The Journal of the Institute of Chinese Studies (The Chinese University of Hong Kong)*, 4.2, December 1972.

Watt, John, *The District Magistrate in Late Imperial China*, New York: Columbia University Press, 1972.

Wei Ch'ing-yuan, *Ch'ing-tai ch'ien-ch'i ti shang-pan kuang-yeh ho tzu-pen chu-i meng-ya* [Merchant operated mining in the early Ch'ing period and the sprouts of capitalism], Peking: Chung-kuo jen-min ta-hsüeh, 1981.

Wu, Silas, *Communication and Imperial Control in China: Evolution of the Palace Memorial System, 1693−1735*, Cambridge: Harvard University Press, 1970.

Yung-cheng chu-p'i yü-chih (CPYC), Wen-yuan shu-chu, 1965.

Yung-cheng hu-k'o t'i-pen (TP), Number One Historical Archives, Peking.

INDEX

An Hsiu-te, 231

Anhui: *chieh-sheng yin* in, 68; deficits in, 298–99; *huo-hao kuei-kung* in, 158–60, 183–84, 283–84; *kung-fei* in, 179, 283, 300; *yang-lien* in, 201. See also Kiangnan; Kiangnan *ch'ing-ch'a*

Annual accounting system. See *Tsou-hsiao* system

Arrears: assigning responsibility for, 233, 248, 253–54, 257–59; in Chekiang, 160; defined, 74; effect on fiscal rationalization, 261–62; falsification of, 51, 242, 244, 314*n*39; in Fukien, 165; in Honan, 46; in Kiangnan, 152, 154, 221–63 passim; and natural disaster, 10–11; and *pao-lan*, 11; remission of, 10, 263, 298; repayment of, 51, 224, 227–28, 232, 259–61, 352*n*68; in Shantung, 150; and tax resistance, 11; traditional attitudes towards, 10, 25; Yung-cheng emperor on, 224; mentioned, 46, 75. See also Deficits; Embezzlement; Tax Remissions

Artisan households: tax on, eliminated, 314*n*34

Board fees, 45, 77–78, 161–62, 163, 214, 286, 327*n*13

Board of Revenue: advises Yung-cheng emperor on *huo-hao*, 189; control of corruption in, 79; and efforts to standardize *huo-hao* rates, 270; and extension of *yang-lien*, 199; memorials of, 310, 319*n*30; supervision of *huo-hao* expenditure, 106–7, 168, 271–72, 277, 284–88, 300, 359*n*67; and *tsou-hsiao* system, 13, 16–17, 76. See also Board fees; Board price

Board price: and inflation, 286, 292, 359*n*67, 360*n*71, 361*n*91; and informal funding network, 53

Brokers, 217, 349*n*163

Bureaucracy, Ch'ing: centralization of, xii–xiv passim, 107; problems of, 6, 84, 107, 186, 304, 306. See also Fiscal administration; *Lou-kuei*

Ch'a Ssu-t'ing, 106–7, 332*n*96

Ch'ai Hu-sheng, 292–93

Chang Ch'ing-tu, 100

Chang Kuang-ssu, 138–39

Chang Tan-lin, 225, 226–27

Chang T'ing-lü, 332*n*87

Chang T'ing-mei, 269–70

Chang T'ing-yü, 332*n*87

Chao Ching-li, 275–76

Chao Hsiang-kuei, 235–37, 239

Charity: allocation of *ts'un-liu* for, 35, 36

Designer: Randall Goodall
Compositor: G & S Typesetters, Inc.
Printer: Braun-Brumfield
Binder: Braun-Brumfield
Text: 11/13 Sabon
Display: Sabon and Rubens